D0701191

Survivors

THE ASIAN AMERICAN EXPERIENCE

Series Editor
Roger Daniels, University of Cincinnati

A list of books in the series appears at the end of this book.

Survivors

CAMBODIAN REFUGEES
IN THE UNITED STATES

Sucheng Chan

UNIVERSITY OF ILLINOIS PRESS

URBANA AND CHICAGO

© 2004 by the Board of Trustees
of the University of Illinois
All rights reserved
Manufactured in the United States of America
1 2 3 4 5 C P 5 4 3 2 1

∞ This book is printed on acid-free paper.

Library of Congress Cataloging-in-Publication Data
Chan, Sucheng.
Survivors : Cambodian refugees in the United States / Sucheng Chan.
p. cm. — (Asian American experience)
Includes bibliographical references and index.
ISBN 0-252-02920-8 (cloth : alk. paper)
ISBN 0-252-07179-4 (paper : alk. paper)
1. Cambodian Americans—Social conditions. 2. Refugees—
United States—Social conditions. 3. Refugees—Cambodia.
4. Cambodian Americans—Biography. 5. Cambodia—History—
20th century. I. Title. II. Series.
E184.K45C48   2004
305.895'93073—dc22   2003021628

TO THE MEMORY OF THE SEVERAL MILLION CAMBODIANS
WHO PERISHED SO NEEDLESSLY—
MAY THEY BE REINCARNATED TO HAPPIER LIVES.

CONTENTS

FOREWORD

Roger Daniels

IN 2003 Sucheng Chan published *Not Just Victims: Conversations with Cambodian Community Leaders in the United States* in which she had protagonists tell their own stories and explain the varied ways in which they were coping with America. In the volume at hand, her second in this series, Chan writes a compelling narrative of the Cambodian experience in both Asia and the United States. This kind of trans-Pacific analysis, which looks at the emigrant homeland as well as the new location, conforms to the ideal of immigration history put forth by one of its progenitors, Marcus Lee Hansen, an ideal infrequently achieved in the literature.

Chan has a tragic story to tell. Unlike most accounts of the killing fields of Cambodia where millions were slaughtered by their own kind, she does more than relate the horror. She places those tragic events within an appropriate perspective of several centuries of Cambodian history and provides a brief account of Cambodian culture.

Her narrative then explains the dangerous process by which hundreds of thousands of Cambodians initially found sanctuary in countries of first asylum and then underwent the complex, frustrating, and tedious process of qualifying for American visas. Her final chapters analyze the challenges and complexities involved in becoming Cambodian Americans and establishing themselves as refugees in the United States, a society quite different from anything they had experienced. Like everything Chan has written, *Survivors* is imbued with her passion for Asian American history and culture and her compassion for other human beings.

A prolific writer and editor, Chan, now emeritus professor of Asian American Studies at the University of California, Santa Barbara, has written separately about Chinese, Hmong, and Cambodian immigrants to the United States. She is surely our most versatile Asian Americanist. *Survivors,* in addition to being what I believe is the finest study we have of any Southeast Asian immigrant group, has some clear messages for our time. Chan reminds us of the price that noncombatant civilians sometimes have to pay for the military exertions of others. Although the final atrocities were committed by Cambodians, the whole complex of events described here are surely another "side effect" of the long Franco-American-Vietnamese military struggle that George Herring has called the war that would not die.

PREFACE

THIS BOOK is a multidisciplinary study of why and how Cambodians have come to this country and how they have fared since their arrival. By emphasizing continuities rather than ruptures, I link their past to their present, unlike some writers who have divided the lives of Indochinese refugees into pre-escape and post-arrival segments. I combine my own research with the information collected and analyzed by scholars in several disciplines, by journalists, and by Cambodian refugees themselves. Even though critics often fault multidisciplinary studies for being "superficial" because such works do not discuss in depth the complex internal debates and theoretical fine points within specific disciplines, multidisciplinary studies do offer more rounded and often more nuanced pictures of phenomena or topics. By juxtaposing the findings and conclusions of scholars in several disciplines, such works can present either explicit or implicit critiques of the limitations inherent in any single discipline.

In synthesizing virtually the entire existing literature, including the findings in almost a hundred unpublished Ph.D. dissertations and M.A. theses, this study contributes to scholarship in at least three ways. First, the scope of this book is broader than those in earlier writings about this new American ethnic group. I provide a full account of the experiences of Cambodian refugees and examine them within the larger contexts of political and social developments that have affected Cambodia and its people in the last century. I begin, in chapter 1, with an account of the events that caused some two million deaths among a population of nearly eight million. Attempts by Cambodians to seek refuge, and the complex politics involved in coping with the refugee outflow, are analyzed in chapter 2. Chapter 3 details the newcomers' arrival and their settlement patterns in the United States. Chapters 4, 5, 6, and 7 discuss their efforts to build ethnic communities; to ensure their economic survival; to negotiate cultures in local, national, and transnational contexts; to cope with multiple disrupting influences that threaten to tear their families apart; and to overcome the severe traumas that have scarred their existence.

Second, in telling their story, I try to reflect as much as possible the perspectives of Cambodians themselves by quoting at length what dozens of Cambodian refugees have written about (in English) or told to oral historians. A great deal has been published about the refugees and immigrants who left Cambodia, Laos, and Vietnam from the mid-1970s to the mid-1990s, because they grabbed the attention of journalists, scholars, and other professionals alike, given the dramatic and heart-wrenching circumstances under which they escaped from their homelands. For almost two decades the refugee exodus created an international crisis of massive proportions that took great effort on the part of many nations, nongovernmental organizations, and concerned individuals to resolve. Many who have written about these refugees had participated in this "rescue operation." Some authors had no formal academic training in Southeast Asian studies, however, and only a few could speak the languages of the people they aided, befriended, researched, and wrote about. Consequently, many publications reflect largely the professional concerns of the authors—that is, they are mostly records of how non-Cambodians perceived the refugee-seekers. To get a sense of the momentous disasters that the refugee-seekers and immigrants experienced, especially how they understand their ordeals in retrospect, we can turn to the dozens of autobiographies and short oral histories they have produced, which focus mainly on the authors' lives *before* they escaped from their homelands and during their flight. These memoirs, however, say little about the challenges the authors have encountered since they set foot on American soil.

Little attempt has been made by anyone to meld the scholarly literature with the personal accounts. Such a synthesis is what I attempt in this book. As the bibliography indicates, the literature emphasizes what might be called the pathological aspects of the Cambodian refugees' experiences—various kinds of mental health problems that continue to haunt this population, the gang warfare that has terrorized them, and the intergenerational conflicts that rend many Cambodian American families asunder. Although I do include these often-sensationalized topics in the present study, I also make an effort to discuss less melodramatic and more mundane subjects.

Third, in writing this book I hope to redress another imbalance in the literature. Although something has been published about each of the refugee groups from Cambodia, Laos, and Vietnam, the writings deal mainly with the Vietnamese—the most numerous and visible group—because Vietnamese are the people whom Americans know best, given the large number of Americans who fought in the war in Vietnam and the extensive mass-media coverage of that war. In contrast, what most Americans old enough to remember the newsmaking events of the late 1970s and the 1980s know about Cambodians is based on a handful of stark images: piles of skulls and bones, bedraggled people straggling across the Thai-Cambodian border, emaciated individuals with vacant stares, and babies with bloated bellies. Scholars began to publish works that explicate various aspects of the lives of Cambodian refugees only in the 1980s. Many more studies about Cambodians, as well as about the Hmong, who have received some scholarly attention, and about the Lao, Iu Mien, Tai Dam, and Cham, about whom virtually nothing has been written, are urgently needed.

During the three decades I taught Asian American studies, I tried my best to be as inclusive as possible in terms of ethnic coverage. I felt strongly that my colleagues and I cannot call our field *Asian* American studies if all we focused on were Chinese and Japanese immigrants and their American-born descendants. Where usable texts on the smaller or newer Asian ethnic groups did not exist, I read everything I could find about them and did original research to supplement the information so I could include their stories in my lectures. I also edited books and wrote articles about them. In short, what I chose to research and to write about has been guided largely by where lacunae existed in the literature. Writing about Cambodian Americans is another attempt on my part to fill one of many still-existing gaps.

In addition to my scholarly concerns, I have a personal reason for wanting to write about Cambodians. To me, Cambodia is not some distant land and Cambodians are not exotic strangers. I spent five years of my childhood in Malaya (now called Malaysia) and one year in Singapore. The schools I attended there taught me the names of the neighboring Southeast Asian countries but little else about them since Malaya and Singapore were still British colonies during the years I lived there, from 1950 to 1956. The history I learned in school was that of the British Empire. My classmates and I had a few lessons on Burma, Malaya, Singapore, and Brunei, which Great Britain had colonized, but we were taught nothing about Vietnam, Laos, and Cambodia, which France had colonized; or about Indonesia, which the Netherlands had colonized; or the Philippines, which first Spain and then the

United States colonized; or Thailand, which had remained independent. It was not until 1964, when I was getting an M.A. degree in Asian studies at the University of Hawaii, that I finally heard the amazing story of the Angkor kingdom when I audited a Southeast Asian history course taught by the late Walter F. Vella. Fascinated by what I heard and read in that course, I decided that I must visit Cambodia. After finishing my course work in Hawaii and doing a year's anthropological fieldwork in the Philippines, I took off for Bangkok in December 1965, hoping to get a visa to Cambodia.

Unfortunately, the Thai-Cambodian border was closed when I got to Bangkok. The staff in the Cambodian embassy told me to keep checking back with them, however, because they expected the border to be reopened "any day." That day came in early February, 1966. With great excitement, visa in hand, I boarded a train and headed for Poipet across the Thai-Cambodian border. But the train arrived late. By the time I disembarked, night had fallen and the last bus to Siem Reap had left hours earlier. There being no hotel in sight, I made my way to the police station, where a kind policeman somehow understood my plight, even though we did not know the language we each spoke, and allowed me to spend the night in the jail!

The two weeks I spent in Cambodia, traveling by local buses and *cyclos* (vehicles drawn by bicycles), remain, to this day, the most memorable two weeks of my life. As a Chinese, I was able to blend into the local scene relatively easily. Although I did not know Khmer, I could communicate in one or more dialects of Chinese with the Sino-Cambodians who owned or managed many of the hotels and eating places in Siem Reap and Phnom Penh. Where no Chinese speakers could be found, I communicated through gestures. I always greeted people by holding my palms together and bringing them to my forehead while bowing, as any well-mannered Khmer would do. Because I knew how to be polite, villagers and townspeople who spoke only Khmer tried to intuit my needs and did what they could to help me.

I was enthralled by the truly awesome stone monuments the Angkorian kings had built and spent days wandering through the temples, some of which are entangled in the sinuous roots of bayan trees. There being virtually no other tourists around at that time, as the war in neighboring Vietnam was in full swing, I felt as though I had the magnificent edifices all to myself—to behold, to marvel at, to imprint forever upon my mind's eye. A performance of the Royal Cambodian Ballet on the grounds of Angkor Wat that I attended in the moonlight was likewise magical. At Tonle Sap, I persuaded a fisherman to row me out to the middle of the lake in his boat so that I could survey the scenes along the shores. In Phnom Penh, I bought delicious food from vendors in the open-air market and strolled along the streets, some of which are broad, tree-lined boulevards—a reflection of the French colonial influence. A cyclo driver pointed out to me the pavilion where Prince Sihanouk periodically interacted with the common people and, through gestures, impressed upon me how an ordinary Cambodian such as himself loved the prince. Even though, in hindsight, things were already beginning to fall apart in Cambodia in early 1966, such societal cleavages were not yet apparent to a visitor like me. I thought the landscape was serenely verdant and the people seemed relatively satisfied with their lives.

Given the deeply favorable impression that Cambodia had made on me, whenever I think of what happened in that country during the last three decades of the twentieth century I cannot help but shudder. It is as though I, too, have suffered a profound and personal loss. For that reason, I hope that this book will, in some small way, help to "rehumanize" (to borrow a concept from anthropologist Alexander Hinton) those who survived by gathering together and including their voices in this book and to honor the memories of those who perished by bearing witness to their immense sufferings.

Writing this book has been difficult. It is impossible to remain cheerful when one is describing manmade horrors of unimaginable proportions. What makes the story of modern Cambodia and its people so tragic is that they suffered not one but multiple catastrophes, one piled on top of another in very short order. That is to say, the relatively well-known atrocities committed by the Khmer Rouge are only a part of the story. So, how can one tell the full story without getting depressed? I certainly could not.

I also encountered difficulty collecting information. The fact that postpolio syndrome (a progressively degenerative neuromuscular disease with no cure) began to afflict me some years before I started work on this book meant that I could not carry out ethnographic fieldwork even though I thought it would be one of the more appropriate methodologies for studying a group such as Cambodian refugees. Thus, I had no choice but to find alternative ways to collect information. I first sought help from my Cambodian American students but encountered unexpected problems. Unlike other Asian American students who gladly shared their life stories and encouraged me to quote from them, Cambodian American students were extremely reluctant to let others read what they had written. As they explained, their reticence came from the fact that they felt "so ashamed" of being Cambodian. Although children of other immigrant groups have also often been embarrassed about their origins, the Cambodian American students had a more poignant reason: They did not want non-Cambodians to read about what the Khmer Rouge had done and to infer that *all* Cambodians are so savagely brutal. I could not persuade the students that it is important to publicize what had happened in order to prevent similar occurrences in the future. Only three of my Cambodian American students of the dozen or more I taught gave permission to quote from their autobiographies.

Next, I hired Khmer-speaking undergraduates to interview older Cambodians, but the students did not know what to do when their interviewees broke down in tears or became silent all of a sudden while telling their stories. I quickly gave up that research method because I realized that no amount of "interviewer training" can help undergraduate research assistants cope with the psychological complexities of asking severely traumatized individuals to talk about their experiences. Moreover, as an ethnic studies scholar, I abide by the unspoken tenet that we must respect those who help us in our research by sharing information with us. We must never pressure them to talk about what they would rather not talk about. We should try our best not to exploit members of our communities for the sake of career advancement.

I made a third attempt to enlist the help of Cambodian American students when I attended a conference in 1996 at California State University, Long Beach, organized by the Cambodian Students Association. Some of the organizers were aware that I was doing research on Cambodian refugees, so they invited me to participate in a panel discussion. I took the opportunity to distribute two hundred copies of a questionnaire, along with two hundred stamped, self-addressed envelopes, to the conference attendees, who came from all over the United States. Even though many individuals expressed great willingness to help me and promised to fill out the two-page form, the response rate turned out to be only 10 percent. Therefore, I did not use the data I collected this way, because the sample was so small.

Due to those difficulties, I resorted to hiring three Asian American graduate students in counseling psychology to assist me in my research. Graduate students in that field are well trained to carry on dyadic conversations. They are good listeners, they know how to make appropriate responses to keep the conversation going, and their manner is simultaneously sympathetic and professional. Moreover, I decided to interview only English-speaking individuals who are used to talking to outsiders and to refrain from asking anyone too many questions about how he or she managed to survive during the Khmer Rouge regime because enough published personal accounts already exist about this topic.

We interviewed Cambodians as well as those who had worked with them. To get a general picture of the situation around the country, we conducted structured sociological interviews over the telephone with the directors of the State Refugee Coordinator's Office in thirty-seven of the fifty states and with almost a hundred staff members in voluntary agencies around the country who had helped to resettle Indochinese refugees. Even more useful were half a dozen individuals who had been deeply involved in the refugee resettlement process overseas. They gave me valuable insights into the policy choices that had to be made under tumultuous conditions. In addition, Audrey Kim, one of my research assistants, traveled to Massachusetts, Rhode Island, Connecticut, New York, Pennsylvania, Maryland, Washington, D.C., Virginia, Washington state, Oregon, and California to collect forty-nine face-to-face oral histories from Cambodian community leaders. Unfortunately, a shortage of funds prevented Audrey from visiting sites in the Midwest and South.

Because I hope this work will be read by students and the reading public as well as by scholars, I have tried to strike a delicate balance in how I present the material. If I leave out explanations of too many intricate political or social developments, specialists will fault me for being simplistic, and the extremely complex story I tell will not be sufficiently nuanced; if I get too tangled up in small details, students and nonspecialists may be confused or, even worse, bored. In an effort to create a work that is well-researched yet accessible, I recount key events and analyze the larger contexts in which they occurred in the same way as I would give a lecture in a university classroom—that is, with "enough" but not an "overwhelming" amount of details—while trying to keep my prose as simple and clear as possible. Although I was trained as a political scientist and know some theoretical jargon, I transformed myself into a historian when I discovered that history is a field that still prizes felicitous expression. In this book I write as a historian while relying a great deal on the research done by social scientists.

A final difficulty that slowed me was that a reviewer, who has a book on a related topic in press, kept my manuscript for almost a year in order, I suspect, to delay its publication. This action is a reflection of the contentious relationship among scholars who study Cambodia and Cambodians. Since the 1990s, "Cambodia experts" have fought over control of the Cambodian Genocide Project funded by the U.S. State Department and the Documentation Center of Cambodia in Phnom Penh (Kiernan 2000; Press 1997) and disagreed over whether the killings carried out by the Khmer Rouge should be called a "genocide."

The word *genocide* has profound legal consequences. If what the Khmer Rouge leaders perpetrated was indeed genocide, as defined by the 1948 Convention for the Prevention and Punishment of the Crime of Genocide, which has no statute of limitations, then they can be tried for this heinous crime against humanity and will suffer consequences. Ben Kiernan has argued that the Khmer Rouge did carry out a genocide, whereas other scholars and journalists have declared that even though the Khmer Rouge committed mass murders, such killings do not constitute a genocide. The debate has been so bitter that even a work such as this, which deals with the experiences of Cambodians who have become refugees and does not purport to address the exact nature of the deaths inflicted by the Khmer Rouge, is in danger of being castigated by colleagues involved in one or the other side of the debate.

Because my aim is to enable readers who are not "Cambodia experts" to learn something about the agonies Cambodians have endured in recent decades and *not* to get sucked into the academic and political quarrels among experts, I could not allow such altercations to prevent me from writing this book as I see fit. Specifically, I am not trying to make individuals of Cambodian ancestry feel ashamed of what the Khmer Rouge had done, nor am I trying to present Cambodians now living in the United States in a negative light when I discuss their dire poverty and the difficulties that they and their children face every day. What I *am* trying to do is present a sympathetic portrait of Cambodian refugees—a picture that brings out their dignity, strength, and will to survive despite all the hardships they have suffered.

ACKNOWLEDGMENTS

FIRST AND FOREMOST, I thank the hundreds of individuals listed at the end of this book who allowed me and my research assistants to interview them by telephone and in person despite their busy schedules. They were informative and most gracious. Although I designed the questionnaires and did some of the pilot interviews, Audrey U. Kim, Christie Fukunaga, and Jeannie Huh-Kim, my teaching as well as research assistants, carried out most of the telephone interviews. Audrey Kim also traveled to the East Coast, the Pacific Northwest, and southern California to interview English-speaking Cambodian community leaders on my behalf because my deteriorating physical condition (brought on by post-polio syndrome) no longer allowed me to travel on my own.

Twelve of the forty-nine in-person interviews she conducted were transcribed, edited, and published in *Not Just Victims: Conversations with Cambodian Community Leaders in the United States* (University of Illinois Press, 2003). The main titles of that book and this one serve as counterpoints to one another. Quotations from the twelve interviews are cited by the interviewees' names and the pertinent page numbers in *Not Just Victims*. All other interviewees are cited anonymously in order to protect the speakers' identities. A copy of the notes that I and my research assistants took during the telephone interviews, as well as the forty-nine face-to-face interviews that Audrey Kim carried out, not all of which were transcribed in full, are on deposit at the Southeast Asian Archive at the University of California, Irvine. I thank Anne Frank, the curator of that archive, for allowing me to deposit my documents there.

Several small grants from the Committee on Research and the Interdisciplinary Humanities Center at the University of California, Santa Barbara, paid the wages of the three extraordinarily able graduate students named above. They completed their Ph.D.s in the late 1990s and are now working as counseling psychologists.

I appreciate the willingness of three former undergraduate students, Chivy Sok, Soy Duong, and Sohko Pich, to allow me to quote from the lengthy and moving autobiographies they wrote while they were taking my courses. A number of other Cambodian American students also shared their life stories with me. Even though they declined to let me quote from their writing, I nevertheless appreciate what they taught me about the horrors that they and their families experienced during the Khmer Rouge era. I also thank Manhao Chhor, another former student, for videotaping his conversations with several teenaged Cambodian Americans. I am quoting a lengthy segment of his exchange with two young women, to whom I gave pseudonyms, in this study. Some of the photographs that Manhao took at a Cambodian New Year's celebration in Long Beach, California, appear in the photo essay that accompanies the text.

I thank the staff at the Library of Congress, the Immigration and Naturalization Service, the U.S. Census Bureau, the Office of Refugee Resettlement, the headquarters of several voluntary agencies, and the Cambodian Network Council for allowing me to photocopy material that could not be borrowed through interlibrary loan. Such material, published and unpublished and not easily accessible, enabled me to tell a fuller story.

Just as I was about to finish the first draft of this book, I discovered that there exists a veritable treasure trove in the Special Collections and University Archives of the University Library at California State University-Sacramento. In 1989, a team of multiethnic oral historians had interviewed sixty Cambodians, most of whom lived in the Stockton area, transcribed the interviews in Khmer, and then translated them into English. I am extremely grateful to Pamela Macas for making a copy of these translated transcripts, which run to more than a thousand pages, for my use. I am even more indebted to Charles Martell, who initiated and directed this oral history project for the CSU-Sacramento library. When I contacted the now-retired Charles Martell to seek permission to quote from the transcripts, he informed me that permission is not needed because the library has placed the material into the public domain. Still, I thought it wise to ask Sheila O'Neill, director of the Special Collections and University Archives, to send me written permission to quote from the transcripts; I deeply appreciate her willingness to do so. Excerpts from these oral histories enrich this book by allowing us to hear the voices of non-English-speaking Cambodians from a variety of backgrounds—voices that we might otherwise never have heard.

I appreciate the generosity of Sheila Pinkel, professor of art at Pomona College, who shared unpublished transcripts of several oral histories she collected in the 1990s. Anonymous quotes from four of the individuals she interviewed add telling details to this book.

I thank Sharon Fiffer, author of *Imagining America: Paul Thai's Journey from the Killing Fields of Cambodia to Freedom in the U.S.A.* and JoAn D. Criddle, author of *To Destroy You Is No Loss: The Odyssey of a Cambodian Family* and *Bamboo and Butterflies: From Refugee to Citizen,* for allowing me to quote long excerpts from these books, which are full of vivid details.

I am truly grateful to Ben Kiernan for saving me from many errors. I also thank David Chandler and another colleague who prefers to remain anonymous for pointing out what they perceived as problems in the manuscript. I chose not to follow all of their suggestions with regard to how certain topics should be presented or interpreted. The usual caveat that the author is responsible for all errors is even more true in this instance.

For two decades Roger Daniels has approved of everything I have written. That approval has been very comforting during periods when I was under stress. Mark Juergensmeyer, my spouse and one of the busiest people I know, has nonetheless assumed more and more household responsibilities as my physical condition worsened so that I could conserve my energy and continue to write. My appreciation for their support—crucial, each in its own way—is greater than words can describe.

Finally, I thank Laurie Matheson, acquisitions editor; Mary Lou Menches, production manager; and Mary Giles, copy editor, at the University of Illinois Press for shepherding my manuscript through the publication process.

TERMINOLOGY

THERE IS NO satisfactory term to refer collectively to people from Vietnam, Laos, and Cambodia. The two most commonly used rubrics are "Southeast Asians" and "Indochinese." Each, however, presents a problem. "Southeast Asian/s" is too broad because Southeast Asians, in addition to residents of Cambodia, Laos, and Vietnam, also include people from Burma, Thailand, Malaysia, Singapore, Indonesia, Brunei, and the Philippines. Even the more specific term *Southeast Asian refugees* is misleading because refugees from Myanmar (formerly known as Burma) have also come to the United States in recent years, yet scholars and journalists who write about "Southeast Asian refugees" do not have them in mind. To scholars such as myself who have an anticolonial attitude, "Indochinese" is also unacceptable because it derives from "French Indochina"—the collective name the French gave their colonies and protectorates in mainland Southeast Asia: Tonkin, Annam, Cochinchina, Cambodia, and Laos. For the sake of brevity, I do use the terms *Indochinese refugees* or *Southeast Asian refugees* interchangeably on the occasions when a collective nomenclature is called for.

Two other words used repeatedly in this book, "refugees" and "culture," are also problematic. Many of my students of Cambodian, Hmong, Lao, and Vietnamese ancestries have told me that they hate to be called "refugees" because that word has so many negative connotations. The cues they have picked up from their social environment tell them that refugees are poor people to be pitied, denigrated, or even attacked. To be sure, American-born youths of Cambodian, Vietnamese, Lao, Hmong, Iu Mien, or Tai Dam ancestries indeed are not refugees. But it cannot be disputed that adults from

Cambodia, Laos, and Vietnam who undertook perilous journeys to find refuge in the United States *are* refugees. To those young people who do not wish to be called refugees, I say, "When you cringe upon hearing the word *refugee,* you are unconsciously accepting the underlying racism that has given the term such a negative meaning. In my opinion, to be a refugee is nothing to be ashamed of. The fact that your families courageously survived colossal ordeals as they made their way to the United States is a testament to their strength and resilience—an achievement that should make you feel very proud rather than ashamed."

I use the word *refugees* sparingly in this book for a different reason. Based on the United Nations' definition, refugees are people who have a well-founded fear of persecution *from their own governments* due to their political ideologies or activities, religious affiliation, or membership in certain groups that the government in question has chosen to persecute. Given this narrow definition, people escaping from other forms of danger, such as natural disasters or famine, are not considered true refugees. Instead, they are often dubbed "economic migrants," "diplaced persons," "illegal aliens," or "evacuees." For that reason, the title of chapter 2 is "Seeking Refuge," which refers to a process, not a group of people because only a fraction of Cambodians who escaped to Vietnam or Thailand in search of sanctuary were classified and treated as "refugees," and it is they who were resettled in the United States, France, Australia, Canada, and other countries. I have coined the term *refuge-seekers* to cover everyone who searches for a safe haven, regardless of whether they qualify formally as "refugees." Because a vast majority of the Cambodians in the United States today did enter as "refugees" (only a small number was admitted as "immigrants" or "humanitarian parolees") the word *refugees* in the subtitle of this book is justified.

A second problematic word is "culture." Since the late 1960s, anthropologists and cultural studies specialists as well as scholars in several other fields have been radically rethinking what that word means. They have rejected older definitions of culture as something that is reified, essentialist, unitary, bounded, and unchanging. The current thinking is that culture is constantly being constructed and reconstructed by individuals, groups, and institutions over time and across geographic spaces. How individuals understand and relate to the cultures of which they are purportedly members depends a great deal on what relative power they possess, what positions they occupy, and the subgroups to which they belong. Cultures have both materialist groundings and symbolic meanings. As the academic debate about this slippery concept becomes ever more complex, ordinary people, including many individuals quoted in this book, continue to think that particular cultures do have salient and distinct characteristics and that there *are* differences among cultures. For lack of a better alternative I do not shy away from saying "culture" in this book, but I usually put "American culture" and "Cambodian/Khmer culture" in quotation marks to signal that I am aware that the contents and forms of all cultures, and the meanings evoked by them, are always under contestation.

I italicize transliterated foreign words when they first appear in the text but not subsequently. I do not add an *s* to the plural form of these words. English or French forms of Cambodian proper nouns, however, carry an *s* when they are plural. Thus, the plural of "Khmer" is "Khmer," but the plural of "Cambodian" is "Cambodians." Following conventional usage in English, I write "Khmer Rouge" in the singular even when the term is used in a plural sense. The word, however, is treated grammatically as plural—thus, "the Khmer Rouge were."

"Cambodians" refers to all people who live or lived in Cambodia, regardless of their ethnicity. "Cambodian" is used either as a singular proper noun or as an adjective for anything pertaining to Cambodia. "Khmer" refers to the major ethnic group in Cambodia and is also the name of their language. "Kampuchea" is a closer approximation of how the country's name is pronounced in Khmer. "Sino-Cambodians" are Cambodians of Chinese ancestry. "Khmer Krom" are Khmer living in the Mekong delta of southern Vietnam, which used to be a part of Cambodian territory. The "Cham" are an ethnic group descended from the kingdom of Champa, which the Vietnamese conquered and absorbed centuries ago. They presently live in both Vietnam and Cambodia. The country's name has changed several times since 1970. Before 1970—the year Prince Norodom Sihanouk was overthrown—Cambodia was a kingdom. From 1970 to 1975, when it was ruled by Lon Nol, the country was called the Khmer Republic. From April 1975 to January 1979, when the Khmer Rouge reigned supreme, it was known as Democratic Kampuchea. Between January 1979 and 1989, when Vietnamese troops occupied the country, its name was the People's Republic of Kampuchea. It became the State of Cambodia in 1989. Then, after the May 1993 United Nations–supervised elections voted in new legislators, the name was changed yet again to the Kingdom of Cambodia. Sihanouk was recrowned king in 1993.

The current official name of "Laos" is the Lao People's Democratic Republic. "Lao" or "lowland Lao" refers to the major ethnic group in Laos. "Lao" is also the name of the language they speak. "Laotians" refers to all people who live or lived in Laos, even though non-Lao ethnic groups prefer to be called by their own names. "Laotian" is used either as a singular proper noun or as an adjective for anything pertaining to Laos. "Hmong," "Iu Mien," and "Tai Dam" are some of the minority ethnic groups living in the hills of Laos, but they are also found in the hills of Vietnam and Thailand.

"Vietnamese" refers to everyone who lives or lived in Vietnam, regardless of his or her ethnic origins. The word has three other meanings. First, the "Vietnamese" are the major ethnic group in Vietnam; second, "Vietnamese" is the name of the language that members of the dominant group speak; and, third, it is an adjective pertaining to all things related to Vietnam. "Sino-Vietnamese" are Vietnamese of Chinese ancestry. "Montagnards" is a collective name the French gave to several dozen groups of hill people in Vietnam. Between 1954 and 1975 Vietnam was divided into two countries—the Democratic Republic of Vietnam (commonly called "North Vietnam") and the Republic of Vietnam (commonly called "South Vietnam"). There were communists in both countries. "Viet Cong" or "Vietcong" is a name South Vietnamese President Ngo Dinh Diem coined to refer to the communists in South Vietnam. However, many people, both in Southeast Asia and the United States, have colloquially used "Viet Cong" as a generic term for all Vietnamese communists. Since 1976 the name of the reunified country has been the Socialist Republic of Vietnam.

Until 1932 "Thailand" was called "Siam." The "Thai" are the major ethnic group in Thailand; that proper noun is also the name of their language.

"Burma" is now called "Myanmar." "Burmese" refers to all residents of Myanmar, regardless of their ethnicity. "Burmans" are the main ethnic group in the country and live in the lowlands. Hill-dwelling minority groups prefer to be called by their own names.

Personal names of Cambodians are given inconsistently in this book because some Cambodians choose to follow the Cambodian order of writing family names first, followed by their given names. Others, particularly those living in the United States or other Western countries, write their given names first, followed by their family names. I have followed the forms that have appeared in publications in the English language or that have been chosen by the individuals cited in this book.

Finally, I use the term *Cambodian Americans* rather selectively because very few adult Cambodians now living in the United States identify themselves as such, much less as "Asian Americans" or "Americans." The most these adults would concede is that they are "American citizens." However, most young people who have grown up in the United States, either because they were born here or because they came when they were very young, do think of themselves as "Cambodian Americans." Given the relatively low rate of immigration from Cambodia since the U.S. State Department ended the Cambodian refugee resettlement program in 1994, American-born children of Cambodian ancestry will in time outnumber Cambodians in the United States who were born in Cambodia or in one of the camps in Thailand. When that day comes, the entire ethnic group may then be properly called "Cambodian Americans" should they so desire. But many of them may not. In this age of globalization, an increasing number of people think of themselves as transmigrants—individuals who maintain on-going relations with people in two or more countries and participate in events in many parts of the world. Many Cambodians already exhibit this tendency, so it can be expected that the trend will continue.

Survivors

1 Cambodia's Darkest Hours

THE WORD *survivors* in the title of this book refers not only to those Cambodians who survived a series of cataclysmic horrors before finding a haven of sorts in the United States and elsewhere in the world but also to the ability of Cambodia and its people to endure invasions, colonial rule, war, and revolution. Indeed, survival can be said to be a leitmotif of Cambodian history. During the last five centuries Cambodia's existence as an independent country has repeatedly hung in the balance as Siam (Thailand's name before 1932), Vietnam, France, Japan, the United States, and China all intervened in its affairs. Since the late 1970s, Cambodians in the homeland as well as those scattered in diasporic communities around the world have struggled to make new lives for themselves. Despite the unremitting assaults on their autonomy, the people, culture, and society of Cambodia have all managed to survive. That resiliency is a testament to the strength of the Cambodian people.

A Historical Sketch

A small country in mainland Southeast Asia, Cambodia was once a kingdom named Angkor (802–1431), which occupied a larger territory than Cambodia does today. The Khmer people have inhabited the area for some two thousand years. Their language, also called Khmer, belongs to the Mon-Khmer family of languages. Indian civilization strongly influenced Khmer culture, which is a unique mix of indigenous and foreign elements. Much of Cambodia's mythology is derived from Hinduism, while a vast majority of Cambodians today continue to practice Theravada Buddhism, a religion that also originated in India.

The Angkorian kings built magnificent stone temples, many of which remain standing. The most famous is Angkor Wat. Occupying an area measuring one square mile, it is one of the largest religious edifices in the world. Intricate bas reliefs decorate the walls of the temples. These monuments are not only mesmerizingly beautiful but also critical for reconstructing Cambodia's history, because what we know about the country's past comes mainly from the temples and the engravings on them, inscriptions carved in stone found elsewhere, and accounts written by Chinese envoys who visited Cambodia (Chandler 1992b; Coedès 1968; Groslier 1966; Groslier and Arthaud 1966; Higham 2001; Krasa and Cifra, 1963; Mabbett and Chandler, 1991; Mannikka, 1996). The historical record is sparse, because paper, cloth, wood, and palm fronds all rot easily in the warm, humid weather. Moreover, as Buddhists, the Cambodians cremate their dead, so there are few grave sites containing human bones, tools, utensils, jewelry, and other items of material culture that might give us glimpses of how Cambodians used to live.

The glory that was Angkor stands in stark contrast to the foreign encroachments that marked the next five centuries of Cambodia's history. The Thai began raiding the Angkor kingdom in the mid-fourteenth century and destroyed many of its waterworks. They sacked Angkor Thom, the capital, in 1431. Thai troops captured four of Cambodia's northwestern provinces in 1593 and reduced Cambodia to a vassal state of Siam by 1603. Between the seventeenth and nineteenth centuries, Cambodia's other neighbor, Vietnam, sent tens of thousands of settlers to the Mekong Delta, which belonged to Cambodia, and gradually gained control over that region. To this day, Cambodians call the area Kampuchea Krom (lower Cambodia). The Khmer who still live there, known as Khmer Krom, form a distinct minority within Vietnam. Not to be outdone by Vietnam, Siam also took more Cambodian territory toward the end of the eighteenth century.

By the mid-nineteenth century Cambodia had become a vassal state to both Siam and Vietnam. Then, France appeared on the scene during the heyday of European imperialism. After the French colonized Cochinchina (the southern part of Vietnam) in 1862, Cambodia in 1863, Annam and Tonkin (the central and northern parts of Vietnam) in 1883, and Laos in 1893, they amalgamated the five territories into an entity called French Indochina. Even though the French allowed the Cambodian monarch to remain on the throne, they controlled virtually all aspects of Cambodian life. French rule ended in

1953 in Cambodia and Laos and in 1954 in Vietnam (Cady 1967; Chandler 1992b; Hall 1968: 436–43; Osborne 1969).

Between 1953 and 1970, King Norodom Sihanouk, who abdicated the throne in 1955 and became Prince Sihanouk so that he could participate actively in politics, dominated Cambodia's political life. He skillfully played domestic political factions against one another and juggled the demands of the superpowers and their respective allies aligned on opposite sides of the cold war. But as the war in Vietnam escalated in the mid-1960s after the United States started sending ground troops there, fighting spilled over into Cambodian territory. After the elections of 1966, which brought politicians who were not beholden to Sihanouk to power, he lost his grip on the politics, economy, and society of his country. General Lon Nol, the prime minister, and Sirik Matak, one of Sihanouk's cousins who was serving as the deputy prime minister, deposed the prince in March 1970 while he was traveling abroad. From 1970 to 1975 Lon Nol's Khmer Republic, which the United States supported, and the Communist Khmer Rouge, which North Vietnam supported, fought a civil war that ravaged the country. Some half a million died, and at least three million people of a total estimated population of more than seven million were displaced from their homes (Corfield 1994; Deac 1997; Osborne 1994).

The Khmer Rouge comprised the most radical faction among Cambodian communists. Communism had come to Cambodia via Vietnam while both were under French rule. The Cambodian communist movement began as a section, with only a small number of members within the Indochinese Communist Party (ICP) that Ho Chi Minh, the Vietnamese revolutionary leader, founded in 1930. The ICP dissolved itself during World War II but reemerged in 1951 as the Vietnamese Workers' Party (VWP). It also helped establish a Khmer People's Revolutionary Party (KPRP) and a Laotian People's Revolutionary Party. When the 1954 Geneva Accords settled the First Indochina War (1946–54), about half of the two thousand KPRP members went to North Vietnam. Sihanouk's police killed many of those who stayed behind. In 1960, twenty-one individuals who had coalesced around Saloth Sar—who later adopted the nom de guerre Pol Pot—changed the KPRP's name to the Workers' Party of Kampuchea and adopted a Marxist-Leninist platform (Chandler 1991b; Kiernan 1985; Kiernan and Boua, eds. 1982; Martin 1994).

In the 1960s, a three-way split emerged among those Cambodian communists who had gone to Hanoi, the ones who had remained behind but followed the revolutionary strategy laid down by Vietnam, and the Saloth Sar group, whose members had few ties to the Vietnamese and believed that the needs of the Cambodian revolution should not be subordinated to the Vietnamese one. After a few years of internecine warfare, the Saloth Sar faction emerged as the most powerful one, and its members became the core of the Khmer Rouge (Chandler 1992a: 69–90; Kiernan 1985: 167–246). Even though Sihanouk, while he was in power, had used repressive measures to control the Khmer Rouge, he formed a partnership with them after his ouster. He did not foresee that such an alliance would bring tragedy upon tragedy to the Cambodian people. The last three decades of the twentieth century were truly Cambodia's darkest hours.

Had these events not occurred, few persons of Cambodian ancestry would be in the United States today, for Cambodians did not have a history of emigration to the United States, unlike the Chinese, Japanese, Koreans, Filipinos, and Indians. The story of Cambodians in America, therefore, must begin with a discussion of the developments that propelled them to leave their homeland. This tragic history is a heavy burden that Cambodians everywhere continue to bear.

The First Cambodian Civil War, 1970–75

When the civil war began, the Khmer Rouge had an estimated four to fifteen thousand guerrillas and controlled about one-sixth of the country's territory. At war's end, they had some sixty thousand troops in their main forces and about two hundred thousand guerrillas (Carney 1989b: 26). Several factors help account for the Khmer Rouge's rapid victory: their mutually opportunistic alliance with Sihanouk, the aid they received from North Vietnam, the destruction caused by the American bombing campaign, and their growing military and political sophistication, which enabled them to defeat the poorly led and demoralized troops of Lon Nol.

Less than a week after his ouster, on March 23, 1970, Sihanouk broadcast a radio message from Beijing announcing the formation of FUNK—the French acronym for Front Uni Nationale du Kampuchea (National United Front of Cambodia)—composed of his own supporters and the Khmer Rouge (Grant, Moss, and Unger, eds. 1971: 105–9, 130–38). Although he had treated the latter as enemies before he was deposed, he now realized that he had to work with them if he hoped to retain any influence over developments in Cambodia. In his broadcast he called upon ordinary Cambodians to fight against the Lon Nol government and its American allies.

Residents of Phnom Penh, who had become extremely critical of Sihanouk by the late 1960s and were glad to see him removed, ignored his message. In the rural areas and some provincial towns, however, tens of thousands of people participated in pro-Sihanouk demonstrations after hearing cassette tapes of his appeal (Osborne 1994: 219). To quell the demonstrators, Lon Nol's soldiers fired into the crowds, killing more than a hundred people (Chandler 1991b: 201–2). The soldiers' behavior made it easier for Khmer Rouge and Vietnamese communist cadres to persuade people that the Lon Nol regime was their enemy. During this period Lon Nol's troops also killed thousands of ethnic Vietnamese living in Cambodia.

Concealing their ideology as well as their ultimate goal, and using Sihanouk's popularity as a cover, the Khmer Rouge quickly increased their ranks by telling potential recruits that they would be fighting to restore Sihanouk to power. As one peasant woman from Battambang told Kate Frieson, "The people were angry at Lon Nol for overthrowing Sihanouk. . . . They joined the revolution because Lon Nol had a lot of people killed. . . . And after that a lot of people ran into the forest to join the Red Khmers in order to help the prince come back again. The people in the villages and in the countryside loved Sihanouk . . . when they overthrew him . . . [we] were very sick hearted about it" (Frieson 1992: 83).

Sihanouk hosted a Summit Conference of Indochinese Peoples in Guangzhou (Canton) in southern China in late April 1970, during which North Vietnam, the National Liberation Front (the formal name of the "Viet Cong"—Communists in South Vietnam), the Pathet Lao (Laotian Communists), and FUNK pledged to cooperate militarily to fight against the government of South Vietnam, the Lon Nol regime in Cambodia, and the United States. Then, on May 5, 1970, Sihanouk and the Khmer Rouge formed a government-in-exile to be located in two places. Sihanouk and his handful of supporters would live in Beijing, play a diplomatic role, and lend political legitimacy to the Khmer Rouge; Khmer Rouge leaders, who monopolized control over the coalition's armed men, would continue to operate militarily from guerrilla bases within Cambodia (Chandler 1992a: 91–109; Norodom Sihanouk and Burchett 1973: 186–214).

It did not take long for Sihanouk to realize that the Khmer Rouge were merely using him, but, living in exile in Beijing, he had few, if any, other options. Even as they relied on his popularity among the peasants to advance their own agenda, Khmer Rouge leaders did not hide their intentions with respect to Sihanouk. Ieng Sary, one of the most powerful Khmer Rouge leaders in the Saloth Sar circle and the latter's brother-in-law, told a journalist, "Sihanouk is one of those aspects of Cambodian tradition, like Buddhism and the monarchy, which we believe unnecessary for the larger union. We will phase out those aspects we do not consider to be progressive and revolutionary" (quoted in Etcheson 1984: 132).

During the first two years of the civil war, the Khmer Rouge's military operations benefitted greatly from North Vietnamese aid (Carney 1989b: 20–23; Chandler 1992a: 95–96). Immediately after the coup that toppled Sihanouk, the North Vietnamese changed their policy regarding the revolutionary path Cambodia was to follow. Instead of holding the Khmer Rouge in check, as they had done up to this point, the North Vietnamese now threw their support behind the Khmer Rouge's armed struggle. The reason was simple. Now that the staunchly anticommunist Lon Nol was in power, Vietnamese communists could no longer easily send supplies to comrades in South Vietnam via the Ho Chi Minh trail that ran along the Laotian-Vietnamese and Cambodian-Vietnamese borders or through the port of Sihanoukville, as they had done during the 1960s.

In addition to American bombing raids over the trail, Vietnamese communists now had to contend with Lon Nol's army. They also anticipated that Lon Nol and his American and South Vietnamese allies would attempt to destroy the sanctuaries in eastern Cambodia to which their forces had retreated whenever they had been under heavy attack by U.S. and South Vietnamese ground troops.

Taking advantage of the turmoil following the coup, the North Vietnamese moved quickly to gain control over a part of Cambodia. By late March 1970, their armed forces had taken over four provinces in northeastern Cambodia as well as several towns in Kompong Cham Province. By June, they controlled one-third of the country. Their troops behaved well and did not molest the local population or wantonly destroy property and crops. Vietnamese cadres who could speak Khmer played a critical role in winning over the people. As one peasant put it, "There was no problem between the Viet Cong and the Khmers there because they . . . could speak our language, and were always very honest and well-behaved. They paid for everything, even the smallest thing so people in the village did not have anything against them" (Frieson 1992: 78).

Such model behavior was practiced not only by the Vietnamese communists but also by the Khmer Rouge. As a Khmer Rouge document instructed cadres and troops, "A revolutionist should be kind and sympathetic to the people; a revolutionist should always use kind words when talking to the people. These words should cause no harm; make the listener sympathetic to the speaker; be easily understood by the listener; sound polite in all circumstances; be pleasing to everyone; and make the listeners happy" (quoted in Chandler 1991b: 208–09).

The Vietnamese communist forces not only captured territory but also helped the Khmer Rouge create an administrative structure in rural areas. Well aware of the Cambodians' historic anti-Vietnamese feelings, however, Vietnamese troops and political cadres kept a low profile. They emphasized "loyalty to Prince Sihanouk, protection of Khmer lives and civilization from American and South Vietnamese invaders, and the overthrow of local tyrants" (Isaacs 1983: 206). Such efforts were not sufficient to dampen the historical enmity between the two groups, however. As early as 1973, and in the midst of the revolution, the Khmer Rouge began referring to the Vietnamese as their "Number One Enemy" (Chandler 1991b: 219).

Between 1970 and 1972, the well-trained North Vietnamese soldiers and cadres provided a shield behind which the Khmer Rouge grew in strength and gained battlefield as well as political experience, but in 1972 they withdrew from Cambodia in order to participate in the 1972 spring offensive against South Vietnam. Moreover, by this time the Khmer Rouge were strong enough to proceed on their own. Their regular forces numbered some twelve to fifteen thousand in late 1970, increased to perhaps twenty-five thousand a year later, and numbered fifty-five to sixty thousand when the war ended in April 1975 (Carney 1989b: 26).

A former U.S. Central Intelligence Agency analyst argued that these figures give an inaccurate picture of Khmer Rouge strength. If guerrillas and militiamen are also included, then they probably had two hundred thousand fighters by 1973 (quoted in Frieson 1992: 173–74). Initially they used Soviet- and Chinese-made weapons and ammunition, which the North Vietnamese gave them; later, they relied mainly on captured U.S. equipment. They also bought contraband weapons, medicine, and gasoline from corrupt government officials and military officers in Lon Nol's regime.

North Vietnam's military support was vital to the Khmer Rouge's survival and growth during the late 1960s and early 1970s (even though in later years Saloth Sar vehemently denied that the Vietnamese communists had contributed anything to his victory) because the United States had begun a secret campaign on March 18, 1969, to bomb Vietnamese communist sanctuaries in eastern Cambodia. The month before, General Creighton Abrams, commander of U.S. forces in South Vietnam, had sought permission from the Joint Chiefs of Staff to bomb "Base Area 353" in the so-called Fish Hook area—a section of eastern Cambodia jutting into South Vietnam—where the Vietnamese communist logistical headquarters, which the Americans dubbed "COSVN" (Central Office for South Vietnam), was supposedly located. Abrams's request was forwarded to President Richard M. Nixon and his national security advisor Henry A. Kissinger. Nixon granted permission but insisted that the bombing be done in total secrecy.

According to journalist William Shawcross, a system of dual reporting made the concealment possible. The initial March 18 raid consisted of sixty sorties flown by B-52s, each carrying thirty tons of bombs dropped between 3 and 7 A.M. Forty-eight of the aircraft, all based in Guam, were diverted to the Fish Hook area after they entered South Vietnamese air space, while the remaining twelve dropped their loads over targets in South Vietnam. Military commanders in charge of the operation did not inform the pilots and navigators about the intended diversion until just before they took off. All they were told was that ground controllers in South Vietnam would give them the coordinates for a different set of targets once they entered the war zone. After completing their missions they were to return to base and say nothing about where they had been. Those in charge ordered the supervisor of the radar crew to destroy every piece of paper and computer tape on which the Cambodian targets had been plotted and to write the coordinates for the original targets in South Vietnam in poststrike reports. Thus, "the bombing was not merely concealed; the offical, secret records showed that it had never happened" (Shawcross 1987: 19–31).

Military personnel who knew about the bombing raids were instructed that should journalists inquire about the bombing, they were to say that U.S. airplanes did strike "routine missions adjacent to the Cambodian border" but neither confirm nor deny that bombs had fallen inside Cambodia. Should there be an official protest from Cambodia, the United States would apologize and offer compensation. Despite all attempts to keep the bombing secret, the American public eventually learned about it because a number of the officers who participated in the action were so disturbed by the effort to falsify the official military record that they decided to inform Congress about what had taken place (Shawcross 1987: 31–33). Nixon justified his decision in part by claiming that Sihanouk did not object to the bombing. Sihanouk has never disclosed whether he actually approved of the aerial destruction of a part of his country or passively pretended not to know about it.

Abrams had initially asked for a single attack, but once that had taken

place it was easy to gain permission for additional ones. Over the next fourteen months, American pilots flew 3,630 B-52 raids over Cambodia. This
bombing campaign was an integral part of Nixon's "Vietnamization" strategy—to turn the fighting increasingly over to South Vietnamese forces. As
more and more American ground troops withdrew from South Vietnam,
American airplanes rained greater and greater destruction on Cambodia in
order to protect the flank of the Army of South Vietnam (ARVN). The number of sorties flown reached a zenith in early 1973—more than a hundred a
day—just as the Paris Peace Agreement to end U.S. involvement in Vietnam
went into effect (Kiernan 1985: 349–57). More bombs were showered on Cambodia than the total tonnage dropped on either Europe or Japan during World
War II, killing more than a hundred thousand civilians.

The bombing was counterproductive, however. Instead of driving Vietnamese communists out of Cambodia, the devastation pushed them deeper
into the Cambodian countryside. Instead of destroying the Khmer Rouge,
the raids strengthened their resolve and enabled them to rally more and more
peasants to their side. Recalled one refugee, "The ordinary people were terrified by the bombing . . . sometimes they literally shit in their pants when
the big bombs and shells came. . . . some people became shell shocked. . . .
Even . . . [after] the shelling had stopped they couldn't hold down a meal.
Their minds just froze up and [they] would wander around mute and not
talk for three or four days. . . . we had never done anything to these Americans. . . . The Khmers didn't even have any airplanes and here the Americans
had brought theirs to bomb us, causing great pain to us" (Frieson 1992: 167–
68, 177).

Unable to destroy the communist sanctuaries from the air, the United
States and South Vietnam invaded Cambodia after Sihanouk was deposed.
On April 29, 1970, thirty-two thousand U.S. troops and forty thousand from
ARVN marched into Cambodia (Kiernan 1985: 304–8; Tran 1978: 51–133). This
ground invasion, too, began in secret. President Nixon did not inform Lon
Nol about the plan beforehand. He also kept the U.S. Congress and most of
his cabinet members and high-ranking military commanders in the dark.
Among those who knew, the secretaries of state and defense expressed severe
reservations about the invasion. A number of Nixon's staff resigned in protest. When Nixon appeared on television to disclose what he had done, anti-
war protests erupted across the United States.

As Nixon promised, American forces did withdraw from Cambodia by
June, but units of ARVN remained. Some of the latter were poorly disciplined
and "often behaved like bandits" (Chandler 1991b: 204). They went on a ram-

page, perhaps in retaliation against the Lon Nol government, which had massacred tens of thousands of ethnic Vietnamese residing in Cambodia just a few weeks earlier. The historical enmity between Cambodians and Vietnamese intensified during this period. During the following two years some three hundred thousand ethnic Vietnamese living in Cambodia fled to South Vietnam.

Like the secret aerial bombing, the ground invasion also backfired. Not only were North Vietnamese communist troops not destroyed, but they also now had an excuse to move farther into Cambodian territory. The reason they could do so, according to Cambodian General Sak Sutsakhan, was that U.S. and ARVN forces primarily used frontal assaults rather than "enveloping maneuvers" (Sak 1980: 173). Thus, instead of surrounding their enemy on all sides in order to deny them any escape routes, the U.S.-ARVN troops drove the communist forces ahead of them into the central plains of Cambodia.

In the initial euphoria following the coup against Sihanouk, thousands of young men volunteered for Lon Nol's army, swelling it from thirty thousand to two hundred thousand men within a year. Despite the army's growth and the fact that its troops were increasingly paid, equipped, and fed by the United States, Cambodian government troops did not perform well because they were poorly paid and fed. They often went for months without pay because some of their officers pocketed a large portion of funds that the United States provided for soldiers' salaries.

The amount of American aid was calculated according to the total number of soldiers in the Khmer Republic's army. Some Cambodian military officers padded the size of the army by inserting the names of soldiers who either did not exist or had died or defected. By thus inflating the number of troops, they increased the amount of funds they received, only a small part of which ever reached the foot soldiers. Commanding officers pocketed the pay of an estimated one hundred thousand soldiers every month. In addition, both civilian officials and military chiefs made money by selling American-supplied weapons, ammunition, and gasoline to their communist enemies (Chandler 1991b: 205, 223).

The troops often went hungry because the Cambodian army did not supply them with rations. Instead, they had to either buy food from village markets or rely on their families to bring food to them. Women and children who accompanied men to the front, however, were placed in the line of fire, thus increasing the civilian casualty rate. They also slowed troop movement, as journalist Arnold A. Isaacs reported from the war front (Isaacs 1983: 208). Furthermore, little medical attention was available for wounded or sick soldiers. As General Sosthene Fernandez, the Cambodian army's commander-in-chief, said sadly to a group of reporters toward the end of the Lon Nol regime, "I am sure that in any country, in your country, if soldiers received the same conditions as our soldiers, they probably would not fight ever" (Isaacs 1983: 191).

Army commanders as well as troops, certainly Lon Nol himself, showed little resolve to fight. Consequently, according to Craig Etcheson, "entire brigades" of the army's "best infantry literally vanished into the mud" (Etcheson 1984: 114–15). As they lost one campaign after another, Khmer Republic soldiers and commanders focused on defending the area around the capital and keeping the Mekong River open, because that waterway was Phnom Penh's lifeline.

In contrast to the Khmer Republic's inept military efforts, the Khmer Rouge's armed might became increasingly effective. At the beginning of the civil war they reorganized their armed forces into three tiers: small guerrilla units to be used to infiltrate, spy on, and harass government offices and military depots; larger and better equipped regional guerrilla units to carry out raids and sabotage missions; and a regular army for conventional warfare (Etcheson 1984: 108–10). The reorganization not only gave them tactical flexibility but also enabled the main forces to turn over captured territory to local units to administer as the regular troops themselves moved on to conquer more territory.

Khmer Rouge forces reached the outskirts of Phnom Penh by mid-1973. But their campaign to take the city took almost two years because the Vietnamese had withdrawn their forces by then, and the Khmer Rouge did not have enough arms to wage an all-out campaign. New supplies were not forthcoming from the United States, because Congress cut off additional military aid to Cambodia.

Before August 1973, U.S. air power helped compensate for the poor performance of the Khmer Republic's ground forces. But the Khmer Republic's army became ever more helpless and demoralized as Congress first reduced and then terminated military aid to Cambodia after the Paris Peace Agreement was signed in January 1973 to end the war in Vietnam. Phnom Penh, where the population had swollen by some two million refugees who had flocked to the city to escape the bombing raids, by now was dependent almost entirely on American airdrops for food and other necessities. After the United States withdrew its air power on August 15, 1973, food, fuel, and medicine in the capital all ran out. Malnutrition and starvation became widespread.

By the end of 1973, Khmer Rouge forces were close enough to fire rockets and shells from captured American 105-mm howitzers at Phnom Penh, killing thousands of people. Some Cambodian leaders tried to persuade Lon Nol to leave the country so that negotiations with the Khmer Rouge could begin, but he refused to do so. The final Khmer Rouge assault, called the Meking River Offensive, began in January 1975. The following month, the Khmer Rouge placed floating mines in the river. Made in the People's Republic of China, the mines were deadly effective. Their use ended all barge convoys bringing supplies to the besieged capital.

Lon Nol finally consented to leave at the beginning of April 1975. He first went to Indonesia and then settled in Hawaii. Thousands of high-ranking officials and well-to-do people likewise left the country. Evacuation by fixed-wing aircraft of Americans and Cambodians whose lives might be at risk once the Khmer Rouge captured Phnom Penh took place between April 4 and 10, 1975. On April 12, the day the American embassy closed, helicopters lifted out Ambassador John Gunther Dean, eighty-four embassy staff, and 203 Cambodians and people of other nationalities. The Americans had reserved a thousand spaces for the Cambodian elite, but only 878, half of them children under the age of twelve, actually accepted the offer (Deac 1997: xii).

Those who declined to leave were nationalists who fervently wished to participate in the reconstruction of their country once peace returned. Prince Sirik Matak, in declining the offer to be evacuated, penned a bitter note to Ambassador Dean, accusing the United States of abandoning Cambodia. Long Boret, Lon Nol's prime minister who had accompanied him to Indonesia, flew back to Phnom Penh, hoping to negotiate a cease-fire and political settlement with the Khmer Rouge. Sadly for both men, they were among the first to be executed by the Khmer Rouge after taking the capital.

On the morning of April 17, 1975, Khmer Rouge troops, many of them young teenagers clad in loose, black clothing, marched somberly into Phnom Penh. Some of the city's residents, relieved that the war was finally over and convinced that different groups of Cambodians could work together, regardless of their political differences, welcomed the victors as they paraded along Phnom Penh's broad, tree-lined streets. Little did anyone suspect that beginning that very afternoon, a tragedy of unimaginable proportions, to be followed by yet other catastrophes, would befall the country and engulf its long-suffering people for years to come.

The Nature of the Khmer Rouge Revolution

A single phrase, "the killing fields," taken from the title of a 1984 film has formed the world's controlling image of Cambodia. Although Cambodians themselves also use the term, more frequently they refer to this dark period in their history as *samay Pol Pot* (the Pol Pot time). Pol Pot, the nom de guerre of Saloth Sar, was also called "Brother Number One" to reflect his paramount status among the leaders of the Democratic Kampuchea (DK) regime that came into being on April 17, 1975.

Although Saloth Sar at first did not disclose that he was Pol Pot, that is the name by which he became known around the world. In retrospect, Cambodian refugees refer to his followers as "the Pol Pots" (Welaratna 1993). Khmer Rouge leaders liked to boast that their efforts were "without precedent." "What we are trying to do," declared Ieng Sary, "has never been done before in history" (Chandler 1991b: 240). Reflecting their French education, the leaders borrowed the concept of "year zero" from the French Revolution to indicate their desire to wipe their society's slate clean and start from scratch as they attempted to transform every aspect of Cambodian society.

It has been difficult for scholars to characterize the revolution that Pol Pot led. According to David Chandler, the Khmer Rouge never resolved "the contradiction between their revolution's being a genuine socialist one (and thus comparable to others) or uniquely Cambodian, without precedents or offsprings" (1991b: 245). Michael Vickery observes that the two major policies of the Khmer Rouge leadership were "poor-peasantism and anti-Vietnamese racism." He defines "peasant populism" as an "anti-intellectual ideology" based on "a belief in the sacredness of the soil and those who till it." Thus, the Khmer Rouge leaders were "petty-bourgeois radicals overcome by peasant romanticism" (1984: 264, 285, 287). Kate Grace Frieson, however, argues that the Khmer Rouge revolution was not a genuine peasant revolution. Relying on oral histories, she demonstrates that "the relationship between the peasantry and the Red Khmers . . . [was] one of mutual mistrust, misunderstanding, and inequality." Moreover, peasants perceived that "[d]eference to whatever side in the war had local power at a given time was . . . their best defense." She concludes that "the Red Khmer movement did not represent the needs of the peasants as they themselves defined them" (1992: iii, 249, 255).

As for whether the Khmer Rouge followed any other country's model, Karl Jackson points out that "[a]lthough it is useful to search for the intellectual antecedents of the Khmer Rouge . . . the ferocity and literalism with which they pursued these formal ideologies cannot be explained merely by reference to abstract formal ideologies. . . . The proclivity toward violence, the fear of contamination by outsiders, the moral self-righteousness, and the literal and doctrinaire way of pursuing goals are what separate the Khmer Rouge from comparable revolutionary phenomena" (1989c: 7). In Jackson's opinion, the Khmer Rouge belonged to a "sectarian movement" guided by a "dichotomous" worldview in which the world is divided into two, "believers, who are good, and nonbelievers, who are evil" (8). Khatharya Um aptly characterizes the Khmer Rouge as a "brotherhood of the pure" (Um 1990 and in press). Fearing pollution or contamination, they savagely went about eradicating all those whom they deemed impure.

In the most detailed study of the Khmer Rouge to date, Ben Kiernan argues that the revolution they led made extensive use of what we would today call "ethnic cleansing," a term not popularized until the civil war in the former Yugoslavia two decades later: "Khmer Rouge conceptions of race overshadowed those of class. . . . Race also overshadowed organizational imperatives. Non-Khmer Cambodians with extensive revolutionary experience and CPK seniority were removed from the leadership and usually murdered. . . . This was neither a Communist proletarian revolution that privileged the working class nor a peasant revolution that favored all farmers. . . . Membership in the single approved race [Khmer] was a condition, though not a sufficient one, of official approval" (1996: 26).

Unlike historians and political scientists, who tend to focus on the Khmer Rouge leadership and its ideology, anthropologist Alexander Laban Hinton analyzes how the Khmer Rouge drew on "preexisting cultural models that were emotionally salient to the perpetuators" to motivate them to kill (1997: 266; 1996; 1998a; 1998b). These include Khmer conceptions of honor, revenge, paranoia, patronage, and obedience—concepts deeply embedded in the hierarchical Khmer social structure. According to Hinton, Khmer Rouge soldiers and cadres followed orders because Cambodians are socialized to obey their elders and patrons. Cambodians generally carry out the wishes of their superiors in order not to lose face (*mukh*)—which depends greatly on the evaluation of others—and to avoid potential punishment. In Democratic Kampuchea, those who actually did the dirty work of killing felt no contrition because they could "deflect responsibility" from themselves as the "orders came from Angkar" ("Angkar" meaning "organization" and referring to the upper echelon of the Khmer Rouge). Those who actually committed the acts of violence, that is, did not do so of their own volition. Moreover, the Khmer concept of *kum* (*kum* or *kam* is the Khmer transliteration of the Indian word *karma*) helped justify a phenomenon that Hinton calls "disproportionate revenge"—revenge that is "much more damaging than the original injury"—because the youthful soldiers and cadres were told that the *kbat* (traitors) were "people who had been responsible for traditional class inequalities and the wartime death of numerous comrades" (1996: 823–28;

Hinton 1998a). Hinton argues that the ethic of gentleness, so observable among Cambodians, has always coexisted with an ethic of violence. What the Khmer Rouge did was legitimize the latter and render the "economic and ecological conditions that had previously necessited cooperation . . . irrelevant" (1996: 823).

To those analyses I would add two others. First, although there were some parallels between the revolutionary conditions in China and Cambodia, based on the extensive research I have done on Maoist revolutionary tactics and strategy I would argue that Mao Zedong and Pol Pot differed in one fundamental way. Mao emphasized the importance of analyzing "concrete conditions" and devising political and military strategies to address them as they evolved stage by stage. Pol Pot, in contrast, attempted to leap-frog over other socialist revolutions and transform Cambodia overnight into the most advanced communist society in the world. Second, Khmer Rouge leaders were not "mad men" in the sense of being irrational. On the contrary, they had a clearly articulated scheme that they carried out methodically in the coldest, most calculating way. They acted as they did because they were idealists in two senses of that word. They had a utopian vision of what they considered to be the perfect society, and they thought about the world not in terms of human strengths and frailties but in abstract categories. That is why they could go about implementing their policies with no regard for the human costs of their actions.

The Killing Fields

Impatient to turn their ideals into reality, the Khmer Rouge began to evacuate Phnom Penh on the very afternoon of the day they captured it. Patients at Phnom Penh's largest civilian hospital were among the first to go. Francois Ponchaud, a French missionary working in the capital at the time, remembered:

> A few moments later a hallucinatory spectacle began. Thousands of the sick and wounded were abandoning the city. The strongest dragged pitifully along, others were carried by friends, and some were lying on beds pushed by their families with their plasma and IV bumping alongside. I shall never forget one cripple who had neither hands nor feet, writhing along the ground like a severed worm, or a weeping father carrying his ten-year-old daughter wrapped in a sheet tied around his neck like a sling, or the man with his foot

dangling at the end of a leg to which it was attached by nothing but the skin.
(1978: 6–7)

In the next few days the entire city's population was on the move. Political cadres told residents that they had to leave because the Americans were going to bomb the city. In reality, the aim of the Khmer Rouge was to prevent any resistance from developing against themselves. By abruptly uprooting the approximately 2.5 million people living in the nation's cities, large and small, the victors hoped to gain complete control over the urban population by dislocating, disorienting, dispossessing, degrading, dehumanizing, and downright terrorizing them.

The decision to evacuate had been made two months earlier. Because the directive was not issued to lower-level cadres until early April, however, and reached various regions of the country at different times, the evacuation lacked coordination. Cadres gave contradictory instructions on what people could take, where they should go, and how they could get there. Also, military and political leaders from various zones had different attitudes toward the people and dealt with them differently. A few Khmer Rouge leaders, such as Hou Yuon, opposed the evacuation. He soon disappeared, however, presumably killed by Pol Pot for daring to oppose the plan.

Told to take only a little food with them because they would be allowed to return shortly, people thought the evacuation would be only temporary. But after a few weeks of coerced wandering, it began to dawn on them that the Khmer Rouge cadres had lied to them. As Teeda Butt Mam realized:

> They forced millions of residents of Phnom Penh and other cities out of their homes. They separated us from our friends and neighbors to keep us off balance, to prevent us from forming any alliance to stand up and win back our rights. . . . They kept moving us around, from the fields into the woods. They purposely did this to disorient us so they could have complete control. They did it to get rid of the "useless people." Those who were too old or too weak to work. Those who did not produce their quota. . . . We were timid and lost. We had to be silent. We not only lost our identities, but we lost our pride, our senses, our religion, our loved ones, our souls, ourselves. (1997: 11–12, 14–15)

Although no one knew what awaited them, many evacuees did have forebodings and took some precautions before leaving their homes. Chivy Sok, a Sino-Cambodian woman whose family lived in Battambang Province where both parents were teachers, was only five at the time. She recalled:

We left everything of value behind. I couldn't understand why Mom cried as she looked at old photos and discarded them. She tossed everything into the pond at the back of our house—all the memories of our family history: pictures of [my brother] Sid as a baby, pictures of her elaborate traditional Cambodian wedding, pictures of us playing in the front yard overlooking the wet rice paddy. Apparently, everyone had to get rid of all their belongings, especially those that would classify them as a bourgeois or traditional intellectual. (1993: 3–4)

Most evacuees tried to go to their ancestral villages, but they were not always welcome there. The villagers who were forced to share their homes and rations with urban evacuees flooding into the countryside were understandably wary and resentful. During the cross-country trek, tens of thousands of people died from execution, illness, exposure to the elements, or starvation and thirst. Political cadres accompanying the crowds forced individuals to tell their life stories in order to identify those who belonged to categories of people chosen for liquidation. They also ordered former government officials or military officers to gather at specified locations at appointed times to receive instructions. Those naive enough to attend never returned from those meetings.

The Khmer Rouge called the evacuees "New People" or "April 17 People" or "Deposit\u00e9es" and treated them as enemies of the revolution. Having dwelled in cities, where Western influences had been strongest, the urbanites were considered paragons of immorality. New People included civilian and military leaders of the Lon Nol regime, who were quickly executed; merchants, who as practitioners of capitalism had profited by exploiting others; landlords, who had oppressed peasants; and professionals of various kinds and even students, whose minds had supposedly been corrupted by Westernized higher education. Wealthy and middle-level peasants who owned some land but lived in areas the Khmer Rouge did not take over until April 1975 were also suspect. They, too, were counted as New People. In contrast, "Old People" or "Base People" or "Full Rights People," most of whom were poor peasants, had lived in areas the Khmer Rouge controlled before April 1975. Henceforth, Full Rights People would hold power, and New People would have no rights at all. A middle category, called "Candidates" and consisting of middle-level peasants and small traders, could attend meetings but not speak at them (Vickery 1986: 29–30).

Six months later, Khmer Rouge leaders ordered a second cross-country move. They moved the largest contingents from the Southwestern Zone to the Northwestern Zone. The regime even provided oxcarts, trucks, trains, and river boats to transport people. Already weakened from the initial evacuation, more people perished, mainly from a lack of food and medical care. Even after they reached their destinations they found no sanctuary. Loung Ung, a young girl at the time, remembers how villagers greeted her family at the end of their second evacuation: "All around the truck, villagers have gathered to take their first look at us new people. . . . 'Capitalists should be shot and killed,' someone yells from the crowd, glaring at us. Another villager walks over and spits at Pa's feet. Pa's shoulders droop low as he holds his palms together in a gesture of greeting. . . . They look very mean, like hungry tigers ready to pounce on us. Their black eyes stare at me, full of contempt" (2000: 57).

Once people arrived at the rural destinations where they were allowed to settle, the Khmer Rouge put them to work cultivating crops but provided few tools and no fertilizer. Men, women, and children moved huge mounds of earth to build dams and irrigation ditches, sometimes with their bare hands. In these endeavors the Khmer Rouge had no use for the technical knowledge that well-educated professionals like Pin Yathay, an engineer, might have provided. He, like everyone else, became a common laborer: "[T]he four-mile canal was to be dug without any machinery at all. Theng and I found ourselves part of a group responsible for making a five hundred–yard section, cutting into the earth with hoes, and carrying the earth to the edge in bamboo baskets, piling it up into levees on either side. It was an enormous operation which involved several villages, with a dozen different teams all in competition with each other, working from dawn until ten or eleven at night" (1987: 61).

Khmer Rouge leaders did not allow people to use machinery because they considered such equipment to be symbols of Western imperialism and wanted to promote total self-reliance. They let cars, trucks, tractors, refrigerators, and other mechanized appliances rust in the humid tropical air. The entire country became one gigantic forced-labor camp. What made the heavy labor more unbearable than it might have been otherwise was the fact that the entire population, with the exception of the Khmer Rouge cadres and soldiers themselves, had to subsist on a near-starvation diet. There was a shortage of food because the regime was exporting rice to China to pay for arms and other goods.

By the second year of the DK regime, more and more people were being fed not rice but only thin rice gruel. People desperately foraged for anything that seemed edible; some died eating poisonous plants. Worse, those caught foraging were accused of stealing from the state and punished. Malnutrition became rampant along with the debilitating conditions that come with it.

Underfed and working long hours with little rest, an increasing number of the old, very young, weak, and even those in their prime working years succumbed. Some exhausted and starving women stopped menstruating. The birth rate declined, and the mortality rate shot up. During the three years and eight months that the DK regime lasted, some 1.7 million people of a population of almost eight million died.

The lives of those who became ill were grim. Unable to work, they were deemed nonproductive, and their meager rations were further reduced. The sick either received no treatment at all or were given medicine the Khmer Rouge had concocted themselves and stored in unsterile containers, thereby increasing the rate of infection. Evacuees who brought along commonly available Western drugs such as aspirin, or traditional Chinese herbs, tried their best to keep them hidden. They feared the medicine would be confiscated—or worse, that they would be punished severely for "counter-revolutionary" behavior. Some ailing individuals tried their best to continue working lest they be accused of malingering. Molyda Szymusiak, who developed night blindness due to a vitamin A deficiency, writes, "After a month or so, it seemed to me that I was going blind. I was digging up the earth with a pickax, and it wasn't necessary to see clearly all the time, but at night, when I had to gather up the dirt in my basket and carry it to the embankment, I needed to be able to guide myself and I couldn't see a thing. I was reduced to feeling around on the ground" (1986: 141–42).

In addition to evacuating cities, the regime abolished markets, money, banks, and private property in order to erase all traces of capitalism. Khmer Rouge leaders also closed all schools, although in a few localities schools and hospitals continued functioning for a while. They extirpated the Buddhist *sangha* (community of monks), defrocked monks and put them to work in fields, and used Buddhist temples for nonreligious purposes.

Along with eliminating Buddhism, a bedrock of Cambodian culture, the Khmer Rouge also tried to destroy that culture's second foundation, the family. They separated children above the age of seven from their parents and placed them into youth work brigades under the supervision of young Khmer Rouge soldiers and political cadres. In some areas they also separated couples from one another. By 1976 everyone had to eat in mess halls, but in some localities New People and Old People were fed separately (the latter received better rations). Worse, the Khmer Rouge used children, who were considered "purer," less corrupt, and more malleable than adults, to spy on their parents and other older relatives. People became afraid to say anything lest it incriminate them. Even though numerous directives designed to turn

Cambodian society completely upside down applied to all areas of the country, the severity of measures differed in the various zones because some Khmer Rouge regional leaders and lower-level cadres did not always agree with what Pol Pot and his closest comrades ordered them to do.

Many *kamaphibal* (local cadres) and *yothea* (soldiers) were still in their teens or early twenties and illiterate. They had the power, however, to punish severely even the smallest infractions, often by killing the accused in brutal ways. To conserve ammunition, they did not shoot some victims but rather broke their necks with clubs, shovels, hoes, or pickaxes. Others were buried alive in holes they had been forced to dig themselves or suffocated with plastic bags. An account given to Marie Alexandrine Martin by a former yothea hints at the psychological mechanism at work among the rule-enforcers—youthful pride in being assigned important tasks mixed with latent yet ever-present fear of being punished themselves should responsibilities not be carried out to the letter:

> In the beginning of 1974 I became a yothea and fought against Lon Nol's soldiers. After 1975 I worked in the rice fields, and, at the same time, Angkar entrusted me with rooting out Lon Nol's agents among the "new people." . . . In the case of former soldiers, Angkar physically liquidated them. . . . We killed those who tried to escape. . . . During the interrogations, electric shocks were used. Children were also killed if they made a lot of mistakes, if they were traitors. . . . I agreed with the executions. If I didn't, they'd have accused me of complicity and arrested me. And those who made mistakes had to take responsibility for their errors. (Martin 1994: 167–68)

An older man whom Alexander Hinton interviewed gave a similar sort of answer: "I did this [killing] so that others wouldn't accuse me of being unable to cut off my heart. . . . When my boss asked me to do this, . . . I couldn't refuse" (1998b: 95).

The early evening was a favorite time for taking people into the woods to be murdered. Khuon Kiv, a thirteen-year-old boy at the time he was placed into a youth work brigade, witnessed such a scene:

> One night it was my turn to guard the camp. . . . As I heard a digging sound, . . . I sneaked out and looked. I saw about ten to fifteen people digging dirt. Some were tied up, blindfolded, with their mouths covered, while others carried chopping shovels on their shoulders. Suddenly, I heard a voice screaming in pain. . . . It was the sound of a human screaming for help because he had just been hit with a shovel by young Khmer Rouge soldiers who

could have been the victims' sons or relatives. It was the sound of living hell, the sound of a really frightening nightmare. . . . A moment later the sound was getting softer and softer, and that was the end of it. I was so scared and shaky that I went to get my friend up. Not only was he not surprised, but his response made me more nervous. He told me, "You better be quiet or we will be next." (1997: 102)

What especially haunts so many survivors of the Khmer Rouge era now is the fact the Khmer Rouge joked with one another and laughed about their barbaric deeds. As Vibol Ouk told Charles Martin Simon, who coauthored a chilling memoir with him:

Mr. Phoen was telling the others how he had trouble cutting off one guy's head because the guy was big and tried to fight back. So he shot him in the stomach, which put him in the right position. Then he chopped his head off without a problem. They all laughed. They were admiring a collection of [human] livers, hearts, and gall bladders strung on a palm fiber rope. . . . They were saying how they wanted to find more enemies to kill, but first they were going to eat. Mr. Chan said he would stir-fry some livers and hearts. . . . One of them said, "Eh! Look! Enemies jumping up and down in the pan!" They laughed; that was their idea of a good joke. Then they ate. Then they went back out to look for more innocent people to slaughter. . . . There would not be any more sleep for us that night. And we could not express our feelings. We could only lay [*sic*] there in horror, afraid to breath, afraid to talk, afraid to think, silent except for the pounding of our hearts which we could not control, and very sorry for the human beings who were being butchered all around us. . . . there was no way to bring back the dead. . . . [these memories] would always be there lurking in the Darkness, . . . wanting and desperate, always waiting for an opportunity to sneak out and take over. (Ouk and Simon 1998: 269–70, 283)

The depravity of the young kamaphibal and yothea is best illustrated by the way they treated women and children. As a Cham woman told Ben Kiernan, "When they came back from killing I was awake. They got together and were talking. They were saying, 'I slashed the stomach of this one, so many months [pregnant].' They were very cruel" (1996: 412). Bunheang Ung told Martin Stuart-Fox that he saw people being "tied up to be slaughtered at dusk with hoes, knives, and axes. . . . All were forced to dig their own shallow graves. . . . The girls were raped first. One named Pheng, a leader of the women's mobile group, was heard to shout before being killed: 'Long live the Communist Party of Kampuchea.' Another, Yim, screamed for justice. A soldier shouted, 'Here is your justice' as he struck her with a machete" (1985: 138).

Sar Chanyan, whose oral history was recorded in 1989, recalled the cruelest incident she witnessed: "If the woman carried her child with her, they killed it, too. . . . They killed the woman first . . . they took all of her clothes off . . . they used a stick and clubbed her on the back of the neck. . . . They took the baby by the legs and swung it against the trunk of a jackfruit tree. . . . They smashed it against the tree—WHOOSH. The baby didn't die then. It was still breathing in and out. After that . . . they threw it up in the air. They took a sharp piece of metal that they called a bayonet . . . and . . . stuck the baby with it when the baby fell on top of it. . . . I was very shocked" (Cambodians in California Project, Sar interview 1989, 57: 10–12).

Women were sometimes forced to marry Khmer Rouge soldiers or cadres. Out of fear, none refused. A now-middle-aged Sino-Cambodian woman told Sheila Pinkel what it was like to be married under duress:

> I was gathered among many other girls—young adults at that time—and we lived in our own youth group. . . . My work depended on the season. Sometimes I placed rice in the field, sometimes I made a dam somewhere, and other times I brought supplies from the city into the countryside. . . . I had to conform because I wanted to live. If I had not conformed . . . they would have killed me. . . . they forced me to get married. . . . I was scared that if I did not do it, I would die. . . . I have never known the man. . . . Twelve women got married the same time as I did. . . . Before the wedding day, all twelve women . . . agreed we all had to get married . . . because two of the grooms-to-be were leaders of the Khmer Rouge. . . . if anyone disagrees, everybody dies. So we all agreed to get married to the men whom we did not love and whom we did not know. . . . We were picked as examples . . . so if we did not follow [orders, it would mean] death for the rest of the group. . . . After we got married, we lived in the married couples section. . . . for five months, occasionally I would meet with him, and then after five months I got pregnant. . . . after I had a child, they put the women in one place and the men in another place. . . . I had to get up at five in the morning and take the baby to the community center where there were elderly baby-sitters. But I had the baby at night. . . . If a person doesn't show up for work for a couple of days because the child is sick, the person would be killed. . . . when my child was two years old, he died. . . . He had some kind of disease, I believe it was chicken pox. There was not adequate medicine. (Anonymous interview, Sheila Pinkel, 1996)

Even children were not spared. The kamaphibal were sadistic in punishing those caught stealing food:

I saw orphans of seven to eight years old . . . who'd stolen rice, salt, and vegetables because they were hungry. A cadre caught them by surprise, and he had them beaten until they bled. Another time they stole salt to eat with tamarind; the chief tied their hands and feet and put them for two hours in a place infested with tiny ants, until blood was pouring out. Then they were beaten with a cane and then put back with the ants. . . . A third time they were so hungry—they were nothing but skin and bones—they stole vegetables from the kitchen. The Khmer Rouge cadre picked eight children to beat them and then bury them alive. (Martin 1994: 197)

A young Sino-Cambodian woman now living in southern California told Sheila Pinkel a similar tale:

Being hungry, I stole a watermelon. It wasn't even a good one, it wasn't ripe, . . . it was a small one. But I was caught, not having even eaten the watermelon; I was just holding it. . . . The man who was in charge of the children's camp . . . yanked my head and asked me why I stole. . . . I said I was hungry. . . . He had this big rope and he tied me to a coconut tree. Under the coconut tree, by its roots, there were a lot of red ants that bite. He asked all the kids to come and watch—I was a bad example, he said, and if anyone else did what I did they would get the same punishment. . . . He took honey and smeared it all over my legs, my arms, and my face, so the ants would crawl up . . . they started biting. I cried and cried. . . . I was left there the whole night. . . . The next morning I went to the river and washed myself, then I went to work. (Anonymous interview, Sheila Pinkel, 1996)

Khmer Rouge leaders exorted young cadres and soldiers to carry out their responsibilities with fervor by teaching them songs with lyrics containing many images of blood and its red color. David Chandler collected one: "Glittering red blood blankets the earth—blood given up to liberate the people; the blood of workers, peasants, and intellectuals; the blood of young men, Buddhist monks, and girls. / The blood swirls away, and flows upward, gently, into the sky, turning into a red revolutionary flag. / Red flag! Red flag! flying now! flying now! / Don't spare a single reactionary imperialist; drive them from Kampuchea! / Strive and strike, strive and strike, win victory, win victory!" (1991a: 142).

The Khmer Rouge singled out the country's minority groups—the Vietnamese, Chinese, Cham, Lao, Thai, Khmer Krom, and various hill-dwellers—for the most stringent punishment, simply because they were not Khmer. More than two hundred thousand ethnic Vietnamese still lived in Cambodia at the time. The Khmer Rouge expelled about 150,000 of them in September 1975 and massacred some of the unfortunate people while they were en route to the Vietnamese-Cambodian border. The remaining Vietnamese almost all died, whether by execution or from starvation and disease. The Khmer Rouge hated the Vietnamese so vehemently that they ordered Khmer men with Vietnamese wives to kill their spouses (Kiernan 1996: 296–98).

About five hundred thousand ethnic Chinese lived in Cambodia during the 1970s. Although Khmer Rouge leaders did not similarly target them for extermination, they segregated the Chinese in separate hamlets, mostly in the Northwestern Zone, and eventually dispersed them around the country. About half of Cambodia's ethnic Chinese perished during the Pol Pot period, but more from hunger and illness than from executions (Kiernan 1996: 288–96). Discrimination against them extended even to children; the young Sino-Cambodian woman interviewed by Sheila Pinkel described how she was treated as "that Chinese girl":

> I lived in a children's camp . . . boys and girls lived together in an old, big, long house where they had beds made of bamboo slats, one stacked on top of the other like a triple bunk bed. . . . Where you slept depended on your color. If you looked Chinese, . . . if you had those almond eyes, if you had a whiter complexion, . . . then you're going to end up at the very bottom. I remember waking up every morning with my hair soaked. . . . It was from the urine—the kids on top would urinate in their sleep and I would be completely soaked. (Anonymous interview, Sheila Pinkel, 1996)

The Khmer Rouge also made special efforts to degrade the Cham, who are Muslim. Their religion, Islam, prohibits them from eating pork. Kamaphibal and yothea forced them to eat this meat and executed those who refused. Worse, they made the Cham raise pigs in their mosques in order to defile those sacred compounds (Martin 1994: 183). Not only could the Cham not practice their religion but they were also forbidden to wear traditional clothing or speak their language. Sos Man, a Cham leader who had been a communist for decades and received political training in Hanoi and Beijing, was removed from office. The Khmer Rouge mercilessly massacred those Cham who rose up in revolt. An estimated one-third of the Cham population met its demise during the DK regime (Kiernan 1996: 252–88).

The Khmer Rouge likewise forbade the Lao and Thai ethnic minorities in Cambodia to speak their languages. Some fled across the border to Laos and Thailand, although the vast majority disappeared. An estimated half of them probably died (Kiernan 1996: 300–302). The nearly five thousand Khmer Krom in Cambodia at the time were also suspect. Even though they were ethnic Khmer, the Khmer Rouge leadership branded them as people with "Khmer bodies but Vietnamese minds." The Khmer Rouge kidnapped tens of thousands more Khmer Krom during raids into Vietnam and took them back to Cambodia to be done away with (Kiernan 1996: 298–300). Finally, although some of the earliest Khmer Rouge recruits were from ethnic groups that lived in the hills, these highlanders scarcely fared better than the lowland Vietnamese, Chinese, Cham, Lao, Thai, and Khmer Krom. Several years before they established the DK regime, the Khmer Rouge had already begun to break up the organizations of the numerous hill-dwelling groups in the Northeastern Zone, forbidding them to practice their animistic rituals and ending their seminomadic way of life (Kiernan 1996: 80–83 and 302–09). Pol Pot did, however, continue to use a few individuals from those hill people as his bodyguards.

Because top Khmer Rouge leaders were extremely secretive, no one knew their identities. They referred to themselves as "Angkar Loeu" (upper organization) or simply "Angkar." Unstinting loyalty to Angkar was to replace all preexisting family bonds. Political cadres taught young children not only to love Angkar but also to use a new vocabulary and value system. As a village chief told Loung Ung:

> The children will change what they call their parents. Father is now "Poh" and not Daddy, Pa, or any other term. Mother is "Meh." . . . The new Khmer have better words for eating, sleeping, working, stranger; all designed to make us equal. . . . In this village, as in the whole of our new and pure society, we all live in a communal system and share everything. There is no private ownership of animals, land, gardens, or even houses. Everything belongs to Angkar. If Angkar suspects you of being a traitor, we will come into your home and go through whatever we like. (2000: 60)

Although anonymous, Angkar had eyes everywhere, like the "eyes of a pineapple." Terrified of the constant surveillance, people survived by pretending to be deaf and mute *tiing moong* (dummies). They stopped trusting anyone, even close family members. As Arn Chorn-Pond recalled:

> I was in a temple where they killed three or four times a day. They told us to watch and not to show any emotion at all. They would kill us if we reacted . . . if we cried, or showed that we cared about the victims. They would kill you right away. So I had to shut it all off. . . . I can shut off everything in my body, practically, physically. I saw them killing people right in front of me. . . . The blood was there, but I didn't smell it. I made myself

numb. . . . The killing was unbearable. You go crazy if you smell the blood.
(Simms and Chorn-Pond 2002: 28)

The Revolution Devours Its Own

Distrust also infested relationships among Khmer Rouge leaders themselves.
Beginning in 1977, the revolution systematically devoured its own as Pol Pot
started purging his suspected potential opponents. A special torture and
extermination center code-named S-21 ("S" for *sala,* or room, and "21" being the code for the *santebal,* or security police) began operating in a former
Phnom Penh high school in May or June of 1976. Its main victims were Khmer Rouge leaders and their followers who were no longer deemed trustwor-
thy. Pol Pot's henchmen accused Chan Chakrey, the army deputy chief-of-
staff, of trying to poison Pol Pot, arrested him, sent him to S-21, and tortured
him into confessing that he had collaborated with the Vietnamese, the Americans, and the Russians—all at the same time. They also arrested and purged
Koy Thuon, a former leader in the Northern Zone who had argued against
the abolition of money but had nevertheless been assigned responsibility for
domestic and foreign trade in the DK regime, as well as the man's followers.
Hundreds of mid- and high-level leaders as well as lower-level political cadres from the Eastern Zone, together with their wives and children, were arrested, incarcerated at S-21, and killed because they were suspected of defy-
ing Pol Pot's extremist policies. So Phim, leader of the Eastern Zone, was
declared a traitor. As he was being hunted down, he shot himself to death.
His wife and children were murdered as they prepared his body for burial.
Other high-ranking victims included Cheng An, the DK minister of industry; May Prang, the minister of communications; and Vorn Vet, the deputy
prime minister (Kiernan 1996: 400, 437).

   Altogether, there are records of more than fourteen thousand men and
women who were tortured and forced to write confessions of varying lengths
detailing their "crimes" against the state before they were killed in S-21. The
total number of victims was considerably larger, but there is no exact count
because records for certain months are missing. Of an estimated twenty thousand incarcerated, only seven are known to have survived (Chandler 1999:
viii). The administrators and guards at S-21 maintained meticulous records,
including mug shots of their victims. In their ledgers, they wrote the word
komtech (smashed) after each victim breathed his or her last.

   The death toll included four-fifths of the approximately one thousand highly educated Cambodians who were abroad—mostly in France, various East European countries, the United States, and Australia—when the Khmer Rouge came to power and returned to their homeland to help reconstruct it. Even though some had heard about the atrocities of the new regime they refused to believe what they had heard. Tragically for them, the Khmer Rouge had no use for their skills. As Khieu Samphan, a high-ranking Khmer Rouge leader, told them, "Intellectuals can help in the reconstruction of the country only if they have acquired a proletarian viewpoint, if they have eliminated all private property, material and sentimental. That is, we have to consider our wives, parents, and children no different from other people, with no special bonds between us" (Martin 1994: 200). Sent to hard labor in the countryside, eventually eight hundred of these well-trained individuals met the same fate as 1.7 million of their compatriots. A few did not wait to be killed—they committed suicide.

In 1978 the bloodletting reached a frenzied pitch. Pol Pot's closest followers arrested and killed commanders and political cadres in the Eastern, Western, and Northern Zones and replaced them with more trusted leaders from the Southwest. Eastern Zone leaders who did not share the extreme anti-Vietnamese chauvinism harbored by Pol Pot and his clique had always been more moderate in their treatment of the population under their control (there was little starvation in that zone, for example). They, too, were accused of having "Vietnamese minds." Pol Pot loyalists gave people in the Eastern Zone blue clothing and blue and white checkered scarves to wear, while everyone else was clothed in black and had either red and white or black and white checkered scarves. It was only after huge numbers of people wearing the distinctive blue had been slaughtered that people in the Eastern Zone realized the new clothing they had gladly accepted (because their old clothes were so worn) was meant to mark them for extinction. At least a hundred thousand—perhaps as many as 250,000—from the Eastern Zone (of a population of about 1.5 million in that region) were killed in just a few months during 1978. Systematic massacres also occured in the North and West (Kiernan 1996: 323–25, 337–48, 369–76, 386–439).

Such savage brutality, even against fellow revolutionaries, served four functions: "to destroy the old society and its social, political, economic, and cultural infrastructure"; "to force the entire society into new socioeconomic patterns"; "to counter revisionism and coups d'etat from within"; and "to eliminate threats posed by Vietnam and perceived collaborators of the Vietnamese" (Quinn 1989b: 180). The terror, for the most part, accomplished those goals because until late 1977 it had been used for more or less rational purposes. By 1978, however, it had become what Roel A. Burgler calls "terror gone mad." It was a "terror that seems to have become an end in itself. Even the bureaucracy administrating the terror became suspect. . . . The terror seems to have become a self-generative conflict, fuelling itself, a vicious spiral of paranoia and violence, the Khmer version of the revolution eating its own children" (1990: 272–73).

Resistance

Such heinous extremism finally aroused resistance, both passive and active. Passive resistance came in the form of individual escape attempts, and active resistance was aimed at overthrowing the DK regime. Beaten down though they were, some individuals found the courage to flee. Many perished during their flight, but some succeeded. Bun Thab (a pseydonym), who escaped in 1977 from a youth work brigade, recounted how he did so:

> None of us knew when we would be killed. . . . One evening, we had just sat down to eat when two soldiers came and chose three people to go to a meeting in the soldiers' house. . . . the leader announced, "Tonight we have three enemies here." We knew that they meant us. Two soldiers grabbed my friends, pulled their arms behind their backs and started to tie them up tightly. I was terrified because I knew what was coming. I needed to urinate. A soldier took me outside. It was dark and raining a little, but suddenly the rain came pelting down. I ran into the darkness. . . . [Later] I saw two other people running away also. Their arms were tied behind their backs; when I got closer I recognized my friends. . . . We kept going day and night . . . we lived on fruits and leaves from the forest trees. . . . One afternoon . . . [one of my friends climbed to] the top of a tree to look for the mountains. . . . A shot rang out. Our friend fell from the tree, screaming with pain. While we watched, the Communist walked up and he chopped our friend to pieces with his ax. We fled, and he shot at us too, but I don't know where the bullets went. We kept on running and we came to a river. We jumped in, and hid under the water. I know the Communist kept running after us because once, as I looked up from under the water, he jumped right over my head. I still have nightmares of that Khmer Rouge jumping over my head, and I wake up shivering with fear. (Welaratna 1993: 125–27)

During the DK regime about thirty-four thousand people successfully escaped westward to Thailand by running through the jungles and over the mountains as Bun Thab had done. An unknown number also perished. In addition, at least 136,000 Khmer, 26,000 ethnic Chinese, and 170,000 ethnic Vietnamese fled eastward to Vietnam (U.S. Senate Committee on the Judiciary 1978: 43); some 20,000 people escaped to Laos. Despite these large numbers, to date nothing has been written about the experiences of the refuge-seekers who sought sanctuary—a vast majority of them temporarily, but a small number permanently—in Vietnam and Laos.

Aside from being caught by Khmer Rouge patrols or attacked by bandits, the greatest danger facing aspiring escapees was land mines. All belligerents in successive stages of the war in Cambodia—Vietnamese communist forces, Lon Nol's troops, and the Khmer Rouge—used mines. During the DK period, the Khmer Rouge laid mines around agricultural collectives, as well as along the Thai-Cambodian and Vietnamese-Cambodian borders, in order to prevent escapes and military incursions.

Land mines are popular because they are cheap and easy to use. There are four types. Blast mines, laid on the ground, are tripped by the pressure of footsteps and cause injury by their explosive force. Fragmentation mines, laid above-ground, are set off by trip wires and maim and kill by spraying shrapnel from their exploding segmented casings. An even more lethal kind of fragmentation mine shoots up into the air before exploding and thereby has a 360-degree kill radius. Another variant called a "directional fragmentation mine" is usually tied to trees and can be detonated either by trip wires or remote command (Davies 1994: 1–3). Manufactured in the former USSR, the People's Republic of China, or North Vietnam, all four kinds were used in Cambodia.

Haing Ngor, a Cambodian doctor who became a movie star in the United States, described his escape party's encounter with such mines:

> A sudden muffled explosion, like an artillery shell, came from ahead. . . . A few minutes later word came back that a mine had gone off and that many people had been killed. . . . [we] came upon the sight of the explosion. It was a blood-spattered scene, an arm dangling from a tree branch, part of a leg caught in bamboo. . . . It was a terrible way to die, or to be maimed, after living through the Khmer Rouge years and coming so close to freedom. The mines appeared on either side of the path, sometimes in the middle. They had coin-sized detonator buttons. . . . From the detonator buttons, trip lines made of nearly invisible white nylon thread led to tying-off points such as trees or rocks nearby. . . . we had to keep our eyes on the trail, searching for white threads. (Ngor 1987: 378–79)

Although individual escapees did not threaten the existence of Democratic Kampuchea, an organized resistance backed by the armed might of the Socialist Republic of Vietnam (the name adopted in 1976 by the reunified country) eventually drove Pol Pot and his colleagues from power. Among Khmer Rouge leaders who opposed Pol Pot's murderous policies were two young men, Heng Samrin and Hun Sen. (In the late 1970s Heng Samrin was in his thirties, and Hun Sen was only in his twenties.) Hun Sen defected to Vietnam in 1977, and Heng Samrin led part of the rebellion in the Eastern Zone during 1978. Border clashes had begun between Cambodia and Vietnam as early as April 1975, just as those two countries' communist movements acquired formal state power. These clashes soon escalated to large-scale incursions by both nations across each other's borders. A full-scale war was in progress by late 1977 and early 1978. So, not surprisingly, when Khmer Rouge dissidents in the Eastern Zone began to plan for the overthrow of Pol Pot and realized they did not have adequate manpower or arms for the purpose they turned to Vietnam for help.

Defectors who had escaped to Vietnam gathered other Cambodians who had also fled eastward. Together, they formed the United Front for the National Salvation of Kampuchea in December 1978. The Vietnamese had three reasons to support this group, according to John Spragens, Jr. First, Khmer Rouge incursions across the Cambodian-Vietnamese border threatened the security of the New Economic Zones that the new government of Vietnam had set up near the border; second, the Vietnamese, who were not friendly with the People's Republic of China, which supported the Khmer Rouge, feared the possibility of having to fight a two-front war against DK and China; and, third, the Vietnamese claimed they had a "humanitarian" desire to "liberate" the Khmer people from further auto-genocide (quoted in Etcheson 1984: 193–94). I put the word *humanitarian* in quotation marks because contemporary observers doubted that humanitarianism was, in fact, a motive. Rather, anti-Vietnamese cynics in the United States, as well as Cambodians, believed (and still believe) that the effort to "liberate" Cambodia was merely a pretext the Vietnamese used to take over their neighboring country.

On December 25, 1978, the front, backed by some 120,000 well-armed Vietnamese troops and tanks, marched into Cambodia. They met no resistance along the way. On January 7, 1979, the invaders took Phnom Penh, and top Khmer Rouge leaders fled northwestward by helicopter, train, and automobile. They coerced tens of thousands of civilians to follow. Prince Sihanouk, who had been placed under house arrest soon after being brought back from China in September 1975 and remained confined under house arrest for more than three years during the DK regime, flew to Beijing on the last flight out of Phnom Penh.

Upon capturing Phnom Penh, Heng Samrin declared in a public speech:

> On January 7, 1979, more than on any other day, the entire Kampuchean people . . . experienced limitless joy; this was a day of historic importance, a day when they overthrew the reactionary and cruel social system headed by the insane clique of the traitors Pol Pot and Ieng Sary, and saved our nation. . . . From now on people can live together with their families and relatives, can reunite and restore family happiness in the national community, exercising their genuine freedoms as citizens of Kampuchea; they can be true masters of society, masters of the fruits of their labour . . . all of us . . . bow our heads in deep respect and sorror in honour of the millions . . . who fell fighting . . . who perished tragically under the blows of the criminal, reactionary Pol Pot-Ieng Sary clique . . . [which] committed countless and indescribable crimes of barbarism and insanity against the people. (Heng 1979: 115–16)

Heng Samrin then cited a long list of crimes that Pol Pot and his colleagues had perpetrated. They had eliminated cities, markets, and money; forced the urban population to evacuate; seized all power in the party and the government; enacted cruel measures against the Cambodian people, depriving them of all freedom and "shutting their eyes, closing their mouths, plugging their ears, hopping [*sic*] off their arms and legs"; prohibited any freedom of movement; prohibited any expression of opinions; eliminated religion and family relationships; arrested, incarcerated, tortured, and killed political opponents using false allegations; murdered millions of innocent civilians, including pregnant women and children, the elderly, and "even the mentally retarded"; scornfully treated peasants and workers, in whose name they supposedly carried out the revolution; squandered the country's natural resources, turning cities and villages "into ashes and ruins"; barbarously murdered educated people; uprooted a "fine civilization that had existed since ancient times"; destroyed all human emotional ties; and pursued a foreign policy that served the interests of a foreign power (i.e., the People's Republic of China) (Heng 1979: 117–24).

Unfortunately for Heng Samrin, Hun Sen, and their fellow dissidents, the fact the Vietnamese had installed them in power stymied their efforts and resulted in dire consequences for Cambodia. For the next dozen years the Cambodian people, tragically, yet one more time, became pawns in the vagaries of international power politics.

The People's Republic of Kampuchea
and the Second Civil War, 1979–91

Heng Samrin became the president and Hun Sen the foreign minister of the new regime called the People's Republic of Kampuchea (PRK). Initially, only the Socialist Republic of Vietnam and two other communist countries recognized that government diplomatically. The Western nations, following the example of the United States, shunned it as a puppet government controlled by the Vietnamese, who maintained an army of more than a hundred thousand troops in Cambodia for the next ten years.

The PRK immediately restored freedom of movement. During the first few months, millions of survivors crisscrossed the country, looking for lost relatives. No one bothered to harvest the ripened rice crop that January. As the specter of famine loomed, tens of thousands of emaciated people began pouring across the Thai-Cambodian border. International aid agencies, which tried to supply these displaced persons with food, shelter, and medicine, had trouble doing so because the new PRK regime told them that all relief had to be delivered directly to Phnom Penh. Western nations, however, wanted nothing to do with the Heng Samrin government, and relief agencies insisted on caring for both people within Cambodia and those who had crossed the Thai-Cambodian border. The PRK was adamantly against such a plan. In time—and after complicated negotiations—the relief organizations delivered approximately the same amount of food and medical aid to Cambodians along the Thai-Cambodian border as to those inside Cambodia, even though the latter population was ten times larger (Davies 1994: 8).

Another hurdle was the fact that the country's infrastructure had been so devastated during the DK period that the port of Kompong Som (Sihanoukville) could no longer function and highways full of potholes could no longer be traversed. Thus even agencies like Oxfam of Great Britain, which defied the PRK and the Western powers' injunctions, could not get supplies to people inside Cambodia. Only after the Soviet Union sent hundreds of engineers, mechanics, and construction workers to repair the highways and port facilities, and hundreds of trucks to transport the piled-up relief goods into the interior of the country, did food begin to trickle in.

Meanwhile, Robert Ashe, a British relief worker, indefatigably persisted until he succeeded in setting up a "land bridge" to distribute food and rice seed for the following year's planting to Cambodians amassed at the Thai-Cambodian border. Some of these starving people transported the sacks of grain by oxcart and on foot back to their villages while others tarried around the border, awaiting the next handout. The land bridge program helped to stave off a potentially widespread famine (Mason and Brown 1983; Shawcross 1984). Perhaps even more critical in assuring the survival of the Cambodian people during this period was the food and other aid that Vietnam gave the PRK, although Western observers as well as Cambodians have not credited Vietnam for such efforts.

While relief agencies worked feverishly to save a population threatened with "extinction," three groups emerged to oppose the new government in Phnom Penh. First, the Khmer Rouge, although routed, still had between thirty and forty thousand men under arms along with an even larger number of civilians under their tight control. They hid out in western Cambodia and Thailand while biding their time to retake Cambodia. Second, Sihanouk and his smaller army of followers, who formed the National United Front for an Independent, Neutral, Peaceful, and Cooperative Cambodia (FUNCINPEC, its French acronym), were also determined to overthrow the Vietnam-backed regime. Third, Son Sann, who had served for a time as a prime minister under Sihanouk, returned from exile in France in October 1979 to gather his followers to form the Kampuchean People's National Liberation Front (KPNLF).

After negotiating with one another for a year and a half, Sihanouk and Son Sann first agreed to form a coalition for "common action" against the Vietnamese. Pressured by the United States and the People's Republic of China as well as by the members of the Association for Southeast Asian Nations (ASEAN), and quite cognizant of the fact that the Khmer Rouge had the only viable fighting force capable of attacking the current Phnom Penh government, the two noncommunist factions subsequently, although reluctantly, formed a larger coalition with the Khmer Rouge.

Leaders of the three groups signed an agreement in June 1982 to establish a government-in-exile: the Coalition Government of Democratic Kampuchea (GCDK, its acronym in French). The arrangement was made possible only after the Khmer Rouge (at least outwardly) supposedly disbanded the Communist Party of Kampuchea, relegated Pol Pot to the background, and elevated the urbane Khieu Samphan to greater visibility—all for the sake of improving the GCDK's international public image. The United States and its allies, as well as China, recognized the GCDK as the "legitimate" government of Cambodia and supported its bid to hold Cambodia's seat in the United Nations, even though it controlled very little territory and was dominated by the Khmer Rouge. Thailand, for its own political reasons, tolerated the presence of Khmer Rouge leaders on its soil. Meanwhile, the Soviet

Union and its East European allies, as well as India, established diplomatic relations with the new Phnom Penh government.

With the emergence of the GCDK, the political and military rehabilitation of the Khmer Rouge progressed apace. Not only were international relief agencies compelled to distribute food and other aid to the population residing in border camps under Khmer Rouge control, but the latter also received armaments directly from China and indirectly from the United States. Congress justified the appropriations by arguing that the aid was intended for the two noncommunist factions. In fact, according to the Congressional Research Service, the military and economic aid the Khmer Rouge received from the United States amounted to $54.55 million in 1980, $18.29 million in 1981, $4.57 million in 1982, and smaller amounts thereafter (Reynell 1989: 41). In the words of William Shawcross, "Much of the world—not just the Western world and ASEAN—has chosen to see the Khmer Rouge first as the defenders of national sovereignty rather than as the perpetrators of mass crimes against man" (1984: 330).

During the 1980s, the three-way coalition and the Phnom Penh government engaged in an on-again, off-again (on during the dry season, off during the rainy season) civil war along the Thai-Cambodian border and inside western Cambodia. (This Second Cambodian Civil War has also been called the "Third Indochina War.") Well-meaning nations and organizations convened numerous international conferences to broker a peace settlement but to no avail. Only after Vietnam withdrew all its occupation forces from Cambodia in 1989 and the PRK renamed itself the State of Cambodia could a "peace process" make headway. In 1990 the United Nations withdrew recognition from the GCDK and gave Cambodia's seat to a newly created Supreme National Council, which included the three factions plus the Phnom Penh government. The four groups finally signed a UN-sponsored peace settlement in October 1991.

During the next year and a half the United Nations Transitional Authority in Cambodia (UNTAC) repatriated more than 360,000 Cambodians along the border to their homeland. In May 1993 UNTAC supervised nationwide elections in which multiple political parties as well as more than 90 percent of eligible voters participated. (The Khmer Rouge, however, refused to disarm or respect the cease-fire and boycotted the elections.) The UN peacekeeping mission cost $2.6 billion—the most expensive peacekeeping effort to that point in world history (Brown and Zasloff 1998).

Many Americans who hear about these events for the first time often ask, "How could we have supported the Khmer Rouge? Didn't we know what they had done?" Certainly, the U.S. government knew, although many Americans initially discounted the atrocity stories by saying that they must be exaggerated because it was the Vietnamese who first disseminated such tales of horror. Skeptics believed that the Vietnamese spread the bloody stories in order to justify their invasion and subsequent military occupation of Cambodia. Only after scholars who had impeccable credentials—notably, Ben Kiernan, David Chandler, Milton Osborne, Stephen Heder, and Kate Frieson—began interviewing hundreds of refugees did accounts of the dire deeds of the Khmer Rouge gain credibility. Even after the American public began to accept the truth of the reports, whatever opprobrium American policymakers might have felt regarding the genocidal Khmer Rouge was overridden by the "great-power politics" of the cold war, especially its offshoot development, the Sino-Soviet split—a development that must be discussed briefly in order to make sense of the enigmatic foreign policy the United States adopted during that period.

A rift developed between the USSR and the People's Republic of China in the late 1950s. After Joseph Stalin died in 1953, a collective leadership was supposed to rule the Soviet Union. Nikita Khrushchev, secretary of the Communist Party of the Soviet Union's (CPSU) Moscow region, soon muscled the other top leaders aside, however. He even managed to arrest and execute Lavrenti Beria, head of the dreaded secret police under Stalin. At the Twentieth Congress of the CPSU in February 1956 he made a secret speech (which was later made public) accusing Stalin of various crimes. That act shook the hitherto monolithic communist bloc to its core. The Poles and the Hungarians rose up in revolt, but the Soviet Red Army brutally suppressed the uprisings. In March 1958, Khrushchev became premier and began to implement "de-Stalinization" policies.

The leaders of the People's Republic of China strongly opposed Khrushchev's stance, mainly for ideological reasons. Relations between the two communist giants turned completely cold when the Soviet Union withdrew all its technicians from China, where they had been aiding China in various economic and military development programs since 1950. The chill between the USSR and China did not thaw until Mikhail Gorbachev came to power in 1985; relations were not normalized until 1989.

Certain U.S. foreign policy makers saw the outbreak of hostility between the two communist powers as an opportunity to play them off against each another in order to obtain greater American leverage in dealing with each. Zbigniew Brzezinski, President Jimmy Carter's national security advisor, strongly advocated playing the "China card." The stage had been set by President Richard Nixon, who visited the People's Republic of China in 1972 and reopened the door to China. Diplomatic relations were not restored, however, until January 1, 1979, almost thirty years after such relations were severed—a delay due mainly to disagreements over the status of the Republic of China on Taiwan.

These international developments affected Cambodia and Vietnam in significant ways. Although the USSR and the People's Republic of China had both aided North Vietnam during its war against the United States and South Vietnam, relations between Vietnam and China deteriorated after the war due to Vietnam's growing friendship with the USSR. China cut off all aid to Vietnam and watched warily as Vietnam signed a Treaty of Friendship and Cooperation with Laos in 1977, which increased Vietnam's influence in that country. Vietnam also joined the Soviet-led Council for Mutual Economic Assistance and signed a Treaty of Friendship and Cooperation with the USSR in 1978.

When Russians gained use of the military bases at Cam Ranh Bay and Danang that Americans had built during the Vietnam War, China felt threatened about being surrounded by unfriendly countries—the USSR to the north and the Socialist Republic of Vietnam to the south. At the same time, quiet negotiations between the United States and Vietnam—talks about the possibility of lifting the U.S. trade embargo against Vietnam and reestablishing diplomatic relations with it—came to a complete halt when U.S. foreign policy began to "tilt" toward China.

Relations between China and Vietnam were also tense during 1977 and 1978 because the Vietnamese government was persecuting its ethnic Chinese residents, driving more than a quarter million of them to seek refuge in four provinces in southern China, where the Chinese government resettled them in agricultural communes. In addition, hundreds of thousands of ethnic Chinese escaped by sea in small boats to neighboring Southeast Asian countries. When Vietnam invaded Cambodia in December 1978, China decided to teach its southern neighbor a lesson by invading several northern provinces in Vietnam in February 1979. The Chinese forces caused extensive destruction before withdrawing after two weeks.

The United States, still smarting over its defeat in Vietnam, perceived Vietnam's invasion of Cambodia as an unforgivable act of aggression. For that reason it led international efforts to isolate the new People's Republic of Kampuchea led by Heng Samrin and Hun Sen. Meanwhile, China increased support for the ousted Khmer Rouge remnants, becoming the latter's main arms supplier. The United States and Thailand also supported the

Khmer Rouge because neither it nor its allies in Western Europe and Southeast Asia wished to send ground troops to fight against the Vietnamese now entrenched in Cambodia. They saw the Khmer Rouge as the group most capable of driving out the Vietnamese. According to Elizabeth Becker, National Security Advisor Zbigniew Brzezinski told her that while "winking semipublicly, . . . I encouraged the Chinese to support Pol Pot. I encouraged the Thai to help D.K. . . . Pol Pot was an abomination. We could never support him but China could" (Becker 1986: 440). In short, U.S. policy in this instance was cynical. The desire to drive the Vietnamese out of Cambodia outweighed American distaste for what the Khmer Rouge had done while in power. A further bonus was that by supporting the Khmer Rouge, China's allies, the United States cemented its now-desired relations with China.

This precarious and opportunistic balance of power began to change after Mikhail Gorbachev introduced *perestroika* (restructuring) and *glasnost* (openness) in the Soviet Union. Perestroika, introduced in 1985, was intended as a moderate measure to reform and rehabilitate the Soviet planned economy; glasnost, introduced in 1986, was intended to give Soviet intellectuals greater freedom of expression, including freedom to criticize the regime. These two measures, perhaps unexpectedly, opened the way to profound political changes in the East European countries that had been under Soviet domination during the cold war and led ultimately to the disintegration of the Soviet Union itself in 1991 after the CPSU disbanded and various former constituent republics within the USSR proclaimed independence one after another.

One consequence of the disintegration of the Soviet empire was that Vietnam lost its major supporter. That, together with the poor harvests Vietnam had suffered since the mid-1980s, made it increasingly difficult for that country to maintain its expensive army of occupation in Cambodia. At the same time, a more moderate group of leaders had come to power in Vietnam in 1986 and adopted a policy of *doi moi* (renovation), liberalizing many of the stringent measures the older leaders had adopted from 1976 onward to impose socialist transformation on the South. When Vietnam pulled all its troops out of Cambodia, having trained a Cambodian army to defend the country, a negotiated peace finally became possible.

During the twelve years that the Second Cambodian Civil War raged, several hundred thousand Cambodians amassed in a no-man's land along the Thai-Cambodian border. Before 1985 the four warring factions repeatedly shelled the camps in which they lived. Hundreds, perhaps thousands, died as a result. This displaced population was pushed back and forth across

the border as the fighting see-sawed. Not only were they repeatedly uprooted, but many were also maimed or killed by land mines. During the 1984–85
dry season offensive, however, Vietnamese forces successfully pushed all camp
residents into Thailand, and from early 1985 onward the camps were located
entirely within Thai territory.

The physical safety of the population living on both sides of the border
continued to be precarious, however, because the civil war intensified after
Vietnam withdrew all its troops from Cambodia in 1989. The departure enabled GCDK resistance forces to push their way across the border into western Cambodia, engaging in a frenzy of mine-laying in the next two years as
they attempted to retake the country (Davies 1994: 9). The story of these
Cambodian refuge-seekers along the Thai-Cambodian border constitutes the
next sad chapter in a saga of sorrows seemingly without end.

2   Seeking Refuge

THE APPROXIMATELY thirty-four thousand Cambodians who reached Thailand alive during 1975–79 were classified as "displaced persons"; treated in the same way as refuge-seekers from Laos and Vietnam; and eventually resettled in France, the United States, Canada, Australia, and elsewhere. Known as "Old Khmer," about six or seven thousand of them—mostly better-educated individuals with prior relationships to the French or Americans—were resettled by the end of 1978, almost three thousand of them in the United States. About another ten thousand rural people from Battambang province and other localities close to the Thai-Cambodian border were resettled in 1979, six thousand of them in the United States.

Right after the Vietnamese toppled the Democratic Kampuchea regime, relatively few people left because their first priority was to return home to look for lost relatives. By late spring of that year, however, large numbers of Cambodians began to flee. Unlike those who had left earlier, the later escapees were not given presumptive refugee status when they reached Thailand. Instead, their fate depended on how Thailand, the United States, and the United Nations dealt with them. Thailand's policy was largely determined by that country's overriding concerns for its internal security during the Second Cambodian Civil War, American refugee policy was a product of the interplay of U.S. foreign policy and domestic politics, and the United Nations followed its own mandates regarding the care of refugees and diplaced persons.

Thailand's Dilemma during the Indochinese Refugee Crisis

As Theravada Buddhists, Thai people try to be compassionate toward other human beings. Historically, Thailand has hosted more refuge-seekers than any other country in Southeast Asia, taking in more than 120,000 persons from neighboring countries in the decades after World War II. During the Chinese Civil War (1945–49), twenty-five thousand men in the Chinese nationalist army of Chiang Kai-shek retreated southward across the Sino-Thai border with the Chinese Communist People's Liberation Army in hot pursuit. These men and their descendants are still living in northern Thailand and have grown prosperous from the profits made by controlling the opium and heroin trade in that region. Another group of refuge-seekers, about fifty-five thousand ethnic Vietnamese who were living in Laos and Cambodia, entered Thailand in 1946–48 to escape the fighting between the Vietnamese and the French (which spilled over into Laos) during the First Indochina War. More than thirty thousand persons belonging to minority groups in Burma and some ten thousand students who opposed the Burmese central government also sought refuge in Thailand during the immediate post–World War II period.

The Thai government treated these groups liberally, but when much larger contingents of escapees from Vietnam, Laos, and Cambodia arrived after 1975, Thai leaders curbed their country's traditional hospitality for political reasons. Thailand is proud of the fact that it is the only country in Southeast Asia that has never been colonized. By skillful diplomacy and a concerted effort at modernization, Thai rulers avoided the fate that befell their neighbors during the heyday of European colonialism. To ensure their nation's independence, Thai leaders are always vigilant about their country's internal security.

The Thai concern with domestic political stability came into play when increasing numbers of Indochinese refuge-seekers began disembarking at its shores and crossing over its land borders (Muntarbhorn 1992: 125). Until 1977 Thailand treated the relatively small influx as a temporary problem and cared for the escapees until they could be resettled elsewhere. But as the exodus increased and continued unabated, the Thai government adopted a hardline policy. According to Ben Kiernan, Thai soldiers killed about a thousand Cambodian refuge-seekers who arrived in Thailand during the second half of 1977 (Kiernan, personal communication 2002).

Thailand could react to the situation relatively autonomously because it was not a signatory to the two UN statutes that delineate how refugees should be treated—the 1951 Convention Relating to the Status of Refugees and the 1967 Protocol Relating to the Status of Refugees. The 1967 protocol removed the time constraint built into the 1951 convention, which applied only to people who feared persecution "as a result of events occurring before 1 January 1951." The 1967 protocol defines a refugee as a person who, "owing to well-founded fear of being persecuted for reasons of race, religion, nationality, membership of a particular social group or political opinion, is outside the country of his nationality and is unable or, owing to such fear, is unwilling to avail himself of the protection of that country; or who, not having a nationality and being outside the country of his former habitual residence as a result of such events, is unable or, owing to such fear, unwilling to return to it" (Office of the United Nations High Commissioner for Refugees 1995a: 11, 39).

Instead of abiding by UN guidelines, the Thai government invoked two of its own laws—the 1954 Regulation Concerning Displaced Persons from Neighboring Countries and the Immigration Act of 1979—to deal with the situation (Muntarbhorn 1992: 128, 132–34). Although Thailand relied on UN agencies and private relief organizations to finance the effort and provide technical support for the Indochinese refuge-seekers who appeared in the late 1970s, it insisted on running the camps with its own civilian officials and military units.

The Thai government's challenge had economic, social, and political dimensions. The number of lowland Lao, Hmong, Tai Dam, Iu Mien, Htin, Vietnamese, and Cambodians on Thai soil hovered around half a million at the height of the influx—a figure that came to about 1 percent of the total Thai population, which was about fifty-five million at that time. Such a huge displaced population created an economic burden that Thailand was unable and unwilling to shoulder. Because the amount of arable land in Thailand is limited and the tenancy rate among Thai peasants is high, Thailand insisted that relief agencies aiding the Indochinese refuge-seekers also offer medical, economic, and other forms of aid to poverty-stricken Thai villagers living near the camps. Such simultaneous donations were designed to reduce the resentment that rural Thai might feel toward the unwanted guests in their midst.

The Thai government also had political reasons not to open its doors wide to refuge-seekers. Before the Indochinese influx began, Thailand had been dealing for years with an internal insurgency mounted by Thai communists—an insurgency largely supported by the People's Republic of China (PRC). Thai leaders took advantage of the Cambodian exodus to strike a deal with the PRC. Barely a week after the Khmer Rouge were driven out of Phnom Penh, Thai Prime Minister Kriangsak Chomanand met secretly with two officials from the PRC. They agreed that in exchange for China's cessation of aid to the Thai Communist Party, Thailand would allow Pol Pot's remnants, whom China strongly supported, to operate on Thai soil (Davies, 1994: 7; Robinson 1998: 66). China also promised to sell arms to Thailand on favorable terms.

The Thai government had an additional reason for tolerating the Khmer Rouge presence. Cambodia had historically served as a buffer state between Vietnam and Thailand. Once Vietnamese troops occupied Cambodia to prop up the Heng Samrin–Hun Sen government, Cambodia lost its traditional function as a buffer. Thai officials, however, realized that the Khmer Rouge and the civilian population along the Thai-Cambodian border under Khmer Rouge control could become a substitute buffer between Thailand and the aggressive Vietnamese army of more than a hundred thousand men now stationed on Cambodian soil, poised to make incursions across the border at will. Moreover, should too many Cambodians cross the border into Thailand, Vietnam could take over a half-empty Cambodia far more easily than one still filled with people. As the Thai Ministry of Foreign Affairs explained Thailand's position:

> The Vietnamese occupation of Kampuchea clearly shows the political and military ambition of Vietnam to dominate Laos and Kampuchea. . . . Vietnam . . . has violated the United Nations Charter and international law, which calls for respect of the independence, sovereignty and territorial integrity of other countries. . . . There is no guarantee that Thailand would not be affected by the Kampuchean conflict if it remained aloof to the problem. . . . The fact that Vietnamese forces frequently intrude into Thai territory on purpose and cause the loss of property and lives is undeniable. (Chulalongkorn University, Institute of Asian Studies, comp. 1985: 2–3, 9).

Defining its foreign policy this way salved the collective conscience of Thai officials in terms of their continuing support for the murderous Khmer Rouge, but it did not provide ready answers on how to deal with the hundreds of thousands of refuge-seekers from Laos, Vietnam, and Cambodia pouring into their country. As the numbers increased the Thai cabinet, in August 1977, adopted a closed-door policy: "There should be detention for the existing displaced persons population and preparation for the return of those who enter. . . . In the event that people sneak into the country by boat, officials should detain the escapees and either force or tow the boat out of territorial waters immediately. If a boat has already reached shore, it should be helped with repairs, food, engine oil, medicines, and other necessary equipments. Then the boat should be towed out of Thai waters without delay" (Robinson 1998: 43).

The Thai government also reached an agreement with the Office of the United Nations High Commissioner for Refugees (UNHCR) to institute a screening program for refuge-seekers from Laos. Screening was never implemented, however, due to strong objections from the United States, which had special concern for the Hmong, whom the U.S. Central Intelligence Agency had recruited as mercenary soldiers from 1959 onward to help fight against the Pathet Lao and the North Vietnamese troops operating in Laos.

The outflow from Vietnam and Laos in 1978 numbered at least ninety thousand Vietnamese "boat people" who touched shore in Hong Kong, Thailand, Malaysia, Indonesia, and the Philippines (the number who escaped was larger because many people drowned at sea) and sixty thousand or more Lao and Hmong "land people" who crossed the Mekong River into Thailand. Prime Minister Kriangsak bemoaned the fact that his country was not being flooded but drowned by refugees (McNamara 1990: 125). The outflow doubled in 1979, with several hundred thousand Cambodians augmenting the number of Vietnamese and Laotians.

The neighboring countries of first asylum became alarmed and took repressive measures. Malaysia adopted a "push-off" policy, denying landing to more than fifty thousand Vietnamese boat people, and threatened to deport seventy thousand who had already been placed into UNHCR holding camps (McNamara 1990: 125; Robinson 1998: 42). The Malaysian home minister insisted that his government was "responsible first and foremost to the people of this country" (Sutter 1990: 54–55). Singapore's foreign minister was even more blunt: "Each junkload of men, women and children sent to our shores is a bomb to destabilize, disrupt, and cause turmoil and dissension in ASEAN [Association of Southeast Asian Nations] states. This is a preliminary invasion [by Vietnam] to pave the way for the final invasion" (Robinson 1998: 53).

The ASEAN countries were not simply being paranoid. All of them have large Chinese minorities; in the case of Singapore, Chinese form the overwhelming majority. With a history of troubled interethnic conflicts between the ethnic Chinese and the indigenous people, especially in Malaysia and Indonesia, any large influx of ethnic Chinese, who composed some 70 percent of the boat people fleeing Vietnam in 1978 and the first half of 1979, was not welcome lest it upset the precarious racial and political balance in those countries.

In early June 1979, Thailand did something that shocked the rest of the world. Thai soldiers cajoled some forty-two thousand refuge-seekers from Cambodia who had reached Thailand in the preceding two months into buses by telling them, "You are all going to America. We have buses to take you" (Fiffer 1991: 66). As the luckless people soon discovered, they were not heading for America but for Preah Vihear in the Dangrek Mountains that straddle Thailand and northwestern Cambodia. Sari Touv described what happened after the people were forced off the buses:

> At dawn, all the buses stopped and the soldiers who were waiting there bullied us to get off and go into the forest. . . . they said, "Go forward and down. There is your country." As soon as they finished saying this, they raised their guns, pointed the muzzles to the sky and fired. Then they pointed the guns at us. . . . The rainy season . . . made the ground and rocks slippery. . . . many people . . . slipped down and rolled over the cliff. . . . there were mines all the way down. Landmines below and the Thai soldiers above. They were coming near the cliff and giving us a volley of shots. Some of us shouted back to them that we could not go forward, because mines were scattered everywhere. The answer was a long continuous barrage directed straight down. . . . The explosions, the dead people, all the terrible scenes filled me with despair. (Robinson 1998: 47)

Another survivor, Pov Thai, who later resettled in the United States, became a member of the Dallas police, changed his first name to Paul, and told his life story to Sharon Fiffer, remembered a horrifying incident:

> A lot of women left babies up on the mountain. Everywhere you saw the babies, heard them crying. . . . One woman, she refused to leave her baby . . . [she] was walking ahead of me. She stepped on a mine. She heard the click and screamed for everyone to get away from her because when she moved again, it was going to blow up. But she begged for someone to come and take the baby. She had made it all the way down the mountain with the baby and now she knew she was going to die, but said she would die happy if someone would just come and take the baby from her. Finally, after a long time, one man stepped forward and said he would. Then I don't know what happened, maybe she got excited or anxious, but she must have moved, because the mine blew. We never even found her body. But we saw the baby's head. I felt terrible. I know everyone felt terrible. But the whole way, the whole time, we had to step over bodies. We went this way through the jungle for thirty days and thirty nights. (Fiffer 1991: 67)

The desperate people tried their best to help one another. Even those whose lives ended brutally proved helpful in a macabre way. As Teeda Butt Mam, a third survivor, told JoAn Criddle:

When someone found signs of a land mine, they stuck a branch in the ground and bent it over to point at the spot and tied a rag to the stick. . . . it was impossible to bury the dead with mines all around. The bodies could only be left to rot. . . . Yet those tragic bodies provided a service to those seeking a way off the treacherous mountain. They marked paths where mines had been but were no longer. It was safe to step near the mangled remains. . . . For over a week, we lay beside, stepped over, ate near, and slept with the mutilated dead. (Criddle 1987: 257–58)

When news of this forced repatriation reached the outside world, concerned foreign individuals and governments exerted severe pressure on Thailand to refrain from taking any more drastic actions in the future.

To deal with the crisis created by the massive movement of so many displaced people, United Nations Secretary General Kurt Waldheim convened a meeting at Geneva in July 1979. The sixty-five nations that participated reached agreement on three key points: the government of Vietnam would stop pushing people out; countries of first asylum would continue to offer temporary refuge to all those who arrived; and countries of second asylum (mainly the United States, Canada, Australia, and France but also dozens of other countries around the world) would dramatically increase their intake of refugees for resettlement. (Countries of second asylum are also called "third countries" or "resettlement countries.")

To facilitate resettlement efforts, the Philippine and Indonesian governments donated land to build two refugee processing centers at Bataan and Galang, respectively. The Thai government set up a third processing center, Phanat Nikhom, next to an existing refugee camp in Chonburi Province. During the next two years these arrangements helped reduce the Vietnamese displaced population in the countries of first asylum by two-thirds.

"Humane Deterrence"

Much to Thailand's chagrin, delegates to the 1979 conference did not discuss the land people from Laos and Cambodia. Thailand had to deal with them on its own. It did so first by a change in labels. Instead of being called "displaced persons," the refuge-seekers would henceforth be considered "illegal immigrants" or "illegal entrants." Labels are significant, because how a person is classified in a society determines how he or she would be treated and what his or her rights would be. Unlike displaced persons who were not subject to Thailand's immigration laws, illegal immigrants could be jailed and deported. Given the large numbers, however, deportation was not practical. So, Thailand reached an agreement with Laos in August 1979 to encourage Laotian citizens who had entered Thailand illegally to repatriate voluntarily. The repatriation program did not work, however, because almost no Laotians—neither lowland Lao nor Hmong—consented to be sent back to Laos (McNamara 1990: 125–26).

Consequently, the Thai government instituted a "humane deterrence" policy that had three components: camps housing the escapees would be operated at an "austere" level, providing only the barest necessities for survival; no new arrivals would be eligible for resettlement in countries of second asylum; and Thailand's borders would be "closed" to any further influx. (In fact, however, it was not possible to close the long and poorly marked borders between Laos and Thailand and between Cambodia and Thailand.) The new policy was designed to reduce the "magnet effect" of UNHCR holding centers and the possibility of being resettled in rich Western countries. Given the poverty and political repression in Vietnam, Laos, and Cambodia, Thai officials feared that if people in those three countries knew they could find refuge so easily, then millions, not hundreds of thousands, might risk escapes in search of a better life. That is, the very existence of UNHCR holding camps themselves—the relative security they provided in terms of shelter, food, medical care, and other social services—would lure people to Thailand.

Because the influx already greatly exceeded the number of resettlement slots available, Thailand had no assurance whatsoever that it would not be permanently saddled with the displaced population. The humane deterrence policy was implemented for lowland Lao in January 1981, for Vietnamese in September of the same year, and for Hmong in April 1982 (McNamara 1990: 127; Muntarbhorn 1992: 129). Existing camps would also be consolidated so that, in time, only one would be used to house each ethnic group.

The Thai government dealt with the Cambodians separately because the Second Cambodian Civil War was raging along Thailand's eastern border, which made the situation extremely complex. Even though Thailand had forcibly repatriated forty-two thousand Cambodians, this drastic action did not deter more from coming. The trek from the interior to the border was long and dangerous. Not only were jungle paths full of land mines, but bandits also robbed travelers while Thai, Khmer Rouge, PRK, Vietnamese, and Khmer Serei soldiers extorted them. (Some "Khmer Serei," the commonly used name for right-wing guerrillas, had been operating along the border for decades and eventually joined Son Sann's KPNLF.) Despite the risks, however, tens of thousands made the journey. At the Thai-Cambodian border, they gathered in camps run by the Khmer Serei. The largest of these camps came to be known by the names of the closest villages: Non Mak Mun, Nong Samet, Nong Chan, and Ban Sangae.

Peasants, small traders, soldiers no longer willing to fight, and former urban dwellers who did not wish to live under yet another communist government came to the border for various reasons. Some hoped to contact relatives and friends who had resettled abroad and might be willing to sponsor them. Others were what Michael Vickery calls "politicals"—people who opposed the Heng Samrin government and wanted to organize a resistance movement against it. Their aim was to remain at the border rather than to be resettled in the West. A third group was made up of people who wished to engage in the cross-border trade that quickly developed. Traders could make large profits by smuggling goods across the Thai-Cambodian border and selling them all over Cambodia and as far as Vietnam (Vickery 1990: 298–99).

Because both Cambodia and Vietnam were extremely short of consumer items, people paid for goods with gold and jewelry that they had somehow managed to hoard despite war and revolution. As Someth May recalls, "Gold was the currency. It came in sheets. If you wanted to pay for something small you snipped a bit off with scissors. . . . the gold was just sucked out in the direction of Thailand. In its place came sarongs and jeans, cloth, proper milled rice, cosmetics, tinned foods, fruit, cigarettes and alcohol. . . . All gold had to be cut before it was accepted, to make sure there was no core of base metal" (May 1986: 245, 255–56).

Some people still possessed gold because they had buried their valuables before the Khmer Rouge forced them to evacuate the cities. Many were lucky enough to find these hidden treasures upon returning to their former abodes in 1979. There was a second, more grisly source of gold, however. Before Teeda Butt Mam and her family made their second escape attempt, they knew they had to find some gold that would enable them to buy food and bribe soldiers and bandits along the way. She revealed to JoAn Criddle how they went about doing that:

Early victims of mass murder under Pol Pot had been searched carefully for possible valuables hidden in their clothing. But as the pace of killing . . . increased . . . there had not been time to search so thoroughly. When the Vietnamese took control of Cambodia, they had paid villagers to lead them to the mass grave sites in order to chronicle Khmer Rouge atrocities. . . . Villagers and soldiers scavenged the decomposing bodies, helping themselves to gold-filled teeth and the gold and jewels they occasionally found in the seams and linings of the victims' rotting clothes. But many burial sites had not yet been searched. Samol's family had known of such a site in the dense jungle near the village of Bor Por . . . Samol went to the eerie spot to see if he could find anything of value. . . . piles of bones and disintegrating clothing remained. The site had not been looted. Riffling among the clothes, Samol found enough gold and jewels to make escape seem possible. (Criddle 1987: 271)

The border trade was brisk. An estimated 50 million [Thai] *bhat* (equivalent to U.S. $2.5 million at the then-prevailing exchange rate) in black market transactions took place each day, with 30 to 40 million bhat deposited daily in banks in Aranyaprathet, the largest Thai town along that part of the border (Vickery 1990: 294). Not everyone engaged in this trade was trying to get rich, however. Some were trying their best to feed their families. Pov Thai, whose family successfully made a second escape to the Thai border after being sent back to the Dangrek Mountains in June 1979, told of a man who lost his life while trying to provide for his family:

This one man that I saw had one small piece of diamond, a very small diamond, and showed it to a high-ranking Thai officer who was carrying a pistol. The officer nodded and said, "Ah, good," and pulled out his pistol and shot the man right in the forehead. The man fell down and his bags went flying off in either direction. Then he got up . . . and was having convulsions, but he was looking for his bag and pole. He found it, picked up everything and got it together, and then fell down and died. . . . Watching this man get up and gather his things together said to me that he was still trying to feed his family—even as he was dying—he was trying to get his things together to give his family. I cried at this. (Fiffer 1991: 63)

Unlike the first arrivals, who were not completely destitute, the next contingents of Cambodians to cross the Thai-Cambodian border, in September and October 1979, were on the verge of death. They consisted of starving, wraithlike Khmer Rouge soldiers and their civilian hostages who emerged from the jungle south of Aranyaprathet after being pursued by Vietnamese troops for months. In October 1979 Prime Minister Kriangsak visited the border and was so visibly shaken by the misery he witnessed that he declared Thailand would open its doors to refuge-seekers. To feed and shelter these people, Thailand asked UNHCR to set up emergency holding centers on Thai soil.

Camp Life

Overnight, Thai and UNHCR workers constructed a camp named Sa Kaeo on a rice paddy. The site had poor drainage, no source of fresh water, and posed multiple public health hazards. As the pit latrines filled up, millions of flies and mosquitoes bred and swarmed everywhere (Swenson and Rahe 1986: 221–28). As Moeun Nhu, who now lives in Stockton, California, recalls, "Flood. The land was low. There were problems with the people and their health was not good and the living was not good because [of] the toilets— this month they dug the ground to make the toilets here, next month there. . . . almost used up the ground . . . the soil too muddy, too filthy . . . too difficult for people's living because that place had mosquitoes and flood. Each time it rained, it flooded some of the houses . . . there were worms and diseases because the toilets were too close to the houses" (Cambodians in California Project, Moeun interview 1989, 8: 14).

In this makeshift holding center, the "houses" under which twenty-five to thirty thousand emaciated and sick people huddled were actually blue plastic sheets strung up in whatever way could be found. When it rained, people lay in inches of mud. Those too weak to hold up their heads suffocated in the mud and died. Due to these unremediable problems, UNHCR eventually set up a new holding center, Sa Kaeo II, nearby.

The appalling conditions at the first Sa Kaeo holding center received worldwide attention when Rosalynn Carter visited the site in November 1979. She brought a sizable entourage, including the U.S. surgeon general, the director of the Centers for Disease Control, and staff from several departments in her husband's cabinet. Dozens of television camera crews trailed the delegation and beamed haunting images around the world of skin-and-bones people with sunken eyes, hollow cheeks, bloated bellies, and flies swarming around them. "Once in the camp," Rosalynn Carter reported, "we discovered a virtual sea of humanity . . . they were lying on the ground, on mats or dirty blankets or rags. All were ill and in various stages of starvation; some, all bones and no flesh; and others with crackled feet and swollen as though to burst. All with serious diseases, such as malaria, dysentery, and tuberculosis. All retching, feverish, and silent. . . . Seeing the children was the most difficult part of all" (Carter 1986: 56–57). Upon her return to Washington, D.C., she worked indefatigably to mobilize Congress, relief agencies, churches, and the general American public to contribute to relief efforts at the Thai-Cambodian border. Most Americans were unaware of the irony—the Cambodians whose plight so touched their hearts were retreating Khmer Rouge troops and their civilian hostages.

Paola Polacco Sandersley, a volunteer relief worker, likewise was stunned by her first encounter with a holding center: "Looking back, I think it was the word *camp* that most misled me. I had visualized tents, drinking water, emergency medical facilities, latrines. What I found was a far cry. Thousands upon thousands of people . . . were squatting apathetically in the scorching sun, some dying, most in appalling conditions, all skeletal. Worst of all was the eerie silence. No one talked; the fetal-looking babies did not cry. There was no communication among these people too ill, too hungry and thirsty, too desperate, to react in any way whatsoever" (1986: 48).

UNHCR set up a larger holding center, named Khao I Dang after a near-by mountain, in late November, thirty kilometers north of Aranyaprathet. Having been given ten days instead of just one by the Thai government to construct the camp, UNHCR was able to plan it better. Khao I Dang had two hospitals, feeding centers for malnourished babies and their mothers, a water supply system, and a network of laterite roads (Mason and Brown 1983: 35). There were also schools for children, adult education classes, feeding programs for infants and their mothers, and dozens of volunteer medical teams from around the world. Esmeralda Luciolli, a doctor who joined Médecins sans Frontières to volunteer her services in Thai camps, explained why the international relief teams were determined to make conditions at Khao I Dang as good as possible: "We were obsessed with the thought that while the whole world was fixing its eyes on this area, Khao I Dang must not become a second Sa Kaeo. This obsession overlooked the facts that the refugees who were about to arrive would be in far better health than the 'skeletons' at Sa Kaeo, and that they would not arrive en masse as they had at Sa Kaeo but came on buses in smaller groups over a period of several weeks" (1986: 67).

In the opinion of Daniel Susott, an international health and preventive medicine specialist who served as the medical coordinator at Khao I Dang in 1979 and 1980, the effort to make that holding center a model camp was not an ideal one: "Khao I Dang experienced the mixed blessing of a glut of medical personnel. At one point, there were more than 20 volags [voluntary agencies] involved in some aspect or another of medical care, with the number of expatriate volag personnel approaching 450. There were almost 100 doctors, a ratio of one doctor to each 1,500 refugees. This was ludicrous since another camp was being served by a single physician who was also responsible for training, public health, and care of the 100,000 Thai villagers in the vicinity" (1986: 77).

After Khao I Dang opened, international aid workers went in buses to meet the people who had managed to make it to the border. But the refuge-seekers had to run yet another gauntlet before they could even get near a bus. A Khmer Krom man interviewed by Sheila Pinkel recalled that the Thai soldiers guarding the border put a lot of pressure on relief workers, who were told:

> "If you're not moving these people, . . . we'll send them back. . . . You got until three o'clock in the afternoon to move these people, process these people . . . [or else] we'll ship them back to Cambodia." There was a loud-speaker that announced, "Military families, please come forward. You can go to the United States. . . ." No one believed that. But since I wanted to go to the United States, I did not hesitate. . . . I was the first in line with my fami-ly, filling out all the forms, signing them. We got into the bus at 9 A.M. We waited and waited but the bus did not leave. . . . The processing got worse and worse. The Thais were beating up people, they started shooting their rifles in the air. . . . The buses were all lined up with fifteen hundred people. . . . Right at three o'clock, right on the dot, they ended the processing. They chased the Americans with guns pointed at their heads and said, "Move!" . . . The French and Americans were running around, trying to get children out, the young children . . . trying to sneak them out the fence. . . . [But] the Thai forced the buses to leave. (Anonymous interview, 1996, Sheila Pinkel)

Under such chaotic conditions, members of families were sometimes sepa-rated. Some adults who lost their children, spouses, or other family mem-bers later returned to the border to search for them, but they were not always successful in finding their loved ones.

Not surprisingly, Cambodians who did make it to Khao I Dang with their families intact felt an enormous sense of relief. Says Kiev Samo, "When we arrived in Khao I Dang, it was a rebirth for my family because we escaped from starvation, and besides the humane organizations were permanently in the camp. When I first arrived, American people helped carry my child, helped my grandmother get off from the bus, and provided us rice, dishes, pots, blankets, oil, and some other food. After that they gave us a bunch of bamboo to build a temporary home. At that time rice was very abundant . . . each section has its own school . . . there was a post office in every sec-tion" (Cambodians in California Project, Kiev interview 1989, 14: 9).

Sin Sopha, who had found temporary refuge in several Khmer Serei camps before entering Khao I Dang, likewise appreciated being there: "For me and most of us Cambodians, Khao I Dang was better because it was safe. We could live there and avoid being shelled. . . . in Chumrum Chas [Old Camp] and Chumrum Thmey [New Camp], sometimes the Vietnamese would shell us. Sometimes we had to flee, to run away from the camp. . . . The Khao I Dang camp was really nice. There was food and everything. There were enough houses to live in, and doctors, and medicine and things" (Cambodians in California Project, Sin interview 1989, 23: 24).

Siphana Sok, a radio operator, who has published a short memoir in English, felt reassured and comforted by the presence of international relief workers:

> My first impression of Khao I Dang was a feeling of security that was quite unknown to me for the previous five years. I stood there in the middle of the crowd, staring at faces full of hope. . . . Here people smiled; they found again the notion of living, and they showed in their faces new rays of hope. The rations of food were not excellent, but they were enough. At least, we refugees could eat with peace with our families without any fear. The presence of foreign relief workers from all over the world brought our morale up and strengthened our sense of security. (Sok 1986: 83)

Seang M. Seng, a medical student who managed to survive the DK period by hiding his identity, worked as a physician's assistant and translator at Khao I Dang. He, too, has published a short memoir in English and echoes Sok: "The presence of the international teams made me feel safe and comfortable. The waving of the UNHCR flags had replaced the flickering light of the torches, under which we were condemned to work and starve. Eyes full of meanness, glaring at us every second, had been replaced by eyes full of tears of compassion, ready to help and provide us care. It was the time we all felt that the nightmare, at last, was going to end" (Seng 1986: 12).

But the initial euphoria dissipated quickly. Chim Ol, a widow who supported her children by weaving and selling baskets, recalled the insecurity and violence that soon came to plague Khao I Dang: "Living at KID [Khao I Dang] I was more scared than when I was at Sa Kaeo [II]. . . . People said there were thieves. . . . When everybody ran, we ran with them. Almost every night. I was crying all the time. . . . Sometimes we ran to the hospital. . . . It was nothing special at the hospital but when everybody went over there, I just went with them. I carried my children over there. . . . It was terrible." (Cambodians in California Project, Chim interview 1989, 3: 20–21). Another woman, Tep Nhim, had a similar experience: "They came to hurt [us] every night. When it was dark they had already come in. The shooting made everyone scatter all over the place. I was so scared every night. I never slept at home. Wherever I went, my group members always followed me" (Cambodians in California Project, Tep interview 1989, 5: 8).

Samkhann Khoeun, who served as executive director of a mutual assistance association in Lowell, Massachusetts, from 1995 to 2002, explained why camp residents felt so insecure:

> The word I would use to describe the camp is that it was like a prison. We were surrounded by barbed wire, two or three layers of barbed wire, and we were guarded by Thai soldiers. Anyone who dared to cross the barbed wire would be subject to death; they were killed. . . . There were also a lot of robberies by Thai soldiers. There were a lot of rapes and other crimes committed against defenseless refugees. . . . In the daytime, [the soldiers] . . . went from place to place, so at night, after the UNHCR staff went back to their residences . . . the Thai guards knew who had daughters and possessions. They took the girls and robbed the refugees at night. (Khoeun interview 1995 in Chan, ed. 2003a: 131)

Other former Khao I Dang residents, however, thought the robberies were not carried out by the soldiers themselves. Rather, soldiers colluded with men they let into camp. Sun Bun asserted, "Robbers came from the Old Camp and the New Camp every night. These robbers were friends with Thai soldiers. After they robbed, they shared with Thai soldiers. Therefore, Thai soldiers opened the way for those robbers to come in" (Cambodians in California Project, Sun interview 1989, 45: 34).

Robberies notwithstanding, bourgeois vices quickly crept back into the lives of Khao I Dang residents. As Someth May recalled, "The tankers arrived every day with water, and their drivers brought cigarettes and cloth. . . . There was a coffee shop and you could even get alcohol, but . . . all this was illegal. . . . There were cardgames in half of the huts, and people gambled with everything they had. There were discreet little brothels, attracting trade by word of mouth" (May 1986: 269–70).

Retrospective accounts by Khao I Dang residents now living in the United States indicate that how they fared depended a great deal on where within the camp they lived and how their section leader behaved. Khao I Dang was divided into more than twenty sections, most of which housed Cambodians, but a handful were set aside for Vietnamese, Sino-Vietnamese, and other ethnic groups. Thai authorities appointed a leader within each section, and section leaders oversaw the distribution of food, water, clothing, and building materials for huts. Some leaders were conscientious and made sure people in their sections received their share of whatever was distributed. Getting enough water was especially problematic, because even though wells were dug in Khao I Dang they provided only about a fifth of the water needed. Water had to be trucked in every day, and people had to line up to get their allotment. Even years later, refugees such as Phon Phan recall with bitterness how his section leader behaved: "The group leaders keep the big fish for themselves. The small fish are for us. . . . The fish about this size are set aside. Oil was also set aside. . . . we had such a greedy person. He slept until six or seven and didn't wake up on time to measure out water for the group members. Other group leaders woke up at dawn and they measured water for their members. . . . He cursed people. . . . He took away chickens and fish from people and kept them for his family" (Cambodians in California Project, Phon interview 1989, 52: 23).

Furthermore, the refuge-seekers' own behavior affected how tolerable their lives would be, especially in terms of how the Thai soldiers who guarded Khao I Dang treated them. In general, the soldiers did not mistreat people who obeyed all the rules and did not go outside the fence. However, they brutally punished those caught leaving the holding center to buy or sell things. They kicked and beat them, threw them in jail, and fined them. As Chhom Pok put it, "They hurt people . . . when Cambodians did things a little bit wrong. . . . They considered us as garbage. . . . They hit us with rifle butts, and they treated us like dogs" (Cambodians in California Project, Chhom interview 1989, 36: 23).

Despite these problems, residents of Khao I Dang tried very hard to bring some normalcy into their lives. An important aspect of Cambodian culture is classical dance. Although between 80 and 90 percent of the dancers and artists perished during the Khmer Rouge period, those who survived taught the art forms to children in the camps. As Mom Kamel, who organized a ballet class as soon as Khao I Dang opened, told Virginia Veach, who coordinated and directed the Family Practice Ward at Khao I Dang, "We cannot survive unless we remember where we have come from—unless we have an identity and a sense of dignity. Many people from all over the world have come to help us with medicines and food, for which we are so grateful that our hearts can never express it; but you are the first people who have come to care how we are as human beings" (Veach 1986: 163).

In addition to Khao I Dang, UNHCR also set up holding centers at Kamput, Mairut, Surin, Buriram, and Kap Choeung. The first contingents admitted into Khao I Dang had to build their own bamboo-and-thatch huts. Often there was not enough housing for everyone. As Khao I Dang became overcrowded, camp administrators moved some residents to the other holding centers. Then people were brought back to Khao I Dang when other centers closed in 1982. Lawlessness in Khao I Dang had increased during the intervening two years, said the Cambodians who entered Khao I Dang when it opened, were moved to other camps for a while, and then returned to Khao I Dang in 1982. Despite the difficulties they faced, Khao I Dang's residents were sustained by the hope that they would be chosen for resettlement in a Western country.

Because Thai leaders did not really wish to have any Cambodian refugee-seekers on its soil, given that their presence gave the Vietnamese army a pretext to make incursions into Thai territory, they closed the border again three months after it had been opened. (A coup had removed Kriangsak in the intervening three months, and a new prime minister less sympathetic to the Cambodian refuge-seekers was now in office.) Thailand officially ceased granting asylum to Cambodians after January 1980. Before that happened, however, more than 160,000 Cambodians had been placed into Khao I Dang and the other UNHCR holding centers (Sutter 1990: 102). Thereafter, Thai officials placed all Cambodians arriving at the border into "border camps" instead of UNHCR holding centers. Because the Thai-Cambodian border was not clearly demarcated at that time, with markers spaced miles apart, Thai officials used vague language to suggest that the border camps were not actually on Thai soil. As Michael Vickery puts it, "The Thai position . . . was to treat the . . . border camps as Cambodian and their inhabitants not only as non-refugees . . . but not even as 'illegal immigrants,' . . . They were Cambodians, under one or more Cambodian administrations" (1990: 301). After Vietnamese forces drove all the Cambodians into undeniably Thai territory during the 1984–85 dry-season offensive, however, Thai officials could no longer maintain that fiction, so they began calling the Cambodians "evacuees" to signal the temporary nature of the refuge being granted. The way Thailand dealt with its dilemma, in turn, created a dilemma for the United Nations.

The Role of UN Agencies

UNHCR holding centers that housed all Vietnamese, Sino-Vietnamese, Lao, Hmong, and other refuge-seekers, as well as the 160,000 Cambodians who managed to get in, were located well inside Thailand and administered jointly by UNHRC and the Thai Ministry of the Interior. In contrast, the Thai army ran the eight border camps. The Khmer Rouge controlled five of them, Son Sann's KPNLF (often known as the Khmer Serei) two, and Sihanouk's followers one.

Given its mandate to care for refugees worldwide, UNHCR's absence from the border camps needs to be explained. Established in 1950 as a small agency within the United Nations and financed largely by voluntary donations, UNHCR first aided Europeans displaced during World War II who had not yet been repatriated to their countries of origin or resettled in another country by the early 1950s. It also helped Palestinians who were displaced in 1948 when the state of Israel was established. But the United Nations soon created a separate agency, the United Nations Relief and Works Agency for Palestinian Refugees, to deal with the Palestinians, who to this day still have not yet been permanently resettled or allowed to return to their homes in what is now Israel. In the late 1950s, UNHCR provided some help to Hungarians, Poles, and Chinese refuge-seekers. In the early 1970s it helped relocate ten million people as East Pakistan became a separate nation, Bangladesh, as well as hundreds of thousands of refuge-seekers from the Sudan and Uganda (Office of the United Nations High Commissioner for Refugees 2000: 13–78). When the exodus from Vietnam, Laos, and Cambodia began, UNHCR was still a small agency with a limited staff and even more limited funding. Moreover, its approach, which favored repatriation where possible, and the political neutrality it insisted on maintaining during the cold war, clashed with the policies of the United States—the major country of second asylum.

Because UNHCR's mandate is to aid all refugees—that is, individuals who qualified for such a designation under the 1951 and 1967 statutes—and displaced persons regardless of their political affiliations, it wanted to ensure that it could function *within* Vietnam, Laos, and Cambodia while also helping refuge-seekers from those countries. That meant it had to maintain a relatively smooth working relationship with the governments of those three countries in order to ensure that it would not be denied access to needy populations within their borders. Following the establishment of communist governments in Cambodia, Vietnam, and Laos, UNHCR helped rehabilitate war-torn families in Vietnam and Laos, transported tens of thousands of Hmong back to the highlands to start new lives by giving them seed rice and farming tools, assisted people in North Vietnam to establish textile production and poultry breeding programs, and helped uprooted people in South Vietnam return to their homes (Robinson 1998: 21). In other words, Cambodians amassed along the Thai-Cambodian border were only one of several populations UNHCR was trying to aid. Thus, it could not allow itself to be sucked into the complicated politics that bedeviled relief operations along that border.

When Thailand denied Cambodian refuge-seekers the right to be interviewed for possible resettlement in countries of second asylum, UNHCR did not protest or intervene because both parties believed that the best solution ultimately would be to repatriate the Cambodians when conditions permitted. Even more important, at that very moment UNHCR was overwhelmed with the Vietnamese boat people exodus that was receiving a lot of media coverage. The crisis created by the boat people was an international one involving half a dozen countries of first asylum in Southeast Asia and the British crown colony of Hong Kong as well as dozens of countries of second asylum around the world. The Cambodian problem, in contrast, was confined to the Thai border.

To serve the border population, the United Nations International Children's Emergency Fund (UNICEF) and the International Committee of the Red Cross (ICRC) assumed responsibility as the "lead agencies" during the initial Cambodian exodus. UNICEF and ICRC asked the World Food Program to buy the needed food, which the Thai military then distributed (Robinson 1998: 66–98). The U.S. Embassy in Bangkok contracted with Catholic Relief Services to deliver additionial food (Reynell 1989: 34). At the beginning of 1982, the United Nations created a new, temporary agency, the United Nations Border Relief Operation (UNBRO), to support Cambodians, whose numbers had stabilized to about three hundred thousand by that time, in border camps. In addition, an unknown number of active combatants belonging to the three resistance factions lived in their own camps near the border. Some of these men visited their families in the UNBRO-supported border camps from time to time and took rations to support their fellow fighters—something that was not supposed to happen. UNBRO also gave aid to about sixty-five thousand Thai villagers adversely affected by the chaotic conditions.

Life in the eight border camps was full of insecurities. In some, virtual warlords controlled food distribution. They kept a substantial portion of the food and sold it on the black market (Mason and Brown 1983: 45–58). Worse, what food did reach its intended recipients was not distributed equally. To maintain the fiction that international food aid was not being given to combatants in the on-going civil war along the border, only females over the age of eight were eligible for rations. That meant families with a large number of boys or men never had enough to eat. The food relief program also assumed that camp residents could supplement their diet of rice, canned or dried fish, and beans with vegetables grown in plots around the camp, but some camps, especially the large camp called Site II controlled by the KPNLF, were so arid and barren that no such cultivation was possible (Reynell 1989:73–123).

Thai rangers belonging to Task Force 80, whose members were poorly paid and even more poorly disciplined, guarded the border camps. Instead of protecting the camp population, some rangers robbed whoever still had anything worth robbing and raped young women. The Lawyers Committee for Human Rights, headquartered in New York, sent investigators to the camps and issued several reports condemning the rampant abuses and violations of human rights there, but it is not clear what effect, if any, the group's investigations had (Lawyers Committee for Human Rights 1987, 1989, 1990, 1992). Those incarcerated in camps that had no markets sometimes sneaked out to buy things from vendors, although Thai guards severely punished people caught doing that or shot them on sight. Bandits, who came freely into the camps at night, and Cambodian camp residents, who had become thugs, both preyed upon the camp population.

Another form of insecurity plagued residents of the five camps controlled by the Khmer Rouge. Some Western observers claimed that these people were, in fact, hostages because most were being held against their will, having been forced by the retreating Khmer Rouge army to serve as porters and a source of new recruits. From time to time the Khmer Rouge moved large groups out of their camps in the middle of the night and marched them toward Cambodia in order to beef up resistance units within western Cambodia (Asia Watch Committee 1989). The People's Republic of Kampuchea and its Vietnamese backers considered such moves as hostile acts and attacked the unfortunate conscripts, wounding many while driving the rest back toward Thailand.

Boredom, dependence, and despair pervaded border camps. The small number of jobs that were available usually went to inmates who had some education or connections to the Khmer leaders chosen by the Thai camp administrators to help run the camps. The rest of the people gossiped to while away time, quarreled with one another within their overcrowded huts, and waited and waited—for food to be distributed, for water to be delivered, for men to return from the front outside the gates, and for the fighting to end. Some men abandoned their wives and children for new girlfriends, not for just sexual reasons but for economic ones as well. As the president of the Women's Association at Site II explained to Sheila Pinkel:

> Here in Site II, men do not get rations, only women do. . . . Each woman
> receives seven kilos of rice. . . . The women have to feed the men. When men

do not get enough food, they get angry. When a man is angry, he uses his power to abuse women because he is stronger. Sometimes they violate children, too. . . . A man can have two, three, four wives in the camp. . . . He gets several wives because he has a lot of needs. The first wife feeds him food, the second one gets him cigarettes, the third one gives him alcohol, the fourth fulfills his other needs. . . . During their escape from Cambodia to the border, a woman faced a lot of dangers. At that time, she sometimes needed a man to protect her. If a woman was violated, raped, she had to accept the man as her husband. She had so many problems that she . . . could think only of the present, not the future, because the danger is right in front of her. When she reached a camp, she wanted to release herself from this man but she could not . . . even if she found out the man has three wives already. (Anonymous interview, 1992, Sheila Pinkel)

Despite the fact they lived in limbo, the Cambodians' will to survive not only as individuals but also as a people and a civilization was very evident. In both UNHCR holding centers and border camps the birth rate was high. Women who had more or less regained their health could once again conceive. Feeling a strong moral obligation to replenish the Cambodian population, they gave birth to many babies.

As the number of children grew, leaders within the eight border camps became concerned about educating them. The education that was offered, however, was not just reading, writing, and arithmetic; rather, camps leaders subjected students to a large dose of political indoctrination. Classes for children, and especially classes for adults, became instruments for influencing people's thinking and political loyalty. KPNLF leaders referred to this aspect of education as "political warfare." It was a program "to augment the military effort by creating a cohesive political cadre for the KPNLF and by soliciting the support of the population," notes educator Jeffrey Dufresne. People who completed the courses received certificates, and only those with certificates were hired for the available jobs (Dufresne 1993: 114).

Because so many teachers had been killed during the Khmer Rouge regime, KPNLF camp leaders asked individuals who had any kind of education at all to "teach what they knew" to the children. Those who agreed to do so "all shared a concern for the children and were willing to assist though they were not trained as teachers." The first classes were conducted under the open sky, "with teachers and students moving as the sun moved. . . . Students sat on mats or large leaves spread on the ground. Cardboard from empty boxes served as individual 'slates' for students, and bigger boxes were opened up, flattened, and put on the trunks of trees to be used as blackboards. . . . charcoal and clay [were used] . . . as chalk. . . . The level of the students was so low that any type of instruction was better than nothing. . . . Basic literacy and arithmetic were the highest priorities" (Dufresne 1993: 162–63, 165).

Camp residents also made efforts to resuscitate Khmer culture. The KPNLF leaders at Site II set up Cambodian classical dance classes, dance and its accompanying music being the most cherished of the performing arts. They also actively supported the revival of Buddhism. As Lindsay French, an anthropologist, observed:

> Many monks who had been monks in the past resumed their ecclesiastical roles and duties on the border before the requisite, properly ordained six monks could be gathered for an official re-ordination. Makeshift temples appeared almost immediately in the early border camps: of the seven wats in Site II in 1990 all but two had been established in 1979, as soon as the Khmer had reached the border. The resumption of Buddhist ritual provided a kind of release for many Khmer that seemed to get right to the heart of their pain. Large numbers of young men were ordained for the first time in 1979 and 1980 as so many wanted to make merit for parents who had died witout the benefit of a cremation or funeral under Pol Pot. (French 1994: 241–42)

Partly because of these efforts at self-help, people living in the three non-Khmer Rouge–controlled camps told international relief workers that despite the prisonlike environment, camps were "infinitely preferable to life under the Khmer Rouge" (Reynell 1989: 18). In general, people in those camps where markets existed were better off because Thai, Vietnamese, Chinese, and Khmer traders brought in all kinds of merchandise for sale (Mason and Brown 1983: 40–41). Instead of being dusty and monotonously drab, life there had some color. Between late 1991 and the spring of 1993, the United Nations, as part of the peace settlement that ended the Second Cambodian Civil War, repatriated the entire border camp population of more than 360,000 individuals who had lived for twelve years in a liminal state during which everything was makeshift and the future totally uncertain.

U.S. Refugee Policy in Historical Perspective

The only Cambodians who eventually found refuge in countries of second asylum after 1978 were people who happened to have entered Thailand during the three months when the border was open, from October 1979 to January 1980, and who were placed into UNHCR holding centers. They were eligible for resettlement abroad because they lived in camps under UNHCR "protection" and could therefore be classified as "refugees"—a status denied those who came in February 1980 and thereafter. (Many people, however, managed to sneak into Khao I Dang after that date.) The ultimate fate of those Cambodians who ended up as refugees in the United States depended largely on U.S. refugee policy and the politics of refugee resettlement.

In the two UN statutes spelling out UNHCR's mandate to protect refugees, *persecution* is the defining concept. People fleeing natural disasters or economic hardship, no matter how destitute they may be, are not considered bona fide refugees. To qualify as a refugee, one must already have been subjected to or fear potential political persecution by one's own government. Moreover, to qualify for resettlement in another country as a refugee, one must have already left one's own country. Because the United States, like Thailand, was not at that time a signatory to these UN statutes, however, it, too, could act independently.

The manner in which the United States has treated refuges has historically been intertwined with the nation's immigration laws and their implementation. Norman Zucker and Naomi Zucker characterize U.S. refugee and immigration policies as "Janus-faced. One face presses for admission, the other urges restriction." They divide the history of U.S. refugee policy into five periods: the era of immigration, from the beginning of the Republic until the 1930s, when no distinction was drawn between immigrants and refugees; the era of fear, from the 1930s to the mid-1940s, when policies regarding aspiring refugees were restrictive; the era of conscience, from the late 1940s to the 1970s, when refugees were admitted initially under short-term, ad hoc programs, later under the seventh preference of the 1965 Immigration Act, and finally under the U.S. attorney general's parole authority; the era of legal obligation, when refugees entered under the provisions of the 1980 Refugee Act; and the present era of redefinition, when policymakers are assessing the 1980 law in order to decide what modifications may be needed in light of the growing number of displaced persons and refuge-seekers around the world (Zucker and Zucker 1992: 54).

U.S. political leaders first encountered a refugee problem when Nazi Germany persecuted millions of Jews in Europe. Although sympathetic to the Jews, the United States admitted relatively few as refugees. After World War II, Congress passed the 1948 Displaced Persons Act, but its provisions did not include specific slots for Jews. Approximately four hundred thousand displaced Europeans, a large percentage composed of people from the Baltic countries that had been taken over by the USSR, entered the United States under this law in the next four years.

By the early 1950s, the United States had become virulently anticommunist. Public sympathy for people fleeing communist rule enabled President
Dwight D. Eisenhower to persuade Congress to establish the President's Es-
capee Program in 1952; pass the Refugee Relief Act in 1953; approve the first
mass-parole program for refugees in 1956; and pass the Refugee-Escapee Act
in 1957, the Refugee Fair Share Act in 1960, and the Migration and Refugee
Assistance Act in 1962. Chinese, Hungarians, and Cubans were the main
groups benefitting from these measures (Loescher and Scanlan 1986: 1–101;
Zucker and Zucker 1992: 55–61). In addition to admitting refugees, the United States also made financial contributions to UNHCR and to the Intergov-
ernmental Committee for European Migration (ICEM), which was later renamed the International Organization for Migration (IOM) to reflect the fact
that it is no longer primarily concerned with aiding Europeans.

U.S. refugee policy has been used as a weapon in the cold war and has
strongly favored people escaping from communism. American leaders think
of refuge-seekers from communist countries as people "voting with their
feet." The United States, however, has not welcomed people fleeing from
repressive right-wing governments, particularly those in Central and South
America and Haiti, with which the United States was or still is on friendly
terms.

In March 1975, when the Khmer Republic and South Vietnam appeared
about to fall, President Gerald Ford created an Interagency Task Force made
up of representatives from pertinent federal agencies to plan the evacuation
of American personnel then working in those two countries, as well as South
Vietnamese and Cambodians whose lives might be at risk should the communists come to power. Congressional committees tried repeatedly but without success to get a firm estimate of how many people might need to be evacuated. Philip Habib, the Ford administration's point man on the issue, was
evasive in his replies when pressed by members of Congress, in part because
the American ambassador to South Vietnam, Graham Martin, feared that
panic might engulf Saigon if an evacuation plan was made public. A ballpark
figure of 130,000 persons was chosen, with 125,000 slots reserved for Vietnamese and 5,000 for Cambodians.

In contrast to the chaotic evacuation from South Vietnam, that from
Phnom Penh went almost unnoticed. Only 878 Cambodians, half of them
children under the age of twelve, flew out in American aircraft, even though
a thousand slots had been authorized for them. Of the five thousand spaces
reserved for Cambodians within the 130,000 authorized for Vietnamese evacuees and "Cambodian diplomats, high level officials, and others whose lives

might be endangered if they returned to Cambodia," only 4,600 were used by individuals who were outside Cambodia when Phnom Penh fell. These two groups of Cambodians fitted both the U.S. criterion that refugees must be escapees from communism and the UN definition. Cambodians who fled between April 17, 1975, and January 7, 1979, were also bona fide refugees because the DK regime not only persecuted but also killed those who dared to escape.

Whether Cambodians who left the country after the People's Republic of Kampuchea was established in January 1979 could be counted as refugees is a perplexing issue. The only people the Heng Samrin regime wished to get rid of were Khmer Rouge political and military personnel. The new government did not persecute middle-class, educated people. In fact, it offered jobs to surviving individuals who possessed skills sorely needed for the reconstruction of the country (Vickery 1990: 298). As Michael Vickery points out, "Had they accepted they would have qualified for state support. . . . They were not driven out of the country by persecution, but found flight easy because the new PRK regime kept the promise made by the Salvation Front in December 1978 to restore freedom of movement" (1990: 324).

A very large proportion of Cambodians amassed at the border were looking for food, or for ways to make money, or to join resistance groups against the Heng Samrin government. That is, they were people who intended to stay at the border. So the Thai government and UNHCR were correct when they declared that such people were not true refugees. During the early months of the exodus, only a relatively small number of Cambodians—mainly former middle-class urban-dwellers who did not wish to live under a communist government of any kind—hoped to be resettled abroad. Yet the government that had persecuted them was the Khmer Rouge's Democratic Kampuchea and not the People's Republic of Kampuchea led by Heng Samrin and Hun Sen. Once DK fell, a question arose as to whether these individuals still had a valid claim to refugee status. Those who joined either the Son Sann–led or Sihanouk-led resistance groups had not been persecuted before they left Cambodia but would have been liable for persecution had they returned because their post-departure activities would have marked them as dissidents out to overthrow the existing government in Phnom Penh. In that sense, they were *refugiés sur place*—people who qualified for refugee status *after* they left their country.

The political and ethical dilemma that confronted American policymakers was this: If the UN definition of "refugee" were taken seriously, then the only persons who would have truly qualified as refugees with respect to the

Heng Samrin government would have been the Khmer Rouge because they composed the only group the new regime was out to eliminate. But no Western government was willing to resettle the Khmer Rouge. The United States and its ASEAN allies were willing to support them with arms and food aid in order to use them to undermine the Vietnam-backed Heng Samrin regime, but there was no concomitant desire to admit them as refugees. Various groups, however, began to pressure the federal government to admit at least *some* Cambodians into the United States as refugees.

Media images of the Cambodians who amassed at the Thai-Cambodian border had aroused the humanitarian impulses of so many Americans that public sentiment became quite sympathetic to these poor, sick, starving people. A Cambodian Crisis Center was formed, chaired by the Reverend Theodore Hesburgh of Notre Dame University, to coordinate private charitable organizations in a massive fund-raising campaign. The public's responsiveness was not just humanitarian, it also had political and moral components. Given the cold war mentality that existed at the time and the strong anti-Vietnamese stance of the U.S. foreign policy establishment, Americans wanted to see Cambodians admitted into the United States as refugees—that is, as people "voting with their feet" against the "illegitimate" Heng Samrin government installed by Vietnam, the aggressor nation. Seeing refuge-seekers pouring out of Vietnam itself, as well as out of Vietnam-dominated Laos and Cambodia, helped justify ex post facto America's military involvement in those countries. In other words, refuge-seekers were the clearest indication of the oppressiveness of communist regimes and the correctness of American foreign policy during the Vietnam wars.

Two effective pressure groups emerged to advocate on behalf of Cambodians. The first was made up of the U.S. ambassador to Thailand, Morton Abramowitz, and selected members of his embassy staff, who formed the Khmer Emergency Group (KEG) to care for Cambodians who were being shortchanged in the frenzy to rescue Vietnamese boat people. KEG had three objectives: to provide humanitarian assistance to Cambodians amassed at the border, to lobby for resettlement slots for them, and to explore the desirability of supporting the various anti-PRK resistance groups (Loescher and Scanlan 1986: 160). A vacuum existed at the Thai-Cambodian border at this time because UNHCR was severely understaffed and underfunded. It had only four field officers in Thailand before October 1978 and not a single refugee protection officer there from October 1978 to June 1979, the height of the crisis (Loescher and Scanlan 1986: 158). KEG filled the vacuum by providing relief of its own as well as involving international relief organizations. The group mounted an effective publicity campaign, briefing journalists and members of Congress and making sure that American visitors met individual Cambodians, each of whom was urged to tell his or her sad story.

Ambassador Abramowitz repeatedly cabled the U.S. State Department and the president, urging an increase of the intake of refugees. President Carter, however, did not need much urging. As a strong advocate of human rights, he doubled the U.S. resettlement quota from seven to fourteen thousand a month, thereby increasing the U.S. annual ceiling to an unprecedented 168,000—a number almost ten times as large as the 17,400 slots earmarked for refugees under the seventh preference of the 1965 Immigration Act. He did so in part to pressure other countries to follow the American lead in terms of increasing their intake of Indochinese refugees, particularly Vietnamese boat people, whose plight was daily broadcast on the world's television screens. He invoked the Holocaust as he called upon Congress and the American public to open their hearts to these new victims.

In October 1979, Carter pledged $70 million of aid over the next year and a half for Cambodians, with $30 million available immediately to those inside Cambodia, $9 million to those at the border, and the rest to come from subsequent supplemental appropriations. (The sum was raised later to $106 million.) The U.S. House of Representatives approved the bill the very next day, and the Senate followed suit shortly thereafter (*Indochinese Refugee Reports*, Oct. 30, 1979, 6). Meanwhile, Senators James Sasser of Tennessee, John Danforth of Missouri, and Max Baucus of Montana met in Phnom Penh with the Heng Samrin government to present a U.S. proposal for delivering food and medical aid. Due to political complications, the aid did not reach the Cambodian people until months later.

A loose coalition of human rights organizations, Christian churches, ethnic associations, and activist lawyers—the same people who had effectively lobbied to admit earlier refugee groups, including Hungarians, Cubans, Czechoslovakians, and Soviet Jews from the 1950s onward—also advocated on behalf of Cambodians. They formed a Citizens' Commission on Indochinese Refugees in December 1977, just as the number of boat people was rising (Loescher and Scanlan 1986: 86–94, 129–30). When Cambodians became a visible presence at the Thai-Cambodian border, the commission broadened its concerns to include them. Leo Cherne, chair of the International Rescue Committee that had been involved in refugee affairs for decades, also chaired the Citizens' Commission on Indochinese Refugees. A man with decades of experience as a refugee advocate, and someone who took up this calling with moral fervor for both humanitarian and political reasons, he testified before

Congress and urged it to include Cambodians among the Indochinese refugees being paroled into the United States.

Unlike UNHCR, which saw three possible options for dealing with refugee outflows—repatriation to countries of origin, integration into countries of first asylum, and resettlement in countries of second asylum—American policymakers found only the third option acceptable for people fleeing communism. In the rhetoric popularized later by President Ronald Reagan, refugees are "freedom fighters"—people who *deserve* to be admitted into the United States as permanent residents. Thus, a vague sympathy for suffering Cambodians quickly translated into political pressure to admit them into the United States as refugees.

Before March 1980, when Congress passed the first comprehensive refugee law in U.S. history, refugees had been admitted through the parole power of the U.S. attorney general, who could authorize individuals to enter the United States outside of normal immigration channels and quotas. Between 1975 and 1979, Vietnamese, Lao, Hmong, and Cambodians all entered the country via parole. But as the boat people crisis developed and President Carter used his executive prerogatives to repeatedly increase the refugee intake through parole (Chan 2003b: 185–86), Congress decided it was time for refugee policy to be brought under its control. After more than a year of debate, Congress, under the strong leadership of Senators Robert Dole of Kansas and Edward Kennedy of Massachusetts and Representative Stephen Solarz of New York, passed the 1980 Refugee Act, formally known as Public Law 96–212, 94 *U.S. Statutes* 102 (1980).

The 1980 Refugee Act has two objectives and six provisions. The first objective is to uphold "the historic policy of the United States to respond to the urgent needs of persons subject to persecution in their homelands . . . [and] to encourage all nations to provide assistance and resettlement opportunities to refugees to the fullest extent possible." The second objective is to provide "a permanent and systematic procedure for the admission to this country of refugees of special humanitarian concern to the United States, and to provide comprehensive and uniform provisions for the effective resettlement and absorption of those refugees who are admitted." The six provisions are: to adopt the UN definition of "refugee"; to set an annual quota of fifty thousand refugees (but that number can be modified through an annual consultation between the president's office and Congress); to provide an orderly but flexible procedure to deal with emergencies if refugees of "special humanitarian concern to the United States" cannot be resettled under the regular ceiling of fifty thousand; to give Congress, rather than the executive branch, control over refugee policy; to provide explicitly for asylum; and to establish federal programs for refugee resettlement and fund them annually (Kennedy 1981).

Even after adopting the UN definition of refugee, the United States continued to favor people escaping from communism. In addition to Cubans, the U.S. government also favored Vietnamese and Soviet Jews. Those three groups took up a large share of the total refugee quota year after year, from 1975 onward. The loophole that has allowed the federal government to admit many more refugees than the fifty thousand per year originally anticipated is the phrase "refugees of special humanitarian concern to the United States," which the 1980 Refugee Act did not define, thereby allowing it to be interpreted flexibly. A hint of who such refugees of special humanitarian concern might be was given by the U.S. Senate when it referred to "countries where . . . the United States has had long historic or cultural ties, or where we have been directly involved or have treaty obligations" (Jorgensen 1989: 131).

Although Cubans and Vietnamese were indeed fleeing countries in which the United States had been deeply involved in multiple ways, it is difficult to make the same argument for Soviet Jews. It is likely, however, that American guilt over the "abandonment" of European Jews during the Nazi era accounts for the generous quotas that Soviet Jews have received. In contrast, few refugees from Afghanistan and various African countries destroyed by civil wars have found sanctuary in the United States, even though some of them may have better claims to refugee status than the favored groups do. Moreover, Haitians have been severely discriminated against.

Once the United States decided to open its doors to Cambodians, the issue arose of who among those amassed at the Thai-Cambodian border should be designated as refugees. Given the divergent, ever-changing motivations that impelled Cambodians to trek to the border, it was a tricky question. The Thai government solved part of the problem when it declared that all those entering after the border closed in late January 1980 would not be eligible for resettlement. But there remained at least 160,000 persons who had been placed into UNHCR-supervised holding centers during the three months when the Thai-Cambodian border was open plus thousands who slipped into Khao I Dang in subsequent years.

The very fact that these persons were under UNHCR "protection" implied that they were refugees. Some, however, were Khmer Rouge troops and their civilian hostages. Among the holding centers, Sa Kaeo I (and at the time it was closed, Sa Kaeo II), Kamput, and Mairut housed almost entirely Khmer

Rouge affiliates. Because no one wished to resettle the Khmer Rouge, the Thai government attempted to repatriate them. Thailand sent the first batch of nine thousand back to Cambodia in late June 1980. Vietnamese troops, who did not want to see Khmer Rouge back in the country, retaliated by entering Nong Chan and Mak Mun villages, whereupon Thai troops opened fire and killed about two hundred people.

As a result of that fracas, Thailand made no further repatriation attempts. Instead, Thai authorities moved most of the Khmer Rouge out of UNHCR holding centers and into the five border camps under Khmer Rouge control. Thousands of Khmer Rouge, however, were also inadvertently transferred to Khao I Dang, where they quietly mingled with the rest of the camp population. Cambodian refugees in the United States still claim that many Khmer Rouge, once housed in Khao I Dang, managed to slip through the screening net and were admitted as refugees despite attempts by representatives of the Joint Voluntary Agency (JVA) and the U.S. Immigration and Naturalization Service (INS)—the two organizations that interviewed applicants for resettlement—to keep them out.

In early 1981, U.S. officials allocated a refugee quota of thirty thousand to Cambodians, and processing began. The first twenty thousand or so chosen for resettlement either had family members in the United States or had some kind of connection with Americans before 1975 (Loescher and Scanlan 1986: 164). After they were chosen, however, the selection process became much more difficult, because, as James W. Tollefson puts it, "Although immigration officials looked for ties with family members already in the United States or for a history of employment with American firms in Cambodia during the war, in fact it was impossible to distinguish refugees from economic migrants. Officials feared that any resettlement program for Cambodians would rapidly escalate into general immigration, given the miserable conditions inside Cambodia" (1989: 6).

Indeed, the resettlement option did become a "magnet." Khmer-speaking Michael Vickery, who interviewed many Cambodians in the spring of 1980, reports that they told him the main impetus that had lured them to the border were Voice of America radio broadcasts (in Khmer) beamed into Cambodia and telling them of the establishment of UNHCR holding centers. In particular, the broadcasts characterized the large camp at Khao I Dang, designed to hold up to three hundred thousand persons, as a place where people could "seek freedom" and stated that it had a market where traders could do business in greater security than at the border (Vickery 1990: 310, 329).

After the other UNHCR holding centers closed, Khao I Dang alone remained as the lodestar to draw Cambodians who wished to be resettled in
the West to Thailand. For that reason, the camp's population increased from
111,000 in January 1980, when the border closed and people were no longer
admitted into any UNHCR holding center, to 136,000 in July of that year. The
increase was due to the fact that people sneaked into camp at night or bribed
their way in. This illegal influx, which continued for the next six years,
changed the socioeconomic composition of the camp's population. Those
with money to bribe the guards were people who had been relatively well-
off before 1975 and had managed to retrieve the valuables they had buried
during the DK period. In the words of Milton Osborne, whom UNHCR
asked to assess the situation, "More than incidentally, the current American
programme is quite clearly having the effect of encouraging a further outflow of former middle class Kampucheans from inside Kampuchea in the
hope of being resettled" (Osborne unpublished report 1981: 4–5, as quoted
in Vickery 1990: 321).

Processing Cambodian Refugees

The U.S. State Department's Bureau for Refugee Programs specified six priorities for accepting refugees for resettlement. (The State Department
specified only four priorities when it first instituted the priority system but
increased that number to six in later years in order to take the greater complexity that emerged into account.) In the late 1970s and 1980s, Priority One
consisted of persons "who are in immediate danger of loss of life and for
whom there appears to be no alternative to resettlement in the United States
or refugees of compelling concern . . . such as former or present political
prisoners and dissidents." Priority Two included individuals U.S. government
agencies had employed for at least one year or, if not so employed, "were so
integrated into U.S. government offices as to have been in effect and appearance U.S. government employees." Priority Three was for spouses, unmarried children, or parents of U.S. citizens, lawful permanent resident aliens,
refugees, asylees, or public interest parolees. Priority Four was divided into
two subgroups: Iranians and Cubans and persons "previously in the civil
service or armed forces of the former governments of Indochina who were
associated with U.S. government policies or U.S.-supported programs" and
"persons who played a meaningful role in the social, economic, political,
religious, intellectual, or artistic life of the former societies of Indochina,

including such persons as professors, philosophers, monks, or other trans-
mitters of the cultural traditions of these societies." Priority Five took in
married children, unmarried and married siblings, grandparents, grandchildren, and more distant relatives of people already in the United States. Priority Six was reserved for persons of special humanitarian concern whose
"admission is in the national interest" (*Refugee Reports,* Dec. 30, 1991, 7).

Before mid-1981, applicants who fit these priorities were not required to
prove individually that they had been or were likely to be targets of persecution. Using such priorities by-passed the definition of "refugee" contained
in the UN declarations and in the 1980 Refugee Act. The Heng Samrin government, for example, did not persecute intellectuals and professionals, yet
such persons automatically qualified for refugee status under Priority Four.
To be sure, their peers in the same professions had been targeted for extinction during the DK period, but the DK government no longer existed, and
the PRK government, although also communist, did not engage in mass
persecution or homicide. In 1981, however, the INS ruled that the 1980 Refugee Act required its officers to consider applicants case by case, which meant
that each applicant had to convince INS interviewers individually that he or
she would face persecution should he or she be returned to Cambodia (*Refugee Reports,* Jan. 28, 1983, 2).

As the rejection rate climbed, conflicts arose between INS field officers
at the Thai-Cambodian border and the U.S. State Department. The State
Department wanted to admit as many Cambodians as possible in order to
cast a negative light on the Vietnam-supported government in Phnom Penh,
but INS officers assumed their traditional stance as guardians of the nation's
borders and preferred to be stricter in selecting whom to admit. Tensions also
developed between INS's field officers and JVA staff with whom the State
Department had contracted to prepare applicants for INS interviews. It was
the JVA staff members who wrote up each applicant's biography and prepared his or her file for presentation to the INS. In July 1983, Dennis Grace,
the JVA director, publicly stated that he was troubled by "inconsistencies" in
INS interview procedures and instructed his staff to write up more detailed
biographies (*Refugee Reports,* Jan. 28, 1983, 3–4).

Meanwhile, the pressure to admit more Cambodians—everyone in UN-
HCR holding centers, regardless of connections to the United States—con-
tinued to mount. Among those who did so were Ambassador Abramowitz;
Lionel Rosenblatt, a junior foreign service officer who co-directed KEG;
Sheppard Lowman, another junior foreign service officer; and Richard Hol-

brooke, the assistant secretary of state for East Asian and Pacific Affairs. They opposed the views of Victor Palmieri, the U.S. coordinator for refugees, and Frank Loy, director of the U.S. State Department's Bureau for Refugee Programs, who worried that a large resettlement program would "constitute a severe drain on the human resources of Cambodia and strip the country of the skilled personnel needed to make Cambodia self-sufficient again" (Loescher and Scanlan 1986: 164–65). The latter view was similar to that held by UNHCR, whose field representatives in Thailand tried to discourage the United States from admitting too many Cambodians.

Within Congress, Senators Edward Kennedy and Mark Hatfield and Representatives Stephen Solarz and Joel Pritchard lobbied on behalf of Cambodians. As Solarz and Pritchard wrote to INS Commissioner Alan Nelson, "It is hard to believe that 50 percent of the Cambodians who fled three years ago from the living hell they were then enduring are not truly refugees. . . . [we request that] every possible humanitarian consideration be carefully weighed in screening refugees . . . particularly . . . the Cambodians who have suffered so much and been so long and painfully separated from their families" (*Refugee Reports*, Sept. 24, 1982, 4).

Leo Cherne of the Citizens' Commission for Indochinese Refugees likewise argued that "there is no legal or numerical rationale for not quickly broadening resettlement opportunities for the Cambodians in the camps in Thailand. There are the strongest humanitarian reasons for doing so. No group . . . has suffered more than they" (Loescher and Scanlan 1986: 165). In short, overall suffering rather than political or religious persecution was proposed as the operating criterion in selecting Cambodians for admission. Senator Hatfield indirectly justified such an approach when he declared, "America will cease to exist [if it resorts to] . . . 'compassion fatigue' as a justification for turning its backs on refugees. . . . We must continue to provide hope . . . to those who have no voice" (*Refugee Reports*, April 20, 1984, 4).

The INS responded to such pressure by providing extra training to its officers; by sending Andrew Carmichael, its chief examiner, to visit its field offices in Thailand; by sending cables with additional guidelines to the field staff; and by dispatching a special team to the Kamput holding center in late November 1982 to speed the processing of Cambodians in that camp. The INS instructed its officers in Thailand to reinterview applicants identified by JVA director Grace or Michael Eiland, the State Department's refugee coordinator in Thailand. In late October and early November, U.S. Attorney General William French Smith visited the Thai border himself. He explained to reporters why it was necessary to conduct case-by-case reviews and declared that applications were not being considered with a specific numerical quota in mind (*Refugee Reports*, Nov. 19, 1982, 3).

In an effort to bridge such differences in government policies and procedures, President Ronald Reagan directed, in May 1983, that a review be carried out of how Indochinese refugees were processed. He asked the attorney general to determine whether there were "categories of persons with common characteristics" that might identify them as potential targets of persecution. In other words, was it really necessary for every applicant to prove *individually* his or her susceptibility to persecution? In response to Reagan's directive, the INS issued more liberal guidelines. The appointment of John Schroeder to the post of INS district director for Southeast Asia, who sought to work more cooperatively with the State Department and with JVA, also helped reduce the intramural acrimony among American officials.

One knotty problem, however, remained: What criteria should be used to determine which applicants had been associated with the Khmer Rouge and were involved in the persecution of fellow Cambodians? U.S. immigration law explicitly denies refugee status and resettlement to "any person who ordered, incited, or otherwise participated in" the persecution of others. Yet the only evidence available in many Cambodian cases was circumstantial. A study mission sent to Thailand by the U.S. Senate Committee on Foreign Relations, which was concerned about the impact that a large residual population in Khao I Dang might have on U.S.-Thai relations, stated what INS field officers, U.S. State Department ethnic affairs officers, and JVA staff lacked:

> the precise, reliable information needed to demonstrate definitively whether or not applicants for resettlement were members of the Khmer Rouge or otherwise participated in the persecution of their fellow Cambodians. U.S. officers must rely almost exclusively on information elicited from the refugees, and few applicants are unwise enough to incriminate themselves. But the processing center does not have the capability to independently investigate suspicious cases. U.S. access to Cambodia today is severely restricted and the events under investigation occurred a minimum of 5 years ago . . . many resource materials and analytical aids that could assist the interviewers in making more informed adjustments do not exist or are in short supply. . . . Absent supplementary information, such as eyewitness accounts, interviewers cannot prove that those they reject are Khmer Rouge, any more than they can demonstrate that those they approve did not persecute others. (U.S. Congress, Senate, Committee on Foreign Relations, 1984, 4–5, 7)

The Senate Committee on Appropriations also weighed in by declaring that "specific acts of inhumanity or persecution of others would have to be credibly alleged" to justify exclusion. In addition, the committee recommended that children who were under sixteen years of age when the DK regime fell in January 1979 could be denied resettlement only for "established acts of inhumanity or persecution of others" (*Refugee Reports*, Sept. 7, 1984, 2). The INS retorted by saying such congressional pronouncements had no legal authority because they had not been enacted into law. Due to this tug of war over how Khmer Rouge affiliation should be determined, some Khmer Rouge did manage to slip into the United States (Dunn 1995).

Not everyone was a bleeding heart liberal with regard to the issue. In an August 1984 staff report, the Senate Committee on the Judiciary's Subcommittee on Immigration and Refugee Policy argued that solutions other than resettlement in the United States should not be ruled out. The authors stated that there had never been any intention for the United States to resettle every resident in Khao I Dang. The Khao I Dang population did not differ in significant ways from the quarter-million Cambodians herded into border camps and deemed ineligible for interviews or resettlement (*Refugee Reports*, Sept. 7, 1984, 5). That is certainly a valid point, but it did not trump the passion with which advocates of Cambodians argued their case for admission.

Due to the fact that people continued to slip into Khao I Dang with the hope of being resettled, by the mid-1980s that holding center contained three types of legal residents: those who entered before February 1982; "family card holders," numbering about 4,300 persons, who found their way into the camp between February 1982 and July 1984; and "ration card holders," numbering 7,100 persons, who entered between August 1984 and October 1985. In addition, the camp also had about three thousand "illegal residents"—people who entered after October 1985.

Va Thareth has described how he managed to slip into Khao I Dang even after it was closed. Va had lived in Sa Kaeo I and II, as well as in Khao I Dang, in 1979 and 1980, but he returned to Phnom Penh in 1980 and remained there for two years. After getting married, he came back to the border and lived in Nong Chan camp for some time. Then:

In 1984 I came back to live in Khao I Dang camp. . . . There were six of us who came . . . we had no money. My wife didn't come with me yet. We all six risked our lives to get in the camp. If Thai soldiers shot us to death, we would be dead. . . . we risked our lives by cutting a wire fence and sneaking into the camp. . . . We got in about four, before the daylight. . . . I then [contacted] . . . my mother who lived in the United States of America. I asked my mother to send some money to me. Then I went out of the camp to get my wife. . . . We walked through the jungle. . . . No new-comers were welcomed or given any food or clothes. We had to be on our own. If we were caught, they would take us back to the border. . . . I lived with my relatives. They . . . always hid us. . . . it was because Cambodians living in the camp loved each other. Every neighbor helped hide us. And there were about seven thousand new-comers in the camp. Later we were given food legally. . . . They gave us food in 1985. (Cambodians in California Project, Va interview 1989, 37: 13–14)

Initially, only members of those groups who entered Khao I Dang before the border was closed were eligible for resettlement. The two groups of card holders received food rations and other services but could not be interviewed by officials of resettlement countries. Illegal entrants received no rations. As advocates of Cambodians continued to exert political pressure, however, both kinds of card holders were eventually placed into the resettlement stream. In 1986, family card holders were interviewed to determine who might fit under Priorities One through Four. A few months later, individuals who fitted Priority Five were also considered (*Refugee Reports,* Sept. 12, 1986, 8). Then, in January 1987, the State Department authorized field officers to also interview ration card holders who had family members among the other two legal groups (*Refugee Reports,* June 12, 1987, 6), again under Priorities One through Five.

Even with these greatly liberalized guidelines, approximately fifteen thousand of the original residents and more than half of the two groups of card holders were deemed ineligible for resettlement. Undeterred by those statistics, Representatives Solarz and James Leach of Iowa tried to further broaden the scope of whom to admit. They wrote to President Reagan in May 1985 to request that Cambodians in border camps, who might have close relatives in the United States, in addition to those in Khao I Dang be resettled. Perhaps the resettlement could be accomplished through an Orderly Departure Program similar to that established in 1979 for Vietnamese, but a State Department spokesperson pointed out that both Thailand and UNHCR had denied resettlement opportunity to these border Cambodians (*Refugee Reports,* June 21, 1985, 8).

Solarz's unrelenting advocacy eventually bore fruit, however. During the 1985 annual consultation between the president and Congress regarding the ceiling for refugee admissions during the ensuing fiscal year, Secretary of State

George P. Schultz announced that "subject to Thai government approval . . . a limited program to unite close family members with relatives already in this country primarily through immigration-type channels" would be initiated. Immigrant visas would be issued to spouses and unmarried minor children, and others who could not be granted entry expeditiously under existing law would be admitted under humanitarian parole (*Refugee Reports*, Oct. 11, 1985, 8–9). The small number admitted initially caused concern among supporters of the Cambodians (Robinson and Wallenstein 1989: 1), but in time more than 2,500 persons did enter the United States as humanitarian and public interest parolees.

The Thai government closed Khao I Dang in December 1986, although the remaining residents were allowed to stay there until they could be moved to border camps. The deadline for emptying Khao I Dang was extended repeatedly, but on July 20, 1988, the Thai government announced that the remaining population of seventeen thousand would be moved from Khao I Dang to the Thai-Cambodian border. During this tense interim period, the United States kept opening its doors wider. American officials reevaluated the files of previously rejected applicants and ultimately approved 24 percent of them for resettlement (*Refugee Reports*, Jan. 31, 1989, 8).

As the Khao I Dang residents grew desperate and despondent, some resorted to various schemes to improve their chances of being chosen for resettlement, while others fell victim to scams:

> You went to the church . . . hoping that your attendance there would speed your departure to America. Cambodians had never been Christians before. Now they were eagerly bringing home Cambodian bibles, which made excellent cigarette papers. . . . A Cambodian U.S. citizen arrived from California offering to get people out in return for a certain sum of gold. He loaded up the gold, made a list of fifty customers, left and was never seen again. . . . There were phantom orphans. The orphanage got the best rations. . . . Parents sent their children to live there, partly for the food and partly in the hope that they would be adopted. Once the child was in the States, the parents hoped to stage a dramatic and touching reunion. I reckoned about forty per cent of the orphans fell into this category. . . . In the evening the orphanage tended to be rather deserted as the children were with their parents. (May 1986: 270–71)

In December 1988 the Thai government further softened its stand, announcing that the fourteen thousand persons still remaining in Khao I Dang would be allowed to stay as long as there was a chance they might be resettled in another country (*Refugee Reports,* Dec. 16, 1989, 3). Finally, by fiscal year 1991, no more Cambodians still in Thailand were deemed admissible as refugees even by the most liberal standards. The last batch of Khao I Dang residents was moved to the border camps, mainly to those controlled by Son Sann and Sihanouk. They were repatriated along with the rest of the border Cambodians under UN supervision in 1992 and 1993.

After the gigantic UN repatriation effort, the only Cambodians still left in neighboring Southeast Asian countries were those who had escaped to Vietnam. In 1995 the Socialist Republic of Vietnam permitted 5,100 ethnic Chinese and twenty-seven thousand ethnic Vietnamese from Cambodia to settle in Vietnam permanently (*World Refugee Survey,* 1995: 96), but thirty-four thousand Khmer continued to be classified as refugees supported by UNHCR (*World Refugee Survey,* 1997: 112). In addition, because the Khmer Rouge never turned in their arms, sporadic fighting continued in western and northwestern Cambodia between them and the new government installed by the May 1993 elections. The new round of fighting once again caused tens of thousands of Cambodians to become temporarily displaced persons. Such population movements did not cease until 1999, when one faction after another of the Khmer Rouge defected to the Phnom Penh government and disbanded their troops.

Those Cambodians accepted as refugees had to go through two more processes before they could fly to the United States. First, they had to pass physical examinations to make sure they did not have communicable diseases. Given the deplorable conditions under which they had lived since 1975, many Cambodians suffered from anemia, tuberculosis, hepatitis, malaria, upper respiratory infections, and various kinds of intestinal parasites. Health officials were especially concerned about tuberculosis. They did not allow individuals who had been accepted for resettlement in the United States to leave until their tuberculosis had been brought under control. Tep Nhim described her suffering and determination to overcome the hurdle posed by the disease:

> We had to have physical and health checked. They told me that I had TB so I got to stay another six months for treatment. . . . I had to take medication for six months. I took it until I had bled on each of my single body hairs. I also lost my memory . . . because I had to take thirteen capsules each time. After I took them, I had seizures and bled again. . . . They took me to ICEM hospital; they saw me vomit after I took my TB medication. Even though I was just like that in front of them, they still wanted me to take them. If we didn't take medicines, we couldn't come to America. So, I had to try hard.

Because of those medicines . . . I almost died. (Cambodians in California
Project, Tep interview 1989, 5: 9–10)

Health officials also held up individuals with lesser medical problems until
those conditions improved. For example, the departure of Heng Chhorn, who
had high blood pressure, was delayed for three months until he got better
(Cambodians in California Project, Heng interview 1989, 49: 10).

Individuals held back for medical reasons experienced extreme distress.
Elizabeth Burki, a nurse and sociologist who worked at the Phanat Nikhom
camp, reports that while she was there three individuals under "medical hold"
committed suicide to enable the rest of their families to be released for resettlement (Burki 1987: 208). Even for those who had no health problems,
physical examinations were stressful, because people had to strip themselves
naked (Cambodians in California Project, Kiev interview 1989, 14: 11). The
experience was especially traumatic for modest Cambodian women, who had
to remove all their clothing to be examined by health professionals, many of
whom were male.

A second process that refugees had to undergo before being allowed to
leave involved five to six months of study to enable them to learn basic English and receive cultural orientation. Designed to prepare them for life in
the United States, this education took place either in the Phanat Nikhom
Refugee Processing Center in Chonburi or the Philippine Refugee Processing Center in Bataan (PRPC). In early 1980, before the processing centers were
running at full steam, there were not enough teachers, so only one person
per family was allowed to attend the English classes for an hour a day at the
PRPC (Cambodians in California Project, Min interview 1989, 12: 7). In time,
however, refugees at Phanat Nikhom and PRPC were introduced to many
aspects of modern life. How much a person learned depended mostly on how
much prior education he or she had received. Nhek Leng remembers that
"they showed us pictures with labels on them like pictures of a human being, fruit, a car, and each one was labeled in English, and the teacher read the
words to us. We also learned to listen to tapes. . . . Learning to listen and
learning to pronounce, but we couldn't even repeat. The teacher would say
something and the Cambodian would say something else. It wasn't the same
at all" (Cambodians in California Project, Nhek interview 1989, 6: 27). Sin
Sopha, who also took the classes at Phanat Nikhom, remembered, "We studied five months . . . about how to live in the U.S. and how to use the things
Americans have, to use the telephone to ask for help like when a thief comes
in, and the way to drive a car, the traffic rules in the U.S., everything. . . . They

taught us how to use appliances and tools and stuff" (Cambodians in California Project, Sin interview 1989, 23: 25).

What many refugees found far more challenging than learning how to use various modern appliances was overcoming the huge gap that divides Cambodian and Western behavior. Something as simple as learning to greet someone proved painful, as Chanrithy Him, a sixteen-year old girl at the time, recalled:

> Our teacher is a Filipino lady. . . . Our first lesson is learning how to greet someone in English, how to shake hands. When it's time to practice, our teacher asks a girl sitting beside me to get up. She is to shake hands with a Cambodian man in our class. The girl shakes her head, her face flushed. The teacher asks another girl, and she too shakes her head. She looks embarrassed just to be called upon, let alone to be shaking hands with a man. . . . No one gets up. Our teacher asks a Cambodian man and a Vietnamese man to come to the front of the class. They introduce themselves, then shake hands. The teacher stares at us and says, "You see, it's not hard to come up and shake hands. Watch me. My name is Marie. How do you do?" She shakes hands with a Vietnamese student. "Here, I'm still shaking hands with him and I'm not going to have a baby. Don't worry. You're not going to have a baby by shaking hands. Now, come on and practice." I'm annoyed by her comments. She should have been informed of our culture, and known that our way of greeting people is to press the palm of our hands together, then raise them to our chins. Even I, who am brave under many circumstances, am embarrassed by the idea of hand shaking. . . . She asks a Vietnamese student named Minh to stand in front of the class. Smiling, she says, "Would someone come up and shake hands with Minh?" I stand up. The teacher smiles. She croons, "Come on, Chanrithy. You can do it!" I reach out to shake his hand. He steps forward to shake mine, but as soon as his hand nears mine, I pull it away. I dash back to my seat. (Him 2000: 312)

Cambodians would face many other such challenges as they resettled in their new homes.

Some Pertinent Numbers

The great fluctuation in the number of persons admitted into UNHCR holding centers (table 1) reflects the vicissitudes in Thai policy with regard to how border Cambodians were to be classified and treated, as well as the ambivalences and contradictions that characterized U.S. policy with regard to how many and what kind of Cambodians to admit. The figures for Cambodians placed into border camps supported by UNBRO are only estimates, because these camps were controlled by the three resistance factions. The Khmer Rouge in particular did not allow international agency personnel to inspect their camps. All that UNBRO could do was accept the figures given by the leaders who controlled the camps and supply them with the amount of rations and other necessities for the population each camp claimed to house. Moreover, as the civil war continued along the border, camp leaders moved people in and out at will, so the population in these camps was never stable. UNHCR camps were closed by 1991, and UNBRO camps emptied in 1992 and 1993.

Altogether, from 1975 to 1994 when the Cambodian refugee resettlement program ended, 157,518 Cambodians entered the United States under three categories: 148,665 as refugees, 6,335 as immigrants, and 2,518 as humanitarian and public interest parolees (table 2). Cambodian refugees stopped en-

Table 1. Number of Cambodians Admitted into UNHCR Holding Centers versus Number Placed into Border Camps

Year	Number Admitted into UNHCR Holding Centers	Number in Border Camps (Cumulative Total)
1975	17,038	
1976	6,428	
1977	7,045	
1978	3,528	
1979	137,894	
1980	43,608	
1981	16	
1982	14	215,000
1983	0	208,000
1984	4,346	242,000
1985	7,989	226,000
1986	197	243,000
1987	39	264,000
1988	0	298,000
1989	4,586	311,000
1990	1,607	307,000
1991	300	329,000

Source: Bangkok offices of the United Nations High Commissioner for Refugees and the United Nations Border Relief Operation, as quoted in Jacqueline Desbarats, *Prolific Survivors: Population Change in Cambodia, 1975–1993* (Tempe: Arizona State University Program for Southeast Asian Studies, 1995), 99.

Table 2. Number of Cambodian Refugees, Immigrants, and Humanitarian and Public Interest Parolees Admitted by Year, 1975–94

Fiscal Year	Refugees	Immigrants	Parolees
1975	4,600	98	
1976	1,100	126	
1977	300	126	
1978	1,300	70	
1979	6,000	66	
1980	16,000	85	
1981	27,100	107	
1982	20,100	129	
1983	13,191	163	
1984	19,849	193	
1985	19,237	198	7
1986	10,054	201	2
1987	1,949	254	7
1988	2,900	374	55
1989	2,200	428	88
1990	2,325	460	178
1991	186	701	314
1992	185	878	998
1993	63	831	726
1994	6	847	143

Source: Unpublished data courtesy of Linda Gordon, Immigration and Naturalization Service.

tering in 1994, and humanitarian parolees soon thereafter. Since then, fewer than one thousand Cambodians have gained admission into the United States each year as immigrants under the provisions of the 1990 Immigration Act.

In terms of their socioeconomic background or political history, most of those admitted as refugees were not that different from the approximately 360,000 border Cambodians whom the United Nations repatriated in 1992–93. The ones who ended up in the United States did so because, by chance, they happened to be in the right place (that is, a UNHCR holding center) at the right time. Those who found their way into Khao I Dang after the border was closed either had a lot of money or a lot of courage. Luck and pluck gave them a future different from that faced by their compatriots who were sent home to Cambodia.

3   Getting Resettled

SOME MAY CALL the 150,000-plus Cambodians who were resettled in the United States the lucky ones; others may think such a label equivocal at best, for many Cambodians who came to the proverbial land of opportunities have not fared well. Most refugees who entered after 1979 were in terrible shape, both physically and mentally, after enduring years of near-starvation, sleep deprivation, unremitting hard labor, and constant terror. Yet new challenges confronted them as soon as they set foot on American soil. In the United States the infrastructure set up by federal, state, and local governments, as well as by voluntary agencies to resettle refugees, shaped their lives.

Still, the refugees have not been passive victims. They have made choices, built communities, and gained a modicum of control over their lives. The communities Cambodians have formed are by no means homogeneous. The variations reflect differences in opportunity in various places. In each locality, opportunities are largely determined by its economy and pattern of social relations. How well refugees and immigrants can respond to opportunities depends on the divergent human capital that different segments of the refugee population bring with them. Finally, regional variations exist, and opportunities change over time. Thus, where newcomers settle and the timing of their arrival often make a big difference in how they fare.

The 1975–79 Arrivals

Unlike the Chinese, Japanese, Koreans, Filipinos, and Indians, virtually no Cambodians immigrated to the United States before 1975. There were fewer than one thousand in April of that year—college students, military officers and professionals undergoing short-term training, staff at the Cambodian embassy in Washington, D.C., employees of the Foreign Languages Institute and the Voice of America, and some anxious individuals scouting for ways to move their families to the United States in anticipation of the fall of Lon Nol's Khmer Republic. These persons were scattered all over America; there was no noticeable cluster of Cambodians anywhere in the United States. In the years to come, these early arrivals, together with people who left Cambodia right after the demise of the Khmer Republic, would play critical roles in caring for the less educated, more rural, and more destitute later arrivals. The early arrivals were well educated and spoke English or French. Even more important, they had not been scarred by the "killing fields" of Pol Pot's Democratic Kampuchea.

During the DK regime, Cambodians in the United States had no news of what was happening in Cambodia. The Khmer Rouge had evicted all Westerners two weeks after coming to power and forbade any other foreigners to visit except advisors from the People's Republic of China. In the words of Cynthia M. Coleman, who served as the project officer of the Khmer Guided Placement Project during the years when the largest number of Cambodians were admitted:

> Everyone was waiting for news from home. . . . But they heard nothing. . . . it was as though Cambodia had fallen into a black hole. . . . The fourteen thousand Cambodians in the United States before 1979 had an informal network that spread across the country and to France—and into the refugee camps along the Thai border. But the network did not extend far into Cambodia. . . . Each new rumor . . . deepened the refugees' sense of aloneness and helplessness. . . . there had been wild, unbelievable rumors of executions [but most Cambodians thought that] Cambodians . . . would never do such things to their own people. . . . Most Cambodians projected a semblance of stability . . . functioning in the American context. But the news from home, and the lack of it, had forced a depression upon them which few people in the world . . . had ever experienced. (1990: 364–66)

As Phnom Penh and Saigon fell in April 1975, the approximately 130,000 Vietnamese and Cambodians who fled with American assistance were processed in Guam and Wake Island and then flown to four military bases hastily prepared to receive them: Camp Pendleton in southern California, Fort Chaffee in Arkansas, Eglin Air Force Base in Florida, and Fort Indiantown Gap in Pennsylvania. The four reception centers closed by the end of 1975, when everyone had been resettled.

The federal government asked private voluntary agencies (often called "volags") that had aided earlier, mostly European, groups of refugees to help resettle the new arrivals. The agencies found sponsors to provide housing, food, and other assistance for a certain period of time. Only refugees who possessed at least $4,000 per family member could leave without sponsors. About eight thousand Vietnamese and Cambodians had the money to do so.

The Migration and Refugee Services of the U.S. Catholic Conference, whose local chapters are called Catholic Charities or Catholic Social Services, resettled more than 40 percent of the total arrivals from the three Southeast Asian countries. The nonsectarian International Rescue Committee and the American Council for Nationalities Service (now the Immigration and Refugee Services of America, with regional branches called International Institutes) each assisted between 11 and 12 percent. Church World Service, an arm of the National Council of Churches of Christ in the United States, resettled slightly under 10 percent. The Lutheran Immigration and Refugee Service and the World Relief Refugee Services of the National Association of World Evangelicals each handled about 5 percent. The Tolstoy Foundation, the Hebrew Immigrant Aid Society, the American Fund for Czechoslovak Refugees, the National Council of the Young Men's Christian Association, the Episcopal Migration Ministries, the Buddhist Council for Refugee Rescue and Resettlement, and the Los Angeles branch of the Chinese Consolidated Benevolent Association each helped smaller numbers. The states of Iowa and Idaho, which set themselves up to function as voluntary agencies, called their state organizations the Iowa Bureau of Refugee Service and the Idaho State Voluntary Agency (Hein 1995: 51–52; Ledgerwood 1990a: 253).

The federal government funded the entire process through the 1975 Indochina Migration and Refugee Assistance Act and gave the voluntary agencies $500 for each refugee processed. Misunderstandings arose over that sum, because some refugees assumed it was all meant for them. In fact, the government had authorized participating agencies to use the money to pay for office overhead costs, transportation for refugees, and other expenses incurred in providing basic necessities and services.

Most refugees, both Vietnamese and Cambodians, left the four centers with American families and individuals or collective sponsors such as churches or employers interested in hiring them. Kolab (a pseudonym), sixteen at the time, told the story of her family's resettlement to Bosseba Kong, a social worker. The daughter of a former official in the Lon Nol government, Kolab and her family arrived in Camp Pendleton in June 1975. She recalled, "My first morning at Pendleton . . . we lined up in front of the cafeteria for our first meal in America. I felt sad and embarrassed because I was not used

to waiting in line for food. Back home in Cambodia we had servants to prepare meals and do all the housework and suddenly, I found myself lining
up . . . asking for food. I realized that this morning marked the turning point
in my life" (Kong 1984: 20–21). She felt a little better when she discovered that
her fellow Cambodians were creating a "little Cambodia" right there in Camp
Pendleton:

> I heard Cambodian songs being played all over the place. . . . Most of the
> people who played these songs were servicemen who had left Cambodia
> before the Communists took over. They brought a few songs to listen to while
> they were out of the country for army training. Now everyone knew we could
> not return home any more, and people played these songs to create an at-
> mosphere similar to the homeland. . . . My mother always warned me to be
> careful while I was outside. . . . She said that I was a grown up girl now and
> must act accordingly . . . especially in front of those single servicemen. . . .
> She said that she did not want to hear other people talk about me and stain
> our family's name. . . . Mother . . . did not want me to make friends with any
> servicemen. (23–24)

Mothers watched their daughters so carefully because there was no privacy
at all in the tent city at Camp Pendleton. Fortunately for Kolab, an American widow with two teenaged children sponsored her family and treated them
kindly after they moved into her home.

Not all refugees had positive experiences with their sponsors. A farm
owner in Georgia sponsored the family of another Cambodian American
woman, also a teenaged girl at the time. Years later she was still resentful:

> When the sponsor took us away, she treated us as slaves. My Mom was work-
> ing in their house, cleaning their house every day. . . . We all worked like crazy.
> We put labels on strawberries. . . . I had to go work in the fields and then
> come back to the house to work every day . . . washing their clothes, clean-
> ing their house, things like that. And I got only $20 a week. . . . My brother
> had problems, he went to the doctor and had operations many times. The
> thing that really pained me, that really hurt me, was that when he arrived
> home, the very next day they asked him when he could start working again.
> We were handicapped. We didn't know where to find help. (Anonymous
> interview 1996)

In part because of such unhappy experiences, Cambodians tried their best
to establish their own ethnic communities. The federal government's dispersal policy, the location of voluntary agencies and sponsors, the whereabouts

of refugees' own families and friends, the refugees' tendency to compare the relative economic opportunities in different states, and the climate all played a role in determining where these communities sprang up.

How Long Beach Became the "Cambodian Capital of America"

By the late 1970s, one identifiably Cambodian enclave had emerged in the United States. It is located in the city of Long Beach, the second-largest city in Los Angeles County and the fifth-largest city in California. During the early years of Long Beach's existence, it attracted many retirees from the Midwest as well as tourists in search of sun, sand, and sea. An oil boom enriched its economy during the 1920s and 1930s, and a U.S. Navy shipyard and the aerospace industry provided jobs for residents from the 1940s to the early 1980s. Long Beach harbor and San Pedro harbor in the southern part of Los Angeles County together handle the third-largest volume of container cargoes in the world today. But the city experienced hard times during the 1980s and 1990s as a result of downsizing in the defense industries, closure of the naval shipyard, and a severe downturn in the southern California real estate market.

Long Beach became the largest Cambodian community in America by chance. During the late 1950s and 1960s, Long Beach State University—now California State University, Long Beach—hosted more than a hundred college students from Cambodia, who came to study engineering and agriculture. In 1958 these students formed the Cambodian Students Association of America. Most returned to Cambodia after they graduated, but as political instability increased during the late 1960s and early 1970s several dozen came back to the United States, some to the Long Beach area.

When they and a handful of Cambodian military officers who were in southern California for training heard that a thousand or more from their country had arrived in Camp Pendleton in April and May 1975, they went to visit the camp. They brought Cambodian food to welcome their compatriots, and those who had the means to do so offered to serve as sponsors. Several Long Beach State University professors who had taught Cambodian students in the past also volunteered as sponsors. Him S. Chhim, executive director of the Cambodian Association of America, which evolved from the Cambodian Students Association in November 1975, estimates that somewhere between one and two thousand Cambodian refugees were resettled in Long Beach as a result of the students' initiative (Chhim interview 1996 in Chan, ed. 2003a: 47–48).

In those days, central Long Beach was a depressed area, as a former Lon Nol government official told anthropologist Usha Welaratna: "Back then, Long Beach looked like a vacant lot. It was occupied mainly by retired people . . . If you walked down Anaheim Street, in a ten-unit apartment building only two or three would be occupied. . . . back then the population was made up of about 30 percent White and 30 percent Black, with the rest being Hispanic, Thai, Japanese, Korean, and Filipino, and just about three Cambodian families" (Welaratna 1998: 56).

Scott Shaw, who studied the Long Beach Cambodian community in the late 1980s, notes, however, that seven Cambodian families resided in Long Beach before the refugees arrived in 1975. By 1980 the local Cambodian population had grown to approximately seven thousand. Some were refugees resettled directly in Long Beach from 1975 to 1979; others arrived as secondary migrants—that is, people who had initially been placed in other states but moved to the new location on their own initiative (Shaw 1989). The secondary migrants were attracted to what may be called the "cultural comfort zone" offered by Long Beach.

By the mid-1980s Long Beach had at least thirty-five thousand—in some estimates, fifty thousand—Cambodians. It is the largest Cambodian community outside of Cambodia. The 2000 census counted only 17,396 Cambodians in Long Beach City, but that is very likely a gross undercount. Cambodian community leaders, voluntary agency staff members, and local and state officials who deal with Indochinese refugees have all said that official census numbers are too low because Cambodians do not speak English well and are wary of government officials and the forms they ask people to fill out. Him S. Chhim maintains that the Cambodian population in Long Beach "stabilized" during the mid-1990s, with few people leaving or coming in (Chhim interview 2001 in Chan, ed. 2003a: 46).

About 70 percent of Long Beach's Cambodian residents have lived in the central area of town since the early 1980s—the so-called inner city bounded roughly by the Pacific Coast Highway to the east, Seventh Street to the west, Long Beach Boulevard to the north, and Redondo Avenue to the south (Shaw 1989: 16). Most are renters, and before welfare reform was introduced in 1996 they depended almost entirely on public assistance for survival. About 15 percent of the better-off Cambodians live in a suburban neighborhood of single-family houses in the northwestern part of the city—an area where about half the residents are European Americans. Another 15 percent live in multistory apartment buildings in a light-industrial area of the city's northeastern section (Tan 1999: 161). These apartment-dwellers consist of both welfare recipients and the working poor.

The heart of the Cambodian community is Anaheim Street or the "Anaheim Corridor," commonly called "Little Phnom Penh." It contains several hundred Cambodian-owned businesses, including restaurants, take-out food stands, bakeries, grocery stores, clothing stores, jewelry stores, souvenir shops, automobile repair shops, and video rental stores. There are also many pawn shops because Cambodians who gamble often pawn jewelry, watches, and other valuables. Many of these stores are owned by Cambodians of Chinese ancestry (Chhim interview 1996 in Chan, ed. 2003a: 57). Various professional services are also found there, including pharmacies, medical clinics, beauty parlors and barber shops, and dressmakers (Tan 1999: 161–62). Few storeowners, who are among the better-off Cambodians, live in the inner city itself, but they go there every day to run their businesses.

Buildings in the area are very run-down, and streets are narrow and dirty. The bustling atmosphere is nevertheless attractive to Cambodians who live elsewhere. As a male teenager interviewed by anthropologist Usha Welaratna commented:

> I lived with my aunt in Riverside, where it was very quiet. All I did was go to school, come back home, and stay home. . . . we hardly did anything. . . . Then my other aunt came to Long Beach. I visited her one time, and I found that in Long Beach, there were people on the streets, they had Cambodian parties, they had everything! So I thought, Wow, I am going to move here . . . I was in eighth grade, and all the teachers liked me. But I was the only Cambodian student at my school . . . I didn't understand English. I found the work real hard, and decided to move to Long Beach. (1998: 74–75)

Cambodians in Long Beach share the inner city with other Asian immigrants and their American-born progeny, African Americans, and Mexican Americans and other Spanish-speakers. Latino Americans compose approximately one-fifth of the city's half-million residents, Asian Americans another fifth, African Americans about a tenth, and European Americans about half. Roughly half the Asian Americans are Cambodians, some 15 percent are Vietnamese, and about 8 percent are Filipinos. Smaller numbers of Koreans, Japanese, Chinese, Lao, Hmong, Thai, Pacific Islanders (mostly Samoans), and Native Americans also live in the area (Chittapalo interview 1996 in Chan, ed. 2003a: 96–97; Welaratna 1998: 3). Such ethnic diversity notwithstanding, the state of California recognized the significance of Long Beach as the capital of Cambodian America and erected a freeway exit sign, "Little Phnom Penh," in 2001 to alert drivers to its whereabouts (Wride 2001).

The Cambodian population in Long Beach reached a plateau in the late 1980s and then began to decline after an earthquake struck the greater Los

Angeles area in October 1987. Frightened by that event, approximately five hundred families, numbering some two thousand persons, moved to the Central Valley of California, the southern half of which is called the San Joaquin Valley and the northern half the Sacramento Valley. They settled in cities such as Fresno, Stockton, Sacramento, Merced, and Modesto (Shaw 1989: 18). As Sam Chittapalo, a former Cambodian police officer in Long Beach, put it, the quake was "not only something to fear on its own, but a powerful reminder of their loss of country and loved ones" (Arax 1988). Ernest Velasquez, assistant director of social services in Fresno County at the time, told a reporter that 350 Cambodians signed up for the welfare rolls in his county in the months following the quake (Arax 1988).

According to the 2000 census, the Central Valley, stretching from Redding in the north to Bakersfield in the south, contains 18,695 Cambodians. As defined by the census bureau, the Central Valley includes the Redding, Chico, Yuba City, Sacramento-Yolo, Stockton-Lodi, Modesto, Merced, Fresno, Visalia-Tulare-Porterville, and Bakersfield metropolitan statistical areas (MSAs). The greater Stockton area has by far the largest concentration, with 9,313 enumerated in the 2000 census (Pfeifer 2002).

Two other regions in California also developed sizable Cambodian communities—the San Francisco Bay area and the greater San Diego area. The San Francisco-Oakland-San Jose metropolitan statistical area reported a Cambodian population of 10,552 in the 2000 census, and the San Diego MSA counted 4,314 (Pfeifer 2002). The 2000 census indicates that 70,232 persons of Cambodian ancestry now live in the state of California, a slight increase from the 68,190 counted in the 1990 census, but their distribution pattern remained the same in the ten-year interval.

Unfortunately, the areas to which Cambodians moved are not free of danger. On January 17, 1989, an unemployed welder named Patrick Purdy found his way onto the playground of Cleveland Elementary School in Stockton. He fired more than one hundred rounds indiscrimately at the children playing there during recess, killing five of them and wounding twenty-nine others as well as a teacher before taking his own life. Four of the children who died were Cambodians; the fifth was Vietnamese. In Or, mother of one of the dead children, had thought the United States would be "a place of peace and freedom" and was distraught when that was not the case. Chun Keut, the father of another victim, collapsed after hearing of his eight-year-old daughter's death and died of an apparent heart attack. "I think his heart broke" explained a relative (Sahagun and Stein 1989).

The event revived the Cambodians' trauma and kindled new anxieties. It also, ultimately, transformed the entire city of Stockton. Social service agencies began paying more attention to the refugees in their midst, comforting the bereaved and helping the needy population in myriad other ways. Perhaps what helped the most was that a respected Cambodian monk who had come to the United States in 1979, Dharmawara Mahathera, went to the schoolyard to chant prayers and sprinkle holy water on the ground where the children had been struck down. "We are going to take away the evil action of an evil man," he said. "We are going to send the good spirit of those who lost their lives and purify this school so the children can come to study again" (Gross 1989).

Then, on October 17, 1989, an earthquake struck the San Francisco Bay area where some four thousand Cambodians lived, most of them in the Tenderloin area. The commotion and chaos that followed the quake made the terrified Cambodians feel like they were "back in the war" said Sophat Pak. When the earth trembled, the English-speaking Pak ran out of his apartment and spent hours translating the news blaring from his car radio to frightened, non-English-speaking neighbors who gathered around him. "I call it my second escape," he said in obvious reference to his escape from Cambodia. As Holbrooke Teter, a psychologist working with Cambodians in San Francisco at the time, observed, "Cambodians were so traumatized under Pol Pot that it's as though they have a well of emotional dislocation that any new trauma, like the earthquake, taps into and re-evokes the original tragedy." A Cambodian social worker, Sam Ath, also described the connection: "Many of them said they didn't trust Pol Pot and now they don't trust the earth" ("Cambodians Flee New Terror" 1989).

The warfare that erupted between Cambodian and Latino gangs during the late 1980s also drove some Cambodians away from Long Beach. As the frequency and intensity of violence increased—a situation discussed in chapter 6—people who desired to live in safer environments began to look for homes elsewhere (Rim interview 1995 in Chan, ed. 2003a: 158; Tauch interviews 1996 and 2001 in Chan, ed. 2003a: 212, 207). As another of Welaratna's respondents revealed, "We came to this country in 1981 and our family went to Chicago. But we could not stand the cold, so we came to California. We moved to a small town first, but life was so hard there . . . we decided to move to Long Beach, . . . [but] before I moved . . . I didn't know that this was a scary place . . . there's shooting at night, drugs sold, extortion . . . and gangs. So now I am doing two jobs, and my wife also works, because we want to get out" (Welaratna 1998: 190).

Even as the pace of out-migration quickened, a new kind of secondary in-migration began in the early 1990s, when Cambodians from other countries began to arrive. The influx has helped prevent the number of Cambodians in Long Beach from declining too much. Sam Chittapalo explained why Cambodians from other countries have found their way to Long Beach:

> Cambodians from Paris, from Australia, from Canada, from all over the world, they come to Long Beach. Even from Cambodia they now come to Long Beach. Cambodians from Japan come to Long Beach, too. . . . We had one Cambodian [Sichan Siv] working in the White House with the Bush administration. . . . he's referred to all over the country, even in Japan, even in France, even in Australia. Cambodian people are starting to see if a guy has ability, he has a chance to work in the White House. Why shouldn't I come here, bring my daughter, my kid, my son, to study here? (Chittapalo interview 1996 in Chan, ed. 2003a: 97)

Many new international secondary migrants bring money to invest. They open businesses and hire local Cambodians as workers. They compose an emerging transnational Cambodian bourgeoisie—a mobile population whose members maintain connections with fellow Cambodians in several countries and go wherever they think the best opportunities for upward socioeconomic mobility may be found. Given their desire to make money and gain social prestige, such people can be easily influenced by stories of successful individuals such as Sichan Siv, a resident of the East Coast.

That a Cambodian on the opposite side of the country helped draw Cambodian entrepreneurs to Long Beach is not as amazing as it sounds, for educated Cambodians around the world tap into transnational information networks that enable them to keep up with what is going on among compatriots in the various countries where Cambodians live.

Siv, a college graduate, was working for CARE in Phnom Penh in 1975. The U.S. embassy staff had offered to evacuate him because Khmer Rouge victory seemed imminent, but he missed the last American helicopter out of Phnom Penh on April 12 by thirty minutes (De Loughry 1989: A22). As a consequence, he and his family lived through the Khmer Rouge horrors. Because it was impossible for the entire family, which included young children, to escape together, the family urged Sichan to flee by himself. He did so but was arrested when he reached the Thai border. By then the border had closed, and Thai authorities considered him an illegal entrant. Luckily, Japanese friends learned of his arrival and contacted CARE, which arranged for him to be resettled in the United States four months later.

The voluntary agency handling Siv's case sent him to a small town in Connecticut, where he picked apples to support himself and declined loans from his sponsor. "Once you've been a slave, then find yourself free, you want very much to earn your own living," he explained to journalist Sheldon Kelly (Kelly 1991: 141). He subsequently worked as a janitor, cab driver, and bank teller, all the while sending letters to various colleges to seek admission with financial aid. His persistence bore fruit when Columbia University's School of International Relations and Public Affairs admitted him and gave him a full scholarship. He earned an M.A. degree there in 1981 and became a naturalized U.S. citizen in 1982.

By then, large numbers of Cambodian refugees were arriving, so Siv went to work at an Episcopalian church that was helping resettle them. He married an American woman in 1983. In the mid-1980s he worked for the Coalition Government of Democratic Kampuchea delegation that held Cambodia's seat at the United Nations but eventually became disillusioned with that group and quit his job in 1987. He did volunteer work in George H. W. Bush's presidential campaign in 1988, during which he caught the eye of Republican Party stalwarts. The Bush White House tapped Siv in February 1989 to serve as a deputy assistant to the president for public liaison. He thus became, at forty-one, the first Asian American to be appointed as a ranking presidential aide (Kelly 1991: 138–42). It is not surprising that his Horatio Alger story inspired ambitious Cambodians in other countries to immigrate to the United States.

Except for those who resettled in Long Beach, the first wave of Cambodian arrivals were scattered across the country. The most important factor determining their settlement pattern was the federal government's dispersal policy to place no more than three thousand Southeast Asian refugees in any one locality in order to minimize their impact upon the budget, social services, and school system in each community. The location of the various regional offices of voluntary agencies was a second factor that influenced where refugees were sent. Although many early sponsors were individuals, families, or Catholic parishes and Protestant congregations, as time passed and problems surfaced between the refugees and their sponsors, agencies increasingly took on the sponsorship role themselves. Thus, later arrivals tended to congregate in the cities where voluntary agencies had branch offices.

The Post-1979 Arrivals

By the time the United States decided to admit Cambodians who had escaped to Thailand after the fall of the DK regime in January 1979, the 1980 Refugee Act had been passed. It mandated the establishment of a national Office of Refugee Resettlement (ORR), located within the Department of Health, Education, and Welfare (later renamed the Department of Health and Human Services), and a State Refugee Coordinator Office in each of the fifty states.

Although the U.S. State Department, working closely with the American Council of Voluntary Agencies for Foreign Service (ACVA), made the key decisions on where to place the refugees, the ORR and state refugee offices oversaw their resettlement after arrival. The state refugee coordinators contracted with local community colleges and other educational institutions to offer English-as-a-second-language (ESL) classes and vocational training. They also arranged with hospitals, clinics, and social service organizations to provide health care, counseling, and other services. The ORR and its state offices disbursed funds and received periodical reports about how the money was being spent.

In the 1980s, Cambodians in the United States who wished to sponsor relatives in UNHCR holding centers in Thailand could choose any voluntary agency they desired to help them file the necessary petitions. These sponsors were known as "anchor relatives." The family members whom they sponsored entered under Priorities Three and Five. Before the refugees arrived, the agency would interview the anchor relatives in order to assess their financial and housing situations. Different agencies had different rules. A Vietnamese refugee who served for some years as deputy director of a large voluntary agency maintains that anchor families needed no set income and/or amount of savings to qualify as sponsors. After the refugees arrived at their destinations, agencies checked up on them periodically to see if children had been enrolled in school, whether adults were attending ESL or vocational training classes, and whether problems had emerged.

For those without families to join, ACVA determined how to distribute them geographically. It forwarded the biographical information on each case (a case usually consisted of several persons, because all members of a family were treated as a single case) compiled by JVA staff in Thailand and reviewed by the U.S. Immigration and Naturalization Service (INS). In the United States, such information was stored centrally in a Refugee Data Center. Several individuals who participated in the distribution process told me in the telephone interviews I conducted that representatives from participating voluntary agencies met every Wednesday to exchange information on where sponsors had been found and how many each location could accept.

Refugees without relatives or friends in the United States were the easiest to place. Called "free cases," they could be resettled anywhere. Refugees with medical conditions, such as tuberculosis or other communicable diseases that required prolonged treatment and monitoring, were sent to localities where the requisite medical facilities were available. Theoretically, people who tested positive for tuberculosis and the human immuno-deficiency virus (HIV) could not be admitted into the country, but if their sponsors filed affidavits promising to care for them, waivers would be issued after the Centers for Disease Control reviewed their files. The International Organization for Migration (IOM), under contract with the U.S. State Department, arranged the refugees' travel—first from Thailand to one of the refugee processing centers and then from there to designated destinations in the United States. The IOM paid for the airline tickets, but refugees had to sign promissory notes to repay these advances when they could afford to do so.

The post-1979 arrivals were far less prepared for life in a highly industrialized country than those who came in 1975. Very few had experience with modern technology, so their first encounters with it filled them with wonder, awe, and fear. Children tend to remember their experiences most vividly. Soy Duong, twelve at the time, recalled the flight that brought her family to the United States:

> When I stepped into the airplane at that airport in Thailand, I was amazed. . . . The rows of seats, . . . the dark red color of the carpet and the seats which glowed lovely made me think, "This is heaven! Nothing is better than this!" . . . I was very excited. . . . There was an earphone next to me. I did not know what that earphone was for. . . . As I put it next to my ears, I heard the sounds of people talking. . . . an attendant frequently came over to me and checked how things were going for my Mom and me. She covered me with blankets as I fell asleep. Oh, I felt like an angel! Since the war, I never had anyone take care of me as well as that attendant. My Mom and Dad couldn't take care of me because I was separated from them and I was forced to live in a community of children. I always had to take care of myself. . . . When I woke up in the middle of the flight, there was a movie showing . . . I was too scared to watch it because there was shooting in that movie. The shooting made me think about the shooting that took place while my family and I were trying to escape . . . I was afraid that the screen might explode and all of us might be killed by the shots that were being fired in the movie . . . I shut my eyes tightly. I could feel my hands shaking. (Duong 1990: 20–21)

Chivy Sok, eleven when her family arrived in San Francisco in 1980, had an equally memorable flight. In particular, she was astonished that "food came to us rather than us looking for food." She thought the airplane "was the nicest and cleanest place we had ever stayed in since 1975." After disembarking, other sensations awaited her:

> San Francisco Airport seemed so large . . . Mom and Dad walked along with the crowd . . . we had to climb on stairs that kept on moving upward. They

were grey and had tiny little teeth at the edge of the corners. I . . . trembled at the thought of the stairs eating my little legs up. . . . Dad got a little impatient with me and told me he would leave me if I didn't try to get on it. "NO! DON'T LEAVE ME!! This place is too big for me." . . . Dad took my left hand and climbed onto the first step. . . . When we reached the top I was scared again because the steps were being swallowed up at the end. My heart pounded rapidly. Dad . . . told me to jump at the end and we would be O.K. People around us must have chuckled when they saw a scared raggedy kid giving it her all to jump off an escalator. . . . I thought we were flying again after we walked into this box. The door automatically shut and I felt us moving upward. I looked at Uncle Yot and asked if we were in another airplane again. . . . He chuckled and said we're going up an elevator. (Sok 1993: 20–21)

Like the earlier arrivals, refugees who came during the 1980s also had mixed experiences with their sponsors. Some remember with everlasting gratitude how the sponsors took care of "everything" for them. Keo Vann recalls how, during her first three months in the United States, her sponsor "helped all the way. He bought things for us. He helped me in registering my children in school and applying for welfare assistance and food stamps. He helped my children enroll in high school. My little ones enrolled in second grade. He helped pay the rent" (Cambodians in California Project, Keo interview 1989, 35: 10).

Roeun Chea, who was taken in by a foster family in Amherst, Massachusetts, in 1982 and has published a short autobiography written in English, was likewise very appreciative of how lovingly his newfound family treated him: "I very much enjoy living with my foster parents. I feel very close to my family. They love me as if I were their real son. They support me in a lot of things, especially my education. Moreover, they help me with my family in Cambodia as much as possible" (Chea 1989: 113).

Although many sponsors did not know the refugees they helped, other Americans went to extraordinary lengths to track down Cambodians they wished to aid—as the story of Sarout Suon Seng reveals. Ross and Lauren Palmer of San Diego had befriended Seng's older brother when the latter was studying engineering in the United States in 1960. After the brother went back to Cambodia, he kept in touch with the Palmers, but they lost touch when the Khmer Rouge came to power in 1975. When Cambodians started fleeing to the Thai-Cambodian border, Lauren Palmer sent the name and picture of Seng's brother to relief agencies in Thailand, indicating that she and her husband would be pleased to sponsor him. Three years passed, but no news came. Then, in 1982, one of Seng's cousins saw the Palmers' notice just before she herself left for Australia, where she was being resettled. After her arrival there, the cousin sent a letter to the Palmers, telling them that some members of the family had died but others were still alive and had moved back to Phnom Penh. Because conditions in Cambodia were chaotic in the early 1980s, however, the Palmers had no way to contact the family.

After Sarout Suon Seng arrived in Khao I Dang, she wrote to the Palmers, asking if they could sponsor her. They did not know if her letter was authentic, so they asked their friend, David Klap, M.D., who was volunteering his services at Khao I Dang, to look for her. It so happened that Seng, who had completed her studies in 1982 at the reopened medical faculty in Phnom Penh, was working at a clinic in Khao I Dang. Dr. Klap found her there and asked many questions in order to determine if she was really the sister of the man the Palmers had befriended. When he was convinced that she was indeed the person she claimed to be, the Palmers began the paperwork to bring her to the United States. While waiting for her to be processed for resettlement, the couple traveled all the way to Thailand to visit Khao I Dang in order to meet her (Cambodians in California Project, Seng interview 1989, 60: 30–31). After Seng arrived in San Diego, Lauren Palmer continued to give her support, not just financially but also emotionally. As Seng said, "I'm here alone, it's confused stage because I try to go to school . . . and try to be . . . responsible for everything by myself, and not having anybody that I can ask, 'Should we do that?' or 'Should we not do that?'. . . Lauren help[s] me all the time" (Cambodians in California Project, Seng interview 1989, 60: 36).

Other refugees were less lucky. Even those sponsored by relatives or friends were sometimes abused. Just because sponsors and refugees were coethnics was no guarantee that sponsors would act with true charity. Soy Duong's family was sponsored by a "friend":

> The first months my family and I lived with my sponsor in his own house. By the time we had received money from welfare, he . . . called us to have a meeting with him. . . . he asked us if we had . . . any gold, diamonds, etc. that we had brought with us. . . . If we had anything we must give it to him. . . . We told him we had nothing because we had been robbed by the Thai soldiers. After discovering we had no valuable items, he told us that it was time for us to pay him rent for living in his house. . . . With the money we received from welfare, we paid him. He said the money was not enough. We told him we will pay him next month when we received some more money from welfare. A few days later, he announced he had lost $100. He asked each of us if we had taken it. We told him we did not take his money nor did we have any

idea where he put his money since we were not allowed to go upstairs at all.
. . . He then told us to find our own apartment. We couldn't say anything
except to receive the accusation of being thieves. (Duong 1990: 23–24)

Some sponsors had grievances of their own. Those whose wards left them
thought they were ungrateful. Aside from the language barrier and cultural
misunderstandings, most sponsors had no prior knowledge of the welfare
system, the job market for people who could not speak English and had no
employment history in the United States, or the local housing situation.
Becoming a sponsor took more out of them than they anticipated. Families
in Amherst, South Hadley, Northampton, and Easthampton in western
Massachusetts, who had enthusiastically agreed to serve as sponsors after
hearing talks by Peter Pond, a Protestant minister advocating on behalf of
Cambodians, told Eve Burton of the IOM that they "never realized the number of small things to be done and how time consuming helping newcomers
would be." Many sponsors felt burned out after only a few months (Burton
1983: 34).

Problems even arose between Cambodian families who acted as sponsors
and their incoming relatives:

> For a number, problems began almost immediately. Cambodians who had
> been here since 1975 and had not lived through the Pol Pot era said that their
> relatives had changed almost beyond recognition. The new arrivals were hard,
> both physically and emotionally. . . . the newly arrived "had seen too
> much." . . . They had lost their humanity and gentleness . . . the new arriv-
> als said that it was as though they had come to family they no longer knew,
> family who had not lived through the experiences that had engulfed their lives
> for five years and who could not possibly understand them now. . . . Many
> left their families' homes and moved into Cambodian urban ghettoes. . . .
> They sought other Cambodians who had not become refugees until 1979 or
> later. They sought the comradeship of those who could understand. (Cole-
> man 1990: 369–70)

Although some refugees moved away because they did not get along with
their sponsors, even larger numbers left their initial places of settlement for
other reasons. In a 1993 survey of Indochinese refugees, 76 percent of secondary migrants indicated the desire to live in a warmer climate as a factor in
their move, 67 percent cited the presence of relatives and friends in other
localities, 33 percent said better employment and vocational training opportunities elsewhere were important enticements, and 20 percent reported
moving in order to obtain higher levels of public assistance (Nguyen 1993

cited in Hein 1995: 53–54). Although the people surveyed included Vietnamese, Cambodians, Lao, Hmong, and other Indochinese refugees, it is likely that the Cambodians mirrored the general picture in terms of why they engaged in secondary migration.

Not surprisingly given its mild weather, large Asian population, generous welfare payments, and the existence of Little Phnom Penh in Long Beach, California became the primary state to which secondary migrants moved. The state houses 40 percent of all Southeast Asian refugees even though only a little more than 20 percent of the 1975 arrivals and subsequent waves had been placed there. Texas ranks second, with approximately 7.5 percent of the total Southeast Asian refugee population. Surprisingly, several cold-weather states also have large numbers of refugees. Minnesota and Wisconsin have the second- and third-largest number of Hmong, and Massachusetts contains the second-largest number of Cambodians. But the desire for warm weather, an important issue for many secondary migrants, was a primary motivating force for moving to California.

The Khmer Guided Placement Project

Five years after the first batch of Vietnamese and Cambodians arrived in the United States, both the federal government and resettlement workers found the rate of secondary migration of Indochinese refugees far higher than they thought desirable. Many people in charge of resettling them also knew that Cambodians had suffered more trauma than any other group and that there were more "free cases" among them.

In light of these factors, the ORR decided in the spring of 1980 to fund a demonstration project, the Khmer Guided Placement Project (KGPP)—sometimes also known as the Khmer Cluster Project. The KGPP aimed to resettle three hundred to a thousand Cambodians each in a dozen localities. It was important that cities and towns to be chosen had not yet been heavily impacted by the influx of Southeast Asian refugees, had cheap or at least reasonably priced housing and plenty of entry-level jobs, and already contained a small number of Cambodians who could serve as the nucleus of a larger ethnic community. Planners anticipated that, taken together, these characteristics would maximize the refugees' economic self-sufficiency and minimize their rate of welfare dependence.

The KGPP's second goal was to improve the delivery of social services and other forms of suppport at the chosen sites. By encouraging public and private agencies to coordinate their work, and by setting up supplementary services, the ORR hoped that a more adequate level of social services would minimize secondary migration. In addition, by creating sufficiently large clusters of coethnics, the ORR expected that refugees themselves would provide each other with social and emotional support. A third goal of the KGPP was to help refugee communities develop a greater organizational capacity for self-help through the establishment of mutual assistance associations (Granville Corporation 1982; Yang 1982). By injecting more "structure" into the resettlement process, the ORR thought it could exercise greater control over the rate at which Cambodian refugees entered the United States, their geographic placement, and their subsequent behavior.

Planning began in the summer of 1980, and the implementation period stretched from January 1981 to March 1982. Altogether, the project placed 1,795 cases involving more than eight thousand individuals in twelve project sites. Atlanta received 149 cases with 766 individuals; Boston took in 232 cases with 994 individuals; Chicago had 154 cases with 718 individuals; Cincinnati hosted 35 cases with 169 individuals; Columbus had 66 cases with 358 individuals; Dallas received 258 cases with 1,269 individuals; Houston accepted 291 cases with 1,148 individuals; Jacksonville, Florida, had 74 cases with 267 individuals; New York City resettled 301 cases with 1,302 indivdiuals; Phoenix absorbed 96 cases with 394 individuals; Richmond, Virginia, got 104 cases with 465 individuals; and Rochester, New York, received 35 cases with 157 individuals. Thus, the Khmer Guided Placement Project resettled almost 30 percent of the more than thirty thousand Cambodian refugees who entered the United States during the early 1980s.

The Cambodian Association of America (CAA), headquartered in Long Beach and contracted by the ORR to serve as one of the two administrators of this project, chose the twelve sites. The other administrator was the ACVA, which created the Khmer Working Group for the purpose. Not only did the CAA scout various potential sites and recommend final locations, but its officers also explained the program to its regional chapters and Cambodian communities in various parts of the country in order to seek their cooperation and support. In addition, Sem Yang, the project director of the Cambodian Mutual Assistance Associations Project—the CAA's name for this effort—visited the Thai camps along with Geraldine Owens, who worked for the U.S. Catholic Conference and represented ACVA, and Carl Harris, a representative of the State Department, to disseminate information about the project to aspiring refugees. About three thousand of the eight thousand or so persons eventually chosen as project participants met with the three-person team during its six-week visit to Thailand. Team members tried to persuade aspiring refugees not to join friends and relatives in Long Beach (Granville Corporation 1982: 22; interview with a team member 1995).

Four problems emerged to plague the project. First, a great deal of time was taken up deciding who was a "free case." When individuals involved in the effort realized that there would not be enough free cases to fill the slots targeted by the project, the ORR and ACVA agreed to scrap the definition that stipulated that free cases were people who had no known relatives or friends in the United States, as an official in a large voluntary agency who participated in the process told me in a telephone interview. Instead, they decided that participants in the KGPP could be anyone who had been associated in any way with U.S. civilian agencies or the American military before April 17, 1975, or had distant relatives in the United States (Granville Corporation 1982: 16).

Second, the INS's 1981 decision to henceforth review refugee applications case by case caused delays in the processing of applicants. Instead of a steady flow of Cambodians spread out over the fifteen-month implementation period, few KGPP refugees arrived before August and September 1981, eight months after the implementation period began and only six months before it was scheduled to end. The U.S. State Department speeded up arrivals in the late summer because it did not want to lose any of that fiscal year's Southeast Asian refugee slots, which would disappear on September 30 if unfilled. Consequently, some Cambodians did not receive the six months of English-as-a-second-language instruction and cultural orientation they were supposed to get before coming to the United States; others already in training were flown to the United States before completing their course of study. That meant that people came even less prepared than they might have been otherwise (Granville Corporation 1982: 15, 23, and 30).

Service providers at the twelve sites were swamped during August and September. They often could do little more than pick up refugees at airports and leave them in empty apartments, not returning until days later to see how the frightened and confused newcomers were doing. Because many refugees had never seen a flush toilet, used electricity, cooked on a gas stove, or warmed themselves by a radiator or central heating system, they sat in the dark, went hungry, or shivered in the cold. Those transported to cold-weather sites as winter approached suffered especially.

The third problem that stymied the project was that the ORR and CAA did not inform, much less consult, voluntary agencies at the chosen sites during the project's planning stage. Local agencies did not know until August 1980 that hundreds—in some cases, thousands—of Cambodians were scheduled to arrive at their localities in a matter of months. The agencies, quite understandably, resented being excluded from the decision-making process. They found it difficult to accept the paramount status that the ORR had conferred on the CAA. As refugees arrived, voluntary agencies at many sites made little attempt to cooperate with the mutual assistance associations that the CAA had set up as part of the project. In some localities an agency would call upon the MAA staff to help orientate new arrivals and serve as translators, but at other sites they used their federal funds to hire their own Khmer-speaking caseworkers, thereby shunting the local Cambodian MAAs to the sidelines (Granville Corporation 1982: 49–54). The KGPP guidelines were not helpful in this regard because the exact role of MAAs was never clearly defined. So the MAAs and voluntary agencies sometimes duplicated services, at other times ignored one another, and more often than not showed outright antagonism to each other.

The fourth problem was internal to Cambodian refugee communities. During this period, the three political factions that vied for the loyalty of Cambodians amassed at the Thai-Cambodian border also had followers among Cambodians in the United States. It was widely known that the CAA supported Prince Sihanouk and General In Tam, who was loyal to the prince but had a large following of his own (Coleman 1990: 371). Thus, when the CAA tried to set up new mutual assistance associations or strengthen existing ones at project sites, it often encountered resistance from the officers of Cambodian organizations who had other political affinities.

Even when conflicting political loyalties were not a factor, the lack of foresight created problems. The situation was especially tense in Columbus, Ohio, where a Cambodian MAA already existed. Founded in 1979, it had successfully launched employment counseling and drivers' education programs and an energy conservation project under a dynamic director. Instead of seeking its participation, the CAA's national headquarters proceeded to form its own branch in that city. Not surprisingly, conflict soon arose, and the newer association survived for only five months. After it closed, the preexisting MAA expanded its activities (Granville Corporation 1982: 138–41).

Despite these problems, the KGPP in the long-run was successful in attaining some of its key goals. Cambodians at the twelve sites found jobs fairly easily, and the out-migration rate was relatively low. Some participants who eventually left KGPP sites were not really "free cases" but in fact had relatives they wanted to join. They had signed up for the program because they thought doing so would enhance their chances of being admitted into the United States (*Refugee Reports*, Nov. 2, 1984, 12).

The only unsuccessful site was New York City. The staff of voluntary agencies there had warned project planners that the urban environment would present innumerable difficulties for refugees unfamiliar with city living. Once the site was chosen, however, the KGPP staff stuck to their decision. In time, a high-ranking local staff member at a voluntary agency told me, at least a third of the Cambodians placed in New York City moved to Massachusetts, Rhode Island, and North Carolina.

The story of seven families whose members numbered forty-four persons illustrates why living in New York was so difficult for Cambodians. Church World Service had resettled them in a neighborhood near Prospect Park in the Flatbush area of Brooklyn in 1981, where some 150 Indochinese refugees were housed. Crime was rampant; between fall 1982 and spring 1983 the group was victimized by twenty-two major crimes, not counting muggings. As Nou Moeu, one of the Cambodian refugees, told a reporter, "I expected that when I got to the United States my children could go safely to school and I would have the ability to work for the future. I was really shocked. I didn't think something like this could happen in the U.S. . . . Those people in the neighborhood knew where we came from. They knew we were weak and that they could do whatever they wanted to do. I don't care much about myself, but I do care about my children. I don't think about revenge or dignity. I just want us to survive" (Norman 1983: B4).

Another Cambodian refugee, Soc Dul, who lived in the same neighborhood with his wife and five children, said, "It was a bad place. My children were beaten. I was mugged and robbed. I was terrified about the future of my wife and children." On February 4, 1983, three masked men with guns and knives forced their way into his apartment and tied him up, along with his wife, daughter, and sister-in-law. After ransacking the apartment, one of the robbers placed a gun against Soc Dul's back and made him knock on the front door of a neighboring apartment, where Mrs. Kim Ly, a widow with four children, lived. Soc Dul was forced to ask her to open the door, whereupon the robbers pushed their way into her apartment and bound her and two of her daughters. When one of the children began whimpering, the gunmen threatened to shoot the girl. They took $630 in cash and $300 in food stamps and then fled. The Cambodians called the police but, unable to speak English, could not explain clearly to the officers what had happened. By the time an interpreter arrived on the scene the robbers had long disappeared.

In March 1983 the terrified families moved to Harrisburg, Pennsylvania, with the help of the Presbyterian Church in New York. They traveled in a chartered bus, carrying their luggage and hundred-pound bags of rice. In

Harrisburg, the Indochinese Service Center, which managed to gather a team of volunteers to clean and put fresh paint on the walls of several apartments to house the new arrivals, assisted them (McFadden 1983; Norman 1983). After the families settled into their new homes, Truong Ngoc Phuong, the director of the Indochinese Service Center and himself a refugee from Vietnam, expressed cautious optimism about their future: "They will need time to adjust. What amazed me most is the fact that they can take so much and still not reach the breaking point. . . . Suffering is a part of life, that is understood. They believe that all human beings will go through a period of it. They endure" (Norman 1983). The ability to endure extreme hardship thus remains a critical asset in the United States, as it was in Cambodia.

Massachusetts as a Refugee-Friendly State

Three other factors also help account for where Cambodian communities sprang up: the initiatives taken by particular individuals, the location of Theravada Buddhist temples and monks, and the degree of "refugee-friendliness" in various states. The importance of these factors is illustrated by the growth of Lowell, Massachusetts, into the second-largest Cambodian community in the United States. At its zenith, the estimated size of Lowell's Cambodian community was twenty-five thousand, or about a quarter of the city's total population. The 1990 U.S. census, however, gave the much lower figure of only 11,493 Asians in Lowell, counting Cambodians, Vietnamese, Lao, and others combined. The 2000 census enumerated only 9,850 even though the former executive director of the Cambodian MAA in Lowell, Samkhann Khoeun, maintains that the city's Cambodian population grew steadily during the 1990s (Khoeun interview 2001 in Chan, ed. 2003a: 128).

Why and how did such a large Cambodian community develop in Lowell? Dr. Daniel Lam, a Sino-Cambodian who served as Massachusetts's refugee coordinator for seven years, explains that the state became home to so many from Cambodia and Vietnam in part because of the deep concern that Kitty Dukakis, the wife of then-governor Michael Dukakis, had for refugees:

> The then first lady of Massachusetts had a lot to do with it. . . . Kitty Dukakis
> . . . is active in the Jewish community; she's Jewish herself. She was involved
> in Jewish holocaust memorial projects. . . . somehow she transferred her
> personal commitment to publicizing the Cambodian genocide. Every year,
> in the state house, there's a memorial service for victims of the Armenian

genocide and the Cambodian genocide. She knew a person by the name of Peter Pond . . . one of the strong advocates for refugees . . . he campaigned to resettle them here. Peter met Kitty and knowing her commitment to commemorating the Holocaust, Peter talked to her. At that time, we had the Cambodian Minors Project . . . children . . . who didn't know where their parents were . . . were brought here to be resettled . . . Kitty got involved with the sponsorship and resettlement of those children. That was her first contact with Cambodians. . . . her heart . . . identified with this. She went to the camps in Thailand and then she began to lobby. . . . At that time, Lowell was unknown. But all of a sudden, in about four years, you have this large number of Cambodians here. At that time, Lowell was a depressed city. Lowell was almost bankrupt. . . . That was before the so-called Massachusetts miracle. We had a depression and then all of a sudden—boom. (Lam interview 1995 in Chan, ed. 2003a: 111–12)

The economic boom in Massachusetts was fueled by the computer and electronics industries, which enabled even non-English-speaking newcomers to find assembly work with relative ease. The land along Highway 128 became home to high-technology industry. In 1976 Wang Laboratories, founded by An Wang, a Chinese American computer entrepreneur, relocated its corporate headquarters to Lowell—historically a textile mill town that some scholars have called the "cradle" of the American industrial revolution. In 1986 Wang Laboratories' sales were $2.88 billion, and it was the largest employer in Lowell (Kiang 1994: 138). Two other electronics manufacturing giants, Raytheon and Digital Equipment, also set up assembly plants in Lowell. Even companies in New Hampshire began hiring the Cambodians, sending vans to take them back and forth between their homes in Lowell and companies' locations.

Even though Cambodian refugees could not speak English, company recruiters thought they had good "hand-eye coordination"—a much-desired trait. The fact that Cambodian refugees were being hired in these modern industries soon acted as a magnet to draw other Cambodians to Lowell. Although Boston was one of the twelve KGPP sites and received almost a thousand of the participants in that project, Lowell, located twenty-five miles northwest of Boston, did not attract many KGPP participants. Michael Ben Ho, a social worker in Lowell, notes that only 150 Cambodian families resided there in 1983. But by 1987, an estimated ten thousand Cambodians resided in the city and had opened fifteen grocery stores and ten restaurants (*Washington Post*, Aug. 12, 1991). A state official estimated that 90 percent of them had come as secondary migrants. Some people, however, think of Lowell's Cambodian population as "original" settlers because they moved to the city soon after being placed elsewhere (Khoeun interview 1995 in Chan, ed. 2003a: 141).

Another fortuitous development was that in 1985 Sao Khon, a much-venerated Theravada Buddhist monk, came to the Lowell area to serve a temple established in North Chelmsford in 1984 (Kiang 1994: 135). He was among a handful of senior monks trained in Cambodia who managed to survive the Khmer Rouge regime. There are now two Buddhist temples in Lowell and its vicinity—the Trairatanaram Temple in North Chelmsford and the Glory Buddhist Temple in Lowell.

Moreover, the city had relatively cheap housing, described by an official in charge of refugee resettlement in Massachusetts as "very affordable . . . especially in an area called the Acre [which housed many groups of earlier immigrant workers]. In addition to the jobs and housing," he added, "a big draw for the Cambodians was the presence of the venerable monk. There are very few older, experienced monks in the U.S. One of them came to Lowell and established a temple early on. . . . That was a huge draw."

Finally, what attracted a large number of Cambodian and other Southeast Asian refugees was the perception that Massachusetts was refugee-friendly. Governor Dukakis authorized a number of programs that benefitted refugees. In April 1983, he signed Executive Order No. 229 to establish the Governor's Council for Refugees and Immigrants. Two and a half years later, following the recommendation of the council and Dr. Daniel Lam, he signed Executive Order No. 257, which instructed state agencies to find ways to assist refugees in finding employment, thereby minimizing their welfare-dependency rate. In 1986 the state legislature funded a Gateway Cities Project to the tune of $10 million in fiscal year 1987. The project, Lam says, had few requirements:

> All you had to do was document how many people were newcomers. And then you, the city, decided—since you know the community—what you wanted to do with the money. Because of that, specialized education and other so-called luxury items became available. For example, the library would have special sections of certain kinds of books, tapes, or whatever. In there, too, was a citizenship training program. . . . One of the most significant developments at that time was a comprehensive refugee service plan. . . . the governor wrote a memo to all the state agencies saying they would have to develop, as part of their agency's policies for the future, a section on how they intend to serve refugees . . . Every year, during those several years, we even had town meetings or hearings . . . in different regions in the state. So refugees could come directly to share in what's going on in that community. So

they're at least acting on the perception that we welcome them here. (Lam interview 1995 in Chan, ed. 2003a: 113, 116–17)

Due to the state's responsiveness to the refugees' needs, existing agencies like the International Institute, Jewish Family Services, and Catholic Charities expanded their services to work with incoming Southeast Asian refugees.

One other aspect of the Massachusetts state refugee policy is relevant. Unlike the federal government and many other state governments that emphasized finding refugees employment as quickly as possible, Massachusetts followed a policy that Lam referred to as "front-end loading." State officials encouraged refugees to study English and get as much training as possible before looking for jobs so they could find better than entry-level ones requiring little skill. When Southeast Asian refugees first arrived in 1975, they were eligible to receive thirty-six months of federal cash and medical assistance. As the influx burgeoned, however, the federal government reduced the eligibility period to eighteen months in 1982, then to twelve months in 1988, and finally to only eight months. Refugees in Massachusetts, however, were not pressured to accept unskilled jobs. If they better-prepared themselves, the philosophy went,

> the likelihood of their returning to public assistance will be reduced. So take whatever time was allowable, give them training, make sure they are really ready for the job market . . . if you were to take the group of people who actually went through the training, you'll see the difference . . . the people who are now doing much better financially are the people who arrived first [when thirty-six months of federal aid was available] . . . the later arrivals did not have the same training . . . [It's either] pay now or pay later [in the form of welfare payments]. (Lam interview 1995 in Chan, ed. 2003a: 117–18)

Unfortunately, other state governments and the federal government did not share that philosophy.

An indication of how much progress the Cambodian residents of Lowell have made is that in the 1999 off-year election, Rithy Uong, a local resident, made history when he became the first Cambodian American in the United States to win elective office. A guidance counselor at Lowell High School, he ran for a seat on the nine-person Lowell City Council and won. Even though Cambodians compose approximately one-quarter of Lowell's population, relatively few of them are eligible to vote. Many refugees have not yet become naturalized U.S. citizens, and their American-born children are still too young to vote. Uong, who emerged victorious because he managed to gain support from mainstream voters, was reelected in 2001. Vesna Noun, who ran for a seat on the school board, failed in that bid (Khoeun interview 2001 in Chan, ed. 2003a: 128).

Aside from Lowell, thousands of Cambodians are also found in Boston; in Chelsea, Revere, and Lynn north of downtown Boston; and in Fall River, located in the southwestern corner of the state. The 2000 census shows 17,074 Cambodians in the combined metropolitan statistical area of Boston, Worcestor, Lawrence, New Hampshire, Maine, and Connecticut and 1,812 in that of Providence, Fall River, and Warwick (Pfeifer 2002). The Khmer Guided Placement Project first introduced a large group of Cambodians to Boston, but some, given the expensive housing in that city, eventually found their ways to Chelsea, Revere, and Lynn.

A former executive director of the Cambodian MAA in one of those towns notes that Lynn, which has a Buddhist temple, was home to an estimated three thousand Cambodians in the mid-1990s. In the same year the Cambodian population in Chelsea was estimated to be between 1,500 and two thousand, and a knowledgeable Cambodian community leader in Chelsea put the number in Revere at between three and four thousand. In this instance as well, census figures are much lower than those estimated by people who serve Cambodian clients.

Cambodians in the greater Boston area hold weddings in the city's Chinese restaurants and do their shopping in its Chinatown. Cambodians in Fall River are mostly secondary migrants, some of whom came from California to escape gang violence (Rim interview 1995 in Chan, ed. 2003a: 158). They attend the temple in Providence, the closest city, even though it is in another state. Central and western Massachusetts have also accommodated several hundred Cambodians each (Burton 1983; Cambodian American Association of Western Massachusetts 1991; Commonwealth of Massachusetts Office for Refugees and Immigrants 1990: 13–14).

Unfortunately, the rosy situation in Massachusetts did not last long. Wang Laboratories began to encounter difficulties in 1988. Its stock prices fell, its work force decreased from 31,500 in 1988 to only 8,000 in 1992, and its losses in fiscal year 1992 came to $140 million. The company filed for Chapter 11 bankruptcy that year and laid off another five hundred employees in 1993 as part of its Chapter 11 reorganizational plan (Kiang 1994: 138–39). As the Massachusetts economy declined, the state had to downsize a whole range of social services. The legislature reduced the appropriation for the Gateway Cities Project to $7 million in fiscal year 1988, $3 million in fiscal year 1989, and zero dollars in fiscal year 1990.

A Survey of Cambodian Communities around the Nation

In addition to Long Beach and Lowell, many small and medium-sized Cambodian communities have sprung up elsewhere in the United States. By the time the 1990 census was taken, Cambodians were living in every one of the fifty states, ranging from a low of four persons in Montana to a high of 68,190 in California. Ten years later, the 2000 census also counted Cambodians in all fifty states, ranging from nine in Montana to 70,232 in California. As was the case in 1990, Cambodians in 2000 were concentrated in the southern tier of the New England states (19,696 in Massachusetts, 4,522 in Rhode Island, and 2,377 in Connecticut); the two largest mid-Atlantic states (2,973 in New York and 8,531 in Pennsylvania); the greater Washington, D.C., area that stretches into Maryland (1,921) and Virginia (4,423); the more prosperous southeastern states (2,232 in North Carolina, 2,905 in Georgia, and 2,447 in Florida); three states in the Midwest (2,725 in Ohio, 2,879 in Illinois, and 5,530 in Minnesota); Texas in the Southwest (8,852); two Rocky Mountain states (1,451 in Colorado and 1,332 in Utah); two Pacific Northwest states (13,899 in Washington and 2,569 in Oregon); and 70,232 in California (Pfeifer 2002). In the ten-year interval, the number had increased in every state except New York and Illinois. The remaining states each had fewer than a thousand Cambodians in 2000.

Although official, these figures are not definitive, not only because of undercounting but also because the census bureau introduced a new complexity into the 2000 enumeration. In addition to counting each individual according to a single ethnic designation, it allowed people of mixed-race or mixed-ethnic origins to so indicate. Thus, if persons who are partially Cambodian are included, the 2000 census figures for "Cambodians" in the United States are larger. The total number of Cambodian-only descent plus mixed-race and mixed-ethnicity Cambodians in the country comes to 206,052, compared to 171,937 persons of Cambodian-only descent. In the eight states with more than five thousand "Cambodians" each, compared to figures for people of Cambodian-only descent cited in the preceding paragraph, the combined number in California is 84,559; in Massachusetts, 22,886; in Washington, 16,630; in Pennsylvania, 10,207; in Texas, 8,225; in Minnesota, 6,533; in Rhode Island, 5,290; and in Virginia, 5,180 (Chhim 2003: 94). Even though no studies have yet been done of the phenomenon, comparison of the two sets of numbers shows that interracial and interethnic marriages are taking place among persons of Cambodian ancestry in the United States.

In states with fewer than a thousand Cambodians, perhaps the most interesting cluster is found in the Mobile Bay area of Alabama, fronting the Gulf of Mexico. The 2000 census counted 429 Cambodians in Mobile—a smaller number than that estimated by researchers working on contract with the ORR in 1989. Although the population may have declined, an equally likely explanation is a census undercount. Regardless of what the actual number may be, Indochinese refugees form a significant proportion of the population of Bayou La Batre and to a lesser extent of Mobile and Irvington. Even though Bayou La Batre is a small community, it is Alabama's most important fishing port and ranks seventh in the United States in terms of the amount of seafood caught and landed there. In addition to the local catch, the town's plants process an even larger amount of seafood caught in other states and in the waters of other countries.

Workers in Bayou La Batre's seafood industry have always been segmented by race and gender. From the beginning, African American women dominated shrimp processing (a task called "heading" because it involves removing the shrimp heads). Until the 1980s, however, most of the workers who picked crabmeat from shells (called "backing") were European American women, supplemented by a small number of seasonally employed African American women. Unlike shrimp, which is landed dead (and much of which is frozen before shipping), crab, by law, must be alive when it is landed. Crabs are cooked before being picked, and their meat is refrigerated but not frozen during shipping. It can be contaminated by bacteria more easily than can shrimp, which means that sanitation standards in crab-processing plants must be higher than in shrimp processing (Moberg and Thomas 1993: 89–93). Hence, owners, some of whom have held the racist stereotype of African Americans being "unclean," have been reluctant to employ them as permanent workers to process crab. European American men own and manage the plants and do the fishing, and African American men do the heavy manual labor at the docks and in the plants.

As the seafood industry expanded due to the changing tastes of American consumers who, for health reasons, began to eat less red meat and more seafood, there developed a shortage of local European American female workers. Instead of hiring additional African American women, plant owners brought in Indochinese refugees to augment the labor supply. A crab processor in Bayou La Batre first hired Vietnamese workers in 1979. Other plant owners soon followed suit even though residents in the area were outraged at their decision. To dampen the uproar, crab-processing plants posted large signs printed in the Vietnamese language, telling workers that they must wear hairnets and wash their hands after using the toilet. The owners also publicized the inspections made by the Alabama Department of Health. The message, obviously, was that the plants were utterly clean even if they employed Indochinese workers.

Owners and managers like employees from Indochina because they are concerned about the relative ease of controlling various groups of workers. As one owner put it, "Asians are the best workers, they listen to you and they do what you tell them. After Asians I'd rather hire blacks; they aren't necessarily good workers, but they'll do what you tell them. Whites on the other hand don't want to work all that hard and won't do what you tell them to do" (Moberg and Thomas 1993: 97).

As more refugees were added to the labor force, the proportion of European American women fell. In the crab industry in Bayou La Batre during the 1990s, 62 percent of workers were female, 70 percent were Indochinese, 15 percent were African American, and 15 percent (including the owners) were European American. In contrast, Indochinese still represent only 1 percent of the workers in shrimp processing, because African American women continue to dominate that segment of the work force. With refugees as a new source of labor, the number of crab-procesing plants in Bayou La Batre increased, and the amount of crabmeat processed each day rose fivefold (Moberg and Thomas 1993: 94).

The refugees, for their part, like working in the crab-processing plants because crab pickers are paid by piece rate, which means that those who work fast can earn wages considerably above minimum wage. An ORR survey in 1989 found that nearly a hundred Cambodian families (containing some six hundred persons) lived in the Mobile Bay area—one and a half times the number the 1990 census showed for the entire state of Alabama. In addition to processing crab, Cambodians shucked oysters. They even owned an oyster-shucking factory, the Interland Seafood Company. More than 80 percent of families that the ORR surveyed were self-sufficient; two-thirds of them had two or more workers who earned a combined income four times as large as what a family on welfare and food stamps could receive at that time. The Cambodians established a Buddhist temple in Irvington, which served their compatriots not only in Alabama but also those in the Gulf Coast areas of Mississippi and Florida (North and Sok 1989: 11–16).

Small Cambodian communities were also established in other unlikely locations, such as Portland, Maine, Rochester, New York, Des Moines, Iowa, Memphis and Nashville, Tennessee, and Charlotte and Greensboro, North Carolina. The existence of such small communities in places that have not been settlement sites for Asian immigrants indicates that the factors governing the demographic distribution of refugees from Vietnam, Laos, and Cambodia differ from those determining the historical settlement patterns of Asian immigrants. The primary difference is that, unlike the situation faced by Indochinese refugees, the federal government and voluntary agencies do not tell Asian immigrants where they can or should live.

Cambodians in Maine live mostly in the state capital, Portland, although there are also small numbers in the towns of Saco, Biddeford, Sanford, and Augusta. An old seaport, Portland has many factories that process seafood, pack meat, sew garments, and assemble electronics equipment. Cambodians found work in all those industries. Even though housing is not cheap, about half of Portland's Cambodians became homeowners a decade after they settled in the city and established a Buddhist temple and a mutual assistance association. The public schools hired Khmer-speaking teachers' aides to help Cambodian youngsters, and the Maine Medical Center in Portland hired Khmer interpreters (North and Sok 1989: 50–53). Census-takers counted 661 Cambodians in the Portland MSA in 2000 (Pfeifer 2002).

A few Cambodians first found their way to Rochester in upstate New York in 1975. By the late 1980s, about four hundred lived in that high-technology city on the shores of Lake Ontario—home of the Xerox, Kodak, and Bausch and Lomb companies. The 2000 census reported 392 Cambodians there (Pfeifer 2002). Rochester had a low unemployment rate when Cambodians first arrived, which enabled three-quarters of Cambodian adults not only to become gainfully employed but also to be relatively well-paid compared to Cambodian workers elsewhere (North and Sok 1989: 57–59).

The 2000 census puts the number of the small but highly self-sufficient Cambodian community in Des Moines, the capital of Iowa, at 358 (Pfeifer 2002). Cambodians first came to Des Moines in 1979. Since 1976 Iowa has provided services to refugees directly rather than contracting the services out to voluntary agencies as other states have done. The state encourages early employment. As soon as Cambodians arrived, Iowa's Bureau of Refugee Programs hired two Khmer-speakers to provide them with short-term vocational counseling and training. The Des Moines school district also employed a Cambodian teacher's aide to make sure the children had help. At that time, the state had an unemployment rate 2 percent below the national average, so new refugees had little trouble finding jobs, even when they spoke little or no English. Located in a productive agricultural state, Des Moines has many meatpacking plants that do not hesitate to employ Cambodians. The local community college offers courses in English as a second language as well as in electronics assembly. Some Cambodians, after taking such courses, found work in the electronics industry. They established a small Buddhist temple in Polk City near Des Moines and the Ankorwat Friendship Association in Des Moines (North and Sok 1989: 47–49).

In Tennessee, the Cambodian influx began in 1979, and the population was split between Memphis and Nashville. It took most refugees only about a month to find their first jobs. In Memphis, they worked in food-processing plants and various kinds of factories and as carpenters. In Nashville, the well-known Opryland Hotel employed a large number of Cambodians and provided transportation from their homes to the hotel—a convenience appreciated by Cambodians who did not own cars. The school systems hired Khmer-speaking teachers' aides who helped the children adjust to the American school system. A Buddhist temple was established in Nashville but not in Memphis (North and Sok 1989: 79–85). The 2000 census reported 483 Cambodians in Memphis and 427 in Nashville (Pfeifer 2002).

In North Carolina, Charlotte has the largest number of Cambodians (754 in the Charlotte-Gastonia-Rock Hill MSA in 2000), and they work in textile mills, electronics and garment factories, and other industries. Greensboro's Cambodian residents work in furniture factories and textile mills, and they set up an MAA and a Buddhist temple to meet their social and religious needs (North and Sok 1989: 60–64). The 2000 census enumerated 1,115 Cambodians in the Greensboro-Winston-Salem-High Point MSA (Pfeifer 2002).

Among states with several thousand Cambodians each, Rhode Island has the distinction of having the largest percentage of Cambodians among its Southeast Asian refugee population. One state official who oversaw refugee resettlement for some years there puts the number of Southeast Asian refugees resettled in Rhode Island, 45 percent of whom were Cambodians, at almost ten thousand. (In other states, Cambodians represent fewer than 5 percent to a maximum of 20 percent of the Southeast Asian refugee population.)

Rhode Island's Cambodians live mainly in Providence, the state capital. The first Cambodians to set foot in the city were men who had come for military training at the U.S. Navy's war college in nearby Newport. The 2000 census reported 4,518 Cambodians in the Providence-Fall River-Warwick MSA (Pfeifer 2002). They reside mostly in the West End (Lind 1989: 7, 28) and in apartments or rental houses rather than in subsidized public housing. Those who can afford to do so have moved to nearby Cranston, where they live in single-family houses that they either rent or own (Breckon 1999: 108). Most gainfully employed Cambodians in the state hold low-skill, low-wage jobs in fish-processing plants, in factories that make costume jewelry and garments, and in electronics-assembly plants. Providence has a small number of Cambodian-owned businesses, including restaurants that cater to the general public.

Cambodians came to Rhode Island because the very first Theravada Buddhist temple on the East Coast was set up in Providence. Even though it was located in a tenement building, its first head monk was a world-renowned Buddhist leader. The Providence temple served as headquarters of the Khmer Buddhist Society of New England (anonymous interview 1995; Lind 1989: 9). The temple's importance is illustrated by the story of Dr. Som Chau Yeung, a retired pediatrician from Phnom Penh who moved from Boston to Providence so he and his wife could go to the temple every day (Lind 1989: 29). One official in the Cambodian MAA whom Audrey Kim interviewed in 1995 maintained, however, that the head monk "turned off" some people because he became too involved in factional politics and was suspected of using donations from New England's Buddhists to support partisan political activities in Cambodia. Due to this controversy, the monk eventually returned to Cambodia.

In Connecticut, Danbury had an estimated population of three thousand Cambodians in 1995, as well as a Buddhist temple served by four monks. Smaller numbers live in Bridgeport, Hartford, New Haven, and New London. Catholic Family Services has an office in Hartford, the International Institute has one in Bridgeport, and Lutheran Immigrant and Refugee Services has a Danbury office, which explains why Southeast Asian and other refugees were placed in those towns. Most of the Cambodians came between 1981 and 1987. Only a few hundred were resettled between 1987 and 1991, note individuals involved in their resettlement, and by 1992 no more Cambodians were being placed in the state. The 2000 census counted only 2,377 Cambodians in Connecticut (Pfeifer 2002). Three European American women health-care professionals and two Cambodian refugee women set up an unusual clinic, Khmer Health Advocates, in West Hartford to treat torture victims. Operating on a shoestring budget, the volunteer staff used a variety of approaches including family therapy, hypnosis, cognitive therapy, massage, and medication. Unfortunately, the clinic faced hard times when funding dried up.

The Connecticut state officials and voluntary agency staff members who my research assistants and I interviewed think Cambodians in their state are doing well. They have seen Cambodians keep their jobs longer than Vietnamese refugees do. They work mainly in factories and machine shops. Many Cambodian women in Connecticut work outside their homes. Some individuals, both men and women, hold two jobs, working eighty or more hours a week, not only because they want to earn higher incomes but also because "they want to forget whatever happened in the past. They get busy, come home, sleep, forget the past," said a Cambodian woman refugee who has helped other refugees for many years.

In the mid-Atlantic states, New York's Cambodian population is concentrated in two boroughs of New York City—about two-thirds of them in the Bronx and most of the rest in Brooklyn. The voluntary agencies placed them there because cheaper housing was available. Some better-off people have since moved to the borough of Queens. Since the initial resettlement, more Cambodians have moved out than in. The Cambodian population continued to fall between the 1990 and 2000 censuses. Those Cambodians who remain in New York City work as porters, janitors, and in factories. Many women work in the garment industry. Some hold two jobs either because they have bought homes and must make mortgage payments or are sending children to college. Cambodian community leaders in New York estimate that two-thirds of the city's Cambodians received welfare during the mid-1990s, but a majority of them were widows with children. There is no reliable information about how many are still relying on public assistance in the post-welfare reform years.

A Buddhist temple in the Bedford section of the Bronx serves Cambodians from all over the metropolitan New York area. Veasna Ngin, treasurer of the Khmer Buddhist Society, who used to teach mathematics in his homeland and studied computer science after his arrival, says that many members of the community, poor though they were, each contributed $5 or more to buy a two-story house to set up the temple (Howe 1985). In addition to its religious functions, the temple attempts to preserve other aspects of Cambodian culture. Weddings and other celebrations such as the Cambodian New Year are held in its large hall (Howe 1985; interviews with temple officials 1995).

In Pennsylvania, the largest number is in Philadelphia, where nine voluntary agencies have offices. Proportionately, the Cambodian population in Pennyslvania grew faster between 1990 and 2000 than in any other state containing a significant number of Cambodians. Smaller groups are found in Pittsburgh, which has many entry-level manufacturing jobs, and in Harrisburg and Lancaster, which are close to Fort Indiantown Gap, one of the four reception centers to which Cambodians were sent in the spring of 1975. A high-ranking voluntary agency official who had been actively involved in Cambodian refugee resettlement told me that about five hundred of the Cambodians at the Fort Indiantown Gap reception center were pilots who escaped Phnom Penh just before it fell by flying out in their Khmer Republic Air Force airplanes. When some of the early arrivals became eligible to serve as sponsors, they brought relatives and friends to Pennsylvania.

Several individuals intimately involved with Cambodians in the greater Philadelphia area estimated that in the mid-1990s some ten thousand Cambodians lived there (anonymous interviews 1995; Sylvester 1997: 41), but that number greatly exceeds the figure given for the entire state of Pennsylvania in the 1990 census. The 2000 census counted only 7,332 Cambodians in the Philadelphia-Wilmington-Atlantic City MSA (Pfeifer 2002). Local observers disagree with that count. Samien Nol, executive director of the Southeast Asian Mutual Assistance Coalition in Philadelphia, observes that the size of the Cambodian population in the greater Philadelphia area grew in the late 1990s due to secondary migration from California and the New England states and was estimated at the turn of the twenty-first century to be somewhere "between 15,000 and 20,000" (Nol interview 2001 in Chan, ed. 2003a: 173).

Given the huge discrepancy between the census figure and Nol's estimate, it is likely that the census undercounted the Cambodians while Nol over-counted them. The poorer Cambodians in Philadelphia, most of whom farmed and fished in their home country, congregate in the Logan neighborhood on 11th Street, a predominantly African American area. Other clusters are found in West Philadelphia and South Philadelphia. Those doing better economically tend to live in North Philadelphia, where some have bought homes (Hein 1995: 84–88; anonymous interview 1995). A monk in the Buddhist temple in Philadelphia told Audrey Kim that he had served in the Providence temple before coming to Philadelphia.

In Pennsylvania, the educated pre-1979 arrivals who went through retraining programs, as well as young people who complete college in the United States, have found professional jobs (Nol interview 1995 in Chan, ed. 2003a: 176–77). The less educated work in factories that make plastic goods, computers, other electronics equipment, and plumbing and heating units. A small number work in hotels. A significant number of Cambodians in the Philadelphia area also earned money in the 1980s and early 1990s harvesting fruit, mostly blueberries and peaches in New Jersey, and vegetables. Cambodians gravitated to such work because their earnings in this occupation were not reported, and they could continue to receive public assistance. Cambodians from other states also joined the summer harvest crews (Nol interview 1995 in Chan, ed. 2003a: 177–78). These farmworkers are called "day-haul laborers" because early every morning crew leaders gather a group of workers and transport them to the fields.

From the 1940s through the 1970s, African Americans made up the bulk of the day-haul laborers in New Jersey. Puerto Ricans and Mexicans began entering the workforce in the 1970s. By the mid-1980s, however, the number of Cambodians peaked as the largest group of them arrived as refugees, and they became the most numerous population in the fields. There were smaller numbers of Hmong, Vietnamese, and Thai. The Southeast Asian workers did not displace African Americans, whose numbers had been declining; the incoming refugees were filling a labor vacuum (Pfeffer 1994: 9–10, 14, 16).

By the early 1990s, however, fewer than 10 percent of Cambodians in the greater Philadelphia area still earned money as day-haul laborers. The refugee influx had ended, and farm owners, as crew leaders hired more and more teenagers, increasingly rejected Cambodian crews because the young people were apparently not good workers. Cambodian crew leaders themselves began to leave the business, because they were paid by piece rate for the total amount harvested and their use of less-efficient young people led to declining incomes (Pfeffer 1994: 20–21). In addition, as more and more Cambodians fell ill from the pesticides sprayed on crops, they realized that day-haul labor was not a desirable way to earn money (Nol interview 1995 in Chan, ed. 2003a: 177–78).

In 1975 the greater Washington, D.C., area contained several dozen Cambodians who worked for the Cambodian embassy or attended college. As additional refugees arrived they spread out to Maryland and Virginia, especially to Hyattsville, Landover, Prince George's County, and Montgomery County, said a European American woman who worked as a volunteer to meet their needs. Estimates vary greatly regarding how many Cambodians are in the metropolitan area. A Cambodian American social worker who has lived in the United States since the 1960s thought there were about five thousand in the mid-1990s, although a Cambodian American artist active in community affairs put the number at more than ten thousand. The number shown in the 2000 census is much lower: 2,606 in the Washington, D.C.-Baltimore MSA (Pfeifer 2002). Cambodians are scattered throughout the region and so do not interact frequently with one another. Although most of them are working, some at more than one job, many still live in rented apartments because other housing is expensive, reports a lay administrator of the Cambodian Buddhist temple in the Washington D.C., area.

The temple, Wat Buddhikarama, in the greater Washington area is located in Silver Spring, Maryland. An employee of the Voice of America who came to the United States in the 1960s together with a monk he had known in Cambodia initiated the building project. The temple has traditional Khmer-style architecture. The first head monk died soon after the building was completed. He was succeeded by a monk who was disrobed during the Pol Pot regime but managed to survive by working diligently in the fields under the watchful eyes of the Khmer Rouge. He became a monk again in 1979 and was invited in the early 1990s to serve the Silver Spring temple. When Audrey Kim interviewed him in 1995, he explained that monks must be recruited from Cambodia because few Cambodians in America are interested in becoming monks.

An important national organization, the Cambodian Network Council (CNC), was also located in the capital and provided leadership for a number of innovative transnational projects (Sam interview 1995 in Chan, ed. 2003a: 188–92). Even though the CNC still exists as an organizational entity, it no longer has the funds to support an office in Washington, D.C., and is presently operating out of the offices of a mutual assistance association in Philadelphia, the Cambodian Community of Greater Philadelphia.

Cambodians entered the southeastern states mostly as a result of the Khmer Guided Placement Project. Three of the twelve chosen sites were in this region: Atlanta, Georgia, Richmond, Virginia, and Jacksonville, Florida. The 2000 census counted 2,727 Cambodians in the greater Atlanta area (Pfeifer 2002). The 1989 ORR survey found that more than 90 percent of Cambodians in Atlanta were economically self-sufficient, and fewer than 10 percent were on welfare. Those employed earned the highest wages among Cambodians in the southeastern states. They worked in electronics and other factories, poultry-packing plants, and janitorial services and in hotel kitchens. They set up a Buddhist temple in Lithonia, about twelve miles east of downtown Atlanta (North and Sok 1989: 35–36).

The 1989 ORR survey reported that Cambodians in Jacksonville, located in the northeastern corner of Florida, were also doing well. More than 90 percent were employed and most of the self-sufficient families had two or more income earners. Many worked in electronics factories and poultry-packing plants, but the largest group, about 250 individuals, male and female, were employed by Excel Industries, which made truck parts. The company employed a Cambodian full time in its personnel department, provided Cambodian workers with on-site English classes, and contributed funds to their annual New Year's celebration (North and Sok 1989: 28–31). The 2000 census found 941 Cambodians in Jacksonville (Pfeifer 2002).

St. Petersburg on the Gulf Coast of Florida and the nearby towns of Clearwater, Largo, Sarasota, and Bradenton together contained an even larger Cambodian community, even though St. Petersburg was not a KGPP site. In 2000, census-takers counted 682 Cambodians in the Tampa-St. Petersburg-Clearwater MSA (Pfeifer 2002). As early as 1989, about 85 percent of the Cambodians in these towns had found employment, and there were two or more workers in 70 percent of the economically self-sufficient families. Most of the men worked in factories. Some leased land to farm, while others processed fish. Women worked in sewing factories, electronics assembly plants, food-processing plants, and hotels (North and Sok 1989: 32–34).

The largest Cambodian community in the Midwest is in Chicago, where most live in the Uptown neighborhood. A smaller number is in Albany Park.

Several hundred Cambodians also live in Joliet, an hour's drive away. An official in the Illinois State Refugee Coordinator's office notes that about six thousand Cambodians resided in the state during the mid-1990s—a figure twice as large as the number counted in the 1990 and 2000 censuses. A 1992 study conducted by the Refugee Substance Abuse Prevention Project of Travelers and Immigrants Aid put the number of Cambodians in Chicago at five thousand (Berry et al. 1992: 5). According to the 2000 census, there are only 2,738 in the Chicago-Gary-Kenosha MSA (Pfeifer 2002), but there has been no research to account for the numerical discrepancy.

Most Cambodians in Illinois came from rural backgrounds. Entry-level jobs were plentiful during the years they arrived in sizable numbers, and they found work in electronics and other factories and as janitors, with some women employed in day-care centers. A small number of men and women have white-collar jobs. Cambodian-owned businesses are located in the Uptown area and constitute a quarter to a third of the businesses owned by Indochinese in that rejuvenated, multiethnic area (Hein 1995: 54). Most of the people living on public assistance are widows who receive Supplemental Security Income (SSI) reports an individual who oversaw refugee resettlement in Illinois. The Cambodian Association of Illinois, an MAA, is strong and active. There is also a Buddhist temple in the Uptown area, and it has several monks.

According to the 2000 census, 1,464 Cambodians live in another KGPP cluster site in the Midwest, Columbus, Ohio (Pfeifer 2002). They work in meatpacking plants and other manufacturing industries, and the women are employed in garment factories. Cambodians also do seasonal farm work, picking strawberries in the spring and apples in the fall. There is an MAA and a Buddhist temple in Columbus to serve the community's needs (North and Sok 1989: 66–67).

Cambodians in Minnesota, the third midwestern state where a sizable number lives, are overshadowed by a much larger number of Hmong. In 1995 an estimated five to six thousand Cambodians resided in Minnesota; the 2000 census counted 5,530 in the state and 4,146 in the Minneapolis-St. Paul MSA (Pfeifer 2002). People familiar with the refugee situation in Minnesota—the staff of voluntary agencies and government offices—report that most Cambodians live in the Twin Cities. Both cities have good public housing, 80 percent of which is now occupied by Southeast Asian refugees. Many Cambodians in Minnesota are secondary migrants from Providence and Philadelphia. There is also some out-migration to California. Even though most came from rural backgrounds and did not have much, if any, education, an estimated 85 percent are employed. Most who receive public assistance are widows and children. A caseworker supervisor in St. Paul whom I interviewed observed that the welfare dependency rate among Cambodians was much lower than that among the Hmong. The United Cambodian Association of Minnesota is very active and offers a wide range of services to the community.

The 2000 census reports that the largest concentration of Cambodians in Texas resides in Dallas—3,310 in the Dallas-Fort Worth MSA (Pfeifer 2002). An ethnographer who did fieldwork there, however, suggests that a more realistic number is five thousand. Cambodians live in East Dallas, an ethnically mixed neighborhood, and in the suburbs. Those in the ethnic enclave have little contact with non-Cambodians and depend a great deal on social workers for help in instances where they have no choice but to interact with institutions of the larger society. As some Cambodians have become economically self-sufficient, they have moved to the suburbs and become slightly more integrated in mainstream society (Rasbridge 2001: 27–32).

Businesses in East Dallas were developed by Vietnamese who had been flown to the reception center at Fort Chaffee, Arkansas, in 1975. Many eventually moved to suburban areas in the northern part of the city but continue to operate businesses in East Dallas's "Little Asia" (Marcucci 1986: 96–97). Four voluntary agencies handled refugee resettlement in the area. They brought about a hundred Cambodians to Dallas between 1975 and 1980. In 1981, as part of the Khmer Guided Placement Project, more than nine hundred were placed in the Dallas area, eight hundred in East Dallas and the rest in Fort Worth. An additional seven hundred came to Dallas in 1982, most of whom were also housed in East Dallas. Four to five hundred came annually during the following two years. Thus, the East Dallas Cambodian community grew rather quickly. Residents soon established a Buddhist temple in Duncanville, fifteen miles away.

Most Cambodians resettled in Texas found jobs within a month of arrival (Marcucci 1986: 101). They work in the electronics industry and for garment factories, janitorial services, and hotels (North and Sok 1989: 87). Those unable to support themselves sometimes moved to California. John Marcucci observed in the mid-1980s that Cambodians in Dallas thought "the California public assistance programs offered them a sense of economic security that Dallas did not provide. In many of these cases, the husband remained in Dallas and the wife and children went to California. Also . . . older parents who could not work and were a financial burden to their children frequently left Dallas for California" (1986: 109–10).

Yani Rose Keo, a Cambodian woman who worked for Catholic Charities, initiated some of the most creative efforts to help Cambodians in Texas get on their feet. Keo was once the secretary to the American ambassador in Phnom Penh. In early 1981, before the first large batch of Cambodians was due to arrive, she talked to church leaders, school administrators, teachers, and police officers in Houston, explaining that Cambodians would soon be arriving but that "we don't want to take anything from you, we just want to survive." She also helped establish Khmer Village—a cluster of cottages owned by someone she persuaded to rent to incoming Cambodians. She arranged for volunteers to teach ESL classes at the village and visited the site regularly herself to deal with problems that might arise (*Refugee Reports*, Feb. 17, 1981, 3–4).

In 1985 Keo established Cambodian Gardens, a project designed to help Cambodians over the age of fifty learn to farm under American conditions, because she realized there was not much else the former peasants could do (Awanohara 1991). She leased idle state land near Houston at a discount and invited Cambodians to plant Asian vegetables there for sale. Unfortunately, the land flooded, and the project stalled. Keo next helped Cambodian families acquire plots in Rosharon, again to grow vegetables to be sold to Houston's major supermarkets. Even though the families lived in old mobile homes, they apparently found great satisfaction in farming their own land (Awanohara 1991).

The largest cluster of Cambodians in the Rocky Mountain states, 1,270, as given in the 2000 census, is in the greater Denver area (Pfeifer 2002). Cambodians first came to Denver in 1975, but the population did not really grow until 1981, when Denver became a KGPP site. Denver has a greater diversity of Cambodian community organizations than elsewhere: the Colorado Cambodian Fine Arts Preservation Group, the Cambodian Buddhist Association of Colorado, the Colorado Cambodian Relief Association, and the Refugee Center. Electronics assembly plants—particularly the IBM plant in Boulder—and sewing factories provide employment to most local Cambodians (North and Sok 1989: 20–21).

The 2000 census also reports 1,011 Cambodians in Salt Lake City (Pfeifer 2002). The first arrived in 1975. Perhaps because of Mormon religious dominance, no Buddhist temple has been established by Cambodians in Salt Lake City, although Lao Buddhists did set up one in Ogden. The Mormon Church donated a building to house the New Hope Center to offer services, including ESL classes, employment counseling, job placement, and health services, to refugees. Probably because of the Mormon influence, the crime rate in Utah is low. That fact, plus the strict discipline imposed in the state's public schools, appeals to Utah's Cambodians, who compare their environment favorably to those in California, Massachusetts, or the nation's large cities. Housing is also inexpensive in Utah. Gainfully employed Cambodians work in electronics assembly plants and for hotels and catering companies (North and Sok 1989: 92–93).

The greater Seattle area contains the largest number of Cambodians in the Pacific Northwest, with 12,391 counted in the 2000 census for the Seattle-Tacoma-Bremerton MSA (Pfeifer 2002). A Cambodian community leader in Seattle told Audrey Kim in 1996 that fewer than a hundred of the Cambodians who came in 1975 had resettled in that city. A Washington state official reports that between 20 and 30 percent of the refugees from Southeast Asia initially resettled in Washington were Cambodian, although, yet another state official notes, virtually none has been placed in Washington since 1986. Instead, many Cambodians who live in Washington are secondary migrants from California, Oregon, and Texas. A significant portion are not working. I and my research assistants, however, interviewed several voluntary agency staff members who maintained that mothers were required to seek employment when their youngest children reached their sixth birthdays, even before the "welfare reform" of 1996 went into effect.

One notable aspect of life in Seattle's Cambodian community is that refugees receive relatively good health and mental health care through the city's excellent network of community clinics. Even more important, there is an Asian Counseling and Referral Service (ACRS) that uses innovative and culturally sensitive methods to help clients. A multiservice organization serving a multiethnic clientele, ACRS's behavioral health department provides counseling for mental health problems, chemical dependency, and domestic violence. ACRS also has a medical clinic, a job training program, an assisted living program, a day-care center, a preschool program, an afterschool program for recreation and tutoring, an adult program, an elderly program, a food bank, and an immigration and naturalization counseling service. In addition, ACRS offers English-as-a-second-language classes. Its 150 staff members serve clients who speak twenty-two Asian languages and dialects (Chea interview 2001 in Chan, ed. 2003a: 241).

Moreover, Seattle has two Cambodian Buddhist temples. An official at one recalled that the first was established in 1982 in a rented house in the downtown area. As the number of supporters grew, it moved to larger premises. Since 1993, however, the temple has faced increasing difficulty supporting itself. After the 1993 United Nations–supervised elections installed a new government in Cambodia—one that promotes the revival of Buddhism—Cambodians in the United States began sending more and more money to their homeland to support family members left behind and rebuild destroyed temples or repair those that had been desecrated. Consequently, support of the temples in the United States waned.

More than 90 percent of the Southeast Asian refugees in Oregon live in Portland. There are 2,360 in the Portland-Salem MSA out of a state total of 2,569, according to the 2000 census (Pfeifer 2002). The first Cambodians to arrive in Portland, sponsored by Catholic Charities, were a half-dozen men from the Khmer Republic's tiny navy who had escaped together in the same ship (Tauch interview 1996 in Chan, ed. 2003a: 208). During the peak years of the refugee influx, about 15 percent of the Indochinese refugees brought to Oregon were Cambodians. Most were placed in southeastern Portland, but those who found jobs elsewhere in metropolitan Portland moved closer to their work sites. The associate director of an organization composed of sponsors who assist refugees has observed that few secondary migrants come to Oregon, which does not have a generous public assistance program. Secondary migrants from California come mainly to escape earthquakes and the gang problem (anonymous interview; Tauch interviews 1996, 2001 in Chan, ed. 2003a: 206, 211).

Portland's gainfully employed Cambodians work in electronics assembly plants and for sewing factories, hotels, and janitorial services (North and Sok 1989: 70–71). Two electronics companies, Tektronix and Intel, hire large numbers of them. By the mid-1990s some Cambodians had learned to do metalwork, such as welding and automobile repair. Portland has only a handful of Cambodian-owned businesses—a few sandwich shops, a grocery store, and two laundromats (Tauch interview 1996 in Chan, ed. 2003a: 208–09).

An official in Oregon's State Refugee Coordinator's office proudly noted that Cambodians in his state are "doing well" because of excellent employment training and placement services. The welfare dependency rate had dropped to under 10 percent by the mid-1990s and became even lower after "welfare reform." As soon as refugees arrive, they must register at the International Refugee Center of Oregon (IRCO). There, they meet with job developers who speak Vietnamese, Khmer, Lao, Hmong, Ethiopian, Russian, Romanian, and other languages and provide preemployment counseling such as how to fill out job applications and behave during interviews. Staff members also explain to the job-seekers what American employers expect in terms of punctuality and other aspects of job performance. IRCO provides an initial six weeks of ESL classes, although attendance can be extended if a student finds employment. If IRCO finds a job for a refugee, that person is obliged to take it (interviews with several voluntary agency staff members; Tauch interviews 1996, 2001 in Chan, ed. 2003a: 207, 210–11).

In Oregon's Refugee Early Employment Program (REEP), an individual's education, work experience, skills, and interests are assessed as soon as he or she arrives. REEP staff then draw up employment plans, writing them in the clients' own languages to ensure they understand them clearly. Those who need job training receive it through either IRCO or other agencies. In this coordinated manner, most refugees quickly acquire the skills needed for available jobs (North and Sok 1989: 71). The small number on public assistance tend to be people with many children or those too ill to work (Tauch interview 1996 in Chan, ed. 2003a: 210).

A European American administrator who has worked closely with refugees in Oregon points out that refugees also benefit by the statewide health plan, which includes all low-income individuals. County health departments employ Khmer-speaking medical case managers and interpreters; the University of Oregon Medical School has a clinic that serves Southeast Asian refugees (North and Sok 1989: 72–73); and the Department of Psychiatry at Oregon Health Sciences University has done pioneering work in diagnosing and treating post-traumatic stress disorder (PTSD) among these refugees, particularly Cambodians (Boehnlein et al. 1985; Boehnlein 1987a, 1987b; Kinzie et al. 1984; Kinzie et al. 1988; Kinzie and Boehnlein 1989; Kinzie and Leung 1989; Kinzie et al. 1990).

The preceding survey of Cambodian communities around the nation shows that, in general, those who were resettled in smaller cities in states that had healthy economies but stringent welfare programs have been more able to support themselves than those who resettled in the run-down neighborhoods of large cities. Refugees placed in states such as Texas and Oregon that offer a minimal amount of public assistance but had plentiful entry-level jobs during the height of the refugee influx were encouraged—indeed, forced—to find work quickly, and most of them remain employed to this day. In such localities, a significant number of families with two or more wage-earners has managed not only to survive but also to acquire the basic markers of a middle-class or lower-middle-class life. They buy homes, however modest, and one or more cars so they can go to work or shop without relying on public transportation or others. Although some working-class Cambodians have suffered downward social mobility in the sense that their current occupations have less prestige than the jobs they held in Cambodia, they are nevertheless proud to have achieved economic self-sufficiency in a relatively short period. The experiences of Cambodian refugees have by no means been homogeneous, however, for Cambodian communities in the United States exhibit a significant degree of internal social stratification.

Cambodian New Year Celebration in Long Beach, California

A Photo Essay by Manhao Chhor

4 Struggling for Economic Survival

ALTHOUGH THE opportunity structure in each locality where Cambodian refugees settled influenced how they fared during the first few years in the United States, the "human capital" that individuals bring with them (or manage to acquire after arrival) determines how much social mobility—either upward or downward—they experience. The degree of mobility affects what ultimate socioeconomic status an individual or a family will attain after the initial period of adjustment. The term *human capital* refers to language competence, education, occupational skills, and transferrable work experiences.

In general, the more human capital a person possesses, the more he or she will be able to take advantage of opportunities and overcome barriers that confront persons of non-European origins in settings where racism and nativism still exist. That is to say, class, race, ethnicity, and gender are intersecting axes that structure stratification systems within multiracial, multiethnic, industrialized societies. These are not, however, fixed categories. They are best seen as social arenas, and individuals and groups constantly vie for power and ascendance across their boundaries. Another source of flux is that self-perception may differ considerably from how others view us. Despite their slippery nature, however, race, ethnicity, class, and gender are useful heuristic concepts that help make sense of the extremely complex and constantly changing world.

Socioeconomic Status

The most extensive statistical information about the socioeconomic status of Cambodian refugees pertains to those who arrived between 1975 and 1981.

Unfortunately, far less information is available about those who came later. When some 125,000 Vietnamese and about five thousand Cambodians first landed in the spring of 1975, the U.S. Department of Health, Education, and Welfare (now called the Department of Health and Human Services) contracted with Opportunity Systems, Inc., a private research organization, to carry out a nationwide telephone survey of refugees from Southeast Asia. Opportunity Systems did so every year from 1975 to 1981. Even though respondents who were Cambodian, Lao, Hmong, and ethnic Chinese (persons of Chinese ancestry living outside China—in this case, Chinese from Vietnam, Cambodia, and Laos) were included in the surveys, Opportunity Systems researchers did not disaggregate data for the smaller groups. Rather, they focused mainly on the Vietnamese, who composed a vast majority of the refugees during those early years.

Opportunities Systems did conduct one survey solely on Cambodians in November and December of 1978. The researchers selected a random sample of 210 households from the federal government's 1975 Evacuee Master File. That is to say, the respondents were "first wave" Cambodians who escaped just as the Khmer Rouge took Phnom Penh. Of the households contacted, 160 heads of households representing a cross-section of all Cambodian refugees admitted into the United States in 1975 consented to be interviewed by telephone.

The households contained 627 persons, 38 percent of whom were under the age of fourteen. Investigators found that among Cambodians admitted in 1975 who were sixteen and older in 1978, 79.4 percent of the men and 45 percent of the women participated in the labor force. (The rate of labor-force participation is defined as the percentage of persons within a particular population who are currently employed or who are not working but are actively seeking employment.) Those figures compare favorably with the U.S. population as a whole. According to the 1980 U.S. census, 75.1 percent of the males and 49.9 percent of the females in the general U.S. population participated in the labor force. That is, slightly more Cambodian men and slightly fewer Cambodian women were working or actively seeking work than Americans in general.

Among Cambodians in the labor force, 94.8 percent had found jobs, and 78 percent of the gainfully employed worked full time at forty or more hours per week. The employment rate of the Cambodian male heads of households was high at every level of educational attainment regardless of previous occupational background in Cambodia. Among the gainfully employed, 58.2 percent had looked for jobs by answering advertisements, 55.4 percent by using employment agencies, 54.8 percent by contacting potential employers directly, and 40 percent by relying on relatives and friends (Opportunity Systems, Inc. 1979: v, 10). The total exceeds 100 percent because respondents could choose more than one answer.

Of refugee households, 70.8 percent in 1978 had only one source of income, 90.9 percent of which came from wages and salaries. Only 9.2 percent of the surveyed households relied entirely on public assistance: 6.7 percent received Refugee Cash Assistance, 1 percent Supplemental Security Income (SSI), and 1.5 percent other kinds of financial help. Of all households, however, 25.1 percent, including those with income-earners, were receiving some kind of federal assistance that contributed to their overall income. That 25.1 percent included the 19.9 percent who qualified for food stamps (Opportunity Systems, Inc. 1979: vi, 9).

The reasons that Cambodian respondents cited most frequently for not working were "attending school" (57.1 percent), "keeping house" (43.2 percent), "poor English" (29.2 percent), and "having other means of support" (20.0 percent). Again, the total exceeds 100 percent because respondents could select more than one reason. As might be expected, young men between the ages of sixteen and twenty-four cited "attending school" most often, most women cited "keeping house," and older men and women said that "poor health" and "poor English" were the major reasons for being unemployed (Opportunity Systems, Inc. 1979: 3).

One surprising finding is that the employment rate of people who spoke good English was only 8.4 percent higher than those with poor English. Those who held white-collar jobs in Cambodia had a slightly higher employment rate than those who held blue-collar jobs. Among those who had been white-collar workers in Cambodia, 70.9 percent worked at blue-collar jobs in the United States, whereas all who held blue-collar jobs in Cambodia continued to earn a living as blue-collar workers in the United States (Opportunity Systems, Inc. 1979: 5–6). In other words, since their arrival in the United States, members of the Cambodian upper and middle classes suffered significant downward social mobility, but those who were blue-collar workers in Cambodia remained in that same socioeconomic slot in the United States. Put another way, a great deal of social leveling had occurred within the Cambodian refugee population.

More than twenty years later, there was still no upper class—as measured by American income, wealth-holding, and social prestige standards—among Cambodians in the United States, even though some in the middle class had been part of Cambodia's elite in their homeland. With very few exceptions, the highest socioeconomic status that former members of the upper class have attained in the United States is middle class in American terms. Their former standing may still command deference from fellow countrymen in the ethnic community, but it has not been transferrable to American society as a whole.

In another study based on nationwide data, social work educator Chi Kwong Law (1988) has analyzed the 5 percent Public Use Microdata Sample (PUMS) of the 1980 U.S. census of population. Law divided his sample into Vietnamese, Khmer, Lao, Hmong, and ethnic Chinese. In contrast to the Opportunity Systems sample, which included only the 1975 cohort, Law's sample included all Cambodians who arrived between 1975 (or even earlier) and 1980. He found that among Khmer aged twenty-five and older, 17.2 percent had no education at all; 35.6 percent had attended elementary school; 24.2 percent, high school; 18.8 percent, college; and 4.3 percent, graduate school. Among ethnic Chinese from all three countries, the comparable figures were 12.1, 32.4, 37.4, 15, and 2.8 percent, respectively. Although proportionately more ethnic Chinese than Khmer had completed high school, fewer had college or postgraduate educations. Educational attainment levels for both groups were considerably lower than those for the U.S. population as a whole. Moreover, the data for ethnic Chinese refugees from Southeast Asia contradict the "model minority" image that has been imposed on Chinese Americans since the late 1960s. Among the Khmer, 57.8 percent could not speak English well, and 17.2 percent did not know English at all, whereas 43.1 percent of ethnic Chinese could not speak English well, and 30.2 percent knew no English (Law 1988: 165, 166).

Among Khmer aged sixteen and older, Law found that 40.8 percent were working, 8.6 percent desired a job but had not yet found one, 1.6 percent (aged sixty-five and above) thought themselves too old to work, 13.6 percent were not working because they were in school, 3.1 percent were not working because they were disabled, and 32.2 percent gave other reasons or no reason for being unemployed. The comparable figures for ethnic Chinese, some of whom were from Cambodia, were 43.2, 7.4, 2.9, 18.8, 1.8, and 26.0 percent, respectively. The Khmer male labor-force participation rate was 67 percent, and the female rate was 27.7 percent. Among ethnic Chinese men, the labor-force participation rate was 61.6 percent; among ethnic Chinese women, it was 38.3 percent (Law 1988: 167). The labor-force participation rate for the Khmer enumerated in the 1980 census was more than 20 percent lower than the rates Opportunities Systems found among the 1975 cohort. The 1980 statistics reflect the lower level of human capital that post-1975 arrivals, many of whom had been in the United States for less than a year when the 1980 census was taken, possessed.

Overall, the Khmer occupational status in 1980 was low. Of the gainfully employed, only 2.2 percent held managerial or administrative positions; 6.5 percent were professionals; 5.9 percent, technicians; 2.2 percent, salespersons; 5.4 percent, clerical workers; 18.3 percent, service workers; and 8.1 percent, farmers or fishermen; 17.2 percent worked in precision production or various crafts, and 34.4 percent were machine operators or common laborers. That is to say, only 8.7 percent held jobs that carry social prestige, another 13.5 percent had white-collar jobs, and 77.8 percent had blue-collar jobs. Among ethnic Chinese, 3.6 percent had managerial or administrative jobs; 5 percent were professionals; 1.9 percent, technicians; 10 percent, salespeople; 9.4 percent, clerical workers; and 20.6 percent, service workers; 2.5 percent farmed or fished, 15 percent worked in precision production and various crafts, and 31.9 percent were machine operators or laborers (Law 1988: 169).

Given that more than half of the Khmer were unemployed and at least four-fifths of those who were working earned low incomes, it is not surprising that 63.8 percent of Khmer refugees lived below the federal poverty line according to the 1980 census. They were, however, by no means the worst off among the Southeast Asian refugees. Among lowland Lao, 69.1 percent lived below the poverty line in 1980; the figure was 68.9 percent among the ethnic Chinese. An astounding 75.7 percent of the Hmong lived below the poverty line. These figures are two to three times higher than those for African Americans and Latino Americans. The Vietnamese did relatively better than the other refugee groups, with 36.9 percent living below the poverty line at the time (Law 1988: 171).

Christine Ryan, a sociologist, analyzed data from both the 1980 census and an Office of Refugee Resettlement (ORR) nationwide survey conducted in September 1981 (the last such survey funded by the federal government). Because I have discussed Law's findings from the 1980 census, I shall only report Ryan's analysis of the ORR data. ORR found that in September 1981, 17.6 percent of Cambodians in the United States had no education at all, 44.2 percent had attended one to six years of elementary school, 20.8 percent had some high school education, 14.9 percent had some college education, and only 2.4 percent had graduate training (Ryan 1987: 96).

The 1981 ORR data, when compared to census figures, show approximately the same percentage of Cambodians with no schooling, a larger percentage with only elementary schooling, and smaller percentages for those with some high school, some college, and some graduate education. It may be recalled that 1981 was the year when the largest number of Cambodians entered the United States. A significant number of them were peasants, fishermen, and laborers, and the lower level of human capital they possessed had already become apparent statistically when ORR did its survey in September of that year. The overall socioeconomic status of Cambodians continued to decline as refugees with similar rural backgrounds continued to arrive during the remainder of the 1980s.

Because many girls in Cambodia did not attend school, a wide discrepancy existed between the educational levels of men and women. In the ORR data that Ryan analyzed, only 5.1 percent of the men had no education compared to 31.8 percent of the women. The percentages concerning seven to ten years of education, however, were almost similar for the two sexes (20.6 percent versus 19.7 percent); 27.2 percent of the men had more than ten years of education compared to only 9.1 percent of the women (Ryan 1987: 100). The mean number of years of education (for men and women combined) was 6.6 among those who arrived between 1975 and 1978 and 5.6 years among those who came between 1979 and 1981—another indication of the declining level of human capital possessed by the post-1979 arrivals (Ryan 1987: 106).

In terms of employment, Ryan found a discernible upward trend based on the number of years in the United States. Although only 10.6 percent of Cambodians who had been in the United States for a year or less in 1981 were employed, 27.3 percent of those who had been in the country for three or four years worked. The rate continues to rise until it reaches 63.2 percent among those who had been in the United States for six years and 75 percent of those who had resided in America for seven years (Ryan 1988: 118).

There is a similar upward trend in terms of English-speaking ability, but the curve does not rise in a straight gradient. Although only 11.5 percent of those who had lived in the United States for a year or less could speak English, the percentage jumps to 41.4 percent among those who had been in the United States for two years. The rate of improvement then levels off, rising to only 47.4 percent among those who had resided in the United States for six years. In other words, the most significant language learning occured in the first two years following initial entry. Of the 1975 arrivals who had been residents for seven years at the time the federal government conducted its last survey, 71.4 percent could speak English well (Ryan 1988: 121). The difference between the sixth- and seventh-year cohorts reflects not so much improvements made over time but the differential in human capital possessed by the 1975 group versus those who came later.

Like their Vietnamese peers, Cambodians who came in 1975 constituted the cream of their society. Their absolute number, however, as well as their percentage among the Cambodian population, is far smaller than corresponding figures for the Vietnamese. The Cambodian elite who survived consists primarily of those who happened to be outside Cambodia at the time Phnom Penh fell. Because the Khmer Rouge killed an estimated 90 percent of the educated people who remained in Cambodia, members of the upper stratum of Cambodian society form a minuscule fraction of the population, both within post-1979 Cambodia and the communities Cambodians have established on American soil.

The data for Cambodians in the United States are comparable to those for Cambodians in Australia and France, a reflection of the fact that the same types of people were resettled in major countries of second asylum during the same periods. The 1981 Australian census indicated that only 10 percent of the Cambodians there held white-collar jobs as professionals, technicians, managers, administrators, or clerks. Blue-collar workers, including craftsmen, processors, and production workers, composed 73 percent. Among Cambodians aged fifteen and above, 27 percent were unemployed. In terms of schooling, 23 percent had left school before the age of fourteen. Half of the women had no schooling at all (Kiernan 1988: 658–59). Early arrivals in France were well educated, and some brought significant amounts of money, which they invested in restaurants, stores, and other businesses, mostly in Paris. French-speaking doctors and nurses found work in the health professions, teachers in schools, and technicians in industries. The less-educated, later arrivals, who had spent long periods in refugee camps, experienced far more problems. Their health was worse, and those who managed to find jobs usually worked in factories. Nonetheless, parents seemed grateful that their children could go to school without having to pay tuition (Lenart 1977).

Two regional studies in the United States supplement the U.S. nationwide data. Perry N. Nicassio and Young Yun Kim studied Cambodians who arrived between 1975 and 1979 and lived in Illinois in 1979. They found that a slightly smaller percentage of the Cambodians in Illinois were uneducated compared to the overall Cambodian population in the United States, but they earned less income than other refugee groups in that state (Kim 1989). In a second regional study done in San Diego, California, in June 1981, Paul J. Strand showed that more than half of the Cambodians there were neither working nor looking for work. Among those unemployed, 53.6 said they could not find work because they did not know any English, and 10.7 percent said they were too ill to work (Strand 1989).

Because employment and income data for Cambodians from the 2000 census have not yet been published, the latest information on their socio-economic status appears in a volume on Asian and Pacific-Islander Americans, published as part of the 1990 U.S. census of population. The 2000 figures will very likely show some improvement in Cambodians' overall socioeconomic status. Part of the reason is that the influx of uneducated rural people began to dwindle during the late 1980s and ended altogether by the early 1990s, when the United States terminated its Cambodian refugee admission program. It is also the case that, having been in the United States for a longer period, those who are gainfully employed, especially young people educated in the United States, have experienced some upward socio-economic mobility.

The education, income, and employment data in the 1990 census show that persons who self-identified as "Cambodian" (a category that included both foreign-born and American-born Khmer and some but not all of the Sino-Cambodians, as the latter variously self-identify as "Chinese" or "Cambodian") had made some progress but not a lot in terms of educational attainment level and employment status since the 1980 census. The 1990 census-takers counted 18,105 "Cambodians" between the ages of eighteen and twenty-four. Of these, 4,674 were high school graduates (25.8 percent), 4,657 had some college (25.7 percent), and 412 had some graduate training (2.3 percent). That means that 8,362 persons in that age group (more than 46 percent) had less than a high school education. There were 61,464 "Cambodians" aged twenty-five and older, of whom 40,035 (65.1 percent) had less than a high school education. There were 7,232 persons who had high school diplomas, including General Equivalency Degrees (11.8 percent), and 7,606 who had attended college but had not obtained a degree (12.4 percent). The 4,776 persons with college and graduate degrees included 1,814 with associate of art degrees in vocational fields, 1,284 with associate of art degrees in academic subjects, 2,530 with bachelor of arts degrees, 543 with master of arts degrees, 257 with degrees in graduate professional fields, and 162 with doctorates. Women represented about two-fifths of those who had less education than an A.A. degree, about a third of the A.A.s and B.A.s, and slightly more than a quarter of the M.A.s. In 1990, however, the census found only four "Cambodian" women in the United States who had a Ph.D. (my computations, based on the 1990 Census of Population, *Asian[s] and Pacific Islanders in the United States* 1993: 87).

There were, in 1990, 85,500 "Cambodians" aged sixteen and above; 39,793 of them, males and females combined, were in the labor force (46.5 percent), and 45,707 (53.5 percent) were not. Of those in the labor force, 90 percent were employed, and 10 percent were unemployed but looking for work. The labor-force participation rate among women was quite high—37.3 percent. Another way of looking at this is to take the family as a unit of analysis. Of the 28,185 families counted among the "Cambodian" population in the United States, 10,745 (38.1 percent) had no gainfully employed member, whereas 5,831 (20.7 percent) had one worker, 7,801 (27.7 percent) had two workers, and 3,808 (13.5 percent) had three or more workers.

The overall occupational status of "Cambodians" had improved since the 1980 census was taken. Among the 35,623 gainfully employed in 1990, 3,504 (9.8 percent) had managerial and professional jobs; 8,309 (23.3 percent) held technical, sales, and administrative support (that is, white-collar) jobs; 6,372 (17.9 percent) had service jobs; 620 (1.4 percent) were farmers and fishermen; 6,143 (17.2 percent) were engaged in various skilled crafts; and 10,675 (30 percent) were machine operators, fabricators, and laborers (my computations, based on the 1990 Census of Population, *Asian[s] and Pacific Islanders in the United States* 1993: 122–23; the percentages do not total 100 percent due to rounding). That is, two-thirds of gainfully employed "Cambodians" were blue-collar workers.

Based on that data, the "Cambodian" population in the United States may now be divided into three classes, as the term *class* is understood by most Americans: a small middle class of professionals and businesspeople, about 5 percent of the population; a large, lower middle class of white-collar and blue-collar workers who can also be characterized in terms of income as the working poor, about 40 percent of the population; and a very large, permanently unemployed group, representing more than half the population in 1990, whose members depend on public assistance for survival. Overall, some 40 percent of Cambodians still live below the poverty line. Since the 1996 "welfare reform" legislation was enacted, those who can hold any kind of job at all have been pushed into the working-poor segment of the ethnic community. The welfare dependency rate is still high, however, and will continue to remain so in the foreseeable future, given the large number who have one kind of disability or another as well as families headed mostly by widows who have no employment skills but children to support.

Portraits of the Middle Class

The small Cambodian middle class in the United States is quite heterogeneous; four segments may be identified. One consists of members of the pre-1975 Cambodian elite: scions of various branches of the royal family, high-level government officials, diplomats, and military officers. The only other rich people in pre-1975 Cambodia were those who had made a lot of money in business, and most of them were Sino-Cambodians. Many members of the former elite have suffered downward social mobility since they came to the United States, both in terms of social prestige and income. Those who are now professionals or businesspeople, however, remain at the top of the socioeconomic pyramid within their ethnic communities, even though they belong, at best, to the middle class in American society as a whole.

A second segment consists of individuals who became professionals before 1975. Even though most of them came from well-to-do elite families, there were some who belonged to middle-class families in Cambodia. They have had to struggle to retain their professional status, although they have suffered less downward social mobility than the former elite.

A third segment is made up of people, some of them former professionals who could not meet the licensing or certification requirements in the United States, who have opened small businesses. Being self-employed—that is, being their own bosses—has allowed them to retain a measure of social status and personal dignity.

The fourth segment of the Cambodian middle class consists of younger professionals who received most or all of their education in the United States. Some arrived when they were children or teenagers; others were born in America. Some young professionals are children of the middle class, whereas others are children of the working poor. There are even a few whose parents are welfare recipients.

Middle-class Cambodians are not very visible demographically. Their number is small, and they usually do not live in areas with heavy concentrations of Cambodians. Instead, they are interspersed among middle-class families of other ethnic backgrounds in mixed or mostly European American neighborhoods. Dr. Sam-Ang Sam, a world-renowned musician, winner of a MacArthur Foundation "genius" fellowship, and executive director of the Cambodian Network Council in Washington, D.C., in the mid-1990s, explains why some middle-class Cambodians prefer not to live among large congregations of compatriots:

> The Cambodians now in the U.S. who are, I guess, a little more sophisticated tend to stay away from the larger communities. They go to work there, go in to help, but don't want to live there. The reason is that a lot of times there is an image—we care about the image—of gang problems, something that we are not proud of . . . I think the more educated people who have more responsibility do not like that. . . . we feel a responsibility as Cambodians. . . .

[yet] we cannot afford to be isolated from the mainstream. . . . [but our fellow Cambodians] cannot be ignored because they are our people. (Sam interview 1995 in Chan, ed. 2003a: 193)

In other words, many members of the middle class, even when they choose not to live among less-well-off compatriots, try nevertheless to do something to care for them.

More often than not, older professionals were educated in Western countries before 1975 and were in the United States or elsewhere when Phnom Penh fell, or they left Cambodia right as it fell. They acquired licenses to practice their professions in the United States only after enormous struggle. As is true elsewhere, the professionals who have the most status in Cambodia are doctors, and it is they who have had the hardest time being recertified.

The story of Hay S. Meas, M.D., F.I.C.S., illustrates the struggles and achievements of the older professionals. Dr. Meas received his training in Cambodia. He did an internship in France before coming to the United States in 1973 with the hope of finding a residency in a hospital, but he had difficulty doing so because the medical education he had received was different from that in the United States. He was working as a newspaper folder at the *Washington Post* when the Khmer Rouge came to power. After seven years of extraordinary persistence, he finally obtained a license to practice medicine in the United States. He worked in Houston, Texas, and in Millersberg, Ohio, for more than a dozen years before his family moved to Tacoma, Washington, in 1994 to join his wife's brother. So far as he knows, he is the only Cambodian doctor to become a Fellow of the International College of Surgeons.

Almost as soon as he arrived in Tacoma, he was invited to serve on the board of directors of the Khmer Community of Tacoma and soon pressed into becoming its president. The responsibility became a second full-time job:

I deliver babies day and night. . . . I have my practice and everything. It's like a storm. I have a lifestyle that I don't think too many people would like. I have a nice wife, she lives like a single parent. That has a sort of negative impact on my children. Sometimes, you know, my wife asks me, "Doctor, do you know the last time you ate with your children?" I say, "Sure, it was just the other day." She says, "No, it was two weeks ago." . . . But my soul tells me I got to do something for the community. . . . I don't know how much I can do, but I will, I have to do something. (Meas interview 1996 in Chan, ed. 2003a: 231)

Despite the fact that Dr. Meas is one of the few Cambodians who has managed to remain in his profession, he disagrees with an American newspaper reporter who told him that he is "lucky." Reflecting on his situation, he says, "Most of our brothers and sisters died in the war. I am here but I am missing something. I should have been with them in happiness, or sadness, or in death. . . . It's just a sense of guilt. When one of . . . your family dies, you will cry. . . . Imagine your whole family is wiped out; your friends are wiped out. . . . This is a serious thing. It stays in your mind and in your heart. I'm not at all lucky" (Meas interview 1996 in Chan, ed. 2003a: 232).

The experience of another medical professional trained in Cambodia, Sarout Suon Seng (chapter 3), shows that although some professionals have managed to remain in the same profession they are forced to accept a lower-status job. When Sarout Suon was a child she did not like to do what girls were "supposed" to do, and she retained her spunk and vivacity as she grew into adulthood. Among a small number of Cambodian women who went to college before 1975, she was studying medicine in Phnom Penh when the Khmer Rouge came to power in 1975. During the DK period she and her family were forced to live in the countryside. After the Vietnamese drove out the Khmer Rouge, she did not try to escape but instead returned to the city to find what had happened to her home. She decided to remain in Phnom Penh in order to complete her medical studies. In 1982, however, just five months after she received her degree, she, two cousins, and a friend escaped to Thailand. They managed to slip into Khao I Dang, even though by that time it was closed to new arrivals (Cambodians in California Project, Seng interview 1989, 60: 23–29).

While in Khao I Dang, even though many French doctors wanted her to assist them because she spoke French, she chose to help American doctors because she wanted to learn English so she could go to the United States. After Ross and Lauren Palmer of San Diego ascertained her identity, they sponsored her entry into the United States. Immediately after she arrived in San Diego in 1985, a doctor she had met in Khao I Dang urged her to join the interns who accompanied him on his daily hospital rounds. Although she was happy to tag along, she quickly realized it would be well-nigh impossible to obtain a licence to practice medicine in the United States: "I was desperate because . . . I do not know how to get into medical school [in the United States] because of my English. I have to go through everything again. Probably take me ten more years . . . before I get my M.D." (Cambodians in California Project, Seng interview 1989, 60: 30–34).

Then Seng learned about programs that train people to become physicians' assistants. She applied to several and was accepted by the one at the University of California, Davis. After receiving a P.A. degree, she remained in Stockton because her fiance (now husband), a former medical student who was initially resettled in New Zealand, eventually joined her in America, and he also decided to get a P.A. degree at the University of California, Davis. Despite the fact that she is not considered a "real" doctor and P.A.s have a much lower status than M.D.s, she finds her job fulfilling because she realizes that her work is extremely important:

> I see a lot of Cambodian patients. . . . You know, American hospitals are very frightening . . . because they can't tell everything they want to tell or they need to tell. . . . It's not only Cambodian[s]. Even Lao, Hmong or Vietnamese . . . it is easier to reach them because I understand . . . I go through the same problem, so it is easier for them to tell about the feeling. . . . The thing that I can do is say, "I went through the same problem, I have survived, this is what I did, I made it, and I know you can [too]." . . . They have to trust you . . . to tell you something. You have to be on their side, because sometimes they don't trust . . . Americans . . . when they come here . . . go to the doctor, they think that the words they tell you [may get them deported]. . . . you have to say, "It is okay to tell everything to the doctor. It has nothing to do with immigration." . . . You have to assure them again and again . . . to tell the truth about diseases, about problems. (Cambodians in California Project, Seng interview 1989: 60: 42)

Despite the critical work that such Khmer-speaking medical personnel can do, they have had an extremely difficult time getting licensed. Some are quite bitter about the hurdles in their way. As Dr. G. Chan, who was resettled in the Bronx in New York City, complained to John Tenhula:

> After six years, I am still trying to get a residency to practice medicine here in America . . . I need to provide the original diploma and a transcript of my university work. Who can produce these things, the way we left? . . . there are six thousand Cambodian refugees in the New York area and not one Cambodian medical doctor. . . . It is as if the U.S. officials opened the gates in this country and let you into the courtyard. But nobody will now open the front door, and that is the door that counts. . . . Almost a third of the population are widows. Most are simple country people. . . . She maybe will hide where the pain comes from to avoid any gynecological exam. This is especially true if it is a male doctor. . . . What you have then are more and more people going to Chinatown for medical treatment. . . . [but] that is not covered by Medicaid, Medicare, and welfare. People give up food money to do this. (Chan 1991: 130–31)

Dr. Chan was also concerned that the American Medical Association seems to favor doctors from Vietnam over doctors from Cambodia. "There is," he observes, "discrimination between the way the AMA treats Cambodians compared to the Vietnamese medical doctors. They recognize many more affidavits and transcripts and in general make it easier to let Vietnamese people to take the . . . exam. There are reasons for all of this. Most Vietnamese escaped with their documents and diplomas. It was a different departure for the Cambodians. Plus the Vietnamese know the system here so much better and they are more aggressive" (Chan 1991: 132).

Instead of being bitter, other Cambodian doctors, such as Haing Ngor, changed their profession. Even though, poignantly, he brought a carton of medical books with him when he came to Los Angeles, thinking he might be able to practice medicine, he reveals:

> My first job was as a night security guard. . . . While looking for something better I took English as a Second Language classes. . . . In November 1980 I became a caseworker for the Chinatown Services Center. . . . Being a caseworker was satisfying. It didn't have the status or the money of being a doctor, but it allowed me to help refugees, which was what I wanted. . . . It was clear that there was a massive mental health problem among Cambodian refugees. I understood it because I had had my share of mental problems too. We had all been traumatized by our experiences. . . . We lost everything—our families, our monks, our villages, our land, all our possessions. Everything. When we came to the United States we couldn't put our old lives back together. We didn't even have the pieces. (Ngor 1987: 431–33)

While he was working as a social worker, Dr. Ngor's friends urged him to audition for a role in a film, *The Killing Fields*. Much to his surprise he was chosen to play Dith Pran, a Cambodian photographer who worked with Sydney Schanberg, a *New York Times* reporter who covered events in Cambodia between 1972 and 1975. Dr. Ngor gained fame when he received an Academy Award as the best supporting actor for his role. Tragically, in February 1996, three Chinese American gang members gunned him down outside his apartment near Chinatown in Los Angeles. His death at age fifty-five dealt a huge blow to efforts he had led to establish an international tribunal to try Khmer Rouge leaders for crimes against humanity (Chang and Malnic 1996; Kang and Leeds 1996a, 1996b; Morrison 1996; Munoz 1996a, 1996b). It is ironic that although he survived the "killing fields" of Cambodia Haing Ngor perished in those of Los Angeles.

Professionals in other fields have also changed occupations in order to serve their fellow Cambodians. Him S. Chhim, the executive director of the Cambodian Association of America, came to the United States in 1962 to study agricultural science at the University of Georgia. After he returned to Cambodia with an M.A., he worked for the Agriculture Department of Lon Nol's Khmer Republic. As people flooded into Phnom Penh during the American bombing campaign, and as runaway inflation made it impossible for his family to survive on his civil service salary, he left his government job and joined the staff of World Vision International to assist internally displaced people. He did not suffer Khmer Rouge atrocities because he and his family escaped to Vietnam just as the Khmer Rouge came to power.

Chhim was resettled in Florida. Despite the fact that he quickly found a minimum-wage job and later earned Florida teaching credentials, he soon moved to Los Angeles, where he worked for Catholic Charities for a year. He then became a social worker in Orange County. Ten years later, he was drafted to be the executive director of the Cambodian Association of America. During this period he attended evening classes and received a second M.A. in public administration from California State University, Long Beach. Like Dr. Meas, Mr. Chhim also recognized that he was in a bind: "Remember, our leadership is stretching very thin. There are very few people in the Cambodian community who are qualified and available for these leadership roles; the same people end up doing everything. . . . It's a Catch-22 because it is hard to just walk away from the community's problems, knowing how great the needs are" (Chhim interview 1996 in Chan, ed. 2003a: 61).

As mediators between two cultures—between their coethnics and the larger society—these Western-educated professionals are now the most visible leaders in Cambodian ethnic communities, but they by no means monopolize the leadership in such groups. Individuals whom social scientists tend to depict as "traditional" leaders also enjoy tremendous social status and exert significant influence on compatriots. Some Buddhist monks, although often perceived as "traditional" by Western scholars, actively serve as culture-brokers between parishioners and the non-Khmer-speaking world. As the Venerable Dharmawara Mahathera, who ministered to the distressed families whose children were gunned down by Patrick Purdy in Stockton, told reporter Jane Gross, "To tell you frankly, wherever I am I consider that place my own. . . . do you know [that] I am a [U.S.] citizen? That is because I do not want to be half—half here and half somewhere else. . . . It is my view that anybody who comes here must respect this country and feel it is their own." Thus he constantly encourages his parishioners "to immerse themselves in American language and culture" (Gross 1989).

An even more vivid example of a cosmopolitan Khmer Theravada Buddhist monk is the Venerable Dr. Chhean Kong, who obtained an M.A. in counseling psychology and a Ph.D. in clinical psychology after he came to the United States, even though he already possessed such degrees. He entered the monkhood as a child. After graduating from Buddhist University in Phnom Penh in 1968, he went to India to study Buddhism and philosophy, receiving an M.A. in 1972 and a Ph.D. in 1975. He remained in India after the Khmer Rouge came to power. As Cambodian refugees began entering the United States in increasing numbers in 1979, Cambodians in Long Beach brought him to California and raised funds "to build a Cambodian Buddhist temple . . . [in order] to preserve their cultural heritage and to revive their community spirit. The new temple was built to provide the Cambodians with a mechanism for holding on to their Buddhist way of life and to discuss the conflicts or problems they face in their new society as they attempt to preserve the past and adapt to the present. . . . we provide to Cambodians the support they need in order to rebuild their self-esteem, dignity, and identity" (Kong interview 1996 in Chan, ed. 2003a: 68).

Not only is he multilingual in Khmer, Pali, French, and English, but in his capacity as a licensed marriage, family, and child counselor Dr. Kong also combines Asian and Western therapeutic approaches to minister to parishioners and clients. He counsels people both at his temple and in a community clinic. Like other Cambodian professionals in America, the Venerable Dr. Kong is overextended. In addition to being the chief executive officer of the Long Beach Cambodian Buddhist Temple, the community services coordinator of the Long Beach Asian Pacific American Mental Health Program, and a practicing therapist, he also chairs the Cambodian-American Senior Citizens Committee on Aging and serves on several advisory boards, including those of the Cambodian Association of America, the Long Beach Health Advisory Committee, the Long Beach Police Department Chaplaincy, the International Institute of Los Angeles, and the VISTA program.

The Venerable Dr. Kong is also an American citizen. He identifies both with Cambodia, his country of origin, and the United States, his country of adoption. His transnational orientation was evident in his response to the September 11, 2001, terrorist attacks on the World Trade Center and the Pentagon. Immediately after the event, he coordinated a campaign to collect donations from his parishioners, raising thousands of dollars from individuals who were unemployed or on public assistance to benefit families of victims on the other side of the continent (Kong interview 2001 in Chan, ed. 2003a: 66). He also set up an altar on which is placed a pot that contains incense sticks, two votive candles, a large bowl of fruit, and a vase of flowers. Behind the altar stands a large piece of posterboard on which is mounted enlarged photographs of the burning buildings. Flanking it are two American flags. Dr. Kong and his parishioners have been praying to the Buddha to bless the families of the victims and send the souls of the departed to auspicious reincarnations.

The younger professionals in the Cambodian middle class belong to the "1.5 generation" whose members came to the United States when they were relatively young. Unlike older professionals, most of whom were out of the country in April 1975 and did not live through the horrors of the "killing fields," many younger professionals suffered through the Khmer Rouge devastations while they were young children. Samkhann Khoeun, who served as executive director of the Cambodian Mutual Assistance Association of Greater Lowell, Inc., from 1995 to 2002, was born in Battambang Province. Because his parents were middle-level farmers who owned only a little land, the Khmer Rouge did not kill them outright, but members of his family were separated from one another. Khoeun toiled in a youth work brigade. When the Vietnamese came, he discovered that many members of his extended family, whom he had not seen for years, had died of starvation. The survivors escaped to the Thai-Cambodian border, where they lived briefly in Nimet camp before entering Khao I Dang in December 1980. The family arrived in the United States in November 1984, sponsored by a church in Evanston, Illinois.

Khoeun first enrolled at a community college in Chicago and then completed a bachelor's degree in engineering at a four-year college, all the while supporting himself with several jobs: "I worked really hard, but compared to what I had gone through, it was nothing. Under the Khmer Rouge, you worked at gunpoint. You didn't have enough to eat. You were starving to death, yet you had to work in order to earn that food ration. Here, in the United States, I had a small car. I had to keep a schedule and make time available for both my work and my studies" (Khoeun interview 1995 in Chan, ed. 2003a: 134).

After graduating from college, he worked as an associate engineer and did volunteer work in Chicago's Cambodian community. Being able to help other refugees was so meaningful that he eventually moved to Lowell, Massachusetts, where at least 30 percent of refugee families are headed by widows and the needs of Cambodians are great indeed. Khoeun has been troubled both by the attitude of the town's political leaders and the orientation of the Cambodian refugees themselves. As he observed in 1995:

> We're talking about twenty-five thousand Cambodians here, a quarter of the city's population, and we have only three Cambodian police officers. Within the city government itself, there's no city councilman, there's no school

board member who's Cambodian. . . . They just use us to get money from
the federal government, saying that they will serve us, when, in fact, they're
not really trying to help us. . . . A lot of the [Cambodian] adults always think
about Cambodia. . . . At times, they forget where they are. They are here. I
find it alarming that they are not focusing on what is going on right here . . .
with their children . . . they're putting more emphasis, more thought, more
time, into what's going on in Cambodia, which is thousands of miles away.
(Khoeun interview 1995 in Chan, ed. 2003a: 150, 155)

Understandably, Khoeun was very happy when Rithy Uong, a fellow
Cambodian, won a seat on the Lowell City Council in 1999. That historic
event symbolizes the fact that Cambodians are finally being accepted in Lowell—a development made possible by a change in attitude by the Cambodians themselves, who are slowly realizing that America is now their home and
they must contribute to its commonweal, as well as by Lowell's European
American residents, who now seem to recognize that Cambodians have
brought positive changes to their city by opening new businesses and revi-
talizing the localities where they live, shop, and work (Khouen interview 2001
in Chan, ed. 2003a: 128).

Dharamuni Phala Svy Chea, a clinical case manager at the Asian Counseling and Referral Service in Seattle, was even younger than Samkhann
Khoeun when she arrived in the United States. Her family escaped to Thailand just as the Khmer Rouge took over the country. They spent a year in a
Thai camp before being resettled in 1976 in York, a small town in Pennsylvania. There, she and her brother were the only Asian children in their school.
In 1980 the family moved to Seattle. She became involved in her ethnic community while still a girl:

I moved here . . . in 1980, when I was in the middle of my eighth grade. . . .
there was a big group of refugees who came . . . [because] I was among the
few who had come earlier . . . the community leaders recruited us to help out,
to take people to different places, to interpret. So, I started interpreting and
volunteering when I was thirteen, and that's how I got involved in the
community. . . . When I was going to college . . . a lot of [my friends] . . . went
into science . . . computer systems, managing computer systems, or . . .
pharmacy . . . or engineering. . . . I was the only social worker. (Chea interview 1996 in Chan, ed. 2003a: 250–51)

Because of her bilingual and bicultural upbringing, Chea is able to provide culturally sensitive service to clients through what she calls a "holistic"
case management approach: "You do anything . . . like if they need food, you

take them to the food bank, if they need housing, you work on housing. If they need counseling, then you do therapy. . . . If you're talking about the American traditional therapy [where] you're sitting there on the couch [we don't use that method but] what we do is therapeutic as well; it's just not the traditional Freudian kind of thing. . . . if you're starving, sitting there talking to them isn't going to help, but if you get food for them, it helps. [If] they're out of clothes, you go and get clothes" (244).

Businesspeople within the Cambodian American middle class either had business experience in Cambodia or were former government officials or professionals who changed occupations after arrival in America in order to earn a living. This segment of the middle class has moved laterally, retaining their socioeconomic status in terms of income and prestige but changing their line of work altogether. Aside from the usual grocery, dry-goods, video rental, and jewelry stores that serve coethnics, Cambodians have become famous in California as owners and managers of doughnut shops.

The trail was blazed by Ted Ngoy, a Sino-Cambodian who arrived in 1975. Ngoy worked as a military attaché at the Cambodian embassy in Bangkok and so was out of Cambodia when the Khmer Rouge took power in Phnom Penh. A Lutheran church in Tustin, California, sponsored him and seven members of his family, providing them with a single room in which to live. In exchange, Ngoy worked as the church's janitor. To make ends meet he found a job as an evening clerk at Builders Emporium and pumped gas at a local service station during the night shift. One evening a fellow worker at the station gave him a doughnut. "I didn't know what it was, but I liked it," he recalled. "I took some home and my kids liked it, too." Ngoy decided to learn to make doughnuts. He became a trainee at a Winchell's doughnut shop and was later promoted to a manager's position at the Winchell's in Newport Beach. By 1977 he had saved enough to buy Christy's, a doughnut shop in La Habra. From such modest beginnings, he eventually became the first Cambodian American millionaire (Haldane 1988b). In the mid-1980s he owned more than fifty doughnut shops throughout California and had expanded his empire by buying taco and hamburger shops as well (Haldane 1988b; Pickwell 1990: 91–92). To Ted Ngoy, the United States is "a miraculous country" (Haldane 1988b).

Hoping to emulate his success, other Cambodians followed Ngoy into the doughnut business. Their entry was eased by the fact that Ted Ngoy's nephew, Bun H. Tao, had opened B & H Distributors, a doughnut supply house in Santa Ana. The company provides instant credit and even lends coffee-making machines to clients. B & H has two branches. One, in southern California, is run by Bun Tao, the other, in northern California, is run by his friend Robert Chau, who is also Sino-Cambodian. Together, the two supply houses serve several thousand clients. Their annual sales came to well over $10 million in the 1990s.

Cambodians own or operate an estimated 80 percent of all the dough-nut shops in California. None, however, has been able to duplicate Ted Ngoy's achievement, because the market soon became glutted. Moreover, Cambo-dian entrepreneurs in the doughnut business are finding it increasingly difficult to break even (Akst 1993). Were it not for the unpaid family labor that sustains these small eateries that cater to a multiethnic clientele, many would have gone under.

Cambodian-owned or -operated doughnut shops are often run by wom-en. Cecilia Vann Noup taught high school in Phnom Penh for twenty-two years. After the Khmer Rouge killed her husband, a government official, she first resettled in Virginia in 1979 and then moved to southern California in 1983. Determined to be self-reliant, she opened a four-table doughnut shop on Hawthorne Boulevard in Lawndale:

> I started this business from almost nothing. . . . I get to the shop at 5:00 in the morning to open for breakfast, and I usually leave around 7:00 P.M. I work behind the counter, serving customers, and do the cleaning and sweeping. I work all by myself most of the time. . . . I hired a young Cambodian man from Long Beach to do the night baking for me. He goes to school during the day. . . . All that the refugees have is our work, our dreams. . . . [One] reason that I work and try to save money is to be able to sponsor my cousin and her family from Cambodia. . . . I would tell the American government that I have some income ready for them. They have a place to work in my shop. They don't have to go on public assistance. That's one of the main rea-sons I want to have this donut shop and try to keep it open. There are three reasons: for my children, for my cousin's family, and for the little house I dream of [buying]. (Santoli 1988: 209, 231, and 233)

Sirathra Som, another businesswoman, has been even more ambitious. She and her husband, who worked for the U.S. Agency for International Development, left Phnom Penh on April 7, 1975, ten days before the Khmer Rouge captured the capital. The rest of her family and her husband's family who remained behind were all killed during the DK period. She recalls:

> We arrived in California with nothing, nothing. . . . My first job was at the Sheraton Hotel in San Francisco as a domestic. . . . One of the first things you learn in America is that you need money. . . . we needed two incomes and I

went to work. I know my husband did not like it, but it could not be helped. . . . I could work easier than he could and I began to do well and I supported the family. I became the breadwinner. He had bad feelings about this. . . . Eventually, we were divorced. . . . Before the U.S., I had never worked. In 1976, I persuaded Winchell's Donuts to give me a manager franchise and to work off the $5,000 fee. Then I started a small Winchell's shop in Berkeley and was able to pay off the franchise fee in four months. I built up one business and I sold it in five months. I doubled the money I had paid for it. . . . I am working every morning at four-thirty in one of my six donut stores. . . . I have helped thirteen families start their own businesses around here. I share my experiences and the lessons I have learned. I get upset with refugees who live too long on welfare. (Som 1991: 180–82)

According to a Cambodian woman who has lived in the United States for decades and directed the Cambodian Business Association in Long Beach during the early 1990s, women run so many small businesses because they "are more patient, more understanding, [they] take time . . . [to] communicate. . . . [When it comes to] selling anything, nobody does it better than a woman. . . . Most [stores] are mom and pop; the family runs the business. . . . People raise money mostly from their family and friends . . . Most businesspeople do not live here [in Long Beach but in places like] Rolling Hills, Rowland Heights, Diamond Bar" (Anonymous interview 1996).

Another woman, who has also directed the Cambodian Business Association, explains why the organization was established and what it tries to do:

The Cambodian Business Association was incorporated in 1984. . . . The concern was when they come over here, they want to start their own business, they are kind of handicapped. They don't know how to operate the business over here . . . we educate those businesspeople to respect the city ordinances . . . comply with the law . . . [as] the gang violence really increased . . . last year, one of the gangs come and shoot one of the travel agents, killed the father, the children. That kind of thing is scaring people. . . . We work very closely with the police department to help improve [the situation] . . . a lot of Chinese Cambodians . . . the majority open grocery businesses. But Cambodians, they go into auto repair. . . . [the businesses are] not actually owned by women, but by the husband and wife, but mostly [it is] the wife who runs the business. . . . women stay patient and do all the hard work. (Anonymous interview 1996)

An estimated two-thirds of Cambodian businesses in southern California are owned by Sino-Cambodians. Their dominance is even greater in other large metropolitan areas where Cambodians have settled. Nancy Smith-

Hefner, an anthropologist, found that 85 percent of the Cambodian businesses in the greater Boston area are owned by Sino-Cambodians even though
that ethnic subgroup forms only about 6 percent of the Cambodian refugee
population in the area (Smith-Hefner 1995: 141). Because Sino-Cambodians
dominated the retail as well as wholesale economy in pre-1975 Cambodia,
they have transferred that centuries-old tradition to the United States. Most
of their families lived in Cambodia for several generations and intermarried
with the Khmer, so almost all of them speak Khmer. In America as in Cambodia they interact easily with both Khmer and Chinese customers.

Anecdotal evidence suggests that the Khmer have a better chance of start-
ing businesses without competition from Sino-Cambodians in the smaller
Cambodian communities in America. In Fall River, a small town in the southwestern corner of Massachusetts, the MAA—the Cambodian Community
of Greater Fall River—formed a community development board, bought an
old textile mill, and named it Angkor Plaza. The MAA rents the space and
provides technical assistance to store owners. All but one of the businesses
at Angkor Plaza are owned by Khmer. As Sambath Rim, who directed the
MAA for some years, puts it, "It's important [for us to have our own build-
ing] because we can pull the community together. . . . Here, people can talk
to each other in their own language without fear. . . . they can go without fear
to the laundromat, the grocery store. I think you should have your own center so that you can perform your cultural activities and also your business
activities there, like Chinatown. . . . if you pay rent here, you're paying to your
own community (Rim interview 1995 in Chan, ed. 2003a: 162–63).

Unfortunately for Rim, some Cambodian residents of Fall River were
antagonized by his behavior when he acted as a resource broker between them
and the larger society. Lydia Breckon, an anthropologist, interviewed individuals who were angry with Rim. He was, they alleged, exploiting both the
American system and the Cambodian ethnic community. Moreover, he was
said to be "hoarding power and patronage and dispensing resources only
when it served his needs, when it clearly built his power." As Breckon observed, "The battle was not over services, but over clients" (1999: 94, 176, 178).
By 2003 Rim was no longer in office (telephone conversation with an anonymous MAA staff member, 2003).

Regardless of the segment of the middle class to which they belong, members of that class, both men and women, share three common traits. They
are determined to be financially independent and are very proud of that fact,
they work hard to overcome obstacles, and they show a great deal of concern
for other Cambodians. As cultural and resource brokers who are not always

able to satisfy all the wants of so many needy compatriots, however, they in some instances reap opprobrium instead of appreciation.

The Working Poor

Members of the lower middle class in Cambodian ethnic communities, who may also be characterized as the working poor, usually live in ethnically mixed, older neighborhoods in downtown areas. Many of them have suffered considerable downward social mobility. They have worked as hard as, or perhaps even harder than, members of the middle class to support themselves. The story of Patrick Medh Keo and Felicia Savanne Im Keo illustrates the trials and tribulations of this group. Medh Keo, whose family owned much land in Cambodia, attended college for several years before he joined the Khmer Republic's air force. On April 12, 1975, as he watched the last American helicopter fly out of Phnom Penh, he realized the Khmer Rouge were about to capture the city. The next day, he put his wife and child in his fighter jet and flew to an American air base in Thailand. Although he had no intention of coming to the United States, he and his family were evacuated to Fort Indiantown Gap, Pennsylvania. There he contacted his former American flight instructor, who sponsored him out of the reception center. For six months the Keo family lived in Fort Walton Beach, Florida, with their sponsor, who worked hard to help them learn to survive in the United States:

> In Cambodia, when flying we must use English to communicate, whether wanting to come in or taking off. Specially, when we flew to Thailand or Vietnam, we used English to communicate. But the vocabulary [for things] in the house I can't understand much. Therefore, the first time when we just arrived, my instructor showed me how to learn. As he entered the kitchen, he . . . started to write down such as what is this bean's name. Uh! Everything was written in English. And frequently I asked him questions. In the house he taught me everything. (Cambodians in California Project, Medh Keo interview 1989, 43: 32)

Keo's sponsor also found him a job delivering flowers in Pensacola. While there, Keo heard from a Cambodian friend in Alabama that he could apprentice to become a welder and earn good wages. So he and his family moved to Alabama. "I went to welding school," he recalled. "After graduating I got a job in New Orleans, Louisiana. I was a ship welder. I worked there for three years. I transferred my job [and became] a crane operator . . . I worked as a forklift driver lifting sections: the pieces of the . . . ship when they were completely welded. . . . both of us worked, my wife and me. . . . each week my wife and I could collect about $1,000, $1,200" (Cambodians in California Project, Medh Keo interview 1989, 43: 30–31).

His wife's first job was in a grocery store. "At the beginning it was so hard because they needed workers with experience," she remembered. "That's why, in order to have experience I did whatever I was told. . . . When the cashiers finished calculating, I put all items in the bags for the customers" (Cambodians in California Project, Savanne Im Keo interview 1989, 39: 7). But she quit after one of their children was hit by a car while she was at work. After staying home for a year to take care of the children, she decided to return to work and found a job in a Chinese restaurant: "I was an order taker . . . I got quite good pay at that place. Each hour I got $4.00 plus tips. . . . But I had to work long hours. . . . My husband worked at the ship welding company at night. . . . We were very busy earning a living" (Cambodians in California Project, Savanne Im Keo interview 1989, 39: 7).

The family bought a house in 1977 and was well on the way to attaining middle-class status. Then a series of misfortunes shattered their lives. The eldest child was killed when a truck rammed into their garage, then Medh Keo had an accident that broke four of his ribs, and soon after that their house was robbed. Unable to continue to live in the house because of their bad experiences there, they moved and eventually sold the property. Next, they bought a restaurant, but it did not do well and they sold it, losing $60,000 to $70,000. Despondent, Medh Keo became a fisherman in the Gulf of Mexico. When Savanne became pregnant again she moved to Stockton, California, and applied for public assistance. But she soon became uneasy about being on welfare and found a job as a waitress, first in a Chinese restaurant and then in a Japanese restaurant. She became the family's main breadwinner because her husband, in an effort to overcome his depression, had become a devout Christian and decided to devote the rest of his life to "the Lord's work." Despite such difficulties the family is in the United States to stay. Perhaps as a symbol of that commitment, when the couple became naturalized U.S. citizens he took Patrick as his given name, and she became Felicia.

A San Diego resident whom Kenji Ima and his colleagues interviewed provides another example of how Cambodians in the lower middle class survive. The man, a commissioned officer in the small Cambodian navy, escaped in the boat under his command. After arriving in the United States he first worked as a gardener for a friend of his sponsor. Then he went to a mechanics' school for six months, not because he was interested in that trade but because he was required to be enrolled in a vocational training course in order to receive public assistance. After graduating, he found a job in a shoe factory, but the labor proved too heavy for him and he quit after three months. He then attended electronics school and found work as an electronics technician after graduating from that. His wife worked first as a receptionist, then as a caseworker for a social service agency, and finally as an instructional aide in an English-as-a-second-language class. To save on child care, she works during the day, and he works at night (Ima et al. 1983: 18–20).

Despite long hours and low pay, some members of the lower middle class seem quite satisfied with their lives and are happy with what they have managed to achieve. Choeun Rim was initially resettled in Michigan but made two subsequent moves, first to Philadelphia and then to Greensboro, North Carolina. He left Philadelphia because many people were being mugged and his wife and children were fearful. He had a friend in Greensboro and decided to move his family there. Although the Cambodian community in Greensboro is small, he considers it "much better than Philadelphia, and my children are very happy here. The older ones seem to talk better, and sleep better at night. . . . We have a very strong MAA here. They try to help newcomers. They meet the new people and spend time with them. If you have a problem, you can go to them. This was not possible in Philadelphia, you see. The city was too big, too many people, and too many problems. . . . What my wife and I feel the most is the kindness of the people we have met here" (Rim 1991: 89–91).

Choeum Rim is also happy with his work, both in terms of the satisfaction he receives from the products he makes and the congenial work environment. He continues:

> I work in a factory that makes furniture. I am a wood-polish person. . . . It is not a difficult job and the money is okay for this kind of work. Most of the people I work with are Cambodian. . . . It is a good group of people; there are many Cambodians and two black people and white people in the shop where I work. We get along. We make jokes . . . I enjoy the carpenter's job. I can see my own work become finished and see it become a beautiful object. . . . To be able to create something that people can use is very important. I do not mind the long hours because to work with my hands clears my head. To feel the wood with my hands is like being an artist. (Rim 1991: 90)

Choeum Rim's words reveal that even though Cambodians are from a country very different from the United States and have experienced horrors that few Americans can begin to imagine, in the end what they desire are very much the same things that all people want—the ability to feed, clothe, and shelter one's family, peace and safety in one's surroundings, satisfaction from the work one does, and a sense of connection with others in their communities.

Having parents who number among the working poor is hard on children. Soy Duong reveals how her family, which had been quite prosperous in Cambodia, managed to survive in Oregon and how the children were all expected to pitch in and earn and save money:

> The money that welfare gave us was not enough for all eight of us. . . . I remember that every time the supermarket had a sale on items such as chicken all eight of us went together to buy it. Because there were limits on . . . [how many of the sale] items you could purchase in these sales, . . . each of us [took] . . . turns going to a different cashier. . . . For clothes, we bought them from the second hand store. I have never had a brand new set of clothes. . . . Every time I saw cans and bottles I picked them up and took them home so that when there got to be a lot, I took them to the supermarket [to get a refund]. . . . every weekend, my sisters and cousins and I went out walking in the streets looking for cans. . . . In the summer, my family and I picked strawberries. Every morning we woke up at 3 o'clock, got ready, and drove our car . . . to the fields. . . . It was cold and chilly. With my body shaking, I knelt down on my knees and . . . was like a turtle which moves at a very slow pace. . . . Each pound of strawberries, I received 8 to 10 cents. By the time I went home, around 5 or 6 o'clock, my back was all bent and I couldn't stand up straight. My back ached and my legs were numb. On a rainy day, my clothes were all soaked. My feet were clogged with mud. . . . After the strawberry season was over, I picked blackberries. Picking blackberries does not require back work but it requires a lot of standing and thorn-touching. My fingers were all cut by scratches. It hurt very much, especially when the juice . . . got into the cuts. It felt like dipping my cut fingers into lemon juice, very painful. . . . When the summer was over, I went back to school. Going to school was great. (Duong 1990: 25–27)

Despite her family's struggle to survive, she did well enough in school to be admitted into the University of California, Santa Barbara. She concluded the autobiography she wrote in an Asian American studies class with these resounding words:

> I came to the United States with nothing . . . I started from scratch and have made it through to now . . . I have lived a harsh existence, I do not want my life to fall back into that lifestyle. I must work hard to be successful, I must

work hard to improve my life, and I must work hard to give myself a trophy for what I have gone through . . . I have nothing to give my family for all the troubles they had gone through . . . except to give them my diploma when I graduate from UCSB and then graduate school. . . . I am the only person in my family who is attending a university. . . . America has saved my life . . . I am grateful to the country and to its people. . . . I shall always honor [their] kindness. (Duong 1990: 30–31)

The Permanently Unemployed

In contrast to the working poor, who are determined to be self-reliant whatever difficulties they may encounter, those who have become a part of the permanently unemployed are found in the poorest sections of town and live among poverty-stricken African Americans or Latino Americans. Many who were placed into cities located in states with relatively generous welfare programs have become dependent on various forms of public assistance or welfare. In California, Massachusetts, Washington, and Minnesota in particular, a large number of Cambodians are trapped in a vicious cycle of welfare dependency, helplessness, hopelessness, and despair; they live in environments that are often filled with crime and violence.

In these states, voluntary agencies and other sponsors followed the path of least resistance and helped refugees apply for public assistance after the money provided by the Refugee Cash Assistance program ran out. The agencies were not purposely trying to create a refugee underclass. Rather, they were overwhelmed between 1979 and 1982 when refugees from Southeast Asia were pouring into the United States in far larger numbers than resettlement workers were prepared to handle and had no choice except to resettle each airplane load as expeditiously as possible. Anthropologist Aihwa Ong, however, has a less benign assessment of social service providers than I do. She maintains that "welfare policy . . . is not just structured positioning but also specific rationalities and techniques that overlap with or deploy pre-existing raced differentations. . . . Cambodian refugees were constituted as particular kinds of unworthy subjects." Following Foucault, she says that social services play a "role in governing less-powerful members of society" through punishment and pedagogy (Ong 2003: 124).

Preexisting arrangements for managing the poor enabled voluntary agencies to resettle refugees expeditiously. In large American metropolises, the cheapest and most run-down housing is usually found in inner cities, which is where the agencies rented blocks of apartment buildings, including subsidized units in federal housing projects, to house the new arrivals.

In the New York City borough of the Bronx, for example, almost all of the six thousand or so Cambodians live in about thirty tenement buildings located on about twenty streets. As Leah Melnick, a photographer, observes, "These buildings, which have seen generations of newcomers, are like miniature villages; neighbors go from apartment to apartment visiting each other, kids play in the courtyard outside, sarongs on clotheslines run between windows and the Khmer grocery stores are practically right downstairs. This has aided their ability to continue some of their cultural traditions, but has isolated them from interaction with the larger community" (Melnick 1990b: 5).

The voluntary agencies also helped refugees apply for financial assistance the day they arrived. Doing so freed the agency staff to take care of the next day's or next week's arrivals. The U.S. economy was in a deep recession in the early 1980s, and even had voluntary agencies wanted to it would have been very, very difficult to find jobs for Cambodian refugees, many of whom did not speak English and were also illiterate in their own language. Thus, without forethought for long-term consequences, the agencies placed refugees into the welfare-dependent stratum of American society, and many have not been able to extricate themselves. This group includes illiterate or minimally educated widows who have children but cannot afford child care even if they wanted to work, individuals who are physically disabled or psychologically too traumatized to work, and people who might have found work had they really tried but felt no pressure to get off welfare—at least before 1996.

The point is not that the more generous public assistance in certain states created a class of permanently unemployed among Cambodian refugees, but rather that the differential level of public assistance among the fifty states has acted as a sorting mechanism to separate those able and willing to work from those who cannot. Although the self-sufficient working poor are spread around the country, most of the unemployed and nonemployable are found in the larger cities of California, Massachusetts, Washington, and Minnesota.

To understand why certain Cambodians have suffered such a fate it is necessary to review how social welfare policies and programs in the United States help insert certain individuals, including refugees, into particular socioeconomic slots. Advanced industrialized countries usually provide a social safety net for their citizens. In the United States, that net has two aspects. The first consists of social insurance programs. A person's eligibility and compensation level for such insurance depends on past contributions, and benefit payments begin at stipulated times. The second consists of welfare or public assistance, which is a means-tested form of assistance based on need and financed from general revenues (taxes) rather than contributions from potential beneficiaries.

The 1935 Social Security Act provided for old-age pension and survivors' and disability insurance. An unemployment insurance program was also established in 1935, but, unlike social security, it is administered by the individual states even though its funding comes primarily from the federal government. The goal is to maintain income at a certain level, even when a worker is laid off or dies and leaves a family. Everyone in the United States over the age of five is assigned a social security number, and participation in the program is mandatory. In 1965, as part of President Lyndon B. Johnson's Great Society package, amendments to the 1935 act created Medicare and Medicaid, which provide medical assistance to people over sixty-five and indigents, respectively. Finally, Supplemental Security Income (SSI) payments became available to the disabled and aged in 1972.

Between 1935 and August 1996 the Aid to Families with Dependent Children (AFDC) program was the major component of welfare. It provided benefits to economically disadvantaged families with children who lacked support from one or both parents due to death, absence, or incapacity. Various kinds of assistance were available: child support, an allowance to cover the cost of child care, food stamps, and, in some instances, federal subsidized housing and assistance in paying energy bills. The eligibility criteria—the amount of cash assistance a family could receive and what mix of benefits it could expect—were determined by each individual state, and benefits varied greatly. Federal law, however, put constraints on a state's ability to terminate benefits on the basis of sanctions or time limits, which meant that AFDC was an entitlement program.

By 1991 AFDC had become the single most costly component of the nation's social safety net, paying out more than $20 billion in state and federal funds to about 4.6 million families a month. To stem the growth of the welfare budget, Congress passed the 1996 Personal Responsibility and Work Opportunity Reconciliation Act, which had bipartisan support to reform the welfare system. Henceforth, federal funds would be given as block grants to individual states, which can administer the funds as they see fit. The 1996 act was designed to change the "culture" of welfare. Temporary Assistance to Needy Families (TANF) replaced AFDC and imposed a lifetime five-year limit on the receipt of public assistance. States, however, can exempt 20 percent of their caseload from the five-year limit, so those who are the most hard-pressed would still be supported. More important, assistance now must be coupled with strong efforts by recipients to prepare themselves for work and find work. The strong emphasis on work is reflected in the names given various state programs. For example, California's TANF program is called Cal-WORKs (California Work Opportunity and Responsibility to Kids), and that in Washington state is called WorkFirst. To encourage people to work, families receiving support can now keep more of their earned income and accumulate more assets.

The 1996 act barred illegal aliens and immigrants from receiving SSI and food stamps and also prohibited immigrants who arrived after August 22, 1996, when welfare reform went into effect, from getting TANF or Medicaid. In response to outcries from advocates for the poor, however, as well as from many governors who feared their state budgets would be overtaxed after federal support for indigent noncitizens was withdrawn, Congress restored some benefits even though 1997 General Accounting Office studies showed that immigrants and recently naturalized citizens indeed used SSI, Medicaid, and TANF at higher rates than do U.S.-born citizens, as anti-immigrant groups have repeatedly alleged (U.S. General Accounting Office 1999: 2).

The 1997 Balanced Budget Act restored SSI eligibility to most non-citizens, and the 1998 Agricultural Research, Extension, and Education Reform Act restored food stamps to immigrants younger than sixteen and older than sixty-five who had arrived in the United States before August 22, 1996, or who, at whatever age, receive SSI for blindness or other disabilities. Most states also decided to continue providing TANF and Medicaid to "new" immigrants (that is, those who came after August 22, 1996), even after they have been in the United States for more than five years. Then, in January 2000, another amendment enabled people to continue receiving food stamps even if they own a car worth more than $4,650, so long as they use that car to get to work.

All these changes have had a profound impact on Cambodian refugees because so many of them receive public assistance. Cambodians on welfare have expressed very different feelings about it. Because patron-client relationships structure Cambodian society, some refugees may perceive their sponsors and the government as their new patrons in America and are not uneasy about accepting help from them. Phon Phan, for example, was greatly relieved to have such support: "I don't worry about anything . . . I am happy . . . the government helps support us . . . by giving us Welfare and SSI assistance, including children. . . . They want our children to be educated. . . . Our children go to school back and forth with free busing. . . . I never go out of my house. I sometimes just walk out . . . but not far away; and sometimes I just throw myself on the sofa and take a nap. . . . There is no stress or difficulty. . . . This is like living in heaven" (Cambodians in California Project, Phon interview 1989, 52: 30–31).

Others, however, regret not being able to repay their patrons or hosts. Nim Heang lost his sight when a Khmer Rouge soldier whipped him with a metal chain, hitting his face repeatedly while he was tied to a post. He, more than anyone else, has a right to receive SSI, yet he cringes at having to do so: "It is difficult to receive welfare because I don't have anything to pay back to this country. I came and ate and didn't go to school or work. I thought about it and got sad but my sponsor told me not to worry about food or sleep. I want to get off [welfare] very much but I can't because of my eyes. If I can see, I can get off welfare because I can work. I do not want to receive welfare even today. I want to work instead" (Cambodians in California Project, Nim interview 1989, 30: 17–18).

Contrary to popular belief, California does not pay out the highest amounts but ranks fourth, after Hawaii, Alaska, and Vermont. As the twenty-first century began, under the CalWORKs program a parent with one child receives $520 per month. The payment is $645 for a parent and two children, $768 for a parent with three children, $874 for a parent with four children, $981 for a parent with five children, $1,079 for a parent with six children, $1,175 for a parent with seven children, $1,260 for a parent with eight children, and $1,363 for a parent with nine children. The amount for families with more than nine children remains at the $1,363 ceiling (interview 2002 with official familiar with CalWORKs). Although given the state's high rents it is difficult to live on $520 a month, it is possible to survive if two or more families— each with, say, three or four children—pool their resources and share rent by squeezing themselves into the same apartment or house, as many Cambodian refugees do in localities where no ordinances restrict the number of persons allowed to occupy a residential unit.

In the past, one reason welfare recipients gave for not trying to find a job was that they would lose eligibility for Medicaid once they started working, a loss that single mothers with children, or sickly refugees in particular, absolutely could not afford given the exorbitant cost of medical care in the United States. Many refugees learned about this quirk in the law the hard way. Moeun Nhu of Stockton found a job washing dishes at a Red Lobster restaurant but decided to quit when assistance was cut off after it was discovered that he was working too many hours: "Some days—worked overtime. . . . Then the welfare office sent me a letter stating that they would discontinue medical and cash aid. They stopped helping because I worked one month over a hundred hours. They only allow sixty hours. . . . Therefore, I stopped working" (Cambodians in California Project, Moeun interview 1989, 8: 19).

To deal with the problem caused by that rule, Congress passed the Ticket to Work and Work Incentives Improvement Act in 1999 to allow people with disabilities (but not able-bodied people) to retain their Medicaid coverage indefinitely, even after they return to work. Now, California residents who do not qualify for any other medical assistance can turn to the Medically Indigent Adult program for help. Even after five years of public assistance, the disabled and individuals over sixty-five will not be left entirely destitute because they will still be eligible for SSI, food stamps, and Medicaid. Moreover, when the five-year limit is reached, only adults are removed from the welfare rolls; children can continue to receive assistance until the age of eighteen.

For indigent and unemployable Cambodians in the United States, the crux of the dilemma is that many have not looked for work, or they were fired because they could not learn even the most rudimentary English despite their best efforts. For example, when Leang Eng first arrived she was hired as a maid in a hotel, but her experience was so exasperating that she quit after three months and never tried to find a job again: "They let me study but I didn't learn anything. My brain was too confused and mixed up . . . they let me work in the hotel . . . I only worked for three months . . . When they [guests] spoke to me, I didn't understand. . . . They put the sign on the door that said DO NOT DISTURB and I did not know [what it meant]. I knocked and they said something to me but I didn't understand" (Cambodians in California Project, Leang interview 1989, 1: 16–17).

Because some Cambodians never learned English, they find it impossible to hold even those jobs that supposedly require little knowledge of the language. It is therefore understandable, from the point of view of caseworkers, that helping refugees such as Mrs. Leang fill out application forms for public assistance is the most expedient thing for voluntary agencies to do. Certainly, it takes far less effort than finding an effective way to teach her English or train her for a job she can handle. Even though unemployed refugees live in poverty, life in America still seems better than in wartorn Cambodia. What no one foresaw, of course, was that a day would come when a limit would be imposed on how long individuals can receive welfare benefits.

Even before welfare reform became a reality, many Cambodians agonized over their lot. The desperation Bith Sann felt because he could not remember even a few words of English is clear even in translation:

I try to learn . . . I couldn't. Allow my children to teach me, I still couldn't do it. Couldn't, couldn't, couldn't. Why I couldn't remember, my brain . . . I used to, in the temple, remember how many monks were present, how many times they chanted and what they chanted, I knew and remember all. I didn't forget . . . I never forget. But now if you recite ten words or one hundred words to me, I remember only one word. . . . I'm in panic. . . . That is why they call me mute . . . I don't know their language, I'm dead. That's why I'm willing to admit I almost go insane, almost insane. . . . My words have no meaning. I would rather die . . . poor people like me, very poor. (Cambodians in California Project, Bith interview 1989, 58: 30–33)

He is not alone in his despair. Fate has not been kind to Cambodians, not even those who were resettled in the proverbial land of opportunity. Those who can support themselves economically still face countless challenges as they attempt to find their way through the maze created by the constant clash between the cultural values and norms of Cambodia and those of America.

5   Negotiating Cultures

BECAUSE THE United States is a nation of immigrants, American scholars have long been interested in how immigrants adapt to life in their new home. For decades scholars used an "assimilation" paradigm to chart newcomers' progress. They assumed that immigrants will gradually discard the cultures of their countries of origin as they adopt American values and behavior. The "melting pot" was a handy metaphor that supposedly captured the essence of this process. Since the 1960s, however, scholars have observed that assimilation is neither unilinear nor monolithic and have proposed new metaphors, such as the "salad bowl," to characterize as well as promote the desirability of a pluralistic society.

Equally important, scholars now recognize that "culture" is not an essentialist, bounded, unchanging phenomenon; rather, it is something that individuals and groups constantly construct and reconstruct as they interact with others. The current scholarly thinking is that instead of assimilating in an unproblematic manner (i.e., discarding an undying, unitary old culture and adopting an unchanging, homogeneous new one), what people actually do is negotiate among different cultures that are in flux. In everyday discourse, however, most people still treat "culture" as a reified phenomenon. For that reason, I will use quotation marks around "Cambodian culture," "Khmer culture," and "American culture" to signify the contested and shifting meaning of those terms.

Cambodian Refugees and Social Science Theories

To understand how studies of Cambodians in America fit the intellectual genealogy of immigrant studies in general and Asian American studies in particular, it is useful to survey briefly the conceptual lenses that researchers have used to perceive Asian immigrants and their offspring. Scholars in several disciplines have been keenly interested in "assimilation" and "ethnic identity," but they have differed with regard to which aspects of those phenomena should be emphasized. In decades past, historians and political scientists focused mainly on how an American national identity (in contrast to specific ethnic identities) was formed, while social scientists were more concerned about how individuals and groups, even as they became Americanized, developed ethnic identities.

As historian Philip Gleason and Hans Kohn, a political scientist, pointed out, American national identity has been based more on ideological principles than on common ethnic or cultural origins—the major principles being liberty, equality, and republicanism (Gleason 1980; Kohn 1957). The Founders stressed ideology because they wished to distinguish themselves from the British against whom they rebelled but with whom they shared a common language and culture. Moreover, because other Europeans, Africans, and Native Americans also inhabited the territory that became the United States, a common language, culture, or religion could not be used as the foundation for an American national identity.

Although liberty, equality, and republicanism were framed as universal principles, in reality not everyone in the United States has enjoyed them. Before 1870, only "free, white persons" could become naturalized citizens. Those immigrants who could not be naturalized were denied the franchise and, hence, participation in electoral politics—the essence of a republican form of government. Persons of African ancestry were not given the right of naturalization until 1870; Asian immigrants did not receive that right until 1943 (for Chinese), 1946 (for Filipinos and Asian Indians), and 1952 (for Japanese and Koreans). In myriad other ways, nonwhite people as well as Catholics, Jews, Mormons, Quakers, and (more recently) Muslims have been discriminated against during much of the nation's history and denied full membership in the American polity.

In contrast to historians and political scientists—who have attempted to delineate the contours of a distinctive American national identity—psychologists, sociologists, and anthropologists have been more interested in how newcomers change values and behaviors as they attempt to fit into the American mold. Values and norms are components of culture, which is often defined as "a way of life." Although some anthropologists now shy away from the term *culture* altogether and prefer to "problematize" it and employ it only in its adjectival form ("cultural"), scholars in other fields less concerned with anthropology's internal debates continue to use the word to refer to how people perceive the natural and social world; how they explain and justify certain patterns of social relationships and actions; how they socialize the young by teaching them what members of that culture consider to be good, beautiful, and true; how they enforce the behavior considered appropriate for individuals, depending on their sex, age, and ascribed or achieved status; how they determine the criteria to be used to differentiate members of the in-group from outsiders; and how they deal with transitions and crises, whether individual or collective, natural or humanmade.

A convergence has occurred since the 1990s among scholars in various disciplines as social scientists have begun to analyze ethnic phenomena diachronically and in an ethnically inclusive way. Ruben Rumbaut and Alejandro Portes, for example, now use "ethnogenesis"—the construction and *evolution* (emphasis added) of American ethnicity—as a framework. Instead of focusing primarily on the changes that individual immigrants, and the particular groups to which they belong, undergo, their unit of analysis is now the American nation. Moreover, instead of looking only at the immigration of Europeans they also consider the "enslavement, annexation, and conquest" of Africans, Mexicans, and Native Americans, respectively, as "originating processes by which American ethnicities were formed and through which, over time, the United States was transformed into one of the world's most ethnically diverse societies" (Rumbaut and Portes 2001: 4). My use of gerunds in the chapter titles of this volume signals the current stress on process and flux.

With regard to Asian immigrants and their descendants, over the course of the twentieth century sociologists Robert E. Park, Ernest W. Burgess, Milton Gordon, Won Moo Hurh, Kwang Chung Kim, Alejandro Portes, Min Zhou, and Yen Le Espiritu and anthropologists Margaret A. Gibson, Aihwa Ong, and Lydia Breckon have proposed important concepts to further understanding of the cultural transformations that Asian immigrants experience as they confront life in American society while maintaining ties to their homelands.

In 1921 Park and Burgess defined "assimilation" as "a process of interpenetration and fusion in which persons and groups acquire the memories, sentiments, and attitudes of other persons or groups." Park then formulated a "race relations cycle" to describe the four successive stages of interaction between immigrants and members of the host society: contact, conflict, accommodation, and assimilation. Park himself realized that this model did not seem applicable to "Negroes" and "Orientals," who were forced to wear what he called a "racial uniform" (1923, 1926). Before the 1970s, however, social scientists made little attempt to investigate how this "racial uniform" constricted the lives of racial minorities. When they did study the issue they focused almost entirely on the experience of African Americans and only incidentally on Asian Americans.

In 1964 Gordon refined the concept of assimilation by identifying its seven variants: (1) acculturation—also called "cultural" or "behavioral" assimilation (when newcomers adopt the cultural patterns of the host society); (2) structural assimilation (when immigrants can enter the major institutions of the host society at the primary-group level); (3) marital assimilation (when people marry individuals of different ethnic, racial, or religious origins); (4) identificational assimilation (when immigrants identify with the host society); (5) attitude receptional assimilation (when immigrants encounter no prejudice from members of the host society); (6) behavior receptional assimilation (when newcomers face no discrimination in the host society); and (7) civic assimilation (when there are no power conflicts between immigrants and members of the host society). Gordon's major contribution is a scheme that explicitly recognizes the fact that whether or not immigrants assimilate is not entirely up to them. They can do so only if members of the host society accept them in various ways (Gordon 1964).

In 1984 Hurh and Kim coined the term *adhesive adaptation* to describe how Korean immigrants simultaneously retain Korean cultural norms *and* adopt selected aspects of American behavior in order to function effectively in the United States (Hurh and Kim 1984). In a 1988 study Gibson pointed to a similar phenomenon among Punjabi immigrants from India and called their behavior "accommodation without assimilation" (Gibson 1988).

In a seminal article, Portes and Zhou (1993), writing about the "new second generation" (children of immigrants who have come to the United States since 1965, when Congress liberalized American immigration law) coined the term *segmented assimilation* to refer to the fact that young immigrants no longer assimilate into a single "American culture" but rather show three different "modes of incorporation." The first mode is acculturation and integration into the European American middle class. The second mode refers to acculturation and integration into the largely nonwhite underclass. The third identifies a strategy that some immigrants adopt in their pursuit of rapid economic advancement. They rely on ethnic solidarity and do everything possible to preserve their cultures of origin (Portes and Zhou 1993). Other scholars have since elaborated on this tripartite scheme by using data from a large variety of ethnic groups (Fernandez-Kelly and Schauffler 1996; Portes and Rumbaut 2001a, 2001b; Rumbaut 1996; Rumbaut and Portes 2001; Zhou and Bankston 1996).

Also during the 1990s, anthropologists introduced transnationalism as a framework for understanding the experiences of "transmigrants"—people who move from one country to another in this age of globalization but retain on-going relationships with people and institutions in two or more countries (Appadurai 1991; Basch, Schiller, and Blanc 1994; Gupta 1992; Ong and Nonini eds. 1997; Takacs 1999). Among Asian American scholars, sociologist Yen Le Espiritu uses transnationalism as a "heuristic device" to make sense of how Filipino Americans live and perceive themselves, but she does not "wish to overstate the frequency of Filipino transnational activities." Among the Filipinos she interviewed in San Diego, she found that most "do not live in transnational 'circuits.' . . . Their lived reality . . . is primarily local." She notes, however, that transnationalism also takes place "at the symbolic level—at the level of imagination, shared memory, and 'inventions of tradition.'" It is mainly at this level that Filipino Americans can be said to lead a transnational existence. Espiritu cautions that "transnationalism must be understood as a contradictory process—one that has the potential to break down borders and traditions and create new cultures and hybrid ways of life but also to fortify traditional hierarchies, homogenize diverse cultural practices, and obscure intragroup differences and differential relationships. . . . transnationalism is at best a compromise—a 'choice' made and lived in a context of scarce options" (2003: 213–14).

In a study of Cambodians in San Francisco and Oakland, anthropologist Aihwa Ong analyzes another kind of contradiction. Relying heavily on the theoretical notions proposed by Michel Foucault, particularly "govermentability," she looks at their experiences through the lens of "citizenship" and observes that although American government officials, social workers, health professionals, law enforcement officers, religious leaders, and employers all urge Cambodian refugees to aspire to become self-reliant and individualistic Americans, in reality American society limits their ability to achieve such a goal (even if they desired it, which many do not) by constraining their options on account of race, ethnicity, and, in the case of women, gender. Ong dissects the dual processes of "being made" and "self-making" as Cambodians absorb and deflect the various lessons they are taught by those who seek to resocialize them (Ong 2003). She explains that "the processes of being made and self-making do not entail a simple opposition of hegemonic American culture and minority culture, but rather a reworking of the tensions between paternalistic compassion and self-reliance, spiritual discipline and racial subordination. . . . This interlacing of assimilation and self-invention always bears the traces of cultural loss" (197).

Lydia Breckon also uses a transnational framework to study Cambodians in Fall River, Massachusetts, but her analysis is less critical and nuanced than those of Espiritu and Ong:

> Cambodians have not "re-settled" in the U.S. at all. Instead they have settled into changeable and transnational lives that link them with Cambodia as well as France, Canada, and Australia. . . . Khmer-Americans travel to and from Khmer "hub-cities" such as Lowell, Massachusetts and Long Beach, California, and to "mainstream" arenas for work, school and residence. . . . Travel along these routes also leads to the Khmer past, to an idealized Khmer culture, to memory. . . . the symbolic processes of imagination, interpretation and representation cannot be separated from movements of capital, physical force, labor, coercion. . . . The reshaping of lives and the redistribution of resources involves [sic] a complex interplay of ideational and material processes. (Breckon 1999: 1, 3)

The main avenues through which Cambodians in America create transnational networks include sending cash remittances to relatives in Cambodia; sending and receiving letters, videotapes, audiotapes, newspapers, and magazines; and traveling to their natal country to visit, choose marriage partners, attend weddings and funerals, set up business ventures, and, for the politically minded, engage in politics (Breckon 1999: 99–135).

In my view, Breckon's analysis is too voluntaristic. She depicts refugees as having more choices than they actually do. Most Cambodians came to the United States out of dire necessity. Although those who arrived as adults do not have strong motivation to adopt America as their new home, they cannot easily "go home" to Cambodia, either, for it is still mired in poverty and political instability. Those who return there to live face daunting challenges. Consequently, some returnees ultimately come back to the United States, where economic survival may be difficult but is still possible. Individuals not completely "at home" in either land end up with their bodies on American soil and their hearts and minds in Cambodia or other places where their loved ones dwell. Developing a transnational identity and lifestyle, therefore, may not be so much the result of a conscious choice as an existential necessity by default.

Moreover, Cambodians who are unemployed and cannot speak English lead rather isolated lives, and their intercultural encounters are relatively limited. Although the better-educated and gainfully employed interact with a wider spectrum of the host society, some do so mainly for pragmatic reasons. That is, they follow an adhesive adaptation pattern, learning only what is needed for survival, but they do so within a transnational context. People, institutions, and events in Cambodia—past, present, and future—continue to be their main reference points, but such connectedness is fraught with ambiguity. As Breckon astutely observes, "Transnational connections for Khmer refugees in the United States are as much about widening and deepening the distance between American and Cambodian Khmer, and between the past and the present, as they are about bridging them" (1994: 103). That is so because some Cambodians now living outside of Cambodia do not support the existing government and are critical of certain social and political practices, such as corruption and violence, that pervade everyday life in that country. Thus they distance themselves from Cambodia as it exists at present or as it existed in the recent past. To many of Breckon's respondents, Cambodia is a "much beloved but presently inaccessible, irretrievable place" (112).

Still, what matters most to a vast majority of Cambodians, regardless of their socioeconomic status, is the urgent need to preserve—indeed, to revive—"Cambodian culture" as they remember and idealize it. They dedicate themselves to that task more assiduously than other immigrants do because the Khmer Rouge so methodically destroyed the most important institutions of pre-1975 Cambodian society. Virtually every Cambodian old enough to remember what happened feels a strong moral obligation to recover what was almost lost. Even though "Khmerness" or "Khmer culture" is itself in flux, that fact does not stop Cambodians in the United States and the rest of the world from trying to reconstruct an ideal as they remember it or as they wish it to be. For that reason, the "Khmer culture" that Cambodians who live outside Cambodia are trying to preserve may be more reified and essentialized than the cultural forms evolving within Cambodia itself.

Religion as an Arena of Cultural Negotiation

How Cambodians try to negotiate cultures is most clearly seen in the way they respond to efforts to convert them to Christianity. Because religion is such an important component of any culture's belief system, conversion to another religion often represents a decisive break with other aspects of the convert's culture of origin as well. Such, however, is not the case for Cambodians, because most of them have a more ecumenical attitude toward religion than do Christians. The latter tend to think that different faiths are incompatible and cannot or should not be adhered to at the same time. For Christians, anyone who converts to their religion must give up all prior religious affiliations and practices. Khmer Buddhists, in contrast, are more accepting of other creeds.

Because a vast majority of Cambodians are Theravada Buddhists, it is important to summarize that faith's basic tenets. The Buddha—Prince Siddhattha Gotama (also transliterated as Siddhartha Gautama)—preached that there are Four Noble Truths: suffering is an inherent part of the life of all sentient beings; suffering is caused by craving for or attachment to the things and persons of this world; suffering can and does cease when one attains nirvana (which literally means "blowing out," an extinction not of the self but of the fires of greed, hatred, delusion, yearning, and lust); and all who follow the way of the Buddha—called the Middle Path or the Eightfold Path—have the potential to reach nirvana. Nirvana is a quality that can be realized while a sentient being is alive; it is not a place (like the heaven of Christianity) where one goes after death. "Eightfold Path" refers to correct understanding, intention, speech, conduct, means of livelihood, effort, mindfulness, and concentration. By following these paths, people can conduct themselves ethically, develop their mental capacities, and eventually attain wisdom.

Theravada Buddhists believe that the best way to improve one's karma (*kam* in Khmer)—the law of cause and effect, of action and its consequences—is to "make merit" by giving food and clothing to monks and money to the *wat* (temples). Despite the fact that Theravada Buddhism is doctrinally austere, in practice it is a truly communal religion that helps adherents cope with the problems of everyday life. During festive celebrations that mark important events, floral arrangements adorn wat compounds, and people carrying lighted candles join processions, burn incense in front of Buddha's statues, listen to monks chant for hours on end the story of Buddha's life, and bring all kinds of food to share with everyone. Moreover, the Buddhism practiced by Cambodians and other mainland Southeast Asians is syncretic. Selected aspects of Hinduism, Buddhism, and indigenous Khmer animistic beliefs and rituals are combined in such a fashion that it is not contradictory to juxtapose them (Ebihara 1966). Such syncretism, however, often poses a problem for Cambodians who convert to Christianity.

Cambodian Christians in the United States convert for different reasons and approach their new faith in different ways. They include people who add

Christianity to their rather diffuse religious orientation, others who convert to Christianity because they think it serves their personal needs better than Buddhism can, and individuals who repudiate Buddhism because, in their view, it had failed their nation both morally and politically.

Christianity was one of the first aspects of "American culture" to influence Cambodian refugees because many individuals who rushed to the Thai-Cambodian border to help them were "good Christians" who believed in alleviating the suffering of other human beings. Some of those volunteers set up churches in UNHCR holding centers as soon as they arrived. Although camp residents were never forced to attend church services, some did so because they thought it was the polite thing to do. When Tep Nhim was asked why she went to church at Khao I Dang, she responded, "Because the United Nations [sic] had a church, and we lived under their support; that's why we had to join them. There's an old proverb that says, 'Wherever you live you must follow the society.' So, I just joined them, including my children" (Cambodians in California Project, Tep interview 1989, 5: 9).

Many refugees who attended church services within the camps, however, also went to Buddhist temples. They saw no contradiction in doing so, because religion in Cambodia has long been syncretist. People comfortably amalgamate beliefs and rituals from several traditions. To Cambodians, Christianity need not replace Buddhism but can be another accretion to their multifaceted belief system. Refugees were exposed to even more Christians after they arrived in the United States, because many voluntary agencies are affiliated with either the Catholic Church or with various Protestant denominations; an overwhelming number of families who stepped forward as sponsors were Christians.

In the United States even more so than in UNHCR holding centers in Thailand, many refugees who go to church have an easy-going, nonexclusionary attitude toward religion. Nim Heang, a former peasant, reported, "I'm in two religions. Sometimes I go to American church . . . later I go to my Khmer religion. . . . There is nothing that differs. Christianity leads people to do good, not to kill or steal or rob from others and in Khmer religion it's the same, not to kill humans, or steal and rob from others. They are the same because there is one God in the world" (Cambodians in California Project, Nim interview 1989, 30: 19). Vann Keo, who also has rural origins, likewise saw no contradiction in the way she has integrated Buddhism and Christianity in her life: "I go to Buddhist temple and sometimes go to church, I am never prejudiced towards others. I never think of caste or status of any kind.

My mind is very clear and clean. I love everything" (Cambodians in California Project, Vann interview 1989, 35: 12).

Some refugees became Christians for social rather than doctrinal reasons. They wanted to show appreciation to their sponsors and gain whatever material advantage that church attendance might bring. As recounted by JoAn Criddle, a small Lutheran Church congregation sponsored the family of Mearadey, Teeda Butt Mam's eldest sister, which had five members. The other eight members of the extended family were sponsored privately by five couples who belong to the Church of Jesus Christ of Latter-day Saints (Mormons). Mearadey explains why her family was baptized: "When we joined the Lutheran Church, Ken and I understood that the baptism ceremony had a religious dimension. To us, however, joining was a way to thank our sponsors for their help. It was a way to fit in. Other refugees had already told us that joining a sponsor's church made them happy. It could help us to learn English and be part of the American community" (Criddle 1992: 190).

A dilemma arose when the family members sponsored by the Mormon couples also decided to become Christians. Torn by conflicting loyalties, they wanted to join the same Lutheran denomination that Mearadey had joined but did not want to hurt the feelings of their Mormon sponsors. Fortunately, they got up the courage to tell both sets of sponsors about the bind they were in. They were greatly relieved when their Mormon sponsors said it would be all right if they chose to become Lutherans. Like her sister, Teeda also converted out of a strong sense of obligation. Moreover, Christianity did not seem all that strange to her. As she explained to JoAn Criddle:

> In Cambodia friendship and other relationships are based on the exchange of favors. We want to do nice things for people who have been thoughtful or helpful to us; it is a way to honor them. . . . In America, we always tried to go to church. It showed respect to our sponsors. Before we got baptized, the pastor came to our house like he had done for Mearaday's family. He read us stories from the Bible . . . To us they were just stories; we never got the concept that they were meant to give us a belief in Christ. . . . In our culture, we also have many myths and legends that explain how the world started and what happens to good people and bad people. . . . Bible stories seemed similar. (Criddle 1992: 195)

A second group of refugees converted because Christianity satisfied their personal needs better than Buddhism, even though they did not see a great deal of difference between the two. Pal Ron, who never went to school, felt that the Christian God, to whom she was introduced while in the Phanat Nikhom Refugee Processing Center in Chonburi, had truly answered her prayers:

> Before, I was Buddhist. I am Christian now. In my opinion, they are not that different. It's just that in one you chant the prayers and in the other you sing. But they all pray to God. Buddhists also pray to God, only they have monks. Christians don't have monks, don't use incense and candles—these are the only differences. . . . Why do I believe? . . . during my period of hardship, I learned to pray as others have done—pray to God to provide for me in my times of hardship: "Oh, God, please help me. I am so miserable, in need of so much, in dire poverty." . . . I have no relatives in America who can help me out. There are only two of us, mother and child. After I prayed, there were people who felt sorry for me, some gave me a little bit of this, others gave me a little bit of that. . . . people kept on giving. That's why I said, this God is true. (Cambodians in California Project, Pal interview 1989, 26: 3–4)

Felicia Keo (chapter 4) found comfort in Christianity because Christians believe that their sins can be forgiven. The notion of finding salvation by being forgiven is quite different from the Theravada Buddhist tenet that says individuals bear full responsibility for all their actions. Because the sins of Buddhists can only be counteracted in the next life by making merit in this one, Buddhism does not offer its believers the possibility of instantaneous redemption. Christianity gives hope to Cambodians who feel weighted down by earthly burdens and allows them to think they can start life afresh. As Keo observed:

> Southeast Asian people don't know anything about God. . . . we are so far away from God. So, [when] a person comes to share the news and tells us about God . . . we must kneel down. . . . God will forgive us. God will bless us. . . . We must kneel down to be forgiven for what we have done in the past. We have had sin since our forefathers: Adam and Eve. . . . God always forgives us. Whatever we had done wrong will be finished. God loves all human beings on earth. Therefore, he had arranged the plan to have Jesus Christ born on earth. And let him die on the cross. It was to wash away our sins. It was to save us. (Cambodians in California Project, F. Keo interview 1989, 39: 21–23)

Christianity has filled other kinds of personal needs in ways that most Americans would not have thought of. These needs arise not out of any desire for individual salvation but rather out of desperation, because many Cambodian parents think they must find ways to control their children now growing up in the United States. These parents, based on what they see on television and in the host society around them, perceive American teenagers as "bad." They particularly disapprove of the lack of respect on the part of American children toward parents and other elders, as evinced in their habit of "talking back" to older people. They also strongly disapprove of sexual promiscuousness among members of the host society. To them, even behavior that Americans consider quite innocent, such as pubescent boys and girls spending time together in various kinds of extracurricular activities, touching each other while they play, or teasing each another, are all forms of sexual permissiveness they find unacceptable. Many Cambodian parents, especially less-educated ones, try their best to minimize their children's contact with youngsters who serve as carriers of such corrosive influences.

So even though they may be Buddhists and would like their children to follow the same religion, Cambodian parents often allow Christian proselytizers to visit their homes because they consider doing so as one more way to keep the children at home. As a respondent in Modesto, California, whom Susan L. Holgate interviewed explained, "Now there is a widespread home-teach movement. My own children receive this teaching and learn about the church every Saturday when they come to our house to teach the children. . . . I feel that by allowing them to play outside and be with the other kids, they will learn some bad things, even worse than [what] they learn from the church" (Holgate 1994: 163).

The third group of Christians among Cambodian refugees, who are generally more educated, tend to see a linkage between religion and politics. They credit Christianity for the prosperity the United States enjoys, and they blame the absence of the Christian faith in Cambodia for the tragedy that befell their ancestral land. According to Lor Kin Naren, a college-educated former teacher from Phnom Penh:

> I am [a] Christian now. . . . I learned in the Bible that I have to believe in God so I can live forever. . . . when I practiced Buddhism I didn't know what Buddhism was. I just went to the ceremony with everybody else . . . we are living in God's country now. . . . I realized that this country is progressive because they believe in Jesus Christ. That's why I've given myself to God for Him to prepare me for everlasting life. . . . Cambodia was destroyed because of bad people, people who did not listen to God. . . . Jesus Christ died on earth for all our sins. . . . Now I spread the word of God, so the word of God [can] come to people who don't yet believe . . . so that they can have happiness . . . in this life and the life to come. (Cambodians in California Project, Lor interview 1989, 7: 23–24)

Hong Sary, who had twelve years of schooling—a rare accomplishment among Cambodian women—saw a similar linkage between Christianity and the well-being of Americans: "I believed in Buddhism since I was young. . . . [but] the country [Cambodia] has been corrupted. I see that in this country they believe in God. They are all happy, and the country improves a lot. . . . I changed religion so that I would receive all good results and happiness in the future" (Cambodians in California Project, Hong interview 1989, 21: 30).

Patrick Keo, Felicia's husband, who became such a devout convert that he quit his job in order to spread God's word full time, explained how he thought Cambodia and its people could attain salvation:

> The reason why God does not let our country be peaceful is because we do not believe in God. So, if each Cambodian has God in his heart, Cambodia will have no problem at all. Then God will bless us and let us live peacefully. . . . God will give us the better things in life. Like other countries which God has blessed. America is an example. The great grandparents of Americans in the past came to seek God. They worshipped God. God blessed them to be a healthier and richer country. Now America is the richest country in the world. . . . Our people didn't have love from the Bible; therefore, Cambodia was corrupted. (Cambodians in California Project, P. M. Keo interview 1989, 43: 49, 51)

According to anthropologist Nancy J. Smith-Hefner, who has done extensive ethnographic research in the Boston area, the Cambodians who have converted to Christianity for truly religious (rather than merely social or political) reasons tend to join evangelical denominations. Six Khmer congregations, each with eighty to a hundred members, are located in eastern Masachusetts. In the Cambridge area there are the Revere Evangelical Church, the Lynn Southern Baptist Church, and the Tremont Temple Southern Baptist Church, and, in Lowell, the Lowell Cambodian Baptist Church, the Elliot Presbyterian Church, and the New Jerusalem Evangelical Church. There are also Catholic and Lutheran congregations, but they are smaller (Smith-Hefner 1994: 35, 27). Members of the more evangelical congregations apparently have made a strong commitment to religious orthodoxy, and they inveigh strongly against the sins of drinking alcohol, smoking tobacco, and engaging in premarital or extramarital sex. Often, Khmer pastors and their flocks are even more orthodox than the American pastors who have mentored them. The strong family values that such churches promote resonate well with the Khmer emphasis on maintaining enduring family ties.

Smith-Hefner also notes that in addition to being attracted to the notion of redemption, some Cambodian Christian converts may be lured by the possibility of a "new structure of status and prestige outside the mainstream Khmer community"—that is, a hierarchy based on Christianity and its linkage to the dominant group in the United States (1994: 32). Churches have a lot of young members who enjoy the weekly youth fellowship programs and other social activities. Parents who can afford to do so send their children to private, Christian schools and strongly encourage them to go to college. Because they tend to be ostracized by Buddhists, some Christian families are distancing themselves from fellow Khmer and interacting more with members of the host society. In short, converting to Christianity and participating in the church's myriad social institutions is increasingly becoming an important channel for upward mobility in American society. Aihwa Ong pinpoints another reason that some Cambodians have converted to Christianity, specifically its Mormon variant: "Many of the converts found special comfort in the Mormon belief in the continuity of family units in the afterlife. . . . [The] Mormon ritual of proxy baptism that allows young converts to become living substitutes for dead souls . . . was . . . meaningful because many Cambodian refugees were unable to return and find the bones of loved ones in order to give them a proper burial. In this way, proxy baptism became an alternative practice to Theravada Buddhist customs commemorating the reciprocal relations between the living and the dead" (Ong 2003: 208).

Some refugees, however, resent the pressure that Christians put on them. Dr. Bunroeun Thach, an outspoken Khmer Krom intellectual whose views are sometimes controversial, expressed such resentment quite clearly:

If you're a refugee or homeless, you become very oppressed and feel degraded. You feel unwanted and lonely and unnoticed. And so you try to reach out, you feel like you're in the middle of the river or something, you try to reach anything that you can hold onto. This is where the Christian groups come in. . . . When I escaped from Cambodia to Thailand, as soon as I arrived there, the first thing they handed me was a Bible, not food. . . . we have over two thousand years of history, two thousand years of civilization. Who are these Christians who came here giving us the Bible? Don't they know we have our own literature, our own great authors, great civilization? . . . Our survival was at stake. You came and put pressure on us in the refugee camps. When we got to the U.S., we were also under a lot of pressure. (Thach interview 1996 in Chan, ed. 2003a: 266–67)

In Oakland, California, where an estimated eight thousand Cambodians lived in the early 1990s (there is no separate figure for Oakland in the 2000 census because it is part of a metropolitan statistical area that also includes San Francisco and San Jose), some community leaders began complaining about the proselytizing tactics of the local Mormon temple when its missionaries became too aggressive. Every week, Mormon missionaries knocked on doors in the large apartment complexes where Cambodian refugees lived, asking if they could come in to discuss their religion. According to Jack Cheevers, a reporter for the *Oakland Tribune,* "Refugees who express interest are showered with free groceries, used furniture and clothing, English classes and other services." When criticized by community leaders for taking advantage of their compatriots' desperate need for social services, a Mormon spokesperson declared, "If we felt we were hurting people more than we were helping, we would withdraw. . . . [but] we're not going to back off because some other person with another cause says he wants to corner the market" (Cheevers 1986).

The "some other person" to whom he was referring were Cambodian community leaders, who charged that the ethnic community's ability to raise sufficient funds to expand the existing Buddhist temple in Oakland was being undermined by the eight hundred Cambodians who had been converted to Mormonism tithing a tenth of their earnings to the Church of Jesus Christ of Latter-day Saints.

The incident that most angered Oakland's Cambodians occurred in 1986, when Mormons entered an apartment where an engagement party was in progress and declared that the ceremony could not continue because the woman had been baptized as a Mormon but her fiance had not. They later whisked the woman off to an unknown destination, causing her mother severe concern. A lawyer representing the Mormons defended his group's actions by claiming that she was being "forced into a marriage against her will" (Cheevers 1986).

Despite such occasional high-pressure tactics, only an estimated 10 to 15 percent of Cambodians in America have adopted variants of the Christian faith. That is a far smaller conversion rate than among other groups of Southeast Asian refugees. An estimated 50 percent of the Hmong in the United States, for example, are now Christians. A vast majority of Cambodians have resisted conversion because their belief in Theravada Buddhism is strong. To most Khmer, Buddhism is not just a religion but an entire way of life. As they put it, "To be Khmer is to be Buddhist." For them, upholding Buddhism is fundamental to the preservation of "Cambodian culture." Even though many average people do not have deep understanding of the complexities of Theravada Buddhist doctrine, the religion's rituals punctuate their lives, and its moral guidelines shape their daily behavior. Thus, to many Cambodians, individuals who convert to Christianity are abandoning not just their religion but the other facets of "Khmer culture" as well.

Because the Khmer Rouge had so savagely uprooted Buddhism, and because Cambodian refugees were so in need of solace, one of the first things they did after arriving in the United States was to set up temples, however modest. Among Theravada Buddhists, it is the local people who raise funds to construct buildings or rent space for temples and who are responsible for finding monks to serve them. Initially in America that was difficult to accomplish, not only because the refugees had no money but also because so many monks perished. The small number who did escape the "killing fields" because they were out of the country during the DK period, or who otherwise managed to survive the Khmer Rouge devastation, have played a critical role in reviving Buddhism, both within Cambodia and among Cambodians scattered around the world. Senior Thai Theravada Buddhist monks have aided in this effort and helped ordain new monks or re-ordain former monks whom the Khmer Rouge defrocked. Cambodians had to depend on the Thai because so few Khmer senior monks survived the Pol Pot period. Buddhists in many countries have also helped by supplying copies of key texts to the reconstructed or newly built temples, because the Khmer Rouge destroyed all the Buddhist scriptures they could.

In Cambodian communities in the United States, even though temples have been established (often in existing buildings whose exteriors give no hint of their function), it has been difficult to retain some Theravada Buddhist practices. Monks in America no longer go door to door to beg for food every morning, as Theravada Buddhist monks do in Sri Lanka, Burma, Thailand, Laos, and Cambodia. In the United States, laypeople bring food to the temples for the monks' morning meal. (They cannot eat after the noon hour.) Some of the food comes cooked, and some is prepared for the monks by devout older women who also clean the temples and the quarters where the monks live. In some small communities where temples are located in outlying areas, however, it is not always possible for laypeople to feed the monks, so the latter sometimes have to prepare their own meals—which they are not supposed to do. Also, due to cold weather, monks in America have to wear sweaters or jackets on top of their saffron robes and put on socks and shoes rather than walk barefoot or wear open-toed sandals. Many drive cars, go shopping, and handle money even though monks are not to handle money at all.

Perhaps even more important, certain ceremonies are held whenever temples are built in Theravada Buddhist Southeast Asian countries, and stones must be blessed and placed in sacralized spots on the temple grounds. It has not been possible, however, to conform to this practice in the United States in many instances because most U.S. temples are housed in preexisting buildings, some of which have no grounds at all. Finally, to accommodate the American work week, major religious events are now scheduled on weekends instead of on the exact dates they are supposed to be celebrated. Moreover, because most temples are quite small, events that attract large crowds have to be held in large rented premises, thereby somewhat obscuring their religious significance. Monks and lay worshippers in America alike have had to accept these modifications for pragmatic reasons (Chan, ed. 2003a: 73, 216–20, 238–39).

Compared to such changes, which most people accept, what older, more devout Khmer Buddhists find hard to concede is the fact that some individuals no longer show the same degree of respect to temples and monks as Theravada Buddhists in Cambodia have always done. In Cambodia, when laypeople talk to monks they use a different vocabulary to signal a reverential attitude. As a respondent whom Maureen Lynch, who has a doctoral degree in human development and family science, interviewed observed:

> We respect our religion. When you walk into pagoda [temple] you have to take your shoes off, your hat off, and you have to bow down. And when the monks start to preach . . . you have to sit down and not stand. And when you talk to the monk you have to show . . . respect . . . but here . . . when they see the monk, they don't care about the shoes. . . . [they] talk to the monk . . . just like that and just use the regular language. And when the monk start[s] the sermon, some women just turn [their] backs on the monk . . . it is annoying to me to see . . . people act not appropriate[ly]. (Lynch 1997: 194)

Devout people find such disrespectful behavior offensive, not only because it violates religious norms but also because it breaches the general Khmer sense of propriety—the belief that interpersonal relationships should be charaterized by politeness above all else.

Milada Kalab, who studied Khmer Buddhist temples in Paris, observed that the authority of monks that derives in part from the hierarchical relationships embedded in Cambodia's Buddhist society has been eroded for another reason in diasporic Cambodian communities. As the state religion in Cambodia (except, of course, during the Khmer Rouge years), Buddhism has a clear institutional structure—one sanctioned by the political system.

Every local temple has a monk, every monastic district has a head monk and a district assembly, and every province has a provincial assembly. At the head of the entire Theravada Buddhist *sangha* (organization of Buddhist monks) is a supreme patriarch. His rank and the ranks of other monks in the higher echelons of this structure are conferred by royal decree. In contrast, no similar structure exists in resettlement countries such as France and the United States (Kalab 1994: 60–61). Thus, the state does not shore up the authority of Buddhist monks in countries where many Cambodians now live; moreover, monks must compete with other sources of moral legitimacy, influence, and prestige.

Cambodian Buddhists in the United States worry that the demands of daily life will cause Buddhism to atrophy. As anthropologist Carol A. Mortland observes, "In America, Cambodians worry that their religion will die, not, they say, because of direct persecution but because it is 'too busy here.'" The pressures of work and the availability of so many other distractions "provide stiff competition to temple attendance" (1994a: 7). Buddhists in diasporic communities also express grave concern about the efficacy of their transplanted religion. Some of Smith-Hefner's respondents wonder whether certain animistic spirits in which they believe, especially those associated with particular localities, have managed to relocate to the United States (1999: 39). Even though such spirits are not a part of formal Buddhist doctrine, they have been integrated into Khmer Buddhist rituals for so long that they have become, for all intents and purposes, prominent facets of the religion. What if these spirits have not found their way to America? In that case, how can they protect the human beings who beseech their aid?

Similarly, as Kalab notes, it troubles the devout that sometimes it is not possible in resettlement countries to perform the *bangsolkaul* ritual—a ceremony in which a white string connects the urn containing the ashes of a dead person to the wrists of four monks as they chant Buddhist scriptures—during *phchum ben* (the fortnight-long ceremonies commemorating the dead) that take place in September and October, when offerings are made to ancestors to honor them. The reason is that the ashes of many dead persons are not available in America. Because some ancestors' ashes remain in Cambodia, and other departed souls have no ashes at all because their bodies were not cremated during the Khmer Rouge period, this ceremony cannot be carried out as it should be. As a substitute, some who wish to pay homage to their ancestors write the latter's names on pieces of paper and burn them to create ashes (Kalab 1994: 68).

Even though Cambodians in the United States worry about transformations in their religion, and even though they cannot visit temples as frequently as they did in Cambodia because their work schedules or lack of transportation will not allow them to do so, they continue to celebrate major Buddhist holidays with joy and fanfare. Cambodian New Year, which occurs in April, draws large throngs, as does phchum ben and Buddha's Day, which commemorates the Buddha's birth, enlightenment, and death. Knowledgeable laymen (*achar*) assist the monks on these occasions and also go to people's houses to officiate at rite-of-passage events.

Those unable to visit a temple regularly still try to live according to Buddhist precepts. Many older refugees, for example, continue to rely on *kru Khmer* (Khmer healers) to mend illness. Said another of Lynch's interviewees, "I may not go to a temple, but . . . [I try to be] compassionate and to help people as much as [I] can. If you can help someone, help them . . . [even though you] never expect anything back . . . one of these days it will come back in another way. . . . That is something that is very Cambodian, to always have compassion for another human being, to feel and respect the other person" (1997: 195).

Despite the noticeable changes in practice, every one of the monks interviewed as part of the research for this book insisted that there have been no doctrinal changes in the Theravada Buddhism propagated within Cambodian communities in America. Whether that is true is difficult to ascertain without an intimate knowledge of Theravada Buddhist doctrine as it originated in India and the form it took in Cambodia. What can be said, however, is that such a claim is a good example of a phenomenon Mortland has identified—that "people reify the ideal while overlooking the actual expanded boundaries of action. What 'should be' becomes more rigid, more stolidly asserted. What 'really is' becomes looser in fact" (1994a: 21).

The greatest challenge facing Khmer Buddhism in America, as well as in France and probably elsewhere in the Cambodian diaspora, is that it is well-nigh impossible to persuade young men to become novice monks (Kalab 1994: 65). At most, a small number of teenagers spend only a few weeks at a temple during summer vacation. For that reason, refugee communities have had to keep inviting monks from Asia to serve in temples they have established. According to an active member of the Khmer Buddhist Society in Seattle, aside from the lukewarm attitude of young Cambodian Americans toward the religion, temples also face stiff competition from Christian churches:

> That's always the question we're thinking about—what are we going to do with our youngsters, the new generation. Over there [in Cambodia] . . . the

way the culture is . . . the man . . . [becomes] a monk for some time . . . to
pay respect to the parents who raised us. Here, we don't have that kind of
thinking. I mean the children . . . you can bring them [to the temple], but
it's hard. They join us in the celebrations . . . [but only because] . . . they
enjoy themselves talking to their friends. . . . [In contrast to the nascent development of Buddhism in America,] Christianity has been established in
this country for so long. . . . when the people came through the resettlement
process, Cambodian families had nothing, no clothes, no pots and pans to
cook with. They came to the temple but it had nothing to offer. So they go
to the church . . . somebody picks them up, somebody takes them to the
doctor, those kinds of services, so that's why these people became Christians.
(Anonymous interview 1996)

Despite the perception that Christianity threatens the continued viabil-
ity of Buddhism, some Christian churches have, in fact, made sincere attempts to help Cambodians establish temples. A Lutheran church in Pennsylvania, for example, allowed Khmer Buddhists to use its building for
worship services whenever an itinerant monk visited that community because Cambodians there had not yet set up a temple. A church in New York
made a small donation to help some refugees sponsor a monk from a refugee camp in Thailand, and another church in Massachusetts helped local
Cambodians plan large Buddhist celebrations (Mortland 1994b: 78).

In contrast to the supportive attitude of some churches, residents of some
towns have been less tolerant. In Maine, for example, Julie Canniff, a professor of education, describes an incident that occurred when Cambodians
bought five acres, with a chicken house on the property, in a small town equi-
distant from two cities in which a majority of Cambodians live. They discussed their plans to convert the facility into a temple with Protestant and
Catholic leaders and parishioners. The state's Council of Churches presided
over four meetings, and after they ended the Cambodians believed they had
dispelled initial apprehensions about the project. Sixty-five local residents,
however, attended the Planning Board's public meeting, at which the Cambodians' application for a zoning variance was reviewed. The residents sub-
mitted a petition stating that "the proposed use does not serve the current
interests of the neighborhood, nor will it favorably impact the neighborhood." When the board responded by tabling the application, news of the
event was broadcast to the entire region. Stunned by this unexpected development, the Cambodians withdrew their application and forfeited the deposit they had made on the property. The following year they bought a small
house in a suburb of the state capital for use as a temple. Perhaps embarassed

by the preceding year's outcry, local churches donated $800 to help remodel the property. In 1993, however, vandals broke into the building and attacked its interior with hatchets, stole all electronic equipment, scattered other items in the yard, and painted hate slogans on walls. Law enforcement officers never caught them, so no one was prosecuted for this act of destruction (Canniff 2001: 93–95). Fortunately for Khmer Buddhists in America, such attempts to desecrate their temples have been the exception rather than the rule.

In spite of occasional setbacks, Khmer Buddhists have tried tirelessly to establish temples in the United States. And because so many of them have held on so tenaciously to beliefs and practices handed down for centuries from their forebears, religion will continue to be an arena of cultural contestation as Cambodians adapt to life in America and interact with non-Buddhist neighbors.

Cultural Cues

Although instructors in "cultural orientation" classes at refugee processing centers in Southeast Asia and resettlement workers in the United States tried their best to teach Cambodian refugees the most rudimentary elements of American life, the refugees have had to learn a lot more on their own. Given that most Cambodians, especially those who do not work or attend school, have few opportunities to acquaint themselves with a cross-section of everyday Americans, they often rely on television as an agent of acculturation. Television programs provide some sense, however skewed, of how Americans live. As Paul Thai, a Cambodian police officer in Dallas, explained to Sharon Fiffer:

> The television and stereo, the programs and the radio and the music all help with language. This is how Cambodians find out about how to act, how to talk, how to get along with the Americans. . . . The television helps us learn about the American culture. My wife . . . watches some of the soap operas . . . she says that they teach her about how Americans act, how they dress, and what their homes, their lives are like. And there are good stories to follow. These programs are her opportunity to visit Americans. . . . They are the tools for survival in America. (Fiffer 1991: 36–37)

Immigrant and refugee children in particular have relied heavily on television to help them learn English and pick up cues about how to behave in

American society. Many of the immigrant and refugee students whom I have taught have told me that *"Sesame Street* saved my life"; without that program, it would have taken them far longer to learn English.

Among the viewing that Cambodian audiences most enjoy are science fiction, action films, boxing and wrestling matches, and situation comedies, all of which provide an unintrusive way to interact with American society in general. Frank Smith, an anthropologist who has studied cultural consumption patterns of Cambodian peasants now living in the United States, has noted that "the main draw of these films seems to be their representations of what peasant refugees see as the bizarre and very foreign behavior of Americans. These programs are the source of endless amusement and fascination for refugees, providing a means for scrutinizing Americans in what appears to be their 'normal,' day-to-day activities without the uncomfortable necessity of face-to-face interaction" (1994: 153). As Stuart Hall and other cultural studies scholars have pointed out, audiences are not passive. Rather, they actively interpret what they see and use the information they absorb in diverse ways. Apparently, Cambodian refugees are no different from other audiences in this regard.

In addition to programs broadcast on television, refugees watch a lot of videos. Researchers have noted that even the poorest Cambodian households in the United States usually have videocassette recorders in addition to television sets. Although the two pieces of audiovisual equipment form a set, they serve opposite functions in terms of how Cambodians negotiate cultures. Refugees use VCRs to tape-record themselves and their activities. They then send the tapes to relatives and friends in Cambodia in order to keep in touch with separated loved ones. They also play the tapes they receive in return.

Audio and videocassette tapes are especially useful to people who may not be able to read and write. Indian and Thai films—especially those featuring modern versions of classical tales—dubbed in Khmer are popular and can be rented from Cambodian-owned video stores. Many non-English-speaking refugees spend hours watching these movies to while away the time and relieve loneliness and homesickness. The films are appealing because both Thai and Khmer myths and legends were derived from Indian epics, particularly the *Ramayana* (which Cambodians call the *Reamker*). Their audiences find the films—"filled with spectacular fight scenes, slapstick comic escapades, and numerous lively love songs and dance numbers"—highly entertaining (Smith 1994: 151). Cambodians in the United States are also avid about martial arts films from Hong Kong, which are dubbed in Khmer. Finally, an increasing number now make and sell their own videos, many of them patterned after American music videos (Smith 1994: 151). Thus, VCRs are vehicles used to maintain contact with loved ones left behind and keep alive the popular culture of the homeland, as well as to express a new Cambodian American artistic sensibility. They serve an opposite function from television programs, which act as windows through which to view "American" society.

"American" popular culture is accessible to Cambodians in every part of the United States, but those who live in Long Beach have the privilege, once in a long while, to reacquaint themselves with the expressive arts of their homeland. At the Cambodian New Year celebration in April 1987, for example, an organization called the Cambodian Arts Preservation Group put on what American journalists David Holley and John Kendall called a "folk opera." Many dancers and singers came from other states days in advance in order to rehearse together before the performance, the first of its kind ever staged in the United States. Until then, according to Leng Hang, the female president of the group, folk opera had existed "only in the memory and the yearning of the Cambodian refugees in the United States. The young people now, they like disco more than going to see people acting like that, but the old people like the old culture. It reminds them of Cambodia" (Holley and Kendall 1987).

Some efforts have also been made to bring Cambodian "high culture" to the United States. Sad to say, many of the efforts have been ill-fated. The first tour, by the Cambodian Classical Dance Company's thirty-six dancers, came in 1990 as part of a cultural exchange program sponsored by the U.S. government. In addition to showcasing Cambodia's most important art form, the tour had symbolic meaning. Proeung Chhieng, director of the Dance School at the Royal University of Fine Arts in Phnom Penh, observed that the troupe's goal in visiting the United States was to show U.S. Cambodians that "we have revived dance and our nation is surviving." Unfortunately, the tour was marred by the defection of four artists, including Yim Devi, the lead dancer (Butterfield 1990). By the time the troupe reached New York after a month on the road, its members had experienced "threats, media mania, and the intrusive presence of burly security types with metal detectors" (Siegel 1990). The situation turned ugly. The U.S.-Indochina Reconciliation Project, which had sponsored the tour, claimed that certain people within Cambodian ethnic communities had pressured the dancers to defect, while the local groups accused the white organizers of trying to prevent would-be defectors from leaving (Conover 1990).

The following year another group, Angkor Dreams, likewise ran into problems. The troupe, which had formed while its members still lived in a refugee camp in Thailand, had planned performances in nineteen cities across the United States. Due to poor publicity and low attendance, however, the tour had to be canceled after only four shows (two in Long Beach, one in San Diego, and one in Fresno) because the troupe had accumulated a debt of $56,000. Yet the fifty-five-member group could not go home immediately, because they had to find ways to settle the debt before departing. Ted Ngoy, the "Cambodian doughnut king," housed the men and boys of the troupe in his luxurious mansion in Mission Viejo, and Evelyn Sak, who had helped to organize the tour, housed the women and girls while Ngoy tried to raise funds to pay off the debt (K. Johnson 1991). After hosting the dancers for three weeks, Ngoy decided to assume full responsibility for their financial affairs. He then rented two buses and a rental moving truck to transport them to New York, Boston, Rhode Island, and Philadelphia, where they still hoped to perform. However, the group canceled its scheduled appearances at the United Nations, Constitution Hall in Washington, D.C., and Disney World in Florida. Ngoy personally accompanied the group to the East Coast. "I want to see them be successful," he explained. "It's not all about money anymore. There's an attachment between us" (Johnson 1991a).

Ten years later, yet another company, the six dancers and musicians who came to present "Dance, the Spirit of Cambodia," defected as well. Proeung Chhieng, the artistic director of that group as well as the Cambodian Classical Dance Company, stated sadly that the artists' refusal to return home was a "big loss for Cambodia." Having trained them since they were very young, he said that all he could hope for was that they would use their talents to "preserve Khmer culture in the United States" (Kaufman 2001).

Although colorful performances onstage are highly visible expressions of a people's culture, they are usually not a source of cultural conflict. As spectacles, they illuminate the values of a people but do not prescribe rules of behavior. Conflicts arise, rather, from the divergent ways in which members of different groups carry on their everyday lives. Simple things that members of a host society take completely for granted often pose almost insurmountable obstacles to some newcomers. Cambodian refugees from rural areas encounter enormous difficulties, not only because they do not know English but also because so many of them are unfamiliar with modern technology and urban life. Paul Thai's story about how he learned to ride the bus illustrates the traps that may ensnare the uninitiated:

> The caseworker told us the numbers of the bus we were supposed to take to the office. . . . But there were many things he didn't mention, like for instance

that you have to pay. It must have looked funny—bus stops, doors open, a group of Asians get on the bus, doors close, doors open, Asians get off the bus. Then when we know we have to pay, we get on with dollar bills and the bus driver won't take them. Must have change. We can't understand driver, driver can't understand us. . . . Then you figure out that you have to get change and get it and get back on bus, but don't know how much you are supposed to put in. So you ask driver and he doesn't understand. Pretty soon, he just wants you off the bus! So we watch. We watch people drop the coins in and we count and learn how much to drop in. Then we ride the bus. But we don't know how to get off, how to make the bus stop. . . . I kept getting lost because I didn't know how to ask the bus driver to stop and let me off. Because I am a good Cambodian boy, I keep my head down, my eyes down, so I never see Americans pull the cord to ring the bell to signal to driver to stop. I hear the bell, and I notice that the bus stops, but by the time I look up . . . the cord has been pulled and I don't see how to do it. Then, one day, I am on the bus . . . when I see an old, old lady. . . . I see her raise her arm, very slow, very shaky, and I wonder what she is doing. I keep watching her as her arm goes up, slowly, slowly, she reaches something by the window, and pulls and I hear the bell, and aha! I know how to make the bell ring. So I don't get lost this time. And I go home and teach everybody. . . . I am so happy that I can help everyone. . . . That old lady was a good teacher to me. (Fiffer 1991: 6–7)

Even after Cambodians learn enough English to find their way around, more subtle factors may still impede their ability to function, because cultural interaction involves not only words but also nonverbal communication. Scholars have identified at least five forms of nonverbal communication, each of which conveys deep meaning: paralanguage (intonation and pauses while speaking), kinesics (body movement and posture or comportment), occulesics (eye movement and contact), proxemics (the amount of space individuals keep between them in order to feel at ease), and haptics (tactile or touching behavior) (Hopkins 1991: 89–90).

Cultures differ in terms of what is deemed appropriate in each of these forms of nonverbal communication. Him Chhim, executive director of the Cambodian Association of America, is concerned about improving the employment rate among Cambodians. He identified a hurdle that would seem to be easily surmountable but, in fact, is not because Cambodian occulesic norms are diametrically opposite to those in American society: "Our culture teaches us to look down when talking to higher-ups. When talking to our own people, we look down and not straight at the other person. It's disrespectful to look at someone straight in the eye in Cambodian culture. Many of our youngsters fail at interviews because of this habit" (Chhim interview 1996 in Chan, ed. 2003a: 60). Americans tend either to distrust people who do not look them in the eye or consider them to lack self-confidence. Little wonder then that Cambodians who cast their eyes downward out of politeness do not interview well when they enter the job market.

Different rules of proxemics and haptics, together with divergent conceptions of appropriate gender roles, likewise can be obstacles to Southeast Asian refugees interested in certain professions. To get into a police academy, for example, applicants have to take a civil service examination, a polygraph test, and a psychological test. Officer Ron Cowart, a Vietnam War veteran and a Dallas police officer who started a storefront police station in the Little Asia neighborhood of that city, explained the difficulty of helping Paul Thai and other Southeast Asian refugees be admitted to the police academy. The reason was one that likely no one else had thought of until that point:

> It's extremely difficult for Asians . . . to successfully get through the psychological exam. For instance, you can't be a homosexual and join the Dallas Police Department. But that isn't what they ask—they don't ask, "Are you a homosexual?" But they do ask if you've ever held hands with a member of your own sex. Or if you ever put your arms around someone of your own sex. Of if you've ever kissed someone and so on. And with Oriental culture as well as some European cultures, men hold hands with each other when they walk. They put their arms around each other. In the river, they've taken baths together. . . . When I was in Vietnam . . . we thought the whole country was gay! . . . they're all holding hands with each other! (Fiffer 1991: 81)

Applicants who honestly answered yes when asked whether they had ever held hands with other men would be considered homosexuals and thus dropped from further consideration.

Community Organizations, Leadership Style, and the Clash of Cultures

More than anyone else, the directors of Cambodian mutual assistance associations (MAAs) have had to modify their behavior as they mediate between their own ethnic communities and the larger American society. Him Chhim, for example, had to change at least the outward manifestations of his personality in order to become an effective advocate for his people: "I used to be very shy myself; I have changed my nature due to this job here. I used to be very calm, passive, and shy, not talking much. Now I almost turn aggressive sometimes and make very blunt statements in front of the elected officials. You have to make your needs known and demand action or these needs will not be met" (Chhim interview 1996 in Chan, ed. 2003a: 60–61).

Another community activist in Long Beach, a Cambodian American woman whom Audrey Kim interviewed, has also learned how to act like an American in order to have the powers-that-be pay attention to her concerns about other Cambodians: "You have to have somebody scream or make a noise all the time, you know, if you want to have something done. . . . [you have] to volunteer, to sit on different boards, get up at six o'clock in the morning to go to meetings, be willing to work late at night, willing to work on Saturdays and Sundays. To be there when they say you have to be there" (anonymous interview 1996).

That is a far cry from the way Cambodian women were (and still are) brought up to behave. Thus, ironically, she is most effective in calling attention to the needs of her ethnic community and securing resources to meet those needs when she behaves in a way that traditional Cambodians most disapprove of. For them, women should be demure and soft-spoken if they speak in public at all. At all times, female comportment should radiate a soothing gentleness; women should never talk loudly, nor should they ever demand anything in an aggressive way.

Differences in "Cambodian" and "American" ways of getting things done have caused serious problems in some community organizations. One example concerns a mutual assistance association in Massachusetts studied by anthropologist William Niedzwiecki (1998). In order to become a participant-observer, Niedzwiecki served as the MAA's assistant director for almost a year. In that manner he gained greater insight into how its board of directors and staff interacted than he could have as an outsider-researcher. The MAA's director was an older Cambodian man who acted very much like a patron in a traditional Southeast Asian patron-client relationship. As James C. Scott (1976) and other students of Southeast Asian societies have noted, the patron-client relationship is an exchange relationship between roles, not one between individuals themselves. Patrons and clients have different socioeconomic statuses, which is what facilitates an exchange of resources or services. The relationship between patrons and clients is not only hierarchical but also diffuse, which means they may call on one another for any service the other can offer. Someone who is a client in one relationship may be a patron in another and vice versa.

In the case of the MAA in Massachusetts, Niedzwiecki found that the director, although very dedicated and willing to work long hours with minimal pay, ran the organization in a way that made it extremely difficult for the staff to meet the bureaucratic requirements of funding agencies (which, as might be expected, treat MAAs as modern American organizations and not as mechanisms for the exchange of services between patrons and clients). The director resisted all efforts to keep track of details, including budgetary matters, and, as a true patron would, personally doled out favors. Younger, more Americanized staff members, especially one who had excellent management skills, in addition to the European Americans brought in as consultants when the organization began to flounder, failed to persuade him to change his ways and ensure continued funding.

To add to the ambiguity and confusion, members of the MAA board of directors also equivocated between an "American" and a "Khmer" style of decision-making. The MAA's inability to function entirely according to either "Khmer" or "American" norms diminished its effectiveness. In Niedzwiecki's opinion, the organization had no choice but to follow "American" standards of management, given its dependence on outside funding. Its existence was threatened because the director continued to act according to patron-client expectations despite all advice to the contrary. Members of the board of directors found it difficult to criticize him due to his age and leadership status (Niedzwiecki 1998: 175–217).

Another MAA that educator Sally Habana-Hafner studied also had difficulty functioning smoothly because of cultural ambiguities. Its executive director was an energetic college graduate educated in the United States, but older members of the board of directors found it hard to accept his leadership because of his youth. According to "Cambodian culture," young people must show complete deference to those who are older. As one elderly board member said, "The old people do not expect the young to do everything for them. We only need and expect the young to tell us how to do things legally" (Habana-Hafner 1993: 102). Moreover:

> The executive director and the outreach worker—both young—felt that the elders accepted their advise only when they acted as translators and interpreters of the legal or formal aspects of the new culture. When they tried to talk about the social implications of being in the new culture . . . the elders were not receptive. . . . The elders who joined the board to regain status and prestige found their traditional role undermined by the younger members. . . . The young members, mindful of the elders' cultural wisdom and knowledge, were conscious of the dilemma that their emerging leadership created. They tried to find leadership images that would be least offen-

sive to their elders, such as using respectful gestures and language. However, they were not always careful and behaved inappropriately by Cambodian standards. (Habana-Hafner 1993: 108, 112–13)

Anthropologist Craig B. Badgasar, who has investigated conflict resolution in Long Beach, has identified three forms of conflict very similar to those found in Massachusetts. Disputes occur between Khmer who maintain their ethnic identity and those who have adopted more European American ways; those who favor hierarchical relations and those who prefer a more egalitarian style; and those who formerly had high status in Cambodia and those who have acquired elite standing after coming to the United States. Although people in Cambodia resolve conflicts mainly by relying on intermediaries such as monks, achar, kru Khmer, or village elders to work out differences, Cambodians in Long Beach apparently do not consider anyone suitable to assume such a role. They do not trust one another and are divided by political factional disputes (Bagdasar 1993).

Judy Ledgerwood, an anthropologist, has also examined the dynamics of a conflict and illuminated how unmet "Khmer cultural expectations" underlay an accusation couched ostensibly in American terms. In the situation she analyzed, several Cambodian foster parents accused a bilingual social service agency staff member of corruption. Investigators, however, found no evidence of that being the case. Instead, what came out was a lot of rancor toward the accused staff member, who was denounced for not showing the proper respect to other Cambodians who considered themselves deserving of such deference (Ledgerwood 1990b).

Despite these intraorganizational problems, many MAAs play a critical role in persuading Cambodian refugees and immigrants that it would be useful—in certain specific instances—to adopt "American" norms. The United Cambodian Community, Inc. (UCC) of Long Beach, for example, applied for and received a grant of $35,000 from the U.S. Department of Health and Human Services in 1997 to make public service announcements in Khmer. The announcements, to be aired on radio and television, would be used in the UCC's campaign to prevent domestic violence and child abuse. Even though some husbands in Cambodia beat wives whenever the latter displease them, and parents believe that whipping is an effective way to discipline misbehaving children—whipping being a form of responsible parental caring rather than "abuse" in Cambodia—the UCC staff obviously did not think such practices should continue in the United States. They wanted to "make the community aware that violence is unacceptable" and suggest that both the victims and victimizers needed help. "We're in a new country now," declared staff member Chetra Keo, "there's new laws, new services available. Let's learn." When the group that made the commercials sought input from community members, the public advised that the videos should sound positive rather than punitive. The message should seem "hopeful" and affirm that people can change and that Cambodians in America can lead a different kind of life (Stewart 1997).

In a number of telephone interviews I conducted during 2001, the executive directors of MAAs in cities large and small on both coasts—notably, Lowell, Fall River, Philadelphia, Long Beach, and Portland—all reported that one of the most encouraging developments of the late 1990s was the fact that many Cambodians finally accept the idea of being "here to stay," at least physically if not mentally or emotionally. They pay more attention to what is going on around them "in the here and now." Fewer people still nurse their wounds or are obsessed with political events in their homeland. More Cambodians in America apparently now recognize that they should make a greater effort to learn English, speak out, interact with non-Cambodians, and participate in public affairs whenever possible, thereby empowering themselves (Chhim interview 2001, Khoeun interview 2001, Nol interview 2001, Rim interview 2001, and Tauch interview 2001 in Chan, ed. 2003a: 46, 128, 174, 158, 207, respectively).

At the same time, MAAs and their staff try to explain the subtleties of "Khmer culture" to non-Cambodians, including why they must not touch the heads of Cambodian refugees and immigrants or hug and kiss them. The organizations and their leaders simultaneously work to preserve "Khmer culture," help their compatriots become effective, functioning members of American society, and sensitize Americans to Cambodian etiquette and values so members of neither group are uncomfortable as they interact with one another.

Confronting Racial Animosity

As Cambodian refugees and immigrants struggle to make a home on American soil, they must deal with racial hostility as well as cultural differences. Such animosity is both subtle and overt. Sombat, who was resettled in Chicago and quickly found a factory job with the help of a woman from a church, has perceptively identified the subtle ways in which prejudice can express itself. His story is told by sociologist Jeremy Hein. According to Sombat, "Cambodians had to work very hard under Pol Pot for no money and almost no food. We know how to work, and if there are jobs we can do them. I have a harder job than any Cambodian I know. My hands look as bad now as they had during the Khmer Rouge" (Hein 1995: 142). Not only has he been a good worker, but he has also tried to fit in with co-workers by joining a bowling league and going fishing with some of them (bowling being, Hein points out, a "fixture of American blue-collar culture").

Nevertheless, as a nonwhite person Sombat is still stereotyped: "When I do something wrong it's because I'm Cambodian. When an American does something wrong it's only because they're Mike or John. That's prejudice, isn't it? I tell new Cambodian workers that Americans are watching them and that they will judge all Cambodians by what they do" (Hein 1995: 143).

But Sombat has not allowed such prejudice to prevent him from realizing the American dream. When Sombat's wife and sister-in-law also got jobs at the same factory, the family was eventually able to save enough money to make a downpayment on a house. When they moved in, they hung a portrait of Jesus in the entryway because, Sombat says, "I . . . pay respect to the woman who found me this job, not really because I'm Christian" (Hein 1995: 143).

Prejudice has made some Cambodians feel sad, but it is violent, anti-Asian activities that have intimidated them. In surveying where hate crimes against refugees have occurred and who has perpetrated them, Hein discovered that "the regions where the refugees are most likely to experience conflict are not those where hate groups are excessively active." Instead, refugees have encountered the most hostility in California and the New England states (Hein 1995: 71).

In other words, the larger their numbers in a region, the more likely it is that Cambodians will be victimized by physical violence. Hein also found that European Americans, rather than minorities, are more likely to destroy property and protest the arrival of refugees, and they do so in more violent ways, such as assaults and arson. Domestic racial minorities, however, have attacked refugees when they perceive that the government has favored the latter with regard to public housing, jobs, and school programs. Therefore, it is primarily the competition for scarce resources that fuels the jealousy, resentment, and antagonism that people of color have expressed toward Indochinese newcomers. Not surprisingly, most incidents perpetrated by domestic minorities have taken place in large cities, where refugees have been placed into neighborhoods hitherto occupied mainly by African Americans and Latino Americans (Hein 1995: 74).

"We have been here four hundred years and what do we have? Nothing," an African American woman in Philadelphia told a journalist. "They came yesterday and they have all the rights and privileges today that we don't have in four hundred years" (Nordland 1983, quoted in Hein 1995: 81). "You're pitting the groups that are suffering the most against each other," explained Joan Weiss, executive director of the National Institute against Prejudice and Violence in the 1980s. Andy Anh, a Vietnamese refugee who directed the Economic and Development Council in Los Angeles, summarized the dilemma that refugees face: "If we are successful in jobs . . . other minorities complain that we take the jobs away from them. But if we aren't successful, they say we rely too much on government assistance" (Lamer 1986).

Some Cambodians have developed a rather nuanced understanding of the attacks against them and realize they are being victimized for a variety of reasons. First, they believe they are easy targets for criminals who perceive them to be quiet, ignorant of American laws, and too unassertive to complain or report crimes. They are also targeted because some Americans continue to harbor lingering hostility toward the "Vietcong" or "gooks"—generic epithets hurled not only against Vietnamese but also against Cambodians, Hmong, and other refugees from Southeast Asia.

Ratha Yem, a Cambodian community liaison officer with the Boston Police Department, pointed out that films such as *Rambo* remind Americans of the horrible experiences they had in Vietnam. The fear of economic competition on the job market is intertwined with a racism that is not amorphous but specific (Lamer 1986). Recognizing that fact, Sambath Rim of Fall River, Massachusetts, frequently talked to organized groups while he directed the MAA there. He was, he told audiences, quite aware that more than fifty-eight thousand Americans lost their lives during the war, but people should remember that a far larger number of people in Vietnam, Cambodia, and Laos also died. Cambodians, he said, did not come to the United States out of their own free will but were forced to do so in order to survive (Rim interview 2001 in Chan, ed. 2003a: 158).

It is clear that negotiating cultures is a difficult process for individuals and ethnic community organizations alike. Unfortunately, the great discomfort of older Cambodians when they interact with Americans of various ethnic backgrounds or even with Americanized young Cambodians, their inability to achieve upward social mobility because they have not fully acculturated to "American" norms, their loss of conflict-resolution mechanisms, the struggles they face as they try to become bicultural and live transnational lives, and even the racial antagonisms that mar their existence are all trivial when compared to the extreme distress caused by the clashes between generations within Cambodian homes in America.

6   Coping with Family Crises

AMONG THE MANY challenges that Cambodians face as they adapt to life in the United States, the most debilitating tensions arise out of the conflicts between men and women and between parents and children. It is not an exaggeration to say that many a Cambodian family in America is a crucible of conflict. Because the concept of family was one of the pillars of "tradition-al" Cambodian society, intrafamilial discord in the country of resettlement causes heartbreak for both parents and children.

Several factors engender such conflicts: (1) a differential rate of accultur-ation among family members, with "American" values and norms that of-ten clash with "Cambodian" beliefs and behavior being introduced into the home via the more acculturated members; (2) changes in gender roles and the reversal of roles between adults and children; and (3) the pattern of seg-mented assimilation experienced by young Cambodian Americans—a divi-sion based largely but not entirely on their families' class backgrounds. Some young people are becoming members of the middle class, while others are joining gangs and terrorizing their communities. In this chapter, as in chap-ter 5, by using the words "American culture" and "Cambodian culture" I am not trying to essentialize those concepts but rather to employ a shorthand way of referring to complex ideas and relationships.

Cambodian Refugee Women and Changing Gender Roles and Relations

Non-Asians who are not familiar with Asian societies often think that all Asian families enjoy close and harmonious relationships. Indeed, many do.

In the United States, however, many families of Asian ancestry experience multiple conflicts among their members. That is true not only in Cambodian ethnic communities but in other Asian ethnic communities as well. The reason is that American practices severely challenge two of the most important organizing principles in Asian societies—gender hierarchy and age hierarchy.

In Asian countries, young people are expected to respect and obey people older than themselves, even when they disagree with their elders' opinions and instructions; girls and women are expected to defer to boys and men. Most Americans, in contrast, value youth more than age, and American women have made substantial headway in claiming greater equality for themselves. In addition, many Cambodian refugee adults are not familiar with what American law delineates as the "boundaries" of "acceptable" behavior. Many Cambodians, as well as adults from other countries, are shocked when they discover that the American legal system and its enforcers have the power to impose limitations on the prerogatives of parents and other elders, even within the privacy of the home.

Although women in certain societies in Southeast Asia—the Philippines, Cambodia, and the lowland areas of Laos, Thailand, and Myanmar (formerly called Burma)—have generally enjoyed more equality than women in societies shaped by Confucian philosophy (China, Japan, Korea, and Vietnam), they are still expected to respect male authority and privilege, especially in public. Historically, women in these Southeast Asian societies, where the kinship system is cognatic or bilateral rather than patrilineal, could retain close relationships with their natal families, inherit property, and engage in economic activities outside the home, such as managing small stores or selling food and other merchandise in public markets—rights that women in Confucian-based societies generally did not enjoy. Today, as in earlier times, married women in lowland Southeast Asian societies control their families' purse strings, and the roles of men and women are considered to be complementary. But it is a complementarity manifested in a sexual division of labor rather than in conferral of equal status in all spheres of life. Among Burmans, Thai, Khmer, Lao, and Filipinos, daughters are generally valued as much as sons—an attitude that differs from the attitude of many Chinese, Japanese, and Korean parents who, to this day, tend to value sons more.

While such a pattern of gender relations has given many Southeast Asian women a modicum of freedom and power, they still lag behind most American women, who enjoy more freedom of speech and movement and a greater ability to choose careers, lifestyles, and sexual partners than women elsewhere in the world. More than anything else, attempts by young women in Asian immigrant and refugee families to imitate the behavior of many young (mostly) European American women—especially the sexual freedom they have claimed as their birthright since the sexual revolution of the 1960s—lead to severe strains between them and their parents. Dating, premarital sex, and the free choice of marital partners are all contested issues.

In the case of refugee women from Cambodia, Laos, and Vietnam, quite aside from cultural differences, the circumstances surrounding their resettlement in the United States greatly affect gender roles and relationships. The difficulties that male refugees encounter in finding jobs—and the meager salaries provided by many jobs they do find—compel women to enter the labor force in order to make ends meet. Although some men appreciate their wives' financial contributions, others are upset about them engaging in paid labor; providing for the family was and still is considered the main responsibility of married men. Thus, having wives who work undermines men's self-esteem. For them, it implies that they are incapable of supporting their families.

Having to rely on their wives' earnings exacerbates the distress many men already feel over the low status of their own current jobs. The situation is especially hard for men who enjoyed high class status in Cambodia. Anthropologist Usha Welaratna interviewed someone in Long Beach who discussed how he felt about the first job he got as a janitor in a hospital: "So here I was, a man who had drunk Hennessey and eaten filet mignon, who had never opened the car door himself or changed a tire, washing floors for $2.15 an hour to buy the cheapest meat and rice! I became very depressed. I don't know how to express how bad I felt. I tried to be patient, to be flexible in my outlook, to have extreme self control, but there were days when I just blew up because I simply could not cope. I couldn't even eat. I drank beer all day, and at night forced myself to sleep" (Welaratna 1998: 57). The man eventually found a white-collar job as an interpreter in the school district and is now self-employed.

Meanwhile, Cambodian refugee women who hold jobs outside their homes generally learn to behave more assertively, although they show a range of reactions to the demands and rewards of paid employment. Florence Mitchell, a psychologist, talked to one woman who found her work dehumanizing even though the pay was good: "Right now I work in [a] company that makes surgery needles. I do mending, polishing, cutting, trimming, drilling. Good pay, but not good job. My job right now, no skill . . . I started only six months ago and I [already] feel like a machine" (Mitchell 1987: 67). Another interviewee, however, was more positive about her job, which gave her not only an income but also enhanced her self-esteem: "Before . . . I didn't have a job, I didn't have money, I didn't have anything. . . . Now . . . I have a job, I get paid, so I don't need anything. I got a car, I got a job, I got the kids, and that's it! In this country you need money. When you got money, you got everything. . . . Sometimes before when I didn't have a job yet, I feel lonely. I feel empty, nothing. But when I get a job I feel happy, I feel good" (Mitchell 1987: 69).

How men react to their wives' paid employment outside the home depends not only on a family's former socioeconomic status but also on the personalities of individual men. Although some feel threatened by their wives' increased economic autonomy, others welcome it. The wife of Sombat, the thoughtful and perceptive factory worker whom Jeremy Hein interviewed, also had a blue-collar job. Sombat not only felt good about treating her as an equal partner but also believed that such partnership would be a good model for their children: "I don't like the Cambodian custom of the man being the boss. I try to share with my wife, and we talk things over when there is a problem. . . . the man cannot say do this or do that like in Cambodia. We have to respect our wife and give an example to our children" (Hein 1995: 143). Individuals like Sombat may feel proud of their new, egalitarian attitude, but their deviation from prescribed behavior can sometimes be subject to gossip and criticism from members of their ethnic communities (Kulig 1991: 109).

The nature of the welfare program in America also affects gender relations within refugee families. The needs of children and their mothers underpinned the Aid to Families of Dependant Children program. That orientation, which also characterizes various state Temporary Assistance to Needy Families programs now, has a destabilizing effect on Indochinese refugee families because welfare payments are a critical, sometimes the only, source of subsistence. In these instances even more so than in two-income families, women hold the key to the families' economic survival.

The American legal system similarly plays a significant role in changing gender relations within Indochinese refugee families. In the United States, women who divorce can either find jobs if they have the requisite skills and determination to support themselves or, if they have good lawyers, collect alimony and child support. They may become poorer after their divorce, as many women—regardless of their ethnic origins—indeed do, but they need not fear starvation. Equally important, negative social sanctions against divorced women have declined since the 1960s. Attitudes in the United States differ considerably from those in Asian countries, where divorcees still experience enormous censure and seemingly unending opprobrium.

Because of these differences, the divorce rate among Cambodian and other Asian immigrants or refugees increased after they arrived in the United States. Moreover, according to anecdotal evidence, more divorce proceedings are initiated by women than by men. American law—at least in theory if not always in practice—also attempts to protect women from physical abuse. Wife-beating, a practice prevalent in many Asian societies even now, can be grounds for legal proceedings in the United States. Finally, in larger towns and cities there are usually facilities where battered women and their children can find temporary shelter. These factors greatly erode the power of men within Indochinese refugee families.

The demands of everyday living likewise help to transform gender roles and relationships in these families. When women work outside their homes, they often drive themselves to their place of employment. Knowing how to drive allows them to enjoy greater mobility and decreases their dependence on others who drive. At work, they come into frequent and close contact with male fellow workers. In some jobs, women are expected to attend occasional meetings in the evenings or even out of town. The social conditions that accompany paid employment—which most American working women take for granted—cause anxiety among some refugee parents, husbands, or fiances who believe that women who participate in such unchaperoned occasions could ruin their families' reputation.

Scholars studying refugee families and communities notice how some of the working women often assume two different personae, depending on whether they are at home or at work and whether older members of their ethnic communities are present. Some women, especially younger ones, are talkative and vivacious at work, but within the four walls of their homes they are quiet and deferential to their husbands and elders. Women who do not behave appropriately according to context are sometimes divorced.

Chinda (a pseudonym), whom educator Julie Canniff got to know quite well, is an example of a divorced Cambodian woman who has come to terms with herself and found ways to rationalize her actions. She now lives an independent life and allows her teenaged daughter far more freedom than most Cambodian parents would. In talking to Canniff, she justified her attitude and behavior by looking for evidence within Cambodian history that indicates women had historically held equal power alongside men. Based on her research, Chinda asserted that it was Indian civilization that introduced gender inequality into Cambodian society and that the oppression of women was not a salient feature of pre-Hindu Cambodian life. Furthermore, she observed, Buddhism does not compel women to remain in abusive marriages: "Buddhism doesn't believe that you [have to] stay with bad people. If the husband is very abusive, Buddhism says stay away from those people . . . The Cambodian culture [today] make[s] the women believe they have to stay married in order to have the good reputation for . . . [their] daughters [but] Buddhism say[s] you don't have to stay with the perpetrator" (Canniff 1999: 152). Buddhist scriptures do not actually discuss divorce, but Chinda is apparently interpreting broad Buddhist tenets in a particular way—one that suits her own situation.

Chinda's efforts at justification provide a good example of how certain Cambodians now living in the United States negotiate cultures. She does not rely on "American" notions of women's liberation to support her behavior but rather plumbs selected elements of "Khmer culture" to defend herself against criticism. In drawing a distinction between Buddhism and Hinduized Khmer cultural norms, she is, in effect, saying that she need not accept every aspects of her cultural heritage in order to be considered an "authentic" Cambodian. As though to prove that her Khmerness is genuine, she exerts enormous efforts to help other refugees in multiple ways despite being a single parent, working to support herself and her daughter, and going to college—all at the same time. She even hosted a local Khmer-language radio program for some time, reporting news from Cambodia as well as from Cambodian communities in America. In these many ways she makes known her desire to be seen as a dedicated and loyal member of her ethnic community. At the same time, however, she insists on her right to behave in a way contrary to the expectations of her cultural legacy. Chinda explained why she does not hesitate to express her thoughts and feelings: "I am too 'Americanized' because I am going out and talking about my feelings. My culture suppresses women, everything about their feelings, about their sexual desires. We are supposed to say nothing about that. . . . I want to change what is bad about my culture, so I have to keep talking about my feelings" (Canniff 1999: 151).

Without extensive comparative studies, it is difficult to gauge how representative Chinda may be. Her critical thinking and independent behavior are probably still relatively rare among middle-aged Cambodian American women who entered the United States as adults. Nonetheless, the fact that she exists at all indicates how dramatically some Cambodian women are changing. At the same time, it must be noted that there are feminists in Cambodia, so it should not be assumed that "American" cultural influences are the main source of change. A woman whom Sheila Pinkel interviewed in the Rithisen section of Site II was, as president of the Women's Association, helping other women become economically self-reliant and change their attitudes about themselves. She declared:

> Until today, Cambodian society makes the man the head of the family. But, in fact, the woman is the head because she takes care of the family budget. She was the head but she never accepted herself as "head." . . . I want to see men and women be equal. But how can we talk to men to get them to consider women as their equals? This is a problem not just in Cambodia but in other countries as well. Men are very stubborn. They don't want to consider us equal but we have to persist bravely. . . . We must talk a lot and spread our viewpoint to other women. We need to keep women strong while educating men in a secret way. . . . We must take time to correct them secretly and smoothly. Women have a very big duty. . . . They must make themselves smarter than they were in the past. Women must be the teachers, the examples, for the children, for the husbands, for the neighbors. Women have to be more clever, more brave, than others. They have to take responsibility and guide the society. (Anonymous interview by Pinkel 1992)

Note that the *method* the speaker recommends resonates with what may be called a "traditional Khmer" cultural prescription that urges women to influence men in a nonconfrontational way, but the ultimate *goal* she seeks—gender equality—is a modern, nonindigenous ideal.

Other women, who are less outspoken, also resort to fundamental Cambodian values to justify their behavior. For example, in Cambodia being a good mother is an essential aspect of being an ideal woman. A good mother not only nurtures, protects, and socializes her children but also welcomes whatever number of them she happens to conceive. In the United States, however, some women realize how costly it is to raise children and consciously limit the size of their families in order to be good mothers—"good mothers" now being defined, in the American context, as women who can provide adequately for their children rather than women who produce many children. Thus, "Khmer cultural ideals" continue to be upheld, but the ways in which they manifest themselves are changing.

Some Cambodian women are also making use of American means to achieve ends sanctioned by "Khmer culture." Said one, "I plan a lot for the kids. Like save money for school . . . and everything the kids need. . . . I buy . . . life insurance. When I die, got $50,000 for the kids. . . . I'm poor now. That's why I don't have so many kids. Just . . . two so I could help them to be happy. I don't want the kids [to be] just like me, you know. I want . . . [them to be] better than us" (Mitchell 1987: 106). Because buying life insurance was not, and still is not, a common practice in Cambodia, this woman is obviously learning about and using new ways to deal with life's uncertainties. She wants to ensure that her responsibility as a good mother will continue to be fulfilled, even if she should die unexpectedly.

Cambodian refugee women are not abandoning their "homeland culture" but are, instead, creatively reconstructing it. It is they who are supposed to "hold"—that is, preserve—the culture. Thus they continue to uphold key cultural symbols, even as they subtly transform their contents. Meanwhile, there *are* occasions when Cambodian women wish that Americans would more readily accommodate to more familiar ethnic practices. One such occasion is when they give birth. Many Cambodian women are disconcerted by the way they are treated in maternity wards. One whom Elizabeth Burki, a sociologist, interviewed obviously had not received prenatal care, nor had she undergone a physical examination until she reached the hospital. Therefore, she was mortified by what happened: "They took off my clothes. They pulled the covers back to examine me. My legs—everything—was in the open. I was so ashamed. . . . I screamed and cried which is not Khmer custom. Finally they brought me into another room and my son was born" (Burki 1987: 274).

Three women interviewed by Doris Dyck and Izabela Plucinska, two nursing educators, explained the differences between Cambodian and American birth practices. One revealed how lonely she was in the maternity ward: "I don't know why they leave the patient alone until the baby comes. . . . Even the nurses come in and out and just check you and say, 'No, you're not ready yet,' and then they leave" (Dyck and Plucinska 1990: 67). The second pointed out how, contrary to the custom in the United States, the birth of a baby in Cambodia is a truly social event: "In Cambodia when you're in labor you have your relatives, or parents, or sister or parents-in-law, you know, to look after you, but over here you just have your husband" (67). The third woman explained why the lack of social support is difficult for mothers, not just emotionally but also physically: "In Cambodia, when the baby [is] born, when [you] feel pain, and the midwife feels the stomach, and . . . say the baby will be born soon, so push . . . they have old people on either side to help push. Here, they just let the mother push by herself, so take a long time, and after the baby born, she [is] tired" (68).

According to Cambodian birth practices, a postpartum mother should be kept very warm. In Cambodia, a fire is built underneath her platform bed for that purpose. The practice is hard to maintain in the United States because "some Cambodian . . . tried to do this with an American bed and it caught on fire!" (Burki 1987: 274). Another way to generate warmth is to drink wine in which herbs have been soaked for weeks, but some of the herbs are difficult to find in America. A fourth woman whom Dyck and Plucinska interviewed was traumatized by how she was treated after her baby's birth. An interpreter relayed her story: "She said the nurses told her . . . to take a shower and she doesn't want to take the shower . . . because [in] her culture not take a shower after you have baby, but you can wash. The nurses . . . [thought it was] disgusting . . . they put cold water in the bath tub and throw her in" (Dyck and Plucinska 1990: 75). It is not difficult to imagine that the shock of the cold water likely was not the only shock the woman felt. The incident is a prime example of cultural insensity on the part of service providers.

The Hard Life of Cambodian American Girls

Cambodian girls growing up in America perhaps have an even more difficult time than adult women because they can be punished even when they are not purposely trying to misbehave in any way. Given the great emphasis that "Cambodian culture" accords female modesty and comportment, some parents do not like it at all when girls are required to participate in athletics. A few even forbid daughters to participate in sports activities, even when such participation is mandated by the school curriculum. A Cambodian father in Massachusetts, interviewed by anthropologist Ronnie J. Booxbaum, was so infuriated by the swimming suit his daughter had to wear in a required swimming class that he cut it to shreds (Booxbaum 1995: 189). As one elderly interviewee said to anthropologist Nancy J. Smith-Hefner, "Girls should talk softly and walk softly without making any noise. No screaming or yelling" (1999: 99). Pity the poor girls who are supposed to behave with quiet decorum while playing sports.

Overnight fieldtrips, especially if they are coeducational, cause even more distress among some Cambodian parents, because these outings provide opportunities for girls to mingle with boys. What horrifies parents most is sex education; they assume that the information their daughters acquire in such classes will automatically encourage them to become sexually active. Booxbaum cites a case of two grandparents who demanded that their son call the school where their granddaughter was receiving sex education and tell the teachers that Cambodian children are not allowed to know such things (1995: 189).

Premarital sex is absolutely forbidden for girls (although it did and does occur in Cambodia) because virginity is so highly prized, not only for moral reasons but for an economic one as well. A virgin can command a high bride price, whereas the parents of a non-virgin can expect nothing. Having a daughter in the family who is known to have lost her virginity is a source of almost unbearable shame. Not only is her family's reputation at stake, but its physical and spiritual well-being may be in jeopardy as well. As Barbara R. Kelley, a public-health professional, learned from interviewees, "A girl's improper behavior will displease the spirits and could lead to harm, sickness, or misfortune elsewhere in the family" (1991: 83). Should a girl become pregnant, she rather than her partner is always blamed.

The moral burden borne by Cambodian American young women is heavy indeed. As Smith-Hefner puts it, "Many Khmer feel very strongly that the continued existence of Khmer identity and culture in the United States is contingent on the purity of Khmer women" (1993: 147). That is why girls, in a vast majority of Cambodian families in America, are not allowed to go to parties unless they are chaperoned—if they are allowed to go at all.

Not surprisingly, the American custom of dating causes more conflicts than any other aspect of life. Tragic incidents have occurred as a result of the prohibition against dating or even close friendship between a girl and a boy. One sad story is told by Paul Thai, the Dallas police officer:

> A young Cambodian girl was walking down the street holding hands with a Cambodian boy. This is very much against our culture. Boys and girls, men and women, do not show affection in public. But this girl's parents saw her with this boy. They were upset and angry. She told them that he was just her friend, that it didn't mean anything serious. But the parents insisted that because there had been such a public display, the girl had to marry this boy. . . . [the] parents met with the other parents and the marriage was arranged. . . . [on] the wedding night, the boy said it was time to go to bed and the girl said no. She liked him as her friend, but she did not want to go to bed with him. He was very angry and went to her parents to demand the money [bride price] back that he had paid them. The parents were very angry and they beat their daughter. This kind of punishment, physical punishment, is common in the Cambodian culture. And this daughter, their daughter, had caused her parents much embarrassment. She had disobeyed them, disgraced them. They had lost face because of her. The girl ended up in the emergency room. (Fiffer 1991: 40)

Similarly, a father interviewed by Smith-Hefner confessed that he severely punished his daughter after finding that she had a boyfriend: "All this time,

I thought she was a good girl. No boys. Just always studying. I even bought her a car so she could go to [a community] college. . . . When I heard that she had a boyfriend at school, I just couldn't stand it. I hit her until she was unconscious" (1999: 117).

Lest it appear that Cambodian parents are cruel and merciless toward their daughters, it should be noted that Cambodians do distinguish between appropriate and inappropriate reasons for corporal punishment. For them, it is proper to beat children in order to impress upon them the necessity of behaving in acceptable ways. It is improper, howeer, for adults to hit family members "like an animal" and without reason. Shamed by such behavior, elders either severely reprimand the adults for letting their anger get out of control or they physically intervene to rescue the children from further torment (Smith-Hefner 1999: 117–20).

Not only are Cambodian girls in America not allowed to go out, but they are also expected to do all the chores at home, to help care for younger siblings, and to serve elders and guests graciously, as girls in Cambodia are taught to do. The ideal, virtuous Cambodian woman, notes Judy L. Ledgerwood, an anthropologist, "must know how to keep order in the house, how to cook delicious food, wash clothes, take care of babies. The virtuous woman is intelligent, advising and assisting her husband in his endeavors. The virtuous woman is beautiful . . . generous . . . [and] obedient" (1994: 121).

In contrast to the softness and housekeeping skills valued in girls and women, physical and moral strength, industriousness, the ability to provide for families, and abstention from excessive drinking, gambling, and cavorting with prostitutes are the traits valued in men and boys. Men are not supposed to engage in these vices, not just for moral reasons, as spelled out in Theravada Buddhism, but for an economic one as well. Overindulgence can drain a family's financial resources. The greatest virtue a boy can demonstrate is to become a novice monk for a certain period. By so doing he accrues merit for himself as well as for his family.

A conversation that two teenaged Cambodian American girls ("Ellen" and "Judy") had with Manhao Chhor, a Sino-Cambodian American male student of mine who interviewed them and other youths for a class project, highlights these themes clearly. (In real life, the girls do have American first names.) Even though some girls resent the differences in the way their parents raise and socialize them, they believe there is little they can do about their subordinate status. They sense the tug of war between obligation toward their families and the desire for a little freedom. The conversation is revealing.

Manhao: You and many other young women I have interviewed have mentioned that a lot of Cambodian women marry very young. Why do you think this is so?

Ellen: You know how they don't allow us to date . . . so getting married is easier. You know how old people talk. If they talk about a young woman who's married, it would be all right because the man is her husband.

Judy: Back in Cambodia where they can't date, if you get caught together, you have to get married, even though you hadn't done anything. . . . Their parents make them.

Manhao: Have your parents ever brought up the subject of marriage?

Ellen: All the time! My mother thinks when a girl goes out, she'll get pregnant.

Judy: They tell you, "I see it on television. I hear it. Look what happened to that girl. I don't want you to be like her."

Manhao: The parents are afraid of losing face?

Judy: Yeah!

Ellen: They think if you go out with guys, you'll have sex. They always think that, even though you only go out and come home late.

Manhao: Do you ever talk about the subject with your parents?

Ellen: It's hard to talk to your parents about something like that. Basically, if you talk about it, they always bring up life in Cambodia.

Judy: Or they lecture you. They say, "When I was your age I never had a chance to do this. Whose child do you think you are?"

Manhao: You mean they are trying to make you feel guilty?

Judy: I guess so. When you get mad, they say, "This is for your own good. I love you, that's why I'm saying this to you."

Manhao: Do either of you have a boyfriend?

Ellen: I don't have a boyfriend.

Judy: I do.

Manhao: Do your parents know about him?

Judy: They know I have a boyfriend but they don't know who he is. Friends and relatives of my parents say, "I saw her with this guy" and they get suspicious. But my parents actually don't mind. My dad says it's natural to love but he is always emphasizing school.

Manhao: Do you want to tell your parents who he is?

Judy: I want to, but I don't think they are ready for it yet.

Manhao (to Ellen): Do you have the same kind of problem?

Ellen: Yeah! It's O.K. for my brothers to go out because they're guys and they don't get pregnant. For me, it's not allowed.

Judy: If you get pregnant, your life is over, is what they say.

Manhao: I'd like to talk more about the different ways young men and women are treated.

Judy: Well, it's not just Asians. I think that's true for all races. Guys are always considered the superior ones. They work, earn money. They can go wherever they want and stay out as late as they want. If you're a girl, you're fragile, you can get hurt, you can get pregnant. We're told we can't take care of ourselves.

Manhao: But you know that's not true?

Judy: Yeah. I mean, if you happen to get pregnant, it's your responsibility. You took the chance to do what you did.

Manhao: You said your parents are not ready to know about your boyfriend. What makes you think that?

Judy: My dad always says, "Talk to me as a friend." I want to, but I'm afraid of his reaction.

Manhao: You're the oldest child in your family, right? Do your parents stress your responsibilities?

Judy: Yeah, I have to set a good example for my younger brothers and sisters.

Manhao: Do you feel that responsibility is a burden?

Judy: Yeah, sometimes I do. When I do something bad, I feel guilty. I think I'm not a good older sister or something.

Manhao: Do you sometimes feel you want to get away from it all?

Judy: Yeah, I've thought about that a lot. I even went to a fortune teller. He said, "If you leave home at this time, it'll bring bad luck for your family." That's why I didn't leave even though I had already packed my clothes.

Manhao: So, it was your sense of responsibility to your family that prevented you from leaving?

Judy: Yeah, of course. If I didn't care about my family, I would have said who cares and would have just left.

Manhao: What made you decide you wanted to leave home?

Judy: A lot of problems. Family problems—they were bugging me a lot. Plus, I was stressed out at school.

Manhao (to Ellen): You have an older brother, right? Are there any differences in your parents' expectations for the two of you?

Ellen: My parents expect me to be a lady—you know, to cook, clean, stuff like that.

Manhao: They don't expect your brothers to do any of that?

Ellen: No. The boys just eat and throw the dishes in the sink.

Judy: And you can't complain about that, either. You're the girl, so you should wash the dishes. We're told, "Don't complain. Your brothers are guys."

Ellen: When my brother washes the dishes once in a while, my mom compliments him. You know, "My son this, my son that," but to my sister and me, she says, "You girls are so lazy." My two sisters and I just stay in our room because if we come out, we'll get lectured. We do our house chores and then retreat to our room.

Judy: Parents emphasize the bad things that girls do, but when you do something good, they don't even notice. That's what stresses me out.

Manhao: I know it must be very difficult for you to tell them the situation is unfair.

Ellen: My mom would probably say, "You're not a guy."

Judy: You can't tell them it's not fair because it would be "wrong" for us to speak our minds.

Ellen: I like to hang out with my brother. I like to go out, but when I do, my mom says, "Don't act like a guy." She says it's O.K. for guys to go out because they're guys. We girls, we're supposed to stay home.

Judy: "They're guys, so they can protect themselves"—that's the argument my parents use against me. But I think guys can get hurt, too. It's like they don't trust you to make the right decisions. They don't think you know what's right from what's wrong.

Manhao: Do you ever talk about this with your friends?

Judy: Yeah. When we say something other girls can identify with, they'll say, "yeah, yeah."

Manhao: Do you ever discuss this topic with young men?

Judy: No, because they'll say, "You're supposed to do that. We're guys, so we can do whatever we want."

Manhao: How do you think Cambodians are being perceived by members of other ethnic groups?

Judy: Well, they don't notice the good things we do, like fund-raisers for charity. They focus on the gangs, the violence, the crimes. I mean, if you listen to the news, if there's any news about Cambodians, it's never good. It's always bad. We get stereotyped. They think all Asians are on welfare and we don't work. You walk into a mall and the salespeople think you have no money. They don't bother to help you. They think you just want to look but not to buy. However, if we want to buy something, we'll buy it.

Ellen: Yesterday we were browsing. The saleswoman just came up and stayed there. She kept walking around us as though she thought we were going to steal something. I got mad and cussed her out. Only then did she walk away.

Although Cambodian girls growing up in America are hurt by the fact that their parents as well as outsiders do not trust them, some parents are mistrustful because their children do sometimes lie about their secret social lives. As a young woman told Susan Holgate, a social scientist, "They don't trust us because we lie to them. We tell them we have to go to a meeting but instead we go to meet boys. If you lie too much they don't want to believe you anymore. That's why. When I tell her [my mother] the truth she says I just made it up. . . . Sometimes she believes me when I lie. It's the only way to get out" (1994: 200).

Young men also use subterfuges to deceive parents, especially girlfriends' parents. "If a boy calls a girl, and her parents find out," a teenaged boy told Holgate, "she'll get in trouble. So you have another girl call for you. If a girl calls me, she has to get permission from her parents first so she has to lie about who she is calling. If my parents answered the phone and it was a girl, they'd talk about her and I'd get a lecture. They might even call her house and give her a lecture. If her parents find out, it's really trouble" (111). The double standard means that young men, despite the necessity of such precautions, experience far fewer restrictions than young women. Another teenaged boy explained, "The guys, even if we did something bad, have a criminal record, whatever, we can change it, clear it. If the Asian people see you do something good later, get a good job, become a lawyer, they forgive you. [But] girls, once they do something bad, they're always bad—all the way. They can't change it" (Holgate 1994: 115).

Several social scientists have observed that the age at marriage of Cambodian young women has fallen in America. Judith C. Kulig, a nursing educator, notes that although women usually marry between the ages of eighteen and twenty-one in the homeland, in the United States many are being married off at sixteen if their parents suspect they have boyfriends (1991: 127). Susan Holgate, who also noticed this phenomenon, explains that lowering the marriage age is "a means of adapting to their social surroundings and the danger it presents, rather than a continuation of a traditional cultural practice" (1994: 181). Some young people, male and female, consent to early marriages because "it is the only way they can obtain the freedom they desire to go out and be with members of the opposite sex." Moreover, married teenagers have a higher status than unmarried ones, whom parents treat as children (180).

There seem to be class differences among Cambodians in the United States with regard to early marriages and the acceptance of bride prices, which can range from $2,000 to $10,000, depending on the bride's education and reputation. Although these customs are still widely followed, an increasing number of well-educated, middle-class Cambodian parents are beginning to frown upon the practices. As one of Elizabeth Burki's interviewees emphatically declared, "We are not living in Cambodia! I will not marry off my daughter to get rid of her or to get money! She will finish high school and college. She must be able to earn a living on her own. I see what happens to women when they have no skill and get divorced" (1987: 288).

In terms of upward mobility American-style, marrying off a teenaged girl, with or without her consent, may save a family's reputation within the ethnic community, but it is also likely to have long-term negative social consequences. Most girls who marry young drop out of school and begin conceiving babies soon after their wedding, although a few now insist that they be allowed to continue their education even after they become mothers. Having so many young women drop out of school will impede the chances for Cambodian families in America to achieve intergenerational upward mobility. As the young women lose the opportunity to complete high school and attend college or vocational school, their chances for finding good jobs, and their ability to help their children do well in school, will be greatly diminished.

In many families of rural origin, parents do not seem upset when daughters and sons drop out of high school. Compared to the parents' own limited schooling, children who complete high school or even junior high school are considered well-educated. Some social scientists offer two additional reasons that many Cambodian parents do not seem to pressure their children to excel academically the way that Vietnamese, Chinese, Japanese, Korean, or Indian parents do. First, in Smith-Hefner's opinion, the Khmer belief in karma leads them to think that the fate of an individual is predetermined. The main responsibility of parents, then, is to observe children carefully in order to decipher their character and destiny rather than make them into something they are not destined to be (1999: 64–69, 82–86). Second, as Canniff and Welaratna remind us, Cambodians who are Theravada Buddhists define "success" differently from the way that European Americans (and more achievement-oriented groups of Asian Americans) do. To the Khmer, a successful person is above all one who helps others and gains their respect. People who earn high salaries or accumulate wealth are expected to share their financial resources with less-fortunate persons (Canniff 2001: 113–41, 150–69, 192–238; Welaratna 1993: 269–77).

Some scholars of Cambodian ancestry, however, do not accept such "culturally deterministic" explanations. A scholar who prefers to remain anonymous notes that children in families from other Buddhist countries do well academically, so Buddhist values cannot be the reason for the school performance of Cambodian American students. She asserts that structural factors are more pertinent, although she does not indicate the nature of those factors (private communication 2002). Chanthou Boua, a Cambodian scholar who taught school in Australia and now lives in the United States, however, has pinpointed some of them. In a study of Cambodian-ancestry adolescents in Australia, she found that "nearly all" Cambodian high school students dropped out "before acquiring useful qualifications. Nearly everywhere they were known as low achievers, but not because they were lazy and unmotivated. In fact the students were usually hard working and had arrived in Australia with high expectations. They wanted to succeed at school. Their parents too usually had a healthy respect for education" (Boua 1990: 1–2). Why, then, can they not shine in school?

Boua argues that the difficulties they encounter in learning English, their traumatic experiences both in Cambodia and during their flight, the fact that they had no formal education in Cambodia and only "haphazard courses" in refugee camps, and their parents' inability to help them with school work account for the inability to keep up in Australian schools. Most disturbing of all, many Cambodian youths are illiterate or only semi-literate in Khmer, even if they speak Khmer at home. That means they cannot read, much less write, any language. Worse, they cannot understand many concepts embedded in lessons (Boua 1990: 2–3, 21–37). In short, to function in school, they must acquire not just the rules of English grammar and a new vocabulary but ideas as well.

Intergenerational Conflicts in Middle-Class Families

Although changing gender roles sometimes cause problems between men and women within families, Cambodians in America find it far more difficult to deal with conflicts between generations—ones caused mainly by the differential rate of acculturation between adults and children. Children learn English more easily so they can communicate with members of the host society much sooner than can their parents. That leads to role reversal as children become de facto spokespersons for their families when dealing with English-speaking outsiders. Even young children sometimes have to decipher and translate documents, help pay bills, answer the telephone, deal with salespeople who knock at the door or telemarketers who call, fill out forms, and respond to inquiries from teachers and school administrators.

In these myriad ways a great deal of power is bestowed unwittingly on children. In the process, some learn to manipulate the system and deceive their parents, especially with regard to reports of their truancy or misbehavior at school. Sambath Rim reported one example of how children outwit parents:

> The kids are smarter than the parents. Let me tell you a story. One of the kids told me he never went to school. The school sent a letter to the parents saying, "What happened to this kid? Why isn't he coming to school? Why is he absent?" The parents told the kid, "You know, I got a letter from I don't know where; can you translate it?" The kid says, "Oh, it's a letter from school saying that I'm a very, very good kid doing a really good job in school." . . . the parents are very excited, until the police calls . . . "This kid is locked up; he was shot." . . . So you have to be smarter than the kids in order to control them. Otherwise, they just do whatever they want. (Rim interview 1995 in Chan, ed. 2003a: 165–66).

The widely accepted Asian value of age hierarchy has been turned on its head to such an extent that social leveling has occurred, not only between classes in Cambodian refugee communities but also between generations. Role reversal causes estrangement among family members, in part because parents continue to control children strictly yet rely on them as intermediaries with society in general. Some youths deeply resent the contradiction between control and responsibility. Youngsters who harbor such resentment sometimes despise or hate their parents, at other times ignore them or stop helping them, and in yet other instances run away from home. Some Christian proselytizers, who "call Buddhism a pagan religion and make fun of the rituals," help fuel the contempt some children develop toward their parents (Welaratna 1998: 135).

Even in instances where no Christians denigrate Buddhism, children who go to school observe, day after day, how their American peers behave and the autonomy they enjoy. Young Cambodian Americans are both more malleable in terms of their personalities and far more vulnerable to peer pressure than are adults. Problems arise because what is considered "normal" behavior on the part of American children is often interpreted as rambunctious, sassy, and disrespectful behavior by Cambodian and other Asian immigrant parents. In some families, children who ask simple questions out of curiosity or express an innocent opinion, as they are encouraged to do at school, are severely reprimanded by parents because young people are not supposed to question or "talk back" to their elders.

Many parents feel enormously frustrated and powerless because in America—unlike in their homeland, where an entire society reinforces what children are taught at home— the outside world contradicts many things Cambodians hold most dear. Moreover, some children know that when their parents use corporal punishment to discipline them, they can call the police or tell their teachers or social workers, who then accuse the parents of child abuse. Countless parents bemoan the fact that American law sides with their misbehaving children. In the words of one of Booxbaum's interviewees, "In Cambodia, the parents have more rights. The parents can shape the children's behavior. They can hit the child a little bit, spank the child. Here, they don't have that kind of rights. If they hit the child, the child will report it to the school or the police. The parents will be in trouble" (1995: 194–95).

Because everything seems stacked against them, some parents give up trying to discipline their children, all the while lamenting the fact that their progeny are completely unmanageable. Others, however, often indulge the children because they regret the severe deprivations of Cambodia during the Khmer Rouge years and the Thai camps. Sok Teang Pin, who was resettled in the Bronx, confessed that she gave her children things because "I felt bad for them because they never had things before." Danh Hum Thi, a Vietnamese refugee participating in the same group conducted by the Indochinese Mental Health Program at the Montefiore Family Health Center in New York City as Sok, echoed the latter's sentiments when she explained why she let her children eat so much junk food after years of near-starvation: "I saw a lot of children [in television advertisements] look chubby and I said, 'Maybe that's good food'" (Chira 1993). Only when the group facilitator told the women that junk food is unhealthy did they begin to think it would be all right for them to try and minimize the amount their children ate. Furthermore, the facilitator said, "You don't have to accept kids saying, 'You don't speak English, so we don't have to tell you [anything].'" The Montefiore staff did emphasize, however, that there are alternatives to hitting children and urged mothers to show affection toward their youngsters.

Rebellion on the part of young Cambodian and other Asian Americans is usually driven by their desire to be "normal" and accepted by American peers rather than by hostility toward their parents. To find such acceptance, however, they often must go against the wishes of parents and the traditions that shaped their attitudes and behavior. In this regard, girls are having a much harder time than boys because they are expected to restrict their activities once they enter puberty. Chivy Sok, a politically active student leader while in college and now deputy director of the University of Iowa's Center for Human Rights, has written an insightful analysis of coming of age:

> My high school years mark the greatest achievement in terms of education but the greatest loss in terms of maintaining my own history, culture, and language. Like most teenagers, I wanted to be like everyone else . . . I wanted to assimilate into American society. . . . The first thing I needed to do was

to get rid of my Asian accent that I still had even after four years of learning English. I needed to sound like an American whenever I opened my mouth. I was so determined to do this that I avoided speaking Khmer at all times. If my Mom spoke to me in Khmer, I answered her in English. Listening to other people, especially to the television or radio, became very important. I also stopped reading or writing Khmer. . . . Second, I tried to distance myself from all aspects of Cambodian culture and history. Being normal meant having a background similar to that of my White American counterparts. Since I didn't have that, I had to create it in my mind. I had to forget who I was and where I came from because being Cambodian made me abnormal. I avoided going to gatherings where there were a lot of Cambodians because it reminded me of myself. I avoided learning about anything that was even remotely related to Cambodia. PBS was airing a documentary about the Cambodian revolution. . . . Mom insisted I sit down to watch it with her . . . [but] I stormed out of the apartment. . . . It must have been hard for her to . . . watch me go through this process of disowning everything she had risked so much to teach me during the Khmer Rouge years. (Sok 1993: 29–30)

What Sok may not have realized is that her mother was probably far more troubled by her rejection of the Khmer language than by her refusal to watch the televsion program on Cambodia. Second only to Buddhism, facility in spoken, if not written, Khmer is considered a true mark of being Cambodian. (Both of Chivy's parents are of Chinese ancestry, but they speak Khmer and not Chinese at home and consider themselves as Cambodians.)

The defiant behavior of Sohko Pich, another former student of mine, likewise pained her mother. The Pich family was initially resettled in Plymouth, Wisconsin, in 1980, where Pich never met other students of color, either at school or in town. Two years later the family moved to Long Beach, where she, for the first time, met and became friends with Asian Americans. As she recalled:

I began dressing like my new friends, which really disgusted my mother. I would always wear black and white clothes everyday and I would style my hair and wear makeup in a manner my mother found disturbing. To my mother I was dressed like a gangster. It was not that she was worried about my life being in danger. A more important concern was that I was disgracing her and the family because it seemed as though she had not raised me properly. Not only did my image disgrace her, but it also reminded her of the Khmer Rouge. I would not listen to my mother about anything. . . . There was nothing my mother could say that would make me listen. . . . I was at a stage where I thought every adult was against me and I was against their traditional ways. My mother would always complain that just because I went to school here and she didn't doesn't make her stupid. I never listened because I thought I knew everything and I was so cool. (Pich 1993: 10)

Cambodian parents pay so much attention to their daughters' clothing for an important cultural reason. Although black clothing upset Sohko's mother because it reminded her of the loose-fitting, black clothes that the Khmer Rouge made everyone wear in order to erase all visual cues of former social distinctions, it is possible that she may also have disliked the cut of her daughter's clothes—a fact Sohko did not mention—because proper Khmer women are not supposed to flaunt their physique in a way that American clothing enables women to do. When a daughter is not properly attired, friends and neighbors or even strangers gossip about her. As one teenaged girl in Modesto, California, told Susan Holgate, "They [the old people] do not like it if you leave the house wearing a tank top or something. They think you're a hooker already. . . . They don't understand the culture, how American kids dress. . . . they won't give us a chance to be ourselves, to fit in. Some girls do act bad because they are always accused of being bad" (1994: 101).

Although parents are less strict with boys, they nevertheless attempt to control their appearance as well. One young man interviewed by educator Terpsichore N. Kapiniaris Tan said, "My dad took my clothes that he did not like or approve [of] and burned them." Another young man reported: "My mom gave me an allowance for clothes, but when she did not like my clothes because they were too baggy (which was fashionable at the time), she took the scissors and cut up my pants. . . . I was trying to prove to her that wearing baggy pants does not mean you are a gangster, but she did not let me get away with it" (Tan 1999: 285).

As young Cambodian Americans grow up, they eventually learn to appreciate their heritage and accept themselves as bicultural. Those who get over their rebellion generally come from middle-class families. Even during the most rebellious phase of their lives they study hard and get good grades. Many go to college and do well academically. By the time they finish high school, they have usually realized that no matter how hard they try, they will never be seen by others as White Americans. So they begin to search for their ethnic roots. Judging from what generations of Asian American students have told me, they generally prefer to learn about their ancestral cultures from books rather than from parents' tiresome lectures. Books provide information without coercing readers to behave in prescribed ways. Information from teachers and professors is also usually acceptable so long as they do not try to act as surrogate parents.

The bicultural Asian American identity that these young people choose is based not only on a creative mixing of two cultures but also (in many although not in all cases) on a conscious commitment to struggles against the racism still endemic in American society as well as against the ethnocentrism and sexism embedded in various "Asian cultures." This hybrid identity is therefore considerably more complex than the ones suggested by the first and third modes of incorporation delineated by Portes and Zhou. In my opinion, the first form of segmented assimilation they identified—full assimilation into the White middle class—cannot occur with respect to Asian Americans, including Cambodian Americans, because most European Americans still do not consider people of Asian ancestry as "real" Americans. Although Asian Americans can and have become part of the *American* middle class or even upper class economically, they can never become a part of the *White* middle class. Being "American" and being "White" are not the same thing. It is possible for people of Asian ancestry to become Americans, but they cannot become Whites. "American" refers to national identity and citizenship, whereas "White" is a racial category. The distinction is a critical facet of contemporary American racial dynamics even though many European Americans—as well as Asian American, Mexican American, and African American middle-class people—often deny that such a distinction exists.

As I see it, the third mode of incorporation specified by Portes and Zhou—using ethnic solidarity as a mechanism for achieving upward socioeconomic mobility—is also problematic from the point of view of many young Asian Americans. Such an adaptational pattern seems to be something that foreign-born grandparents, parents, uncles, aunts, older siblings, teachers, and professors try to impose on young people raised in America more than an end the latter desire of their own free will.

Although middle-class Asian American youths actively fashion a distinctive identity for themselves, they differ little from peers in the multiethnic American middle class in terms of career patterns and lifestyle. In that sense, they are acculturating, but they do so in an adhesive rather than an all-or-nothing way. The cultural mix in their form of adhesive adaptation, however, is the reverse of that followed by adults. Although immigrants or refugees who entered the United States as adults usually add selected aspects of middle-class "American culture" to their ethnic cultural base, their children, whether American-born or American-raised, are more likely to sprinkle elements from their parents' cultures—mainly those that strike their fancy and do not threaten to restrict behavior—onto a largely European American cultural base. The adhesive pattern of adaptation they are following fuses

Portes's and Zhou's first and third modes of incorporation, which means that segmented assimilation consists of two, rather than three, distinct and separate pathways of incorporation into American society.

Compared to middle-class youths, the acculturation pattern of children of the working poor is more unpredictable. Their future depends mainly on how well they do in school and who their friends are. They may graduate from high school and go to college, find white-collar jobs, and join the middle class; or they may remain among the working poor; or they may descend to the multiply-disadvantaged underclass. Since the 1970s, as manufacturing jobs moved overseas to countries with cheaper, nonunionized labor and the United States deindustrialized, opportunities for the intergenerational upward mobility that earlier generations of European immigrants had enjoyed became scarcer and scarcer (Portes and Zhou 1993).

In the past, blue-collar jobs, especially unionized ones, paid good wages and enabled hardworking immigrant parents to support their families, buy homes, and send their children to college. Today, the American economy is shaped like an hour glass, and the passageway from the working poor upward into the middle class is becoming ever more constricted. The number of jobs in the United States has grown, but the new jobs are not in the heavy-industry sector of the economy. They are, rather, in the poorly paid service sector and the well-paid, information-based sector. People who hope to find jobs in the latter must have at least a college degree, which means that education has become even more critical now than in the past for families aspiring to intergenerational upward mobility (Portes and Zhou 1993: 76, 83–85). Thus immigrant and refugee families whose children do not perform well academically are condemned to remain in the two lowest strata of American society—the working poor and the permanently unemployed.

A family whom Julie Canniff studied in a city in Maine illustrates how much the achievements of siblings can differ. In determining outcomes, the personality and social networks that an individual develops can sometimes be more important than a family's class background. This family lived in a low-income neighborhood, and the mother worked as a sea urchin processor during the fall and winter and as a farmworker in the summer. Her eldest son Kusal (a pseudonym) hung out with the "wrong crowd" and was constantly in trouble while in high school, getting drunk and into fights, taking drugs, and having run-ins with the police. He left home at age seventeen and drifted around for several years before his mother persuaded him to return home to help care for his younger siblings while she worked. After bouncing from job to job, he eventually found one and worked the second shift in a food processing plant. Then he married, had a child, and finally settled down.

Other individuals, however, can overcome the structural constraints into which they are born. The second son in the family, Touch (a pseudonym), received a four-year scholarship to attend an elite prep school, where he was the only Cambodian and only one of five students of color. Not only did he do exceptionally well there, but he also became the president of his senior class and captain of the junior varsity team. Although he socialized with rich young men at school, he was too ashamed of his home to invite them to visit. During the summers he washed dishes at a local country club, where he had further opportunity to become acquainted with wealthy people and observe their affluent lifestyle. During the process he developed the fluid social skills needed to bridge divergent cultures as well as disparate socioeconomic classes. Moreover, he was willing to work incredibly hard. The summer before he entered Clark University, he held three separate jobs simultaneously: "I work at the Country Club. . . . I also work at supermarkets. . . . I am able to provide for myself and help support my family. A lot of people don't have that kind of drive, you know. A lot of my friends say I am a workaholic because I put in like eighty-two . . . hours a week. For me, I don't mind [because it gives me] the option to do whatever I want with . . . [the money], like save it or go shopping or buy stuff for the family" (Canniff 2001: 184).

The American dream, although considerably harder to realize in today's hour-glass economy, can still be within reach. Touch is an excellent example of how personality and drive still matter. His older brother Kusal is fortunate in a different way. The city in which his family lives does not have a severe gang problem, which was what enabled him to return home at his mother's entreaty and start a new life as a blue-collar worker under the watchful eyes of his mother and wife.

Cambodian American Gangs

Cambodian children from homes with welfare-dependent parents or widowed mothers who live in inner-city neighborhoods are less fortunate than Kusal because they are exposed to, and almost inevitably drawn into, "the adversarial subculture developed by marginalized native youth to cope with their own difficult situation," the second mode of incorporation delineated by Portes and Zhou (1993: 83). The greatest agony that many Cambodian parents, especially widowed mothers, face in these neighborhoods is that their children join gangs and engage in violent criminal behavior, usually robbing and intimidating fellow Cambodians. Scholars, journalists, police officers, social service providers, and Cambodian community leaders have all offered the same analysis of why Cambodian youngsters have joined gangs. First, they initially formed gangs to protect themselves in school and on the streets. Second, because some youths feel alienated in school and at home, gangs offer the camaraderie they find nowhere else. Third, after young people start hauling in bounty, they quickly become addicted to the fast life.

Children who live in rough neighborhoods feel a need for protection as soon as they start elementary school. One boy spoke poignantly to the executive director of a mutual assistance association in a Massachusetts town. "You try to help me in the office," he said to the former school counselor, "try to help me in school, but you never try to help me on the street. I walk from school to home and from home to school, and I have a lot of difficulty."

His words are echoed by several young Cambodian gang members whom Kimberly Kang, a social worker, interviewed in Long Beach, California. In explaining why he joined a gang, one youngster said, "We get jumped everyday, at bus stops, getting out of school, out on the street." Added another, "You know, every time they see Asian, they keep messing with you." A third revealed that "whether you're a gang member or not, you may be innocent, . . . still they're trying to get you because you're Asian." "Growing up in Long Beach in the east side . . . ghetto," observed the fourth, "we can't go to school without getting beat" (Kang 1999: 58, 55, 85). David Chum, who joined a gang at age twelve, told reporter Seth Mydans, "On my first day of school I got beat up. I had to go and get an X-ray and then when I went back to school I got beat up again. So I went and joined a gang" (Mydans 1991a). A fourteen-year-old female gang member maintained that even girls are physically threatened: "Everyday when I walk home from school I get threatened, and I talk back to them. When they start swinging their hands, I don't just let people hit me and I start swinging my hands too. . . . I always get my butt kicked" (Mydans 1991a).

A "retired" Cambodian gang member nicknamed Mad Dog, talking to journalist James Willwerth, touched on another motive for gang formation: envious imitation of other youths. "We saw," he said, "that American people had groups, white with white, black with black. We decided to become more famous. If they could steal cars and do drive-by shootings, so could we" (Willwerth 1991: 103). Another of Kang's young interviewees affirmed why gang membership makes him feel good: "People before [treat me] like I'm nobody. I got respect when I joined a gang" (Kang 1999: 84).

In addition to a perceived need for protection and recognition, gang members mention that gangs satisfy their social and psychological needs by giving them the attention, approval, and affection that their parents and teachers do not. As one young man put it, "Every time you look at your parents, damn, they having a frown on their face." Another added, "My mom and dad yelling at me when I come home, school was bad for me, my parents get mad at me, I can't go out. A lot of pressure. I can't stand it. That's why I decided . . . it's time for me to go, it's time for me to go" (Kang 1999: 56).

In contrast to the distrust between many parents and their children, members of a gang trust and look out for one another. As one of Kang's interviewees observed, "My friends tight because you can trust them, you know, I got your back, you got my back." Another put it even more starkly: "They die for me, I die for them. If a bullet comes, I get for them, they get for me" (Kang 1999: 66, 73). Their members consider gangs to be surrogate families. "Once your blood [family] don't get with you, you gonna look for your homeboys. Family comes first, but when the family ain't there for you, boom, there you go, a new family" (Kang 1999: 66). Finally, gang membership often helps provide the basic needs for those who are poverty-stricken: "If I need food, they gave me money to get food. It's like a family in the streets" (Kang 1999: 85).

Him Chhim, executive director of the Cambodian Association of America in Long Beach, puts the gang members' pithy explanations in more sophisticated terms:

> Due to the lack of a nurturing home environment, the lack of role models in the home, too many of our children drop out of school and join gangs by the thousands. . . . they don't find comfort, love, or anything interesting for them to do inside their homes. They live in crowded neighborhoods, crowded apartments, unsanitary conditions, and spill over into the streets. That's where the gangs recruit them. . . . Cambodian gangs started out with good intentions— to protect their own kind from other youth. Small children get beat up or somebody stole their bike or something like that. Some protection is needed. That's how it started. . . . later on, . . . they [got] involved in all kinds of violent activities. (Chhim interview 1996 in Chan, ed. 2003a: 58–59)

By listening carefully to the gang members, we catch glimpses of how they, too, are negotiating cultures. One, who obviously cannot stand being nagged at by his mother and consequently adopts a defiant attitude, told Kang: "My mom tells me, you know, Cambodian tradition this and that. I always tell them that's in Cambodia, this is America. I do what I got to do." A second is upset because his family always judges him and his peers negatively. He is also exasperated by the fact that adults do not seem to understand how difficult it is for young people to cope with their environment: "I'm just getting tired of old Cambodian folks . . . putting us youngsters down and not having faith in us. . . . . They're scared of us. Seeing us walk down in front of their house they locking up the door. [But] we're just trying to survive." A third explained that belonging to a gang is a form of ethnic solidarity: "It makes me close to Cambodian culture . . . that's why I joined a Cambodian gang, to back my Cambodian people up against the Mexicans." A fourth recognized the ironic twist that ethnic solidarity is taking among his peers: "I'm trying to help my people not the legal way but in the fuckin' illegal way. It's helping them . . . put Cambodian[s] up, my race up, my culture up" (Kang 1999: 62, 86, 78, 84). These gang members consider themselves to be affirming their Khmerness or Cambodianness rather than rejecting it, whether or not their parents and the older members of their ethnic communities approve of the disturbing form that affirmation takes.

As Cambodian gang members in Long Beach became more experienced during the late 1980s, they involved themselves in criminal activities in order to acquire all the material things money can buy. Sam Chittapalo, the former Asian affairs liaison officer in the Long Beach Police Department, discussed the relationships among different ethnic gangs and why Cambodian gangs transformed themselves from youth cliques to criminal groups:

> When the Cambodians [first] formed a gang, the gang is always led by Vietnamese . . . Vietnamese are the Asian gang organizers, mobilizers. Not just in Long Beach and L.A., but all over the United States—Chicago, New York. After they formed the gangs here, Cambodians became stronger. . . . From 1988 to '90, '92, the Cambodian kids . . . formed their own gangs: TRG [Tiny Rascal Gang], Cambodian Boyz, Lazy Boyz. . . . TRG is all Cambodians, they don't want anybody else. . . . If you're on welfare, welfare doesn't give you enough food to eat, barely enough day to day, month to month. And the kids, like you and me, want good cars and want good clothes, want to get out of there and live, and the parents cannot support that. . . . The Vietnamese gangs [approach them and say]: "Friend, you have no money. Come to my team. You join me, I buy you good clothes. You can buy a good car. You can drink whatever you want." But one day, the gang leader says, ". . . You have to pay back." . . . Right now . . . Cambodian gangs fight each other and fight with Vietnamese gangs, fight with Latino gangs, fight with black gangs. (Chittapalo interview 1996 in Chan, ed. 2003a: 99–101)

According to Detective Norm Sorenson of the Long Beach Police Department's Gang Violence Suppression Unit, many Vietnamese gang leaders who recruit Cambodian children and teenagers are former military men and expert in the use of weapons. They can, therefore, easily teach the young recruits how to use assault rifles and machine guns (Haldane 1991; Vollmann 1996). Because the boys begin hanging around gang members from a very young age (eight or nine), it is easy to see how they would become entranced by seemingly glamorous, gun-toting, macho men.

One of Welaratna's interviewees explained how gang members are initiated: "Usually if a kid is a 'wannabe' and keeps hanging around the TRG saying he wants to join them, the gang leaders and members will talk about it, and they will meet that kid at a certain place after school . . . and they'll jump him in. It basically means the kid will get really beaten up by three or four older TRGs who might be about sixteen, seventeen, eighteen years old. They usually time it [the beating] and they do it to see if you can endure that kind of strain, to see if you can fight to protect the others. And if you can, you are in" (Welaratna 1998: 91–92). It is easy to see why young people who survive that ritual are proud of themselves. They now have "homies"; they're tough; they're men.

Cambodian gangs began to form around 1985, but it was not until 1989 that violence flared between them and Latino gangs, whose members felt their turf was being invaded. Jerome Torres, a board member of the Long Beach chapter of the League of United Latin American Citizens, one of the oldest Mexican American civil rights organizations in the United States, observes, "It's a problem of cultural misunderstanding. The Latino kids feel displaced" (Haldane 1991). But, sadly, "The Cambodians have nowhere to go," observes Song S. Kamsath, the Cambodian director of the Boys and Girls Club of Long Beach. "We Cambodians have no country to go back to. Our homeland is a war zone," laments Kamsath (Mydans 1991b).

According to Welaratna, "Hispanic gang members [also] resent that graffiti and other features of the *cholo* subculture have been appropriated by Cambodians, and it adds further fuel to the rivalries between the two groups" (1998: 115) A probation officer who worked with Asian American, African American, and Latino American youths told Welaratna that Cambodian gangs imitate not just Latino gangs but African American ones as well:

The Khmer kids have adopted certain aspects of both African American and Latino sides. . . . They almost talk like Black gangs. They refer to each other in terms that African American gangs use all the time, such as "Cuz." That's basically street vernacular for a Crip. That's how Crips call to one another, "What's up, Cuz?" Cambodians have picked that up. But their dress is pretty much adapted after Latino gangs. Their monikers or their nicknames are almost exactly like Latino gangs. These are usually nick-names like "Sleepy," "Droopy," "Sniper." (1998: 119)

But there is one thing Cambodian gang members do not copy, Sorenson observed: "A Hispanic gang pulling a drive-by shooting will yell out their gang moniker. The Asians think that's stupid. They don't want to get caught" (Vollmann 1996: 32).

The most violent gang warfare in Long Beach occurred during the late 1980s and early 1990s, and it was during those years that the mass media broadcast a truly negative image of Cambodian youths. The violence peaked in 1996, when there were sixty-five gang-related homicides. In the mid-1990s, the largest Latino gang was the East Side Longo, which had more than five thousand members and fourteen cliques. The second-largest Latino gang was called the West Side Longo, and there were many smaller Latino gangs as well. The largest African American gang, the Insane Crips, had some 850 active members, and the largest Cambodian gang, the Tiny Rascal Gang, had more than four hundred. Second in size to that was the Asian Boyz (which also admitted non-Cambodian Asians), with at least three hundred members.

Tired of being used by the Ultimate Wave Warriors, a Vietnamese gang, to do its dirty work, Cambodians splintered off and formed two separate gangs, the TRG and the Asian Boyz, because there happened to be two gang leaders at the time the split occurred, and each wanted his own group. Other Cambodian gangs included the Exotic Foreign Creation Coterie, whose members tended to be younger than those in TRG; the Crazy Brothers Clan, which originated in Fresno; the Eazy Boy Gang, which came from San Bernardino; the Asian Brotherhood; and the Oriental Boys.

Youths of Filipino, Laotian, Samoan, and Guamanian ancestries also had their own gangs in Long Beach. In those years the East Side Longo was at war with all the Cambodian gangs and with other Latino gangs (Long Beach Police Department handout 1996; Mydans 1991a). Although the Cambodian youths were greatly outnumbered, they were ferocious fighters and, as one gang member told journalist William T. Vollmann, they were unafraid of going to jail: "People in there [jail] wanna get out but people out there wanna go in, to be tough. They think it's cool" (1996: 32).

In a telephone interview I conducted in July 2003, Detective Sorenson reported that gang membership began to decline after 1996 for a number of reasons. First, the Long Beach Police Department received grants from federal and state agencies to beef up programs to suppress gang violence. The number of officers assigned to the gang detail increased from five to forty. The city of Long Beach imposed a curfew on youths under the age of eighteen that lasts from 10 P.M. until dawn. Young people who are out after 10 must be accompanied by an adult. Otherwise, the police can arrest them and detain them in juvenile hall until a responsible adult comes to pick them up. A youth who is arrested a second time must appear in court. Second, there are now eight Cambodian police officers in the Long Beach Police Department, and the language barrier between police and the city's Cambodian residents is no longer as insurmountable as it was in the late 1980s and early 1990s. Third, the police department has managed to persuade more Cambodian parents to help monitor the activities of their children. Fourth, the number of registered gang members has declined because the government has issued stricter criteria on who can be counted as a gang member. The criteria are now codified in the Penal Code of California, section 186.22(a) and (b). Youths are counted as gang members when they themselves declare they are members of a gang; hang around with identified gang members; are tattooed with the distinctive patterns unique to each gang; wear bandanas, hairnets, and other accessories of gang attire; walk with the aggressive gait favored by gang members; flash the hand signs used by their gangs; and evince a half dozen other, less visible traits.

The Long Beach Police Department's computer database on gang members is never completely up to date because the names of individuals who leave gangs and change lifestyles, move to other locations, are imprisoned, or die are not immediately removed from the database. The database does, however, have a built-in "purge system" that deletes the names of gang members who have had no contact with the police for three years (Sorenson interview 2003). Finally, because the Long Beach Police Department has been so efficient, Cambodian gang members have been leaving for Fresno, Stockton, Modesto, and Oakland, California and Lowell, Massachusetts—all of which have sizable Cambodian-ancestry populations (Chittapalo interview 1996 in Chan, ed. 2003a: 104).

As of 2003, the East Side Longo was still the largest, most criminally active Latino gang. The smaller West Side Longo still exists, but the gang has made peace with the East Side Longo. The Insane Crips remain the largest, most violent African American gang. Among Cambodian gangs, only the TRG, Asian Boyz, Exotic Foreign Creation Coterie (which has changed the last word of its name to "Crips"), and Crazy Brothers Clan are still active (Sorenson interview 2003).

The three types of crime in which Cambodian gangs engage most frequently are home invasion, auto theft, and extorting local businesses. According to Sam Chittapalo, "Asian gangs, Cambodian gangs, never rob Latinos, never rob Blacks. They know they don't have money inside the house, they don't have jewelry, they don't have diamonds, anything expensive." Instead, they prefer to rob Asian immigrant or refugee families who tend to keep cash and jewelry at home because they are not familiar with or do not trust banks. "The kids ask other gang members to rob their own families. They do that!" said Chittapalo in disgust (Chittapalo interview 1996 in Chan, ed. 2003a: 102). As for auto theft, Sorenson estimated that about half of the cars stolen in Long Beach in the mid-1990s were taken by Cambodian gangs. Extortions continue because it has been difficult to help business people; they are too afraid to report that gangs are collecting "protection money" from them. The merchants' fear of reprisal is justified because gang members often drive by and shoot into their stores or enter the shops and threaten shopkeepers by brandishing guns.

Even in a metropolitan area like Washington, D.C., where a relatively large proportion of the Cambodian residents belong to the middle class or working poor, and where far fewer Cambodian families are on public assistance, gangs have made their appearance. The Tiny Rascal Gang operates mainly in Virginia and the Asian Boyz in Maryland. Two smaller gangs, the Sworn Brothers and Sworn Sisters, each has its own turf. Members of all four gangs hang out at malls, pool halls, skating rinks, and nightclubs. As is the case in southern California, gang warfare occurs mainly between Asian and Latino gangs in the areas surrounding the nation's capital (Sun 1995). A Cambodian American woman who has lived in the United States since the 1960s and became a social worker in order to help her compatriots when large numbers of Cambodians started entering the country has a different take on gangs than do some other community leaders and law enforcement officers. She told Audrey Kim, who interviewed her in 1995:

> I don't feel we should be so alarmed about Cambodian kids in gangs. . . . [In each gang in the Washington, D.C., metropolitan area,] there are only about five or six, perhaps ten at the most, who are seriously involved. The others, they just hang out because their friends are there and many of their families have no structure. There *are* some who are in jail now. They're eighteen, nineteen, twenty years old. Because of their trauma experience during Pol Pot time, they withdrew into themselves. During their escape, they had to protect themselves, so they learned to be violent. . . . Coming here, they carry

around with them all this violence. I think we're lucky there's not that great a number [here]. I'm sure that a lot of my friends would disagree with me. They think this is very serious.

In 2002, the families of gang members who had been convicted of aggravated felonies faced new agony. The former felons, even if they had already served their sentences in jail, became deportable if they were not U.S. citizens. Before 1996, aliens convicted of felonies involving fraud in excess of $200,000 could be deported. The 1996 "welfare reform" legislation reduced that amount to $10,000, thereby greatly enlarging the range and number of deportable felons.

Until March 2002 the more stringent deportation criterion did not affect alien Cambodian felons because Cambodia and the United States had no repatriation agreement, which meant that Cambodia could refuse to take back the Cambodian-ancestry gang members or criminals. After the September 11, 2001, terrorist attacks on the United States, however, the federal government increased efforts to get rid of undesirable foreigners. As part of that effort, the United States put tremendous pressure on Cambodia to sign a repatriation agreement. As soon as the agreement was signed in March 2002, approximately 1,400 noncitizen felons and former felons of Cambodian ancestry became subject to deportation. Most of them are in their twenties and live in southern California. In an effort to stave off deportation, they point out that because they left Cambodia at a young age or have never set foot in that country, having been born in Thai camps, and because they can barely speak Khmer, they will not be able to function in a land they never knew. Moreover, about half of the potential deportees are their families' main breadwinners, and a third have American-born children to support.

Despite such pleas, four dozen individuals were deported during the first year after the repatriation agreement went into effect. To reduce the negative impact of foisting 1,400 gang members and criminals on Cambodia, the United States agreed to deport only ten persons a month. Still, concerned observers are worried that the deportees will introduce gang warfare to Cambodia—a country that can scarcely tolerate yet another form of violence (Paddock 2003; Watanabe 2003).

As an antidote to this grim picture, it is important to note that even in Long Beach, a majority of the Cambodian young people do not belong to gangs and are doing well in school, even though it is gangs that receive the sensationalized media coverage. Terpsichore N. Kapiniaris Tan (1999) has surveyed 135 Cambodian American seniors enrolled in six high schools in the

Long Beach Unified School District and conducted in-depth interviews with forty of them. She found that only 49 percent of the students live in two-parent families, whereas 40 percent have only mothers and 10 percent only fathers. Despite the existence of so many single-parent families, a majority of the students get average or above-average grades.

Tan also tabulated the grade point averages of all Cambodian American high school graduates in Long Beach from 1992 to 1997 and found that 40 percent graduated with grade point averages of 3.0 and above, which in high school is considered honors level. A significant portion of them had GPAs of 3.5 and above. In every year for the period she studied, there were valedictorians of Cambodian ancestry. Some of these high-achieving students are now attending prestigious universities that are extremely difficult to get into, such as Harvard, Columbia, Stanford, and the University of California, Berkeley (Tan 1999: 48–49). Tan found, however (194), that a vast majority of the high-achievers have at least one Chinese or part-Chinese parent, the implication being that it is "Chinese" rather than "Khmer cultural values" that drive students to do well academically.

When Tan asked the students why Cambodian youths join gangs, their answers were very similar to those of Kang's interviewees. Tan also asked for suggestions on how gang membership can be reduced. The replies can be summarized by two statements: "Parents should talk to their kids more often, ask them questions, don't leave them isolated on their own," and "Sometimes parents expect too much, and their kids run away to gangs" (291).

Cambodian parents are increasingly recognizing the importance of parent-child communication. Some now advocate following a "middle way"—not too strict, not too lenient—in terms of raising children so family unity can be preserved. Because the "middle way" is a key Buddhist concept, it is clear that in this instance, too, Cambodians in America are trying their best to negotiate between cultures that collide.

Unfortunately, however, not all Cambodian parents are in a position to act so rationally. Dozens of studies have shown that Cambodians suffer from the highest rates of post-traumatic stress disorder, major depression, and other psychological ailments of any ethnic group in America. Parents who have such deep-seated problems must somehow transcend the tragedies they have experienced before they can deal reasonably with their children in a land that, to many of them, seems so alien in so many ways.

7 Transcending Tragedy

LIKE MOST SOCIETIES, Cambodian ethnic communities in the United States are segmented by class, gender, age, religion, and other markers of social difference. But one axis of demarcation is unique to Cambodians—the disjuncture between those who have managed to cope with the traumas of the Pol Pot period and those who have not. More has been written about the psychological consequences of the "massive traumas" experienced by Cambodians since the 1970s than about any other topic related to them. Psychiatrists, psychologists, social workers, and anthropologists have produced more than twenty Ph.D. dissertations and M.A. theses, and more than sixty articles about the abysmal mental health of Cambodian refugees have appeared in scientific journals.

During the 1980s, psychiatrists and psychologists used clinical models to analyze Cambodian patients, but in the 1990s anthropologists and social workers began to propose alternative frameworks for understanding the mental health problems that Cambodians continue to face more than a quarter century after being traumatized. The anthropologists and social workers, recognizing the Eurocentric assumptions that often underlie clinical diagnoses, believe it important to use "Khmer cultural beliefs" about illness and misfortune in the therapeutic process because doing so will empower survivors to participate more actively in their healing. Even Cambodians not directly traumatized feel obliged to heal themselves and their people by participating in the reconstruction of their ancestral land.

Trauma and Its Aftermath

Although much has been written about the post-traumatic stress disorder (PTSD), major depression, dissociative experiences, and anxieties that afflict

Cambodian refugees, it is relatively easy to summarize the studies because they all paint the same general picture: Cambodians in the United States (and very likely elsewhere) suffer from a higher incidence of severe mental health problems than any other group. Although it is not surprising that such high rates characterize those undergoing psychiatric treatment, it is disturbing that nonpatients—individuals not receiving any medical attention—show equally high or even higher rates. Worst of all, some studies show that the trauma has intergenerational effects and now affects some children of the trauma victims.

PTSD was explicitly named as a psychiatric diagnostic category only in 1980, when the third edition of the American Psychiatric Association's *Diagnostic and Statistical Manual of Mental Health Disorders* (DSM-III, 1980) listed its defining characteristics. The manual's fourth edition, DSM-IV, published in 1994, states:

> The essential feature [of PTSD] is the development of characteristic symptoms following exposure to an extreme traumatic stressor involving direct personal experience of an event that involves actual or threatened death or serious injury or threat to one's physical integrity; or witnessing an event that involves death, injury or threat to the physical integrity of another person; or learning about unexpected or violent death, serious harm or threat of death or injury experienced by a family member or other close associate. The individual's response to the event involves intense fear, helplessness or horror, in children it involves disorganized or agitated behavior. (American Psychiatric Association 1994: 427)

Individuals with PTSD have three kinds of symptoms. First, they frequently reexperience the trauma by remembering it while they are awake or having nightmares about it while they are asleep. They can become dissociated from reality and act as though they are actually experiencing the trauma right that moment. They are also liable to feel intense psychological distress or become physically ill when present events remind them of the past trauma. Second, as much as possible, they avoid thoughts, feelings, and conversations about—or interactions with—others who might remind them of the trauma. They are psychically "numb," feel detached from other human beings, and show little interest in activities. Third, they are always anxious and excessively vigilant. They cannot sleep well, often have angry outbursts, cannot concentrate, and are easily startled. Individuals are diagnosed as having PTSD only after they have exhibited these symptoms for at least a month and the symptoms seem to impair their ability to function in daily life (American Psychiatric Association 1994: 427–29).

J. David Kinzie, M.D., first diagnosed Cambodians as suffering from PTSD in 1984, six years after he and his colleagues in the Department of Psychiatry at Oregon Health Sciences University opened a clinic for Indochinese refugees in Portland. With an influx of refugees from Bosnia and Somalia in the 1990s the clinic now also serves those groups and has changed its name to the Intercultural Psychiatric Program to reflect that fact.

From the clinic's beginning, psychiatrists have been assisted by well-trained mental health counselors who speak Khmer, Vietnamese, Lao, and Hmong. As the caseload grew to the hundreds, Kinzie and his colleagues collected the most systematic longitudinal data available on Cambodians who suffer from PTSD and major depression. Although many did improve with medication and talk therapy, Kinzie et al. report that the Cambodians' symptoms have persisted longer than those of other Indochinese refugees. Moreover, many Cambodians have found no relief through talk therapy (Boehnlein et al. 1985; Kinzie et al. 1984). Unlike others with PTSD who can rely on social support networks to help speed their recoveries, many Cambodians have family members who suffer from the same problems as they do (Kinzie 1988: 78).

People with PTSD are extremely vulnerable to any kind of stress, including accidents, assaults, surgery, and even violent scenes on television or in movies. A survey of patients at the Oregon clinic who watched television images of the September 11, 2001, terrorist attacks on the World Trade Center and the Pentagon indicates that they experienced "secondary traumatization" during which their PTSD symptoms were reactivated. They had recurrent nightmares and intrusive memories, and were depressed. They also felt it unsafe to be in the United States. It took two to three months for them to return to their "baseline clinical status" (Kinzie et al. 2002). Dr. Chhean Kong—a Buddhist monk and psychotherapist—likewise reports treating many Cambodians at the Long Beach Asian Pacific Mental Health Program and says that their trauma symptoms were reactivated in the weeks following the terrorist attacks (Kong interview 2001 in Chan, ed. 2003a: 66).

Twelve years after the clinic in Oregon first opened, a survey of all the Indochinese refugees ever treated there shows that 70 percent met the criteria for a current diagnosis of PTSD, and an additional 5 percent met the criteria for a past diagnosis (Kinzie et al. 1990). Had data for the various refugee groups been disaggregated, the percentages would have been even higher for Cambodians. Other studies have shown that, as a group, the Vietnamese suffer from much lower rates of PTSD than do Cambodians.

Studies done elsewhere show similar results. Psychiatrists at the Central Health Center in Providence, Rhode Island, screened Cambodian patients in 1989 and found that 63 percent showed positive depression scores and 56 percent had positive anxiety scores (Chow and Krumholtz 1989). In Brighton, Massachusetts, Richard F. Mollica, M.D., and his colleagues at the Indochinese Psychiatry Clinic treated and studied fifty-two Southeast Asian patients, twenty-one of them Cambodian. They discovered that Cambodians were more traumatized than the Vietnamese, Lao, or Hmong. The Cambodians experienced a mean number of sixteen trauma events, compared to eleven for the Lao and Hmong and only two for the Vietnamese. Before treatment began, the Cambodians had feelings of extreme hopelessness and worthlessness, but after six months of treatment they showed slight improvement in their depressive symptoms (Mollica et al. 1990).

In Utah, Robert G. Blair (1996) found that 45 percent of his sample of 124 Cambodians met the criteria for PTSD and 51 percent for major depression. The rates indicated in these studies are all much higher than comparable figures for the U.S. population as a whole. By way of a rough comparison, according to doctors studying how various kinds of severe trauma may lead to PTSD and physically damage the brain, only about 15 percent of trauma victims in the general U.S. population—regardless of the nature of the trauma—are likely to have long-lasting, severe PTSD effects (Goleman 1995).

Social workers and psychologists have found that among Cambodian refugees, PTSD can also result from the trauma caused by events other than those related to the Khmer Rouge carnage. Josette M. Rosas, a social worker, reports (1999) that among the eighty-four patients whom she interviewed at the Southern California Mental Health Program in Long Beach, there was a positive correlation between the number of years spent at a holding camp for refuge-seekers and the severity of PTSD symptoms. The longer refugees had lived in a camp in Thailand, the more likely they were to develop PTSD. Furthermore, having family members still in Cambodia and worrying about them constantly also worsens their PTSD symptoms. Psychologist Lani Chow, who interviewed seventy-seven Indochinese refugees, of whom twenty-three were Cambodians, found (1995) that those who have lost a spouse, who cannot speak English well, and who do not attend religious services show the highest levels of anxiety and depression. Gary J. Rezowalli (1990), also a psychologist, who surveyed 136 Cambodian refugees in San Jose, California, found that symptoms of depression and anxiety as well as somatic complaints are most numerous among those who are old, have little education, cannot speak English, have large families, and are on public assistance.

PTSD and major depression both affect the ability of refugees to acculturate. Susan B. Strober (1990), a social worker, has noted that among the 102 Cambodian refugees she interviewed in the Washington, D.C., area, those who did not suffer from severe psychological distress experienced a smoother adjustment to life in the United States. Psychologist Tali K. Walters's study (1994) yielded similar results, although she states her findings in an opposite way: Cambodians who experienced severe trauma show higher levels of acculturative stress.

Studies of nonpatients show that people who are not seeking help have even higher rates of severe psychological symptoms than individuals who do receive treatment. Educator Rhonda L. Rosser-Hogan examined fifty Cambodians in Greensboro, North Carolina. Using four different scales to measure PTSD, depression, anxiety, and dissociative states, she and her coauthor Eve B. Carlson report that 86 percent of the subjects they surveyed met the criteria for PTSD, 80 percent could be classified as suffering from clinical depression, and 96 percent had high dissociative scores. Correlations between the respondents' trauma scores and symptom scores were moderate to large (Carlson and Rosser-Hogan 1991, 1993; Rosser-Hogan 1991). In another study of nonpatients, psychologists Laura Uba and Rita C. Chung (1991) found that trauma experiences have a negative impact on the incomes of Cambodian refugees and are also related to more physical health problems.

Although symptoms of psychological distress need not impair an individual's ability to care for himself or herself or others or even to work, there are reported cases of how a flashback of a trauma event can cause someone to go into a psychotic state. (In the longitudinal data collected by Kinzie et al., 7 percent of the patients with PTSD became psychotic and had to be restrained and hospitalized.) An official in North Carolina in charge of refugee affairs told me a tragic story of a Cambodian man who found a job in a meatpacking plant. When he saw the raw meat and blood, he had a flashback of the "killing fields" and his near-death experience and went into a catatonic state from which he never recovered.

The psychological problems of Cambodian mental health patients often manifest themselves in somatic ways. Florentius Chan, a Chinese American psychologist who served as the first director of the Asian Pacific Mental Health Center in Los Angeles, which opened its doors in 1986, indicated that 80 percent of his Cambodian clients had chronic headaches, 62 percent experienced dizziness, 49 percent had sleep disturbances, and 30 percent dealt with chronic pain and poor memory. Moreover, 73 percent lost siblings and/ or parents during the Pol Pot years, 57 percent experienced extreme hunger, 50 percent had been tortured, 35 percent lost spouses, and 24 percent lost children. These people's symptoms increased after they arrived in America because, according to Chan, their struggles for daily survival overshadow the trauma they experienced while still in Cambodia and Thailand. To survive physically, people in such circumstances tend to suppress grief, anger, resentment, and desire for revenge. Only after reaching a safe haven do they allow these feelings to surface. Up to that point they had "swallowed their tears," Chan explains. Perhaps psychotherapy can enable them to retrieve those experiences and, ultimately, "move beyond those tears" (Haldane 1987).

Two subgroups of Cambodian refugees have received special attention from researchers—adolescents and women. William H. Sack, M.D., and his team at Oregon Health Sciences University studied adolescents in Portland and Salt Lake City. They found that adolescents, like adults, show a strong correlation between PTSD and the trauma experienced during the Khmer Rouge period as well as stresses experienced during resettlement. Among the young people, major depression (a different diagnostic condition than PTSD, although the two often coexist) is strongly related to more recent stressful events. Sack and his colleagues also interviewed the adults who took care of the adolescents, which enabled them to see how the young people assess the state of their personal mental health compared to how their parents, foster parents, or teachers evaluate it. The researchers discovered that the youths are suffering more than the adults realize (Sack et al. 1986).

A similar finding was made by Cecile Rousseau and Aline Drapeau at the Psychiatry Department of Children's Hospital in Montreal. Among their Cambodian clients, they measured the extent of parent-child agreement on the children's psychiatric symptoms and discovered that the parents report far fewer symptoms in their children than do the children themselves. They hypothesized that the discrepancy is likely because Cambodians are socialized to refrain from showing their feelings. Thus, adults who care about family honor may underreport forms of behavior, such as overt displays of psychological stress, that they consider socially unacceptable (Rousseau and Drapeau 1998).

In a three-year follow-up study, Sack's team found that 48 percent of the adolescents in 1989 were still suffering from PTSD and 41 percent from major depression (Kinzie et al. 1989). In a six-year follow-up study of the same youths, PTSD symptoms were still present although less intense, with a prevalence rate of 38 percent; the prevalence of depression had dropped markedly (Sack et al. 1993).

The correlation between PTSD in parents and PTSD in their adolescent children is significant. In families in which neither parent has PTSD, only 13 percent of adolescents suffer from it. In families in which one parent has PTSD, 23 percent of youths have it as well. In homes where both parents have PTSD, 41 percent of children have the condition (Sack, Clarke, and Seeley 1995). In their twelve-year follow-up study, Sack, Him, and Dickason (1999) found that PTSD and depression among their patients appear to have followed different pathways over time. Whereas 35 percent of the group still had PTSD, the prevalence rate of depression actually increased between the sixth and the twelfth years, from 7 percent to 14 percent. They also found great variability in the "chronicity" of PTSD itself. For some clients, the disorder developed early but eventually disappeared; in others, symptoms made a delayed appearance. PTSD's long-term effects seem related to specific traumatic experiences rather than to a generalized sense of loss or displacement. Finally, despite the persistence of symptoms, individuals in the study seem to have made the "transition into American culture quite successfully."

Researchers in the Division of Child and Adolescent Psychiatry and the Institute of Child Development at the University of Minnesota have also examined adolescents. George M. Realmuto and his colleagues (1992) studied forty-seven Cambodian adolescents at a summer camp and found that 37 percent of them met the PTSD criteria. The older children in the sample recalled more exposure to trauma than did the younger ones; 91 percent of the boys and 89 percent of the girls had experienced starvation and seen dead bodies, and 57 percent of the boys and 40 percent of the girls had witnessed the torture of someone they knew. The same research team later studied fifty-nine adolescents in Minneapolis and St. Paul and found that 24 percent of them suffered from PTSD at the time they were interviewed; 59 percent could be classified as having a lifetime diagnosis. Girls showed a significantly higher rate than boys for both the current and lifetime diagnoses. Of the adolescents with current signs of PTSD, 57 percent had at least one additional psychiatric disorder (Hubbard et al. 1995).

Psychologist Andrea K. Northwood likewise found that the girls she studied had more symptoms than did the boys (1996). A slightly brighter picture is presented by Jon J. Hubbard (1997), also a psychologist, who discovered in studying forty young people that general trauma exposure is only moderately related to academic, social, work, and romantic competence. The academic

and work competence of Cambodian adolescents, however, is definitely negatively affected by PTSD and depression. In other words, exposure to trauma, in and of itself, does not always impair children. Yet those who develop
psychological problems because of the trauma show less ability to deal with
various aspects of adolescent life. Hubbard also reported that youths who are
bicultural—that is, connected to both Cambodian and American cultures—
have the highest overall competence scores. A similar conclusion was reached
by Tow Yee Yau (1995), another psychologist. Among his sample in Denver,
those who retain aspects of their ethnic culture while simultaneously identifying with the American mainstream have higher self-esteem and self-efficacy than those who identify with only one culture.

American society is itself full of dangers and can thus be a source of trauma (chapter 6). Social worker Sarah M. Berthold (1998) has analyzed Cambodian youth in southern California and supports that point. A third of her interviewees had symptoms of PTSD, whereas two-thirds showed symptoms of
major depression. She found that the violence that youngsters encounter in
school and on the streets of American cities has affected them as negatively as
the trauma they experienced before arriving in the United States. As might be
expected, Cambodian children and teenagers in families living on welfare in
crime-ridden neighborhoods are exposed to the most violence—violence that
both endangers their lives and causes them severe mental health problems.

Studies that include Cambodian female subjects consistently show that
women suffer psychological distress more than men do. The Rhode Island
study (Chow 1989) shows that a significantly larger percentage of women
suffer from anxiety. Angela S. Ryan (1985), a social worker who surveyed 158
Indochinese refugees including Cambodians (although she did not specify
how many) in New York City, found that high emotional distress correlates
strongly with five factors: being female, unemployed, Buddhist, in poor
health, and unable to speak English. The data collected by psychologist Eric
A. Egli (1989) on 193 Cambodians in Minnesota show that women scored
significantly higher than men in all the measures Egli used. Women's distress
is so pervasive that he calls it "global distress." Egli, however, also asked respondents about their general ability to function and whether they had any
pleasurable experiences. Fewer than 20 percent rated their ability to function
as less than average, and most felt their energy level and enjoyment of life to
be comparable to those of others.

The most puzzling disorder that Cambodian women refugees experience
is psychosomatic blindness— individuals claim they cannot see even though
opthalmological tests show no organic or physiological basis for blindness

or partial blindness. Patricia D. Rozee, a psychologist, and Gretchen B. Van Boemel, director of clinical electrophysiology at the Doheny Eye Institute at the University of Southern California, have written a number of articles about this strange condition after examining 150 elderly Cambodian women who claimed to have such a loss of visual acuity (Rozee and Van Boemel 1990; Van Boemel and Rozee, 1992). They disagree with medical doctors who dismiss the women as malingerers—people who use their eye problem as an excuse not to work. Unlike the cases of "hysterical blindness" that Sigmund Freud reported (a condition Freud attributed to childhood sexual trauma and subsequent psychosexual maladjustment), Rozee and Van Boemel hypothesize that the elderly Cambodian women's condition may be related to the multiple traumas that they experienced under the Khmer Rouge, during their arduous escapes to Thailand, and the stressful years in the holding camps in Thailand. They quote an estimate made by Richard F. Mollica, M.D., that perhaps as many as 95 percent of the Indochinese refugee female psychiatric patients he has seen had been raped not once but many times, even though most of them are too ashamed to reveal that fact. Dr. Chheang Kong also indicates that it can be estimated, based on his conversations with parishoners and clients, that 80 to 90 percent of the women had been raped (Kong 1996 interview in Chan, ed. 2003a: 76–77).

In short, women suffered even more horror than men did. Rozee and Van Boemel assert the importance of recognizing the inner strength these women must possess—strength that enabled them to have survived at all. Although there seems to be no cure for them, Rozee and Van Boemel argue that they should at least be given a psychiatric examination to see if they qualify for disability benefits.

Journalist Alec Wilkinson has told of two such women whom he met in Long Beach. During the Khmer Rouge period, Mrs. Im Cheann was given the responsibility for gathering together the inhabitants of her work camp to witness executions. The Khmer Rouge soldiers forced people, including family members of victims, to watch mutely as individuals were beaten to death, disemboweled, beheaded, or hanged. Those who showed emotion would themselves be liable for death because expressing emotion meant they cared more about their family members than about the wishes of the Khmer Rouge leadership. Perhaps in response to her gruesome task, Im Cheann soon lost her sight, but she was afraid to let the Khmer Rouge know lest they killed her, too. She told Wilkinson that the beatings she received caused her spirit to leave her body, and she thought that was the reason she could no longer see (Wilkinson 1994: 53).

Mrs. Long Eang suddenly lost her sight after a villager led her to a spot splattered with dried, caked blood, near which stood a pile of clothing. She recognized the clothes as those her brother and his family had worn on the day they were taken away. After the shock of recognition, she remained completely blind for many days. Since then, she has gone in and out of blindness. On any particular day how much she can see depends on how frightened she is. She can make out blurred images on some days, but on others she cannot see at all and feels as though needles are piercing her eyes (Wilkinson 1994: 56–57).

Women like Im Cheann and Long Eang are frustrated that no one can tell them why they went blind and how they might be cured. Even though they cannot see the world around them, what remains crystal clear in their minds are images of the atrocities they witnessed. Long Eang told Wilkinson that the only faces she sees when she closes her eyes are those of the Khmer Rouge. As Wilkinson puts it, "They are pursued by their memories; their memories harass them, and they cannot get rid of them except by the most contrived and mechanical resolve to forget, which takes all their energy and leaves them feeling cheerless and drained" (1994: 68).

I suggest that we may interpret psychosomatic blindness in two opposite ways. We can think of it as a pathology and try to determine whether it is another manifestation of PTSD or as a coping mechanism that the afflicted women have developed. As a coping mechanism, people who have gone "blind" no longer have to witness grim events. During the Khmer Rouge period, people acted as though they were deaf and mute in order to survive. Now, perhaps some women have gone "blind" in order to screen out further traumatic images and carry on with their lives.

Alternative Perspectives on Trauma and Healing

Some psychiatrists who treat Cambodian patients are well aware of cultural differences and the need to take them into account. That is particularly true of David Kinzie and James Boehnlein, who have written insightful articles on the challenges facing cross-cultural therapy (Boehnlein 1987a, 1987b; Kinzie and Boehnlein 1989; Kinzie 1989). Still, the model underlying their approach is based on a Western notion of pathology. During the 1990s, a number of scholars proposed getting away from this pathological model if people in the helping professions are to treat Cambodians who have mental health problems more effectively.

Such a new direction was initiated by doctors treating American Vietnam War veterans who suffered from PTSD. They argued that their patients' symptoms should not be construed as abnormal but rather as normal responses to abnormal events. When individuals experience brutality or witness monstrosities, they should be shocked, dismayed, and depresssed, not just momentarily but for a prolonged period. As sociologist Martha Kay Parker concludes (1996), Indochinese refugees, including Cambodians, have suffered not one but four "domains of loss": the loss of an entire way of life, the loss of key relationships, the loss of the roles into which they had been socialized, and the loss of the ability to transmit their cultural heritage to children and grandchildren. Most people who suffer from just one such "domain of loss" would be extremely upset. What must it be like to suffer all those losses simultaneously? In other words, Cambodians who show an exceptionally high incidence of PTSD, major depression, dissociative states, or anxiety are not abnormal. Rather, these so-called pathological conditions can be interpreted as normal responses to the extraordinarily abnormal situations they faced and survived.

Cambodians themselves say that what they call the "Khmer illness" is caused by "thinking too much." It is a manifestation at the individual level of an overall "cultural breakdown," observes Johara M. Chapman, an anthropologist (1995). Cambodians attribute that condition to severe war trauma as well as to current sources of stress, especially violence in their present neighborhoods and extreme worries over their children. Chapman's respondents believe they suffer from a uniquely Cambodian illness and that Americans cannot get it (62). As one who lost both his parents and all six siblings explained his dilemma: "A few [Cambodians] think too much about the war and their lost family. . . . Sometimes I want to die, too, but suicide is not reasonable. Why should I have survived the Khmer Rouge only to kill myself now? . . . I believe I must endure the pain in my body. . . . If I were to kill myself . . . I would be nowhere, not in this life or in the next. . . . I feel very frustrated, very nervous, but I must keep struggling" (Chapman 1995: 36). Sometimes living can be more difficult than dying.

Chapman interviewed a psychiatrist who pointed out another dimension of the condition that afflicts so many Cambodian refugees. "Very few Cambodians," he said, "are seriously incapacitated by PTSD or depression. The major problem is boredom. Back in Cambodia they were farmers. They went to bed at 8 p.m. and rose at 4 a.m. and went to work in the fields all day. Here . . . they have nowhere to go, nothing to do. . . . They tend to stay in their small apartments all day so they do not get . . . tired and then have difficulty sleeping—not because of PTSD or depression but because of boredom" (Chapman 1995: 53–54). In other words, the refugees' current lives—their social isolation and feelings of being worthless—may be part of the problem. Being socially marginal is not conducive to developing a strong motivation to heal.

Other service providers note that the U.S. welfare system also discourages recipients from participating fully in society. Even after welfare reform began, those who are ill can still continue to receive SSI payments if they remain disabled. According to individuals who are critical of the welfare system, mental health services may actually be "harmful in that they tend to perpetuate a sense of victimhood and inappropriate entitlement" (Chapman 1995: 57–58).

Maurice Eisenbruch, an anthropologist, maintains that it is important to explore the meaning that refugees give to their suffering and the strategies they use to overcome it. He suggests that in certain instances it is more appropriate to call the condition "cultural bereavement" rather than PTSD. He also thinks that "refugee distress . . . may be a normal, even constructive, existential response rather than a psychiatric illness." Eisenbruch defines cultural bereavement as "the experience of the uprooted person—or group—resulting from loss of social structures, cultural values and self-identity." The syndrome of pain, morbid thoughts, and anxieties "is not of itself a disease but an understandable response to catastrophic loss." In his view, antidotes should include active attempts to revive the cultural practices that once gave meaning to refugees' lives (Eisenbruch 1991: 673–74).

Eisenbruch tells of a Cambodian refugee woman in Australia who suffered from nightmares, blackouts, shortness of breath, and tingling extremities. Doctors diagnosed her as having PTSD. When Eisenbruch talked to her in Khmer, however, she reported three kinds of worries. First, she never had a chance to conduct proper rituals after her parents died during the Khmer Rouge period. Second, because she gave birth in a hospital, her baby arrived on "the wrong day" after doctors delivered the baby by caesarean section. Moreover, they had thrown out the placenta instead of letting her family bury it according to traditional Cambodian postpartum practices. Third, she lived in a neighborhood where she thought evil spirits visited. Eisenbruch took her to see a kru Khmer who performed rituals to expel the evil spirits from her surroundings. The kru also placed a protective marker around her house. Soon thereafter the woman stopped having nightmares, and her physical symptoms also subsided (Eisenbruch 1991: 675–76).

In this instance, Eisenbruch is not advocating that we believe in spirits.

Rather, he is arguing that because cultural beliefs underlie conceptions of illness and health, tapping into those beliefs will do no harm and may even bring positive results. If a person suffers from mental illness, and if the rituals of a traditional healer allow that person to think something efficacious is being done, then that more hopeful frame of mind may become a positive factor in the healing process. Eisenbruch is fully aware that a culturally bereft person may indeed have PTSD or other psychiatric disorders, but he maintains that it is also important to determine whether some symptoms are "mimicking" PTSD. He points out that although some symptoms of PTSD (e.g., nightmares, chronic insomnia, and startle reactions) can be treated with Western drugs, other symptoms (e.g., avoidance behavior, shame, and withdrawal from social interactions) may respond better to the methods used by kru Khmer. He concludes that "when grief occurs in response to loss of culture—in other words, the bereavement is no longer just personal but cultural—the cultural meaning of the loss cannot be dismissed" (Eisenbruch 1991: 676).

Some Cambodians apparently think that the "Khmer illness" is incurable and all that can be done is to protect individuals who have it from further distress. Protection is provided mainly by having someone stay with and watch over a sick person at all times (Chapman 1995: 64, 71). Providing constant companionship is one of the main treatment modalities that kru Khmer use. Anthropologist Julianne S. Duncan, who closely observed four extended families in Tacoma, Washington, discovered that Cambodians use both Western doctors and traditional healers to alleviate mental illness. Some people try Western medicine first, and when that seems ineffective they resort to traditional methods. Others see Western doctors and kru Khmer simultaneously. Kru Khmer characterize mental illness as a "weakness of spirit," which means that sufferers are too weak to prevent malevolent spirits from invading their bodies and making them ill. Therefore, kru Khmer perform rituals to drive out the evil spirits. They chant, spray holy water on the afflicted, blow across their heads, and stroke their limbs to prevent their own spirits from leaving their bodies and keep evil spirits from entering them. Some kru Khmer allow a sufferer to sleep for a few days in the room where the altar honoring the kru's guardian spirit is located. During this time the kru or a relative sleeps in the same room, near the door to guard it against intruding spirits. Kru Khmer often perform rituals in the homes of clients while family members take precautions to prevent the sufferers from harming themselves (Duncan 1987: 173–262).

Some believe that neither Western doctors nor kru Khmer can cure them.

"I don't think they can heal me!" a person social worker Paula T. Tanemura Morelli interviewed declared emphatically. "The only time that this suffering will go away is when I die" (1996: 135). Based on an intensive study of four cases, Morelli notes that some doctors make matters worse when they belittle or dismiss a sufferer's symptoms because there seems no biological basis for them. The patients' problems are real enough; their "suffering may diminish, but never completely go away, and seems to recur in full measure when exacerbating circumstances or events trigger the survivor's recall of traumatic times in Cambodia" (Morelli 1996: 170). She observes that individuals who see their suffering in collective rather than individual terms seem best able to find meaning in their experiences and derive strength from them.

Barbara L. Nicholson, a social worker who designed and co-led a Cambodian women's support group with a Khmer-speaking colleague, likewise points to the effectiveness of a collective approach. As she puts it, "The most important curative factor of support groups is the mutual aid and *normalization* of experience by members, whereas the most important goal is the enhancement of coping skills gained through this mutual aid and sharing" (Nicholson and Kay 1999: 471, emphasis added). By having the opportunity to articulate and share feelings with others in similar circumstances, some individuals in support groups begin to realize they are not suffering alone and that their suffering is not due to a character weakness.

The theme of strength likewise underpins the research done by Cheryl D. West, a psychologist (2000); by Theanvy Kuoch, Richard A. Miller, M.D., and Mary F. Scully, R.N. (1992) in therapy they offer at the Khmer Health Advocates in West Hartford, Connecticut; by Patricia K. R. Herbst (1992) in the therapeutic work she does at the Majorie Kovler Center for the Treatment of Torture Survivors in Chicago; and by Celine Rousseau and her colleagues at Children's Hospital in Montreal (Rousseau and Drapeau 1998; Rousseau, Drapeau, and Platt 1999).

West, who interviewed people in Lowell, Massachusetts, as well as in Phnom Penh, sought to find personality traits common to survivors who have not succumbed to mental illness. Interviewees report that the same coping strategies they used during the Khmer Rouge period—self-reliance, patience, and persistence—are what helped them survive during the years that followed. Some people also mention that emotional denial was an important survival mechanism during the Khmer Rouge years. They echo the words of many others when they say that what kept them alive were "becoming numb to feelings, not being able to hear, not being able to see, not being able to speak or smile, or pretending to know nothing" (West 2000: 69). The interviewees emphasize that being able to ask for help has been critical in the ability to prevail. "Asking for help was described as being able to have compassion for oneself in times of need or challenge" (73). Compassion, of course, is a key Buddhist value.

Cambodians who have not developed debilitating mental health problems have managed to transform their losses into strengths. They have grown and even thrived rather than suffered. Thus adversity has two faces. It can be a catalyst for growth, or it can lead to dysfunctional illnesses. As one woman declared, "Trauma destroys our personal landscape but the landscape isn't just trauma" (West 2000: 6). West argues that labeling refugees as "victims" supports vulnerability or a deficit model of human behavior and does disservice to individuals who have developed enormous strength and optimism— not in spite of but because of traumatic experiences.

Kuoch, Miller, and Scully used the contextual model of family therapy when they ran Khmer Health Associates. (Sad to say, funding for the clinic has dried up, forcing the organization to curtail its services.) They point out that because it was dangerous to tell the truth during the *Mahantdori* (a time of great destruction) in the 1970s, Cambodian refugees continue to be afraid to say anything. Thus, therapists must overcome clients' fear that it is not "safe" to reveal details about themselves or their families to anyone. Their verbal reticence is not an aspect of Cambodian normative behavior but the outcome of specific historical experiences and structural factors. At the same time, the three therapists, including Kuoch—a survivor of the Mahantdori— firmly believe that it is important for each individual to tell his or her story. The Khmer term for depression is *thlek tuk chet* (the heart and mind are no longer connected). Therefore, "telling their stories which reconnect the hearts and minds of survivors has a powerful effect on mobilizing them to help find solutions for today's problems" (Kuoch, Miller, and Scully 1992: 203).

To minimize the survivor guilt that so many Cambodians feel—their belief that family members perished because they had not done enough to help them or because those who survived had only looked out for themselves—Kuoch, Miller, and Scully urge clients to talk about ways in which they *had* tried to help their families. In their view, "Survivor guilt . . . is the single most immobilizing force in Cambodian family relationships" (1992: 202) and must be dealt with frontally yet creatively. They encourage clients to refocus and move from feeling guilty toward a recollection of their efforts to help. In a 1995 interview with Audrey Kim, one of the clinic's founders offered another insight: "There are two groups of people. There are those who are in denial and don't want to talk about their traumatic experiences. Then there are those who want to talk. Cambodians are actually so desperate that they are willing to seek help but the services just aren't available. . . . Anybody who is judgmental or blames a Cambodian for something will not be tolerated. Cambodians associate being blamed with being killed by the Khmer Rouge. So, any time there is a threat of being blamed or judged, they will withdraw." That observation underscores the underlying philosophy of therapists at Khmer Health Advocates: Focus on the positive rather than the negative.

Patricia Herbst, who worked with the Cambodian Therapeutic Group at the Kovler Center for the Treatment of Torture Survivors, also maintains that "trauma is only part of their experience . . . survivors are more than victims: they are strong. . . . They can use their strength to help in the recovery process" (1992: 148). She uses oral history as a form of therapy because she thinks that encouraging survivors to tell their full life stories (even though doing so may take an extraordinary amount of coaxing) instead of only discussing their medical problems is critical to the recovery process. When the Cambodian group was formed, its members said to each other, "Don't talk about it, it's over, don't cry, put it away." But Herbst persisted, encouraging them to talk because she believes that telling their life stories "immediately put[s] the clients in the position of teachers, an empowered position rather than that of the helpless victim" (Herbst 1992: 150).

Herbst's hope is that by having them discuss their experiences in a group setting they can begin to feel they are not alone and can rebuild a new community among themselves, even though their former communities have been destroyed. When Herbst discovered how deeply ashamed group members were about what the Khmer Rouge—their fellow Khmer—had done, she showed them a book of pictures of Nazi concentration camps, where six million Jews were exterminated. Then she invited a Holocaust survivor to share her story. She stressed that survivors have "the power to denounce what happened . . . and to educate the world about it" (Herbst 1992: 152–53). None of the group's members wished to return to Cambodia before therapy began, but some, after it had been in progress for a while, expressed a desire to return and "help their people" (153). To Herbst, the group's desire to help indicates that members think they have the ability to do so. They no longer see themselves as victims but as survivors who have valuable skills that can be used to aid others.

Celine Rousseau and her colleagues likewise emphasize trauma's "dual nature"; it can be both a burden and a source of strength. Instead of focusing on suffering and its symptoms, they urge clinicians and researchers to underscore the "recuperative powers" that trauma victims may possess. In their study of Cambodian adolescents, the researchers discovered that the subjects show relatively few behavioral problems, such as alcohol and drug abuse, violent behavior, membership in street gangs, and criminal activities. They hypothesize that "the traumatic experiences of the family before the child's birth may play a protective role," in the sense that children in such families will try to "overcompensate." They are compelled "to succeed for the sake of those no longer among the living . . . [in order to] restore the family honor. . . . and to appease the spirits of relatives who died without a proper burial" (Rousseau, Drapeau, and Platt 1999: 1270). What a pity that such culturally sensitive, historically informed therapeutic approaches are available to only a small number of Cambodians.

Participating in Cambodia's Reconstruction

Persons of Cambodian ancestry living in diasporic Cambodian communities around the world have also used various nonclinical ways to deal with the tragedies that befell their homeland. Middle-aged, better-educated Cambodian refugees as well as young, college-educated Cambodian Americans overcome or compensate for their sorrowful history by returning to Cambodia to participate in its reconstruction. The return migration of Cambodians who live in the United States, France, Australia, and elsewhere to Cambodia began during the eighteen-month period when the United Nations Transitional Authority in Cambodia (UNTAC) was administering the country. UNTAC needed Khmer-speakers to serve as interpreters and administrative and technical staff. One of UNTAC's chief tasks was to prepare the country for the elections scheduled for 1993, and a Cambodian from the United States was charged with setting up the computer system for processing election returns.

Some of the earliest returnees wished to participate in Cambodian politics. Cambodians residing abroad could vote in the 1993 elections if they could show proof of being "natives of Cambodia" or having at least one Cambodian parent. Few were able to do so, however, because people could register to vote only in Cambodia itself. Moreover, even after registrating, aspiring voters in the United States had to travel to New York City, where the only polling place on American soil was located. Many who wished to vote could not do so because they could not afford the travel expenses.

Some better-off Cambodians in the United States, however, did launch eight of the twenty-one political parties that registered with UNTAC to field candidates. For example, General Sak Sutsakhan, the defense minister in Lon Nol's Khmer Republic and owner of a Dairy Queen restaurant in Anaheim, California, at the time, established the Liberal Democratic Party; Dr. Sean-glim Bit, a resident of El Cerrito, California, and author of *The Warrior Heritage: A Psychological Perspective of Cambodian Trauma* (1991), set up the Free Republican Party; Ted Ngoy, California's doughnut king, founded the Free Development Republican Party in order to bring to Cambodia "the kind of freedom and democracy that makes America great" (Wallace 1993b); and Kim Kethavy, who owned two gas stations in Lakewood, California, initiated the Republic Democracy Khmer Party.

Despite the fact that U.S. law forbids American citizens from holding public office in a foreign country, more than two dozen Cambodians from the United States ran for office during the 1993 election. Two even won seats in the National Assembly: Por Bun Sroeu of Long Beach, who ran as a member of FUNCINPEC in Kompong Cham Province, and Ahmad Yhya, a Cham who also ran on the FUNCINPEC ticket.

Ted Ngoy, however, did not win a seat in the National Assembly. Having worked in the 1988 Bush campaign and visited President George H. W. Bush in the White House, he liked to brag about how well he knew various U.S. politicians. Although he displayed photographs of himself with them, the ploy did not work. After the elections he stayed on in Cambodia to run for the chairmanship of the Cambodian Chamber of Commerce but lost that race as well (Poethig 1997: 145, 147–48). Neither did Kim Kethavy succeed in his bid for office, even though he sold his gas stations in southern California in order to finance the $350,000 campaign. A third losing candidate, Nanda Chamroeun, ran on the Liberal Democratic Party ticket. She had, she said, "learned how to campaign from the Republican Party in Orange County. They taught me how to get the message out and how to raise money. These are skills nobody knows in Cambodia. Women have never been recognized for their hard work here, and the men never really talk about women's issues" (Wallace 1993b). Prince Norodom Ranarridh, head of FUNCINPEC, echoed her negative assessment of the campaign skills of most Cambodian candidates: "The people who came from California have a lot of skills for a campaign that you don't find anywhere else." FUNCINPEC eagerly made use of what these individuals had to offer. The party's radio and television advertisements, for example, were designed by a Cambodian American, Lay-sreng Lu, who had learned financial and marketing skills while managing his doughnut shop in Long Beach (Wallace 1993b).

After the elections, a number of Cambodian professionals who had been active in mutual assistance associations (MAAs) in the United States and knew how to write grant proposals and run agencies returned to Cambodia to serve as consultants or take up executive or staff positions in the new government's bureaucracy and in various nongovernmental organizations (NGOs). As religious studies scholar Kathryn A. Poethig notes, these professionals, called "Khmer experts," many of whom hold U.S. and Cambodian, French and Cambodian, or Australian and Cambodian dual citizenships, are replicating the mediator role they played in the countries where they were resettled. After they return to Cambodia, they serve as cultural brokers between Cambodian government officials and international development agencies, human rights organizations, and NGOs (Poethig 1997: 156).

During the late 1990s, a more quixotic attempt to use the United States as a base from which to launch political activities in Cambodia came to light. Like some Vietnamese expatriates who hope to overthrow the exising government in the Socialist Republic of Vietnam, Cambodians who call themselves "Cambodian Freedom Fighters" have tried to destabilize the present Cambodian government. The group is headed by Yasith Chhun, who claims the organization has some five hundred members. He likes to show visitors an elaborate spread sheet that lists the 291 targets of "Operation Volcano"— the Cambodian Freedom Fighters' project to attack hospitals, bridges, and the homes of high-ranking government officials in Cambodia. The Cambodian government reacted swiftly in November 2000 after an assault on the building that housed the Defense Department in Phnom Penh. A court convicted Yasith Chhun in absentia and sentenced two other Cambodian Americans—one a resident of Oregon and the other a resident of Long Beach— for the attack. Because there was no extradition treaty between Cambodia and the United States at the time, however, the U.S. government declined to hand over these individuals. All the U.S. State Department did was declare that the United States "strongly deplores and condemns the attack" and ask the FBI to investigate the group (Chandrasekaran 2001).

A larger number of returnees involved themselves in nonpolitical activities. During the mid-1990s, the Cambodian Network Council (CNC) played a key role in encouraging younger Cambodian Americans to visit Cambodia as volunteers in order to teach English and other subjects and provide various kinds of technical assistance as the country rebuilds itself. The CNC was organized in Chicago in 1988 and incorporated in Texas as a nonprofit organization in 1989. The following year, and with funding from the Office of Refugee Resettlement, it moved its offices to Washington, D.C., in order to be closer to national developments. As Dr. Sam-Ang Sam, who served as its executive director for five years, explains, "In order to do anything, you have to be in Washington. . . . When you need to go to the White House for briefings, you can go, step on the metro and go. And we do go to hearings, testimonies on the Hill and all that. The big institutions and government offices are practically all here. The Cambodian embassy is here in Washington. So, it is very, very important that we be here" (Sam interview 1995 in Chan, ed. 2003a: 193–94). The CNC concerned itself with domestic issues in the United States and with the reconstruction and development of Cambodia. One of its programs, the Cambodian Network Development Project, coordinated MAAs in the United States and helped them to build institutional capacities.

A second subunit, the Cambodian-American National Development Organization (CANDO), sent Americans, particularly those of Cambodian ancestry, to Cambodia to aid in its reconstruction. Founded by a dynamic Cambodian American woman named Thida Khus and modeled after the Peace Corps, CANDO accepted applications from individuals over the age of eighteen who were in good health and fluent in English, could speak Khmer at the intermediate level, and were U.S. citizens. Applicants had to commit to a full year's service. Those accepted had their travel expenses paid if they completed a one-year term. They also had health insurance, including medical emergency evacuation, and received a stipend that was modest by American standards but many times the salary Cambodian nationals in comparable positions received. CANDO volunteers were not allowed to participate in politics, proselytize any religion, or engage in personal business activities (Cambodian Network Council 1993: 2–3). CANDO received funding via Private Agencies Collaborating Together (PACT), a main conduit for funds from the U.S. Agency for International Development (USAID) (Sam interview 1995 in Chan, ed. 2003a: 188). Volunteers were housed in a group-living arrangement in Phnom Penh, where the headquarters of CANDO was located. Individuals had their own rooms within a compound containing four houses.

Given the insecure conditions in the countryside, almost all volunteers worked in the capital, although some went out to job sites in rural areas whenever necessary. The first volunteer to work outside Phnom Penh was Dec Ly of Houston, Texas, who had gone back to Cambodia before CANDO was established. After CANDO volunteers began to arrive he signed up locally and was sent to Siem Reap, where the Angkor monuments are located. With a B.A. in art and geography and great savvy in computer technology, he worked in a UNESCO project that was training local Cambodians to preserve and protect the cultural and natural resources of the area where Angkor Wat and the other temples are located (*Motherland: CANDO Quarterly Newsletter* 1994: 1–2).

During its first year of operation, CANDO sent twenty-two volunteers to Cambodia and recruited three Cambodian Americans already in Phnom Penh. Almost all of them were in their twenties, although the first year's group also included forty-three-year-old Richard Kiri Kim from Beaverton, Oregon, who taught English at a rural development and income-generating organization and also wrote grant proposals and networked on behalf of it.

During the four years of its existence, from 1993 to 1997, CANDO sent eighty-seven volunteers, a handful of them European American, from the United States to Cambodia. They came from all over the country—from Massachusetts and New Hampshire in the East to Washington state in the West, and from Minnesota in the North to Texas in the South. Compared to the distribution of the general Cambodian-ancestry population in the United States, California and Massachusetts were underrepresented. For some reason a disproportionately large number of volunteers were from Minnesota and Oregon.

The volunteers were filled with idealism. Many went to Cambodia to repay their debts to humanity. Darwin Pan, who worked with an unaccompanied minors program in Minnesota before joining CANDO, stated, "When I arrived in the U.S. twelve years ago, someone helped me. Now, [the least I can do] is to help others in return." Sova Niev, who has a degree in political science, declared, "I have gone through tremendous challenging life experiences, but I have managed to turn those negative events in my life into positive ones. I feel that I cannot be at peace until I serve the Cambodian people." And Heng Chhour, a certified nursing assistant, added, "I am fortunate to have had the opportunity to be educated in the U.S., and as a former citizen of Cambodia, I wish to share the work of rebuilding the country of my birth" (*Cambodian Community Focus* 1993: 5).

Volunteers had B.A. or M.A. degrees in a wide variety of fields, including accounting, architecture, art, Asian studies, biology, business administration, computer science, dietics, economics, education, various branches of engineering, English as a second language, geography, graphic design, history, human services administration, international studies, management, mathematics, nursing, political science, psychology, urban policy and planning, and wood science technology. They worked mainly with international NGOs or in various units of the Cambodian government. Regardless of their primary responsibility, almost all of them taught English to the Cambodians with whom they interacted daily. Some found their service so meaningful that they extended their stays.

Some of the volunteers experienced culture shock when they first arrived in Cambodia. Even though they are of Khmer ancestry, they had grown up in the United States and become more Americanized than they realized. Their senses were immediately assaulted by heat, dirt, and signs of poverty everywhere. Even though they were supposed to know how to speak Khmer, many of the American-reared young people could not read the Khmer script. Some nearly panicked when they stepped off the airplane and saw Khmer signs everywhere. While in Cambodia, many wrestled with their identity. "In the States," said one, "I never really labeled myself Cambodian American. . . . I just said, . . . 'I'm Cambodian.' I never thought of myself as American. But then coming here . . . I realized that I am Cambodian American because it's so different. It was a rude awakening for me" (Poethig 1997: 199).

In an essay published in the CANDO newsletter, Sokunthea Sok, who has a B.A. in international studies and political science and was assigned to the Ministry for Rural Development as a technical consultant and administrative assistant, reflected on the same question: "I returned to Cambodia for several personal reasons. This is the place of my birth. I returned to fill a twenty-year void. I left Cambodia . . . when I was ten or eleven years old. . . . My education began in Minnesota, U.S.A., a place where I am considered as [a] 'minority,' a foreigner living in someone else's land, not an American. . . . Since 1980 . . . I received my education in English, based on Western history, culture, customs, traditions, and people. Now I must pick up where I left off . . . I am here to learn about me!" (*Motherland* 1994: 20).

Ronnie (formerly Ranachith) Yimsut, who left Cambodia in 1979 as a fifteen-year-old orphan after witnessing the murder of his entire family, is now a landscape architect who works for the U.S. Forest Service in Oregon. His discussion of why he felt compelled to spend time in Cambodia is poignantly eloquent:

> Although I am a naturalized United States citizen with a successful professional practice and a loving family of my own, I felt something was missing in my life. I was drawn back to Cambodia to explore my roots. I know that I could never feel totally comfortable living in Cambodia again; the urge to return was very instinctive, like salmon wanting to return to the old stream once more. This urge or instinct is very strong, almost overpowering. I have changed a lot since my youth in Cambodia, but there was something deep inside of me, a nagging feeling of emptiness, a whisper that told me to look

back. I am no longer a Khmer, but neither am I an American. . . . I am caught in a very uncomfortable wedge. And I will always be called *anickarchun* [alien or foreigner] . . . by . . . local Khmer and Americans alike. . . . I once felt that I could never return to the place where I have nothing left except terrifying memories of great suffering, starvation, and death. I thought that I could never return to a place where I once bared [*sic*] witness to . . . the cold-blooded murder of my family . . . [but] each time I visit Cambodia, I find a sense of strong inner peace and of reconciling with myself. I am able to finally deal with my past and accept that it did happen. The immense pain I learned to endure over the years began to subside. The nightmares began to ease and then disappear altogether. . . . I eventually ended up taking a year of sabbatical leave from my busy professional practice to serve as a volunteer . . . to help with the rebuilding of Cambodia. My . . . return to Cambodia was . . . to help fill the gaps of my identity. It was something I had to do before I could move forward with my life. (Yimsut 1997)

Thida Khus, the founder and director of CANDO, is still working in Cambodia for an NGO in order to "continue the spirit of the CANDO program." When I contacted her in October 2001 and asked her to assess CANDO, she responded via e-mail:

Most of the volunteers adapted fairly well to the program. We had problems in the first year because . . . we did not take enough time to screen applicants and prepare them for life in Cambodia. . . . Most of them faced culture shock when they first arrived. Their body language, their behavior, and their thinking were perceived [by Cambodians] to be very different. They were not readily accepted as Cambodians because of that and it bothered most of them very much. We gave them cultural orientation, trained them to behave [appropriately] in their roles, and [explained to them] what they were expected to do in their host organizations. . . . Most of them adapted well to life in Cambodia; in fact, some of them adapted too well to the lifestyle that we as a program did not want to condone, such as visiting prostitutes, marrying young girls, etc. While they lived in the housing we provided, they were forbidden to do those things. . . . After two or three months in the country, all of them could communicate easily in Khmer. They also took classes to learn how to write Khmer. The most difficult problem they had to face was the expectations of their relatives. They each got a small stipend but their relatives thought they were rich Americans. Most of them had to spend all their stipend to help their relatives and had difficulty making ends meet towards the end of each month. During our first year of operations, we did not withhold any part of their stipend so that they could buy a ticket home. From the second year onward, we kept $250 a month from their allowance for their fare home when they finished with the program. [Looking back,] . . . we should have sent more of them out to the provinces. The program was conceptualized as a short-term one, so we did not set up the structure for provincial placement, hoping at that time the Peace Corps would come in and do that. . . . CNC [Cambodian Network Council] board members had wanted to send older volunteers and pay them larger stipends but that was not the kind of program USAID [which funded CANDO] envisioned. We could not raise funds from Cambodian American communities because they mostly send money back to help their own relatives and to rebuild temples.

CANDO was only one of many venues through which Cambodians abroad have attempted to offer assistance to Cambodia. For example, Than Pok, executive director of the United Cambodian Community, Inc. (UCC), a large multiservice MAA in Long Beach, received a $400,000 grant in the early 1990s to teach disabled Cambodians to repair motorcycles and raise poultry. In addition, UCC's fundraising efforts garnered some $60,000 from southern California's ethnic Cambodian communities to provide loans to disabled people in Cambodia who wished to start their own businesses. Said Than Pok, "I . . . feel I am making a difference over there. We're helping them when they're most in need. It's exciting" (Miller and Glauberman 1992: E3).

Like the CANDO volunteers, however, some who return to visit on their own are shocked by the poverty they encounter. Referring to the dire needs of relatives in Cambodia, Narin Long of Long Beach, who visited them in 1990, told journalist Charles P. Wallace, "I couldn't believe it. They have nothing at all. They think I'm rich, and now I have to feed them" (Wallace 1990).

Cambodian Americans who return to run for office, serve as volunteers, or open their own businesses have obviously developed a transnational consciousness. They no longer behave as citizens of just one country; rather, they are citizens of the world. By breaking out of the parochial boundaries of ethnicity and nationality and doing their part to aid Cambodia's development (however they may define that development), they are also helping heal their own psychic wounds and transcending tragedy.

Seeking Explanations, Deflecting Guilt

Even when they choose not to talk about them, many Cambodians try in myriad ways to make sense of their experiences. When asked by Audrey Kim whether Buddhism can help explain events that transpired during the Pol Pot period, a monk at the Khmer Theravada Buddhist temple in Silver Spring,

Maryland, declared flatly, "There can be no explanation for Pol Pot within the Buddhist framework. Pot Pot was not a Buddhist." Dr. Chhean Kong of Long Beach offers a lengthier discourse on the same subject:

> The Khmer Rouge leaders forgot [the] . . . ideals [taught by Buddha.] . . . Buddha's teachings of great compassion and great wisdom are excellent, noble, and sublime, but they were not practiced by the Khmer Rouge. [Instead,] . . . the Khmer Rouge practice was to promote hate between Cambodian and Cambodian, to kill one another, to live in eternal fear, tension, and suspicion, like wild animals in a jungle. . . . According to Buddhism, hatred is appeased by love and kindness, evil is won over by goodness, and war is appeased by non-war. The Khmer Rouge's politics and propaganda were deceptive and blind. . . . The Khmer Rouge policy toward Cambodia was abetted by foreigners. Foreigners taught the Khmer Rouge leaders to execute all Cambodian intellectuals, to separate families. When the whole population was very weak, it became possible for foreigners to invade Cambodia very easily. (Kong interview 1996 in Chan, ed. 2003a: 79–80)

Unlike Dr. Kong, who did not name the "foreigners" explicitly, the authors of *Buddhism and the Future of Cambodia* (Khmer Buddhist Research Center, comp. 1986) in Rithisen, a section within the Site II border camp controlled by Son Sann, did not hesitate to point their fingers at the Vietnamese. In a section entitled "Why the Genocide?" Ieng Mouly, one of the authors, offers four explanations for the massive killings. The first and fourth reasons have to do with the Vietnamese, and the second and third with the practices of the Khmer Rouge. First, according to the collective authors, "The Khmer Rouge learned the use of violence from the Communist Vietnamese" (59). In fact, Ieng says, the Vietnamese introduced violence into Cambodia centuries ago when they invaded the country—long before they turned communist.

Second, in the years before they took Phnom Penh, various military leaders among the Khmer Rouge shared power, and each commander controlled his own region. When the party's top leaders tried to impose their will on regional leaders, the latter resisted that effort. This led to a power struggle. Pol Pot carried out one purge after another until he had eliminated most would-be rivals. Purges of fellow revolutionaries increased the death toll.

Third, the Khmer Rouge succeeded because they used both physical and psychological methods to recruit several kinds of people: individuals who had "sadistic and brutal inclinations," members of "social categories which were most backward," immoral people, and uneducated people. Khmer Rouge

leaders promoted members of these groups, who became their faithful min-
ions, and infused a spirit of competition among them so they vied with one
another in efforts to destroy the old society. "The desire to do better encouraged the Khmer Rouge to go even further in their brutality." The Khmer
Rouge leaders praised and promoted those "who could murder without having the victim cry too much . . . or without using guns" (1986: 60–61).

Fourth, even though the Vietnamese had helped the Khmer Rouge in the
late 1960s and 1970s, Cambodia became a political pawn when the Sino-Soviet conflict developed worldwide ramifications. The Khmer Rouge sided
with the People's Republic of China and against the former Soviet Union and
its political protege, Vietnam. Accordingly, the Khmer Rouge set out to destroy the "pro-Vietnamese network in Cambodia, which took the life [sic]
of a considerable number of Khmer Viet Minh and of Khmers who were
trained in Vietnam." Given Vietnam's role, Ieng concluded that "the most
urgent task of the Cambodians at the present hour is the liberation of Cambodia from the Vietnamese yoke" (1986: 61–63).

It is clear that the historic animosity between Vietnam and Cambodia
colored the preceding analysis. Although it is true that the first Cambodians
who learned about communism did so under the tutelege of the Vietnam-
ese-dominated Indochinese Communist Party, Pol Pot and his comrades
learned Marxist theory while studying in France. Moreover, the People's
Republic of China has aided the Khmer Rouge more than Vietnam has. Yet
nowhere are the French or the Chinese mentioned by the Buddhist authors
at Rithisen. For them, the only foreign villain is Vietnam.

Like Buddhist monks, laypeople are also searching for answers. For ordinary Cambodians, the Buddhist concept of karma (kam) does not provide
a satisfactory explanation for what happened, because, as a young woman
interviewed by anthropologist Carol Mortland asks, "Babies who were just
born, why did communists throw them against the rock to shatter their
skulls? . . . How could three million people have bad karma at the same
time? . . . If it had been only myself, I could believe the explanation was my
karma, but I cannot believe this for my whole country" (Mortland 1994b: 85–
86).

Another anthropologist, Frank Smith, interviewed dozens of former peasants who now live in Wisconsin and asked why they thought the killings of
the Pol Pot period could have occurred. They had three explanations that
echo those of the Buddhist authors at Rithisen. First, they thought that a
period of great destruction had been prophesized long ago in the *put tum-
niay* (translations of Buddhist scriptures from Pali, the sacred language of

Theravada Buddhism). These writings predicted a time when uneducated people would rise to power, when houses and streets would be emptied, and when Buddhists would be persecuted and a general catastrophe would occur. People would have no food or water, and both monks and laity would die in great numbers. Many Cambodians believe that these prophesies accurately predicted what transpired during the Pol Pot years (Smith 1989: 19–20).

Second, there are Khmer folk tales about *yeak* (ogres) who eat people's livers as a form of black magic. Although the extent of that practice can never be known, some eyewitness accounts claim the Khmer Rouge did indeed eat the livers of those they killed (Ouk and Simon 1998: 270). One of Smith's respondents asserted, "The Khmer Rouge ate human livers—did you know that? They were just like *yeak*." Another said, "I saw the Khmer Rouge throw babies up in the air, and impale them on knives . . . they cut the livers out of the children they killed . . . oh, god, they were so evil" (Smith 1989: 26–27). According to Khmer folk belief, those who eat human livers gain tremendous courage. The practice, Smith's respondents explained, was what gave the Khmer Rouge courage to kill so relentlessly.

Third, the former peasants maintain that the Khmer Rouge were not civilized Khmer but "dark country people" from the jungles where wild beasts dwell. "Those black people just came out of the forest; they couldn't read; they had no manners; they were just like wild animals." Others believe the Khmer Rouge were not Khmer at all but Vietnamese. A few even consider the Khmer Rouge to be Chinese. Upon seeing Pol Pot's picture for the first time, several of Smith's respondents observed, "He's not Khmer! He looks Chinese to me!" (Smith 1989: 33–34).

Explanations such as these serve two functions. Saying that events had occurred according to prophesy allows people to remove the burden of personal responsibility from their own shoulders. What happened, that is, was not their fault. By claiming that the Khmer Rouge were not real Khmer, or at least uncivilized ones, they exculpate properly socialized Khmer from complicity in the bestial crimes of Pol Pot and his henchmen. Alternately, by asserting that the Khmer Rouge were not Buddhists, the point is made that Khmer Buddhists would never have behaved as the Khmer Rouge did.

Defections and Denials

Pol Pot's erstwhile comrades have resorted to the same strategy of denial, as the complex and treacherous political maneuvers that occurred between 1996 and 1999 so graphically reveal. In the 1993 elections, FUNCINPEC, led by Prince Ranarridh, one of Sihanouk's sons, won fifty-eight seats in the 120-member National Assembly. The Cambodian People's Party (CPP), led by Hun Sen, won fifty-one. Because the CPP controlled much of the administrative machinery in the country, not only at the national but also at the provincial and local levels and in the military, Ranariddh was coerced into sharing power with Hun Sen. Ranariddh became the first prime minister, and Hun Sen became the second prime minister. Each ministry likewise was headed by two chiefs, one representing FUNCINPEC and the other, the CCP.

To tip the balance of power in his own favor, Ranariddh and Hun Sen each ousted potential rivals from his own party as a prelude to the ultimate struggle that would be waged between themselves. In March 1996 the two began to engage in a war of words. They eventually toned down their verbal sparring, but each began to court different factions within the remnants of the Khmer Rouge, which still controlled thousands of soldiers even though an estimated three thousand of its troops defected to the government between 1993 and 1996. During this same period, discord developed within the Khmer Rouge leadership; some individuals seemed ready to strike a deal with the government, whereas Pol Pot adamantly opposed such a move.

In August 1996, Ieng Sary, Pol Pot's brother-in-law and comrade-in-arms since their student days in France, defected to the Phnom Penh government after Hun Sen announced that he was willing to forgive him and lift the death sentence that had been imposed on him in 1979. Ieng Sary cagily surrendered to both Hun Sen and Ranariddh. About ten days before Hun Sen made his announcement, the schism within the Khmer Rouge had surfaced when the Khmer Rouge radio, which was in the hands of cadres loyal to Pol Pot, called Ieng Sary "an agent of the Vietnamese" and condemned him to death. Ieng Sary retaliated by calling Pol Pot "the cruellest and most savage murderer" and labeled the regime they had jointly led "fascist." Ieng Sary, who controlled the Khmer Rouge base at Pailin, in a region rich in precious gems and timber, also gave orders to arrest Ta Mok, the chief of staff in the Khmer Rouge army, and Son Sen, the defense minister, but they eluded his dragnet (Thayer 1996a: 21–22).

After defecting, Ieng Sary distributed a pamphlet to reporters in which he proclaimed, without a trace of irony, that he "had nothing to do with ordering the execution of anyone or even suggesting it. . . . It is Pol Pot and his handful of henchmen—Nuon Chea, Ta Mok, Son Sen—who are the mass murderers of the people of Cambodia, committing until now enormous crimes against mankind" (Lee 1996: 20). On September 14, Ieng Sary received a royal pardon.

The following year, on March 30, a grenade was thrown into a crowd of people—supporters of opposition leader Sam Rainsy, who was critical of both Ranarridh and Hun Sen—gathered for a demonstration in front of the National Assembly building. The blast killed nineteen and wounded more than a hundred. Observers suspected that the grenade had been thrown by Hun Sen's followers. Hun Sen rebutted that his followers had no reason to get violent, because his party was running the country (Tasker 1997: 20). Meanwhile, Ranarridh and Sam Rainsy formed a National United Front, allying themselves against Hun Sen. In the midst of these developments, both Ranarridh and Hun Sen continued to court the Khmer Rouge. Spokespersons for the prince, however, told the Khmer Rouge representatives with whom they were negotiating that FUNCINPEC could not be allied with any Khmer Rouge faction that contained Pol Pot. On June 1, Ranarridh met secretly with Khieu Samphan, another close comrade-in-arms of Pol Pot's, at Preah Vihear in northern Cambodia. On June 18, Hun Sen issued an ultimatum to Ranarridh, asking the prince to choose between the Khmer Rouge or the government (Thayer 1997a: 25).

Meanwhile, aware of the maneuvers going on behind his back, Pol Pot, in an attempt to scuttle additional defections, ordered his loyalists, on June 9, 1997, to track down and execute Son Sen (his former defense minister) and all sixteen members of his family. For good measure, after shooting them dead, the executioners ran a truck repeatedly over the bodies of Son Sen and his family. Ta Mok was also on the death list but managed to escape. Ta Mok then turned around and caught Pol Pot on June 19 as the latter, his second wife, twelve-year old daughter, and about three hundred still-loyal followers were trekking northward through the jungle. The band had Khieu Samphan with them as a hostage. Ta Mok brought Pol Pot back to Anlong Veng and placed him under house arrest (Thayer 1997b: 16).

Negotiations with the Khmer Rouge continued apace. On June 22, the Khmer Rouge faction under Khieu Samphan and Ta Mok agreed to dissolve their provisional government (Thayer and Chanda 1997: 15). Khmer Rouge troops would be allowed to remain in the territory they controlled if they changed into government uniforms and swore allegiance to King Sihanouk (who had reascended the throne in 1993), the Phnom Penh government, and the constitution. Ta Mok—his nickname "the one-legged butcher" notwithstanding—disingenuously declared to FUNCINPEC negotiators: "From the beginning of the struggle to now I have never issued an order to kill anyone. All orders were decided by Pol Pot alone!" (Thayer 1997d: 17). Later, he told a reporter, "It is clear that Pol Pot has committed crimes against humanity. I don't agree with the American figure that millions died, but hundreds of thousands, yes" (Thayer 1997e: 23).

Hun Sen knew that the Khmer Rouge had little use for him because of his close ties to Vietnam, so he took a preemptive strike once he got wind of the arrangement. On July 4 his troops attacked and took FUNCINPEC's headquarters as well as Ranarridh's residence, gaining total control over Phnom Penh by July 7. Ranarridh escaped to France even as Hun Sen's men arrested and executed Generals Ho Sok and Chau Sambath, two of Ranarridh's top military commanders. Ranarridh then flew to New York and Washington, D.C., to ask the United Nations and the U.S. government, respectively, to intervene on his behalf—but to no avail.

In late July 1997, Ta Mok put Pol Pot on trial, an event observed by Nate Thayer, a reporter for the *Far Eastern Economic Review* who had been tracking and reporting on the Khmer Rouge for years. People present at the open-air trial chanted, "Crush! Crush! Crush! Pol Pot and his murderous clique!" and the governor of the area proclaimed, "Our ultimate goal today is that the international community should understand that we are no longer Khmer Rouge and not Pol Potists!" Pol Pot was accused of murdering Son Sen, of attempting to murder Ta Mok and Nuon Chea, and of trying to destroy "the policy of national reconciliation." The tribunal sentenced Pol Pot to life imprisonment (Thayer 1997b: 14–18).

On October 16, 1997, Pol Pot allowed Thayer to interview him after months of negotiation. During the two-hour interview, Pol Pot showed no remorse but declared:

> I came to carry out the struggle, not to kill people. . . . Even now, . . . look at me, am I a savage person? My conscience is clear. . . . I do not reject re-sponsibility—our movement made mistakes, like every other movement in the world. But there was another aspect that was outside our control—the enemy's activities against us. . . . I'm quite satisfied on one thing: If we had not carried out our struggle, Cambodia would have become another Kampuchea Krom in 1975. . . . We had no other choice. Naturally we had to defend ourselves. The Vietnamese . . . wanted to assassinate me because they knew without me they could easily swallow up Cambodia. . . . I want you to know that everything I did, I did for my country. (Thayer 1997c: 14–20)

Pol Pot died on April 15, 1998 at the age of seventy-three. At first, it was thought he died from a heart attack, but Nate Thayer later discovered that he in fact committed suicide because he apparently did not want to give Ta Mok the satisfaction of using him as a bargaining chip by turning him over to an international tribunal (Thayer 1998c: 14; Thayer 1999a: 24). As though to show their contempt for their former supreme leader, Ta Mok's men used broken furniture as fuel for the funeral pyre that cremated Pol Pot's body. Again, the sole Western reporter allowed to witness the event was Nate Thayer.

The day after Pol Pot died, Khmer Rouge representatives met with the Phnom Penh government's defense minister. Ta Mok reportedly said, "Yes, we are prepared to negotiate. . . . But I'm not going to be a running dog of Vietnam like Ieng Sary" (Thayer 1998a: 20). In the ensuing months, those Khmer Rouge leaders willing to negotiate met repeatedly with military commanders representing the Phnom Penh government. On December 4, 1998, some five thousand Khmer Rouge soldiers laid down their arms. Along with about thirty thousand civilians still under Khmer Rouge control, they received food and clothing and were permitted to return to civilian life.

Khieu Samphan, Nuon Chea, and Ta Mok were nowhere to be seen on that day, however. Then, on December 25, Khieu Samphan and Nuon Chea finally agreed to surrender, but Ta Mok did not. Thai authorities, who had been holding the three, turned Khieu Samphan and Nuon Chea over to their former comrades in Pailin (Thayer 1999d: 24–25). Hun Sen received the two royally; the government paid for their stay in a luxury hotel in Phnom Penh and at a seaside resort in Sihanoukville. In a public statement, Khieu Samphan asked Cambodians to "let bygones be bygones" but accepted no responsibility for what the Khmer Rouge had done. "If we have to say who was wrong and who was right, etc., etc., we cannot have national reconciliation," he declared. Hun Sen had initially granted amnesty to the two men but later withdrew it after King Sihanouk refused to approve it and outcries arose from the international community ("Cambodia King Refuses. . . ." 1998). Ta Mok was finally captured in March 1999. In September of that year, a military court charged him with genocide.

These top Khmer Rouge leaders are living as free men in Pailin, Ieng Sary's old fiefdom. Conveniently for them, they can blame everything on the dead Pol Pot. The only two high-ranking Khmer Rouge leaders who are in jail are Ta Mok and Kang Kek Ieu (commonly known as "Duch"), who ran the Tuol Sleng torture and execution center. Photo-journalist Nic Dunlop tracked down Duch in late April 1999. He and Nate Thayer found out that Duch had become a born-again Christian. After being baptized in Battambang River by missionaries from the American Pacific College in 1996, he worked with the missionaries, who were unaware of his true identity or his past. At the time the journalists discovered him, Duch was a "senior health worker" for the privately run American Refugee Committee. He told them:

My unique fault is that I did not serve God, I served men, I served communism. I feel very sorry about the killings and the past. I wanted to be a good communist. Now, in the second half of my life, I want to serve God by doing God's work to help people. . . . I am so sorry. The people who died were good people. . . . I am here now. God will decide my future. . . . There were many men who were innocent. . . . I have great difficulty . . . thinking that the people who died did nothing wrong. . . . For the present and future, I want three things: schools for the children, for my stomach to be full, and I want to finish my life to pray to God, to bring the spirit of God to everybody in Cambodia. (Dunlop and Thayer 1999b: 19–20)

When shown copies of documents from Tuol Sleng, Duch admitted that the signatures authorizing the executions were his but claimed he had no pleasure from his work. He revealed that he and his staff did not use bullets to kill prisoners; rather, they slit their throats ("like a chicken"). He said he was merely a "technician" for the Khmer Rouge—"a waterboy for Nuon Chea." "All the confessions of the prisoners—I worried, is that true or not?" (Thayer 1999b). Calling himself the "chief of the sinners," Duch said that his life resembles that of the Apostle Paul and said that he, too, is remorseful and prays for redemption.

In addition to confessing to his own sins, Duch implicated his fellow Khmer Rouge leaders. He identified Pol Pot, Nuon Chea, and Ta Mok as the main culprits. Pol Pot, according to Duch, never directly ordered the killings. Rather, he relied on Nuon Chea to carry out the dirty work. Ieng Sary, Duch claimed, "knew nothing. He only knew a little of the internal situation in the country because his work was outside Cambodia." (Ieng Sary served as the Khmer Rouge foreign minister for many years.) "Khieu Samphan knew of the killings, but less than the others," continued Duch, who characterized Samphan as a "note-taker" at the party's central committee meetings where important decisions were made. In late September 1999, a military court charged Duch with genocide a few days after it had made the same charge against Ta Mok.

Attempts by the international community to hold a war crimes tribunal to pass judgment on the surviving Khmer Rouge leaders have not yet borne fruit. Even though many individuals who now hold power in Cambodia's national government, including Hun Sen himself, and thousands of provincial and local officials are all former members of the Khmer Rouge, some have opposed Pol Pot's genocidal policies since 1977 and are not against having a tribunal to investigate the crimes against humanity committed by Pol Pot and his inner circle.

In June 1997, Hun Sen and Ranariddh (before their split) wrote to the general secretary of the United Nations, asking the international organization to assist Cambodia in setting up a tribunal. The United Nations appointed a Committee of Experts, which looked into the matter and presented a report in March 1999 to recommend that an Ad Hoc International Criminal Tribunal be established with trials to be held outside of Cambodia (Kiernan 2000: 101). In this tribunal, Cambodians would be allowed to participate only as defendants or witnesses. Arguing that such an arrangement would impugn its sovereignty, the Cambodian government rejected the recommendation, insisting that trials must be held within Cambodia. After months of negotiation, the two parties compromised on creating something called "Extraordinary Chambers" within the Cambodian judicial system. The chambers would include foreign judges and prosecutors serving as advisors to Cambodian judges, but Cambodian prosecutors would form a majority at all levels of procedure (Jarvis 2002: 608).

Meanwhile, Hun Sen ruled out the possibility that Khieu Samphan and Nuon Chea would face trial in whatever court might be set up. Appalled by that decision, about five thousand demonstrators led by Sam Rainsy marched through Phnom Penh in early September 1999, demanding that the United Nations establish an independent tribunal. Despite the protests, the National Assembly, on January 2, 2001, and the Senate, on January 15, 2001, approved a bill to create the "Extraordinary Chambers" in order "to bring to trial senior leaders of Democratic Kampuchea and those who were most responsible for the crimes and serious violations of Cambodian penal law, international humanitarian law and customs, and international conventions recognized by Cambodia, that were committed during the period from 17 April 1975 to 6 January 1979." The Constitutional Council, however, recommended an amendment to remove the possibility that death penalties might be imposed because capital punishment is not sanctioned by prevailing Cambodian law. The National Assembly and the Senate adopted an amended bill in July, the Constitutional Council pronounced it in full compliance with Cambodia's constitution, and King Sihanouk signed it into law in August 2001 (*Bulletin of Concerned Asian Scholars* Web-site).

A new hurdle, however, emerged: The UN representative insisted that "Articles of Cooperation" between the world body and Cambodia must be drawn up and that such articles must take precedence over Cambodian law in case of disagreement between the two. The Cambodian negotiator responded that no such "hierarchy" need exist; moreover, the articles could not "modify, let alone prevail over a law that has just been promulgated" (Jarvis 2002: 609; "Letter from Sok An to Hans Corell," Nov. 23, 2001).

Unable to overcome the impasse, the United Nations ended negotiations with the Cambodian government in February 2002, citing inadequate assurances of judicial "independence, impartiality and objectivity." Six months later, at the prodding of many UN member states, the two sides resumed talks (Kiernan 2002: 492). Then, on January 17, 2004, Nuon Chea admitted he had made "mistakes" and said he is ready to face an international tribunal. To Cambodians, however, national reconciliation is more important than retribution.

Cultural Preservation and Revival

Cambodians attempting to revive the traditional arts have followed another approach in trying to come to terms with their country's tragic recent history. The task has been difficult. Not only were an estimated 90 percent of the classical dancers and musicians killed, but the Khmer Rouge also destroyed their musical instruments, theater props, dance masks, and costumes. The only instruments and theatrical items that survived destruction were those their owners successfully hid, mainly by burying them.

The effort to revive the arts began even as people were streaming toward the Thai-Cambodian border. An Italian ethnomusicologist, Giovanni Giuriati, has written about the Khmer Classical Dance Troupe (1988). The dancers and musicians in the troupe first encountered each other while they were escaping to Thailand. The troupe included a few individuals who had been members of the prestigious and internationally acclaimed Cambodian Royal Ballet before 1975. They were joined by musicians who had previously played for their own pleasure. All had survived by concealing their true identities during the Khmer Rouge period. Once they reached Khao I Dang, they started making masks and costumes from whatever materials were available. Those who knew how also began to craft instruments. More important, they recruited students and began training them. They held daily rehearsals and caught the attention of Jean Daniel Bloesch, a Swiss filmmaker who was doing volunteer work at the camp. He contacted officials in various embassies in Bangkok as well as other individuals who might be able to help resettle the troupe as a group, which the United States eventually agreed to do. The national Cambodian Crisis Committee, Buddhist Social Charities, and the National Council for the Traditional Arts served jointly as their sponsors.

Members of the troupe and their families arrived in the United States between September 1980 and April 1981 and settled in Wheaton, Maryland, a suburb of Washington, D.C. The troupe, which had about twenty dancers and ten musicians, gave its first American public performance at the 1981 National Folk Festival, held in a park just outside the capital. In the early 1980s it went on a ten-day tour to California and also performed at Disneyworld in Orlando, Florida, the World's Fair at Knoxville, Tennessee, and the Library of Congress, Smithsonian Institution, and Kennedy Center in Washington, D.C.

After this initial flurry of public interest, however, the troupe encountered increasing difficulties staying together as a performing group. Because it is virtually impossible to earn a living as dancers and musicians in the United States, and the cost of living in the Washington, D.C., area is high, members soon drifted away. As people found jobs, scheduling common times for rehearsals became a problem. After Nuth Rachana, the troupe's choreographer and lead dancer, died in a car accident, no one with equal expertise and enthusiasm took his place. Another inhibiting factor was that general public interest in this "exotic" art form could not be sustained. Cambodian musicians and dancers now perform mainly at events within the refugee communities, at Cambodian New Year celebrations, weddings, fund-raisers, and other parties (Giuriati 1988).

In this endeavor to keep the traditional arts alive, the Cambodian Network Council for a time played a key role, mainly because its executive director during the critical years of the organization's development in the mid-1990s was Dr. Sam-Ang Sam, a performer and ethnomusicologist. Dr. Sam did not experience the atrocities of the Pol Pot period because he was studying in the Philippines in 1975. After arriving in the United States, he continued his education and received a Ph.D. in music from Wesleyan University in Connecticut. In 1994, in recognition of both his artistic achievements and community work, the MacArthur Foundation awarded him a "genius" grant. After serving as executive director of the CNC for five years, he returned to Cambodia. Then he spent some time as a visiting scholar at the National Museum of Ethnology in Osaka, Japan. Now back in the United States, he and his wife, the classical dancer Chan Moly Sam, and some of their children continue to travel as performers, teachers, and cultural ambassadors (Jowitt 1996). He has written about classical Khmer music and recorded it on compact discs, videotapes, and film. In 1995 he discussed how the CNC was working to revive and preserve the Cambodian artistic heritage:

> There are three things. One is local residencies and local teaching programs. For example, I am involved with an organization here called Cambodian American Heritage. . . . I coordinate artists . . . across the country. I have a

database of artists who can serve as resources so we know what we have. . . .
Another component of CNC is supporting programs in Cambodia. We have
the Mentorship Apprenticeship Program and the Khmer Artists Support
Project. The third . . . is the cultural exchange program. . . . we have brought
artists from Cambodia for residencies here. . . . we [also] have a reverse flow.
We send master artists from here to Cambodia to provide master classes and
also to work on collaborative projects. [Due to the death of so many of the
old artists,] . . . we have suffered in the quality of performace in terms of the
skill of musicians and dancers but in terms of numbers we are recovering.
Now we have many more people practicing the arts than ever before. But it
will take . . . years . . . for them to reach the quality level of teachers in the
past. (Sam interview 1995 in Chan, ed. 2003a: 189–90)

Dr. Sam admits that it has been difficult to interest young Cambodian
Americans in classical Khmer music and dance: "In my music appreciation
class, I play Khmer music with several types of Khmer ensembles; Khmer
youth find these pieces 'slow' and 'boring.' During breaks, they form small
groups, some singing rap music and doing break dancing. . . . No one dances
a Khmer dance or sings a Khmer song" (Sam 1994: 44).

It is mainly in Cambodia itself that artistic revitalization efforts have
borne fruit. There, modern technology has proved helpful but has had some
unintended effects. Given the shortage of master dancers and musicians, students are now "learning in new ways, using tapes and records rather than
learning directly from a master. This approach results in a limited repertoire
as well as musical mutations of original pieces" (Sam 1994: 44). Outside
Cambodia, in addition to the CNC and Cambodian American Heritage, the
Khmer Studies Institute and the Cambodian Studies Center in the United
States as well as the Centre de Documentation et de Recherche sur la Civil-
isation Khmère in France are actively working to ensure that classical Khmer
culture does not disappear.

The Cambodian government has supported cultural revival, but during
the Vietnamese occupation it did so in a highly politicized way. In a survey
of novels, short stories, poems, and sketches, written in Khmer and published
in Cambodia as well as France and Thailand since 1979, Khing Hoc Dy discovered that although most of the material depicts the harsh existence under the Khmer Rouge, the writing published under government aegis in
Cambodia differs in one significant way from that published by Cambodians outside their natal country. Within the People's Republic of Kampuchea,
four organizations (a newspaper, *Kampuchea,* the Institute of Sociology, the

Ministry of Information and Culture, and a publishing house established by that ministry) have issued serialized novels, short stories, poems, and plays that contrast the dark years of terror under the Khmer Rouge with life under the new, Vietnamese-supported regime. The latter is depicted as a government that has reinstated light, plenty, cleanliness, and joy. The government was obviously using art to shore up its own legitimacy. In contrast, Cambodians outside the country have put greater effort into reprinting pre-1975 texts such as Khmer literary classics, legends, and textbooks in order to recover what had been destroyed (Khing 1994).

Some artists use their creative powers to ensure the survival of Khmer cultural identity by employing distinctly modern media. Chanthou Oeur, for example, has loved to draw ever since he was a young boy. His parents died when he was only a year old, and he was initially raised by various relatives but later became a novice monk and lived in a temple. Not having access to paper and canvas, he drew on whatever surfaces he could find, including his skin. When the Khmer Rouge took over the country, he buried his sketches. He survived the Khmer Rouge years, he told Audrey Kim, who interviewed him in 1995, by successfully hiding the fact that he had been a soldier in Lon Nol's army. After the Vietnamese invasion, he escaped to Thailand. He spent two years in Khao I Dang, where he taught art to the camp's children with materials provided by UNHCR. He also worked with the classical dance troupe as its technical director. He recalls that "teaching art was more than a personal thing, it was a conscious effort to preserve Cambodian culture."

After arriving in the United States and settling down in Hyattsville, Maryland, Chanthou Oeur painted a picture of a flat tire because he felt "empty . . . like an old car with a flat tire" (Stone 1992: A4). He was self-taught until he enrolled in art classes, his first, at a local college. Oeur supported his family with two part-time jobs, one at a print shop and another at a grocery store. Eventually, he found a full-time job at a factory, producing sculpture that other artists had designed. In his spare time he creates his own sculptures and paintings.

In his basement studio are numerous stone sculptures of human skulls and figures, their heads bent and their feet in chains, hovering over empty plates. One of his pieces, *Innocent Prisoner,* won first prize at a Cambodian festival in California and was exhibited at the Smithsonian Museum of Natural History. In a flyer advertising that exhibit, Oeur said, "Lives of my poor innocent people were swept away—they were gone, just like leaves during a fall season. . . . I am here surviving in the land of freedom, of peace, and best of all in the land of the absolutely, possibly positive life. I will sacrifice everything to let the world experience the recent Cambodian tragedy through my art work."

Oeur returned to Cambodia in 1991 for a three-month visit, during which he relived the horror. He did manage, however, to locate the spot where his house had stood, and—incredibly—when he dug into the earth he found the sketches he had buried sixteen years earlier. Those pictures, now framed, are on the walls of his home. The sculpture he created after the trip reflects the disturbing scenes he saw: a man with no legs (tens of thousands of Cambodians have lost one or more limbs to land mines) begs in the streets, and a woman holding a suckling baby with one arm and stretching the other skyward, imploring help (Stone 1992: A4). Oeur is also a community leader who has devoted a great deal of time to helping other refugees in the greater Washington, D.C., area.

Efforts to come to terms with the Khmer Rouge years through art are now transnational. In "Continuum—Beyond the Killing Fields," three Cambodian classical dancers, Em Theay, Thong Kim Ann, and Bun Thom, and a shadow puppeteer, Mann Kosal, who survived the horrors, tell their stories through dance, song, and words. The performance was conceived by Ong Keng Sen, artistic director of Singapore's Theatreworks, who hoped that a public telling would provide a means for healing. To dramatize the dances and songs, Ong juxtaposes Cambodian classical art forms with modern media, including video sequences by Noorlinah Mohamed, a video artist from Singapore, and an electronic soundtrack by Yen, a Japanese sound artist. Ong declares that the tales, although painful, are important "not only for those who remember them but for all of humanity. The horrors of the Khmer Rouge belong to the world: they act as a grim reminder of depravity that we can ill afford to forget" (Turnbull 2001).

In these many ways, Cambodians around the world as well as the non-Cambodians who empathize with and support them are trying to find meaning in their shattered lives and the will to carry on. As individuals, as a people, and as a nation, they were trampled upon and beaten down, but they were not vanquished. They have shown others how human beings have the strength to transcend tragedies that smite them. They have also taught us that people can still feel compassion and see beauty despite experiencing utter devastation. These courageous survivors—men and women, young and old, rich and poor, healthy and sick, well-educated and illiterate, Buddhists and Christians—all deserve respect.

APPENDIX A:
INTERVIEWS AND ORAL HISTORIES

(The positions listed refer to the position held by each individual at the time the interview took place.)

Cambodian American Community Leaders

Sam Becker. President, Cambodian Mutual Assistance Association, Providence, R.I.; Aug. 22, 1995.

Seang Chan. President, Cambodian Buddhist Temple, the Bronx, N.Y.; Aug. 18, 1995.

Vanly Chau. Executive director, Connecticut Federation of Refugee Assistance Associations, Inc.; Aug. 21, 1995.

John Pha Chea. President, Cambodian Preservation Society, San Diego, Calif.; July 31, 1996.

Rev. Barnaby Chêung. President, Chinese Americans from Vietnam, Laos, and Cambodia; Aug. 6, 1995.

Rithey Chey. Executive director, Cambodian Community of Massachusetts, Inc., Chelsea, Mass.; Aug. 24, 1995.

The Venerable Chhen. Buddhist monk, the "Old Temple," San Diego, Calif.; Aug. 1, 1996.

Him S. Chhim. Executive director, Cambodian Association of America, Long Beach, Calif.; July 24, 1996. Follow-up telephone interview, Sept. 24, 2001.

Wutha Chin. Executive director, Cambodian Association of Greater Philadelphia; Aug. 9, 1995.

Sam Chittapalo. Police officer, Long Beach Police Department, Community Relations Division, Long Beach, Calif.; Aug. 15, 1996.

Linchy Higham. Massage therapist, Khmer Health Associates, West Hartford, Conn.; Aug. 21, 1995.

Ngy Hul. Associate director, Refugee Federation Service Center, Seattle, Wash.; Sept. 12, 1996.

Tarun Khemradhipati. Administrator, Cambodian Buddhist Temple, Silver Spring, Md.; Aug. 5, 1995.

Daniel Samouen Khim. Former president, Cambodian Studies Center, Seattle, Wash.; Sept. 11, 1996.

Samkhann Khoeun. Executive director, Cambodian Mutual Assistance Association of Greater Lowell, Inc., Lowell, Mass.; Aug. 23, 1995. Follow-up telephone interview, Sept. 26, 2001.

Rinh Kien. Member, Khmer Krom Association, Des Moines, Wash.; Sept. 12, 1996.

Kim Huot Kiet. Founder, Cambodian Mutual Assistance Association of New York City; Aug. 15, 1995.

Pheng Kol. Assistant director, Competitive Issues Division, Office of Regulatory Affairs, Public Utility Commission of Texas, Austin; Jan. 6, 1996. (Although he lives in Texas, I interviewed Mr. Kol in Long Beach.)

The Venerable Dr. Chhean Kong. Head monk, Khemara Buddhikaram, Long Beach, Calif., and community services coordinator, Long Beach Asian Pacific Mental Health Program; July 25, 1996. Follow-up telephone interview, Sept. 27, 2001.

Dr. Daniel Lam. Former deputy director, Massachusetts State Refugee Coordinator's Office, and special assistant to the district attorney, Norfolk District, Mass.; Aug. 25, 1995.

Lany Lang. Social worker; director, Angkor Association; director, Multicultural Mental Health Outreach Program, Prince George County; and member of the State of Maryland Governor's Advisory Committee on Asian Pacific American Affairs, Arlington, Va.; Aug. 3, 1995.

Chhong Lao. Oregon Cambodian American Federation (formerly the Cambodian Association of Oregon), Portland; Sept. 10, 1996.

Dr. Hay San Meas. Executive director, Khmer Community of Tacoma; Sept. 12, 1996. Follow-up telephone interview, Sept. 25, 2001.

Chantha Mey. Secretary, Cambodian Buddhist Temple, the Bronx, N.Y.; Aug. 18, 1995.

Meantwo Mut. Novice monk, Cambodian Buddhist Society, Long Beach, Calif.; July 26, 1996.

The Venerable Vene-Khiev Narin. Head monk, Cambodian Buddhist Temple, the Bronx, N.Y.; Aug. 18, 1995.

Khat Neang. Job developer, International Refugee Center of Oregon, Portland; Sept. 9, 1996.

Nicholas Chhea Ngo. Caseworker, San Diego Department of Social Services; Aug. 1, 1996.

Samien Nol. Executive director, Southeast Asian Mutual Assistance Associations Coalition, Philadelphia; Aug. 8, 1995. Follow-up telephone interview, Sept. 25, 2001.

Chantou Oeur. Artist. Hyattsville, Md.; Aug. 5, 1995.

Vathara Oung. Caseworker, Asian Family Center (a component of the International Refugee Center of Oregon), Portland; Sept. 10, 1996.

Sereivuth Prak. Member, Khmer Krom Association of Long Beach; Aug. 15, 1996.

Vitou Reat. Cambodian counselor, Southeast Asian Project, SAY San Diego, Inc.; Aug. 1, 1996.

Dharamuni Phala Svy Chea. Mental health specialist, Asian Counseling and Referral

Service, Seattle, Wash.; Sept. 11, 1996. Follow-up telephone interview, Sept. 26, 2001.

Sambath Rim. Executive director, Cambodian Community of Greater Fall River, Inc., Mass.; Aug. 22, 1995. Follow-up telephone interview, Oct. 17, 2001.

Dr. Sam-Ang Sam. Executive director, Cambodian Network Council, Washington, D.C.; Aug. 7, 1995.

Sandy Arun San-Blankenship. Former director, Cambodian Business Association, and member, Community Development Advisory Council, City of Long Beach, Calif.; July 25, 1996.

Sopha Sar. Khmer Buddhist Society, Seattle, Wash.; Sept. 11, 1996.

Mony Sing. Executive director, Cambodian Business Association, Long Beach, Calif.; July 26, 1996.

The Venerable Pin Sem Sirisuvanno. Head monk, Cambodian Buddhist Temple, Silver Spring, Md.; Aug. 5, 1995.

Khom Som. Cambodian counselor, Southeast Asian Project, SAY San Diego, Inc.; Aug. 1, 1996.

Edward Tuon Son. Member, Khmer Krom Association of Long Beach, Calif.; Aug. 15, 1996.

The Venerable Sam Sukhuen. Head monk, Cambodian Buddhist Temple of Philadelphia; Aug. 9, 1995.

Vun Kim Suos. Former executive director, Chelsea Mutual Assistance Association; currently, caseworker, Tri-County Mental Health, Lynn, Mass.; Aug. 25, 1995.

Sokhom Tauch. Executive director, International Refugee Center of Oregon, Portland; Sept. 9, 1996. Follow-up telephone interview, Oct. 1, 2001.

Alvin Thach. Police officer, San Diego Police Department; July 31, 1996.

Dr. Bunroeun Thach. Member, Khmer Krom Association of Washington State, Des Moines, Wash.; Sept. 13, 1996.

Sarah Thang. Youth leader, 4–H Club. Arlington, Va., Aug. 6, 1995.

Sovann Tith. Executive director, United Cambodian Community, Long Beach, Calif.; July 24, 1996.

Sengha Uth. Officer, Santa Pheap, Beaverton, Ore.; Sept. 9, 1996.

European Americans Knowledgeable about Indochinese Refugees

Roger E. Harmon. Former project director, Peace Corps, Thailand; former consultant, United Nations High Commissioner for Refugees; former consultant, Center for Applied Linguistics Refugee Service Center. Interviewed by telephone on Aug. 17, 1995.

Ginger Jeffries. Volunteer, Catholic Charities, Arlington, Va.; Aug. 3, 1995.

Pamela Lewis. U.S. State Department, Washington, D.C. Interviewed by telephone on June 2, 1995.

Roy Moody. Police officer, San Diego Police Department; July 31, 1996.

Geraldine Owens. Director, Migration and Refugee Services, U.S. Catholic Conference, New York City; Aug. 17, 1995.

Mary Scully. Psychiatric nurse, cofounder of Khmer Health Advocates. West Hartford, Conn.; Aug. 21, 1995.

Bertram Norman Sorenson. Retired detective, Gang Violence Suppression Unit, Long Beach Police Department, Long Beach, Calif. Interviewed by telephone; July 12, 2003.

Robert Watts. CalWORKS administrator, Santa Barbara, Calif.; Nov. 20, 2000.

Officials in State Refugee Coordinators' Offices

Ron Amos. Refugee program manager, Department of Human Services, Oklahoma City; Nov. 30, 1995.

Laurie Bagan. State refugee coordinator, Department of Social Services, Refugee and Immigrant Services Program, Denver, Colo.; July 11, 1995.

Frank Bien. State refugee coordinator, Maryland Office of Refugee Affairs, Department of Human Services, Baltimore; July 13, 1995.

Doris Brasher. Program administrator, Department of Human Services, Columbus, Ohio; July 21, 1995.

Phuoc Cao. Human services program planner, Office for Refugees and Immigrants, Boston, Mass.; June 29, 1995.

Quy Dam. Supervisor of refugee programs, Refugee and Immigration Assistance Division, St. Paul, Minn.; June 5 and June 6, 1995.

Maria Diaz. Coordinator of refugee affairs, Department of Social Services, Lincoln, Neb.; Dec. 7, 1995.

Leo Dorsey. Program specialist, Refugee Resettlement Program, Pennsylvania Heritage Affairs Commission, Harrisburg; July 19, 1995.

Binh Duong. Program manager, Office of State Refugee Coordinator, Department of Social and Health Services, Office of Immmigrant and Refugee Assistance, Olympia, Wash.; Nov. 29, 1995.

Linda Faulk. Refugee coordinator, Refugee Program, Catholic Community Services of Nevada, Las Vegas; June 6, 1995.

Thomas Ford. Deputy director, Massachusetts State Refugee Coordinator's Office, Boston; Aug. 23, 1995.

Judi Hall. State refugee coordinator, Detroit, Mich.; July 17, 1995.

Celina Hill. Management analyst, Office of the Refugee Coordinator, Division of Economic Services, Department of Health and Social Services, New Castle, Del.; July 6, 1995.

Moon W. Ji. Assistant state refugee coordinator, Department of Human Services, Salt Lake City, Utah; July 13, 1995.

Wayne Johnson. Chief, Bureau for Refugee Programs, Iowa Department of Human Services, Des Moines; July 5, 1995.

Louis Kimsey. Refugee resettlement coordinator, Department of Social and Rehabilitation Services, Topeka, Kan.; Dec. 4, 1995.

Christine Marshall. State refugee coordinator, Department of Human Services, Providence, R.I.; June 29, 1995.

Steven Meinbresse. State refugee coordinator, Department of Human Services, Nashville, Tenn.; July 19, 1995.

Paul Pladera. Program specialist, Office of Community Services, Honolulu, Hawaii; Dec. 4, 1995.

William Rufflett. State refugee coordinator, Special Programs Division, Department of Social Services, Hartford, Conn.; July 13, 1995.

Tim Shedd. State refugee coordinator, Department of Human Resources, Montgomery, Ala.; Dec. 8, 1995.

Dr. Edwin Silverman. State coordinator, Refugee Resettlement Program, Illinois Department of Public Aid, Chicago; July 5, 1995.

Olga Skow. State refugee coordinator, Division of Human Services, Concord, N.H.; July 17, 1995.

Betts Smith. Associate government program analyst, Department of Social Services, Sacramento, Calif.; June 29, 1995.

Don Snyder. State refugee coordinator, Children and Family Services Division, Department of Human Services, Bismark, N.D.; Dec. 11, 1995.

Ron Spendal. State refugee coordinator, Department of Human Resources, Adult Family Services Division, Salem, Ore.; Dec. 7, 1995.

Steve Thibodeaux. State refugee coordinator, Office of Community Relations, New Orleans, La.; July 6, 1995.

Regina Turley. State refugee coordinator, Division of Family Services, Refugee Assistance Program, Jefferson City, Mo.; July 17, 1995.

Hyginus Ukadike. State coordinator for refugee resettlement, Division of Human Services, Little Rock, Ark.; Nov. 30, 1995.

Valerie Zadzielski. Director of refugee resettlement, Division of Family and Children's Services, Department of Human Services, Jackson, Miss.; Dec. 8, 1995.

Staff in Voluntary Agencies

Rahim Aurang. Director of refugee settlement, International Institute of the East Bay, Oakland, Calif.; June 21, 1995.

Kham Baccam. Resettlement director, Catholic Charities, Stockton, Calif.; Nov. 16, 1995.

Marianne Blank. Executive director, St. Anselm's Cross Cultural Community Center, Garden Grove, Calif.; Aug. 4, 1995.

Hoa Bui. Refugee coordinator, Don Bosco Nationalities Service Center, Kansas City, Mo.; June 27, 1995.

Sandra Burnett. Caseworker, American Civic Association, Birmingham, N.Y.; July 10, 1995.

Phan Calk. Case manager, Migration and Refugee Services, Fort Worth, Tex.; Nov. 28, 1995.

Barbara Carr. Director, Catholic Charities Immigration Services, Denver, Colo.; Nov. 14, 1995.

Thongsy Chan. Assistant division director, International Institute of Los Angeles, El Monte, Calif.; June 26, 1995.

Don Climent. Regional director for northern California, International Rescue Committee, San Francisco, Calif.; June 21, 1995.

Alicia Cooper. Regional director, Orange County International Rescue Committee, Santa Ana, Calif.; July 11, 1995.

Lieu Thi Dang. Regional director, International Rescue Committee, San Jose, Calif.; July 10, 1995.

Martha Deputy. Executive director, West Kentucky Refugee Mutual Assistance, Bowling Green; June 26, 1995.

Lich Do. Refugee resettlement caseworker, International Services Center, Cleveland, Ohio; June 22, 1995.

Al Durtka. President, International Institute of Wisconsin, Milwaukee; June 21, 1995.

Christina Erevera. Resettlement director, Catholic Charities, Dallas, Tex.; Nov. 21, 1995.

Marge Flaherty. Regional director, International Rescue Committee, Decatur, Ga.; July 13, 1995.

Kathy Flynn. Refugee resettlement director, International Institute of Lowell, Lowell, Mass.; June 22, 1995.

Felicidad Frenette. Program supervisor, International Institute of Buffalo, Buffalo, N.Y.; June 23, 1995.

Miguel Garcia-Vidal. Refugee program coordinator, Catholic Charities of San Francisco, San Francisco, Calif.; Nov. 29, 1995.

John Gordon. Caseworkers' supervisor, International Institute of Minnesota, St. Paul; June 26, 1995.

Marty Hansen. Director of community development, Interchurch Refugee and Immigration Ministries, Chicago, Ill.; Aug. 18, 1995.

Pat Hatch. Executive director, Foreign-born Information and Referral Network, Columbia, Md.; July 12, 1995.

Brigitte Helmer. Resettlement director, Catholic Charities, San Bernardino, Calif.; Nov. 14, 1995.

Greg Hope. Director, Refugee Resettlement Office, Seattle, Wash.; Nov. 13, 1995.

Kathleen Howe. Director of affiliate office, Interfaith Community Services, New York, N.Y.; Aug. 18, 1995.

Maureen Huang. Director of refugee programs, Interfaith Service Bureau, Sacramento, Calif.; Aug. 18, 1995.

Dan Hunter. Caseworker, Catholic Charities, Lombard, Ill.; Nov. 16, 1995.

Dennis Hunthansen. Resettlement director, Catholic Community Services, Tacoma, Wash.; Nov. 22, 1995.

Barbara Irving. Diocesan refugee coordinator, Episcopal Migration Ministries, Media, Pa.; July 23, 1995.

Gintare Ivaska. Supervisor, refugee resettlement, International Institute of Connecticut, Bridgeport; June 23, 1995.

Bob Johnson. Regional director, International Rescue Committee, Seattle, Wash.; June 21, 1995.

By Kang. Director of region, International Rescue Committee, Sacramento, Calif.; July 10, 1995.

Joyce Kanoebber. Education coordinator, Travelers Aid International of Greater Cincinnati, Cincinnati, Ohio; July 12, 1995.

Yani Rose Keo. Resettlement coordinator, Refugee Service Alliance, Houston, Tex.; July 10, 1995.

Helen Koba. Associate director, Sponsors Organized to Assist Refugees, Ecumenical Ministries of Oregon, Portland; Aug. 17, 1995.

Thomas Kosel. Program manager, Migration and Refugee Services, St. Paul, Minn.; Dec. 11, 1995.

Toua Kue. Case manager, Catholic Social Services, Providence, R.I.; Nov. 30, 1995.

Elizabeth Lang. Resettlement director, Catholic Charities, Oakland, Calif.; Dec. 8, 1995.

Cau Lao. Refugee resettlement director, Catholic Charities, Sacramento, Calif.; Nov. 14, 1995.

Sarah Leung. Director of social work, International Institute of Metropolitan St. Louis, St. Louis, Mo.; June 27, 1995.

Hoeum Mak. Refugee resettlement coordinator, International Institute of Rhode Island, Providence; June 22, 1995.

Paul Martin. Resettlement director, Catholic Charities, New York, N.Y.; Nov. 20, 1995.

Gail Maureen. Director of program, Greater Rochester Community Churches, Rochester, N.Y.; Sept. 6, 1995.

Rev. David Montanye. Diocesan refugee coordinator, Virginia Council of Churches Refugee Program, Richmond; July 19, 1995.

Dr. Robert Moser. Resettlement director, Refugee and Immigrant Services, Catholic Charities, San Diego, Calif.; Dec. 6, 1995.

Chris Nash. Caseworker, Ecumenical Refugee Service, Denver, Colo.; Nov. 14, 1995.

Lang Ngan. Deputy director, International Rescue Committee, New York, N.Y.; July 11, 1995.

Lisa Nguyen. Refugee receptionist, Immigrant Center, Honolulu, Hawaii; July 12, 1995.

Nga Nguyen. Executive director, Interfaith Refugee Services of Ohio, Columbus; Aug. 23, Nov. 16, 1995.

Tam Nguyen. Resettlement director, Catholic Charities, Fresno, Calif.; Nov. 21, 1995.

Thuc Nguyen. Director of operations, Y.M.C.A. International Services, Houston, Tex.; June 27, 1995.

Trong Nguyen. Administrator, Travelers and Immigrants Aid of Chicago, Chicago, Ill.; June 20, 1995.

Silen Nhok. Program coordinator, Refugee Information and Referral Services, International Institute of San Francisco, San Francisco, Calif.; June 20, 1995.

Rev. Basil Nichols. Refugee director, Florida Council of Churches, Orlando; Aug. 22, 1995.

Stephen Nofel. Coordinator of refugee resettlement, Interchurch Ministries of Nebraska, Lincoln; Aug. 16, 1995.

Robert Palm. Program director for refugee services, Interfaith Ministries for Greater Houston, Houston, Tex.; Aug. 24, 1995.

Cathy Pham. Co-director, Episcopal Service Alliance, Westminister, Calif.; Nov. 20, 1995.

Cira Ponce. Resettlement director, Catholic Social Service, Charlotteville, N.C.; Nov. 21, 1995.

Debbie Rad. Refugee coordinator, International Institute of Erie, Pennsylvania, Erie, Pa.; July 10, 1995.

Mai Ramey. Indochinese refugee case specialist, Christian Refugee Outreach, Church World Services, Arlington, Va.; Aug. 17, 1995.

Joe Robertson. Director, Virginia Council of Churches Refugee Program, Richmond; Nov. 14, 1995.

Jamie Roskie. Director, Sponsors Organized to Assist Refugees, Ecumenical Ministries of Oregon, Portland; Nov. 16, 1995.

Shahrokh Samadi. Caseworker, Catholic Charities, Los Angeles, Calif.; Nov. 21, 1995.

Dr. Howard Schipper. Executive director, Freedom Flight Task Force, Grand Rapids, Mich.; Aug. 15, 1995.

Janet Shabon. Director, Prime Ecumenical Commitment to Refugees, Clifton Heights, Pa.; Aug. 15, 1995.

Larry Sharp. Executive director, International Institute of Northwest Indiana, Gary; June 23, 1995.

Kham Sing. Caseworker, Migration and Refugee Resettlement Services, Columbus, Ohio; Dec. 7, 1995.

Michael Sirois. Assistant director, International Rescue Committee, Boston, Mass.; July 14, 1995.

Helene Smith. Executive director, International Center of the Capital Region, Albany, N.Y.; July 21, 1995.

Jerry Smith. Employment coordinator, Vermont Refugee Resettlement Program, Burlington; June 20, 1995.

Madonna Snyder. Sponsorship developer, Exodus Refugee and Immigration Program, Indianapolis, Ind.; Aug. 18, 1995.

Silai Son. Resettlement caseworker, International Institute of Boston, Boston, Mass.; June 21, 1995.

Nona Stewart. Director, Interreligious Council of Central New York, Syracuse; Aug. 16, 1995.

Bui Tam. Discesan director, Catholic Social Services, Atlanta, Ga.; Dec. 4, 1995.

Ann Tran. Case manager, Washington Refugee Resettlement, Seattle; Aug. 7, 1995.

Leng Tran. Deputy director, International Rescue Committee, Los Angeles, Calif.; July 11, 1995.

Minh Ha Tran. Case manager, Catholic Community Services, Portland, Ore.; Nov. 27, 1995.

Thu Tran. Resettlement director, Catholic Charities, Santa Ana, Calif.; Nov. 20, 1995.

Alison Tucker-Yi. Area coordinator for South Carolina, Lutheran Family Services in the Carolinas, Columbus; Sept. 23, 1995.

Peter Ving. Case manager, Catholic Social Services, Merced, Calif.; Dec. 6, 1995.

Scott Wasmuth. Resettlement coordinator, International Institute of New Jersey, Jersey City; July 11, 1995.

Maureen Webster. Director, Catholic Social Service, Phoenix, Ariz.; Nov. 17, 1995.

Lynda Williamson. Caseworker, Virginia Council of Churches Refugee Program, Richmond; Nov. 14, 1995.

John Winter. Director, Lutheran Immigration and Refugee Services, New York; June 7, 1995.

Caroline Wong. Vice president, Nationalities Service Center, Philadelphia, Pa.; July 5, 1995.

Chu Ning Yang. Director of branch, International Rescue Committee, Fresno, Calif.; July 12, 1995.

Carol Young. Case manager, Kentucky Refugee Ministries, Louisville; Aug. 17, 1995.

Marilyn Zurek. Associate director, Refugee Resettlement Office, Jacksonville, Fla.; Dec. 4, 1995.

APPENDIX B:
ORAL HISTORIES COLLECTED BY OTHER SCHOLARS

Cambodians in California Project, the Library,
California State University-Sacramento

This project conducted sixty oral history interviews in Khmer. All except Number 53 were transcribed in Khmer and then translated into English. The narrators are listed in alphabetical order according to their family names, which precede their given names. The number in brackets following each name is the number that the research team gave to the transcript of that particular oral history. In my citations of these oral histories, this number is the one that follows the comma, and the page numbers follow colons. Each narrator's occupation or his or her father's or spouse's occupation in Cambodia, as well as his or her sex, is noted in the list. All the oral histories were collected in Stockton, California, except where noted.

Bhanti Bharmawara [59], monk, male; Sept. 14, 1989.
Bith Sann [58], farmer, male; West Sacramento, Calif., Nov. 26, 1989.
Chim Ol [3], daughter of farmer, female; Sept. 17, 1989.
Chhom Pok [36], vegetable grower, male; Sept. 23, 1989.
Da Noy [40], farmer and soldier, male; Aug. 17, 1989.
Heng Chhorn [49], farmer, cyclo-peddler, policeman, male; Sept. 23, 1989.
Hinn Chhea [28], monk, male; Aug. 3, 1989.
Hong Sary [21], daughter of carpenter and cattle raiser, female; Aug. 17, 1989.
Kek Poeun [38], farmer and monk, male; Aug. 21, 1989.
Keo Felicia Im [39], wife of pilot, female; Aug. 1, 1989.
Keo Medh Patrick [43], pilot, male; Aug. 3, 1989.
Keo Sarith [29], son of farmer, male; Aug. 18, 1989.
Kiev Samo [14], soldier, male; Sept. 24, 1989.
Krit Mon [27], farmer, female; Modesto, Calif., Aug. 31, 1989.
Leang Eng [1], farmer, female; Aug. 10, 1989.

Lor Kin Naren [7], teacher, female; Sept. 24, 1989.

Loeur Samboeun [47], son of farmer, male; Aug. 4, 1989.

Ly Chheav [22], daughter of soldier, female; Sept. 26, 1989.

May Chea [15], healer, male; Sept. 30, 1989.

May Kheam [56], fisherman, woodcutter, farmer, and miner of rubies, male; Oct. 29, 1989.

Min Man [12], soldier, male; Sept. 23, 1989.

Moeun Nhu [8], son of farmer, male; Sept. 29, 1989.

Moeung Ro [16], farmer and soldier, male; Sept. 10, 1989.

Neth Sam Phuong [4], farmer, male; Sept. 17, 1989.

Ngoeuth S. [20], farmer, male; April 24, 1989.

Nhiem Peter [44], teacher, male; Aug. 16, 1989.

Nhek Leng [6], carpenter and cart maker, male; Sept. 23, 1989.

Nim Heang [30], farmer, male. Aug. 2, 1989.

Norm Phoeun [11], farmer, male. Aug. 18, 1989.

Noun Hoeun [34], farmer, male. Sept. 1, 1989.

Noun Van [19], wife of soldier, female; Sacramento, Calif.; Aug. 2, 1989.

Oeun Pheap [25], wife of soldier, female; Aug. 8, 1989.

Pal Ron [26], wife of textile worker, female; Aug. 8, 1989.

Phon Phan [52], noodle maker, male; Aug. 25, 1989.

Qung Rem [54], daughter of farmer, female; Aug. 19, 1989.

Ran Chhum [41], occupational information not given, female; Aug. 18, 1989.

Rath Sarey [50], monk, farmer, and soldier, male; Sept. 21, 1989.

Ray May [48], farmer, male; Aug. 27, 1989.

Ros Roeun [42], farmer and carpenter, male; Sept. 1, 1989.

Sam Sokcheat [46], artist and soldier, male; Oct. 3, 1989.

Sar Chanyan [57], vegetable seller, female; Nov. 4, 1989.

Seng Sarout Suon [60], doctor, female; Sept. 1, 1989.

Sin Sopha [23], son of pedicab driver, male; Sacramento, Calif., Sept. 30, 1989.

So Rerom [17], occupation not given, male; Sept. 30, 1989.

So Sophal [18], factory worker and soldier, male; Sept. 30, 1989.

Sok Khorn [2], wife of soldier, female; Aug. 18, 1989.

Sok Sithy [24], son of teacher, male; Aug. 2, 1989.

Sous San [10], teacher, male; Sacramento, Calif., Aug. 2, 1989.

Srey Kien [31], Khmer Rouge soldier, male; Aug. 10, 1989.

Sun Bun [45], monk and soldier, male; Aug. 1, 1989.

Tep Nhim [5], farmer, female; Sept. 19, 1989.

Thir Hin [13], farmer, female; Sept. 23, 1989.

Ton Savoeun [33], farmer, male; Aug. 6, 1989.

Va Thareth [37], son of soldier, male; Sept. 20, 1989.

Vann Keo [35], occupation not given, female; Aug. 21, 1989.

Vann Ong [51], monk, male; Sept. 8, 1989.

Y Chanthan [9], occupation not given, male; Aug. 3, 1989.

Yim Pisith [32], occupation not given, male; Aug. 4, 1989.

Young Keath [55], factory worker, male; Oct. 21, 1989.

Oral Histories Collected by Sheila Pinkel, Department of Art, Pomona College

Anonymous (*head of Women's Association*). Rithisen, Thailand, 1992.
Helen Fu. Long Beach, Calif., 1996.
Samantha Fu. Long Beach, Calif., 1996.
Sovan. Boston, Mass., 1996.

SELECTED BIBLIOGRAPHY

THE LITERATURE on Cambodian history, culture, and politics is voluminous. However, because the focus of this book is on Cambodian refugees in the United States, and not on Cambodia itself, only works cited directly in the text (in addition to a handful of other pertinent items about Cambodia) are listed below. Thousands of short articles about Cambodia and Cambodian refugees have been published in newspapers and periodicals, but only those that are cited are included in this bibliography. Social science writings that have nothing to do with Cambodians in the United States but that are discussed in this book to indicate how scholars have perceived Asian Americans are also listed.

Ablin, David A., and Marlowe Hood, eds. 1990. *The Cambodian Agony*. Armonk: M. E. Sharpe.

Adler, J., Ed. Bodner, S. Bornstein, J. Goldfarb, D. Engelhard, N. Naparstek, B. Nordin, J. Sack, S. Shemer, and D. Weiler. 1981. "Medical Mission to a Refugee Camp in Thailand." *Disasters* 5(2): 23–31.

Agency for International Development. 1975. *Operation Babylift: A Report on the Emergency Movement of Vietnamese and Cambodian Orphans for Intercountry Adoption*. Washington: Agency for International Development.

Ahn, Helen Noh. 1990. "Intimacy and Discipline in Family Life: A Cross-Cultural Analysis with Implications for Theory and Practice in Child Abuse Prevention." Ph.D. diss., University of California, Berkeley.

Akst, Daniel. 1993. "Cruller Fates: Cambodians Find Slim Profit in Doughnuts." *Los Angeles Times,* March 9.

Allegra, Donald T., and Phillip Nieburg. 1986. "The Role of Epidemiology in Disease Prevention." In *Years of Horror, Days of Hope: Responding to the Cambodian Refugee Crisis*. Ed. Barry S. Levy and Daniel C. Susott, 189–99. Millwood, N.Y.: Associated University Press.

Allegra, Donald T., Phillip Nieburg, and Magnus Grabe. 1984. *Emergency Refugee Health Care: A Chronicle of the Khmer Refugee Assistance Operation, 1979–1980*. Atlanta: Centers for Disease Control.

American Psychiatric Association. 1994. *Diagnostic and Statistical Manual of Mental Disorders* (DSM-IV). 4th ed. Washington: American Psychiatric Association.

Appadurai, Arjun. 1991. "Global Ethnoscapes: Notes and Queries for a Transnational Anthropology." In *Recapturing Anthropology*. Ed. Richard Fox, 191–210. Santa Fe: School of American Research Press.

Arax, Mark. 1988. "Cambodians in L.A. Area Flee, Fearing Quake." *Los Angeles Times,* May 20.

Argiros, Rita M. 1994. "Kinship, Work and Welfare: An Event History Analysis of Southeast Asian Refugee Resettlement." Ph.D. diss., State University of New York, Binghamton.

Aronson, Louise. 1987. "Health Care for Cambodian Refugees: The Role of Refugee Intermediaries." *Practicing Anthropology* 9(4): 10–11, 17.

Ashe, Var Hong. 1988. *From Phnom Penh to Paradise: Escape from Cambodia*. London: Hodder and Stoughton.

Asia Watch Committee. 1989. *Khmer Rouge Abuses along the Thai-Cambodian Border*. Washington: Human Rights Watch.

Asia Watch, and Physicians for Human Rights. 1991. *Land Mines in Cambodia: The Coward's War*. New York: Human Rights Watch.

Awanohara, Susumu. 1991. "Rouge, White, and Blue." *Far Eastern Economic Review,* Nov. 21, 55–56.

Aylesworth, Lawrence S. 1980. "Stress, Mental Health and Need Satisfaction among Indochinese in Colorado." Ph.D. diss., University of Colorado, Boulder.

Bagdasar, Craig B. 1993. "Khmer Conflict Style: Cultural Foundations and Forms of Resolution." Ph.D. diss., Union Institute.

Baizerman, Michael, and Glenn Hendricks. N.d. "A Study of Southeast Asian Refugee Youth in the Twin Cities of Minneapolis and St. Paul, Minnesota." Minneapolis: University of Minnesota, Center for Urban and Regional Affairs, Southeast Asian Refugee Studies Project.

Baker, Amy Brooke. 1987. "For Cambodians, Trek's End Is Just a Start." *Christian Science Monitor,* Oct. 20.

Basch, Linda, Nina Glick Schiller, and Cristina Szanton Blanc. 1994. *Nations Unbound: Transnational Projects, Postcolonial Predicaments, and Deterritorialized Nation-States*. Utretch, Netherlands: Gordon and Breach.

Baughan, David M. et al. 1990. "Primary Care Needs of Cambodian Refugees." *Journal of Family Practice* 30(5): 565–68.

Becker, Elizabeth. 1986. *When the War Was Over: The Voices of Cambodia's Revolution and Its People*. New York: Simon and Schuster.

Becker, Gay, Yewoubdar Beyene, and Pauline Ken. 2000. "Memory, Trauma, and Embodied Distress: The Management of Disruption in the Stories of Cambodians in Exile." *Ethos* 28(3): 320–45.

Benson, Janet. 1994. "Reinterpreting Gender: Southeast Asian Refugees and American Society." In *Reconstructing Lives, Recapturing Meaning: Refugee Identity,*

Gender, and Culture Change. Ed. Linda A. Camino and Ruth M. Krulfeld, 75–96. Basel, Switzerland: Gordon and Breach.

Berner, Diane. 1992. "The Indochinese Refugees: A Perspective from Various Stress Theories." *Journal of Multicultural Social Work* 2(1): 15–30.

Berry, Lila, Samorn Nil, Nancy Locke, Stanley McCracken, Kompha Seth, and Virginia Koch. 1992. "Cambodian Oral History Research: Preliminary Findings on Alcohol and Other Drugs in Cambodia and in the United States." Chicago: Travelers and Immigrants Aid, Refugee Substance Abuse Prevention Project.

Berthold, Sarah M. 1998. "The Effects of Exposure to Violence and Social Support on Psychological and Behavioral Outcomes among Khmer Refugee Adolescents." Ph.D. diss., University of California, Los Angeles.

Biellik, Robin J. 1983. "The Evaluation of Public Health Components of International Disaster Relief Operations: Indochinese Refugees in Thailand, 1979–1982." D.P.H. diss., University of Texas, Houston.

Bit, Seanglim. 1991. *The Warrior Heritage: A Psychological Perspective of Cambodian Trauma*. El Cerrito, Calif: the author.

Blair, Robert G. 1996. "Risk and Protective Factors in the Mental Health Status of Cambodian Refugees in Utah." Ph.D. diss., University of Minnesota.

Blakely, Mary M. 1984. "Refugees and American Schools: A Field Study of Southeast Asians in One Community." Ph.D. diss., University of Oregon.

Boehnlein, James K. 1987a. "Clinical Relevance of Grief and Mourning among Cambodian Refugees." *Social Science and Medicine* 25(7): 765–72.

———. 1987b. "Culture and Society in Posttraumatic Stress Disorder: Implications for Psychotherapy." *American Journal of Psychotherapy* 41(4): 519–30.

Boehnlein, James K., J. David Kinzie, Rath Ben, and Jenelle Fleck. 1985. "One-Year Follow-Up Study of Posttraumatic Stress Disorder among Survivors of Cambodian Concentration Camps." *American Journal of Psychiatry* 142(8): 956–59.

Boothby, Neil. 1982. "Khmer Children: Alone at the Border." *Indochina Issues* 13 (Dec.): 1–7.

Booxbaum, Ronnie J. 1995. "The Fabric of Cambodian Life: Sarongs at Home, Dungarees at Work." Ph.D. diss., University of Massachusetts.

Borisenko, Laurel. 1991. "Preparation for Refugee Resettlement: Refugee and Agency Goals." M.Ed. thesis, University of Alberta.

Boua, Chanthou. 1990. *Children of the Killing Fields: Cambodian Adolescents in New South Wales*. Wollongong, NSW: University of Wollongong, Centre for Multicultural Studies.

Boucher, Norman. 1988. "The Struggle Goes On: Southeast Asians in America." *Boston Globe Magazine*, Sept. 25, 18–21, 52–59, 68–74.

Bradish, Cheryl N. 1995. "Perceived Functional Social Support as a Buffer of Acculturative Stress among Cambodian Refugees." Ph.D. diss., California School of Professional Psychology, San Diego.

Breckon, Lydia A. 1999. "The Other Side: Ethnic and Transnational Identity among Khmer Americans in Southern New England." Ph.D. diss., Yale University.

Bromley, Mary Ann. 1987. "New Beginnings for Cambodian Refugees—or Further Disruptions?" *Social Work* 32 (May–June): 236–39.

Brown, MacAlister, and Joseph J. Zasloff. 1998. *Cambodia Confounds the Peacemakers, 1979–1998.* Ithaca: Cornell University Press.

Brown, Phyllida. 1991. "Natural Distress or Mental Illness?" *New Scientist,* Dec. 7, 21.

Brown, Sharon E. 1991. "Supported Employment as a Vocational Option for Khmers with Mental Health Retardation Living in a Displaced Persons Camp along the Thai-Cambodian Border." Ed.D. diss., University of Washington.

Brown, William A. 1988. "Indochinese Refugees and Relations with Thailand." *Current Policy* No. 1052. Washington: U.S. Department of State, Bureau of Public Affairs.

Bruno, Ellen. 1984. "Acculturation Difficulties of the Khmer in New York City." New York: Cambodian Women's Program, American Friends Service Committee.

Bryan, Terri G. 1990. "Southeast Asian Refugee Resettlement in San Diego, California and Albuquerque, New Mexico." M.A. thesis, University of New Mexico.

Bui, Diana D., Le Xuan Khoa, and Nguyen Can Hien. 1981. *The Indochinese Mutual Assistance Associations.* Washington: Indochina Refugee Action Center.

Buist, Neil R. M. 1980. "Perspective from Khao I Dang Refugee Camp." *British Medical Journal,* July 5, 36–37.

Bulletin of Concerned Asian Scholars. Web-site at <http://csf.colorado.edu/bcas/> accessed on Aug. 25, 2003.

Burgler, Roel A. 1990. *The Eye of the Pineapple: Revolutionary Intellectuals and Terror in Democratic Kampuchea.* Saarbrucken–Fort Lauderdale: Verlag Breitenbach.

Burke, Georgine S. 1986. "Sociocultural Determinants of Nutrient Intake and Arterial Blood Pressure among Cambodian Refugees in Utah." Ph.D. diss., University of Connecticut.

Burki, Elizabeth A. 1987. "Cambodian and Laotian Mothers and Daughters in Chicago: Surviving Crises and Renegotiating Identities." Ph.D. diss., Northwestern University.

Burros, Marian. 1992. "A Family's Odyssey Brings a Taste of Cambodia." *New York Times,* April 1.

Burton, Eve. 1983. "Khmer Refugees in Western Massachusetts: Their Impact on Local Communities." *Migration Today* 11(2–3): 29–34.

Butterfield, Fox. 1990. "Cambodia's Troupe's Star Dancer Stays in U.S." *New York Times,* Oct. 18.

Cady, John F. 1967. *The Roots of French Imperialism in Eastern Asia.* Rev. ed. Ithaca: Cornell University Press.

"Cambodia King Refuses to OK Khmer Rouge Amnesty Offer." 1998. *Los Angeles Times,* Dec. 30.

Cambodian American Association of Western Massachusetts. 1991. *Assessment of the Cambodian Community in Western Massachusetts.* Boston: Commonwealth of Massachusetts, Executive Office of Health and Human Services, Office for Refugees and Immigrants.

Cambodian Community Focus. 1993–95. Issues 12–15. Washington: Cambodian Network Development Project.

Cambodian Network Council. 1993. *Annual Report.* Washington: Cambodian Network Council.

"Cambodians Flee New Terror: Quake." 1989. *New York Times,* Oct. 31.

Canda, Edward R., and Thitiya Phaobtong. 1992. "Buddhism as a Support System for Southeast Asian Refugees." *Social Work* 37(1): 61–67.

Canniff, Julie G. 1999. "Traveling the Middle Path: The Cultural Epistemology of Success, a Case Study of Three Cambodian Families." Ed.D. diss., Harvard University.

———. 2001. *Cambodian Refugees' Pathways to Success: Developing a Bi-Cultural Identity.* New York: LFB Scholarly Publishing.

Canty, Judy. 1985. *Survivor in a New Land: A Cambodian Family's Resettlement Story.* Washington: United States Catholic Conference, Migration and Refugee Services.

Carlson, Eve B., and Rhonda Rosser-Hogan. 1991. "Trauma Experiences, Posttraumatic Stress, Dissociation, and Depression in Cambodian Refugees." *American Journal of Psychiatry* 148(11): 1548–51.

———. 1993. "Mental Health Status of Cambodian Refugees Ten Years after Leaving Their Homes." *American Journal of Orthopsychiatry* 63(2): 223–31.

Carney, Timothy. 1989a. "The Organization of Power." In *Cambodia 1975–1978: Rendevous with Death.* Ed. Karl D. Jackson, 75–108. Princeton: Princeton University Press.

———. 1989b. "The Unexpected Victory." In *Cambodia 1975–1978: Rendevous with Death.* Ed. Karl D. Jackson, 13–36. Princeton: Princeton University Press.

Carol, Eileen M. 1991. "Interpreting Information: Health Care Communication among Family Nurse Practioners, Interpreters, and Cambodian Refugee Patients." Ph.D. diss., University of California, San Francisco.

Carter, Rosalynn. 1986. "When the Statistics Become Human Beings." In *Years of Horror, Days of Hope: Responding to the Cambodian Refugee Crisis.* Ed. Barry S. Levy and Daniel C. Susott, 53–61. Millwood, N.Y.: Associated Faculty Press.

Chan, G. 1991. "Medical Needs in the Bronx." In *Voices from Southeast Asia: The Refugee Experience in the United States.* Ed. John Tenhula, 130–33. New York: Holmes and Meier.

Chan, Sucheng, ed. 2003a. *Not Just Victims: Conversations with Cambodian Community Leaders in the United States.* Urbana: University of Illinois Press.

———. 2003b. "Politics and the Indochinese Refugee Exodus, 1975–1997." In *Remapping Asian American History.* Ed. Sucheng Chan, 171–222. Walnut Creek, Calif.: AltaMira Press.

Chanda, Nayan. 1986. *Brother Enemy: The War after the War.* San Diego, Calif.: Harcourt Brace Jovanovich.

———. 1998. "Legacy of Hate." *Far Eastern Economic Review,* April 30.

Chandler, David P. 1991a. *The Land and People of Cambodia.* New York: HarperCollins.

———. 1991b. *The Tragedy of Cambodian History: Politics, War, and Revolution since 1945.* New Haven: Yale University Press.

———. 1992a. *Brother Number One: A Political Biography of Pol Pot.* Boulder: Westview Press.

———. 1992b. *A History of Cambodia.* 2d. ed. Boulder: Westview Press.

———. 1999. *Voices from S-21: Terror and History in Pol Pot's Secret Prison.* Berkeley: University of California Press.

Chandrasekaran, Rajiv. 2001. "Waging War from California: Vietnam, Cambodia Urge U.S. to Curb Exile Groups." *Washington Post*, July 30.

Chang, Kenneth, and Eric Malnic. 1996. "Cambodian Star of 'Killing Fields' Shot to Death in L.A." *Los Angeles Times*, Feb. 27.

Chantavanich, S., and P. Rabe. 1990. "Thailand and the Indochinese Refugees: Fifteen Years of Compromise and Uncertainty." *Southeast Asian Journal of Social Science* 18(1): 60–80.

Chapman, Johara M. 1995. "'Thinking Too Much': Cambodian Refugee Health in Urban California." M.A. thesis, California Institute of Integral Studies.

Chea, Roeun. 1989. "My Unforgettable Experiences." In *The Far East Comes Near: Autobiographical Accounts of Southeast Asian Students in America*. Ed. Lucy Nguyen-Hong-Nhiem and Joel Martin Halperin, 105–14. Amherst: University of Massachusetts Press.

Cheevers, Jack. 1986. "Mormon Recruiting Stirs Up Refugees." *Oakland Tribune*, July 27.

Chhim, Porthira. 2003. "The Invisible Immigrants: Cambodian Americans." In *The New Face of Asian America: Numbers, Diversity and Change in the 21st Century*. Ed. Eric Lai and Dennis Arguelles, 93–96. San Francisco: AsianWeek.

Chira, Susan. 1993. "For Refugees, Help with Double Burden of Child-Rearing." *New York Times*, Dec. 9.

Chow, Lani. 1995. "Depression and Anxiety among Cambodian, Laotian, and Vietnamese Refugees." Ph.D. diss., California School of Professional Psychology, Alameda/Berkeley.

Chow, Robert T. P., and Seba Krumholtz. 1989. "Health Screening of a Rhode Island Cambodian Refugee Population." *Rhode Island Medical Journal* 72(8): 273–77.

Chow, Robert T. P. et al. 1989. "Psychological Screening of Cambodian Refugees in a RI Primary Care Clinic." *Rhode Island Medical Journal* 72(8): 179–81.

Chulalongkorn University, Institute of Asian Studies. 1988. *Thailand: A First Asylum Country for Indochinese Refugees*. Asian Studies Monograph No. 038. Bangkok: Chulalongkorn University, Institute of Asian Studies.

Chung, Rita C. Y., and Marjorie Kagawa-Singer. 1993. "Predictors of Psychological Distress among Southeast Asian Refugees." *Social Science and Medicine* 36(5): 631–40.

Clarke, Gregory N., William H. Sack, and Brian Goff. 1993. "Three Forms of Stress in Cambodian Adolescent Refugees." *Journal of Abnormal Child Psychology* 21(1): 65–77.

Coedès, George. 1968. *The Indianized States of Southeast Asia*. Trans. Susan Brown Cowing. Ed. Walter F. Vella. Honolulu: East-West Center Press.

Coleman, Cynthia M. 1990. "Cambodians in the United States." In *The Cambodian Agony*. Ed. David A. Ablin and Marlowe Hood, 354–74. Armonk: M. E. Sharpe.

Commonwealth of Massachusetts Office for Refugees and Immigrants. 1990. "Refugees and Immigrants Demographic Update." Vol. 1, no. 1. Boston: Office for Refugees and Immigrants.

Conover, Kirsten. 1990. "Questions Linger over Dancers' Defections." *Christian Science Monitor*, Oct. 16.

Corfield, Justin. 1994. *Khmers Stand Up! A History of the Cambodian Government,*

1970–1975. Monash Papers on Southeast Asia No. 32. Melbourne: Monash University, Centre of Southeast Asian Studies.

Criddle, JoAn D. 1987. *To Destroy You Is No Loss: The Odyssey of a Cambodian Family*. New York: Atlantic Monthly.

———. 1992. *Bamboo and Butterflies: From Refugee to Citizen*. Dixon, Calif.: East/West Bridge Publishing House.

Crosette, Barbara. 1988. "After the Killing Fields: Cambodia's Forgotten Refugees." *New York Times Magazine*, June 26.

———. 1995. "Ex-Official's Life in U.S. Evokes Fear." *New York Times*, Aug. 14.

Crow, Georgia K. 1988. "Toward a Theory of Therapeutic Syncretism—The Southeast Asian Experience: A Study of the Cambodians' Use of Traditional and Cosmopolitan Health Systems." Ph.D. diss., University of Utah.

Cumming-Bruce, Nicholas. 1989. "A Life of War and Waiting." *U.S. News and World Report* 107(16): 44–45.

Dahlberg, Keith. 1980. "Medical Care of Cambodian Refugees." *Journal of the American Medical Association* 243(10): 1062–65.

D'Avanzo, Carolyn E., Barbara Frye, and Robin Froman. 1994a. "Culture, Stress and Substance Use in Cambodian Refugee Women." *Journal of Studies on Alcohol* 55(4): 420–26.

———. 1994b. "Stress in Cambodian Refugee Families." *Image: The Journal of Nursing Scholarship* 26(2): 101–5.

Davies, Paul, with photographs by Nic Dunlop. 1994. *War of the Mines: Cambodia, Landmines and the Impoverishment of a Nation*. Boulder: Pluto Press.

Deac, Wilfred P. 1997. *Road to the Killing Fields: The Cambodian War of 1970–1975*. College Station: Texas A&M University Press.

"Death in L.A.'s Killing Fields; Haign Ngor, Who Helped Save Fellow Cambodians, Is Slain." 1996. *Los Angeles Times*, Feb. 28.

Dechawan, Prachuab. 1988. "Church Management from an Asian Perspective: A Case Study of the Lao-Cambodian Ministry of Southern California." D.Min. diss., School of Theology at Claremont.

DeLoughry, Thomas J. 1989. "Former Prisoner of Khmer Rouge Now Provides Higher Education." *Chronical of Higher Education* 36(1): A21–22.

Desbarat, Jacqueline. 1995. *Prolific Survivors: Population Change in Cambodia, 1975–1993*. Tempe: Arizona State University, Program for Southeast Asian Studies.

DeVoe, Pamela A. 1994. "Refugees in an Educational Setting: A Cross-Cultural Model of Success." In *Reconstructing Lives, Recapturing Meaning: Refugee Identity, Gender, and Culture Change*. Ed. Linda A. Camino and Ruth M. Krulfeld, 235–49. Basel, Switzerland: Gordon and Breach.

Dhawan, Gita. 1986. "An Education, Employment and Health Needs Assessment of Southeast Asian Refugee Women Living in Central Iowa." Ph.D. diss., Iowa State University.

DiMarzio, Nicholas. 1985. "Reflections on a Field Visit to Southeast Asia." *Migration Today* 13(3): 35–38.

Dith Pran, comp. 1997. *Children of Cambodia's Killing Fields: Memoirs by Survivors*, ed. Kim DePaul, with an introduction by Ben Kiernan. New Haven: Yale University Press.

Drabble, Margaret. 1989. "Killing Time: A Visit to a Cambodian Refugee Camp." *Harper's* 278 (April): 69–72.

DuBois, Thomas A. 1990. "Growing Up in Education: An Ethnography of Southeast Asian Adolescent Life in Philadelphia Schools." Ph.D. diss., University of Pennsylvania.

———. 1993. "Constructions Construed: The Representation of Southeast Asian Refugees in Academic, Popular, and Adolescent Discourse." *Amerasia Journal* 19(3): 1–26.

Dufresne, Jeffrey R. 1993. "Rebuilding Cambodia: Education, Political Warfare, and the Khmer People's National Liberation Front." Ed.D. diss., University of St. Thomas.

Duncan, Julianne S. 1987. "Cambodian Refugee Use of Indigenous and Western Healers to Prevent or Alleviate Mental Illness." Ph.D. diss., University of Washington.

Dunlop, Nic, and Nate Thayer. 1999a. "'Chief of the Sinners.'" *Far Eastern Economic Review,* May 6, 22–23.

———. 1999b. "Duch Confesses." *Far Eastern Economic Review,* May 6, 18–20.

Dunn, Ashley. 1995. "Cambodians in the U.S. Say the Dark Shadow of the Khmer Rouge Is Back." *New York Times,* Aug. 14.

Duong, Soy. 1990. "The Account of My Life." Unpublished term paper for Asian American Studies 2, University of California, Santa Barbara.

Dyck, Doris, and Izabela Plucinska. 1990. "Perinatal Beliefs and Practices of Cambodian-American Women." M.S.N. thesis, MGH Institute of Health Professions.

Ebihara, May. 1966. "Interrelationships between Buddhism and Social Systems in Cambodian Peasant Culture." In *Anthropological Studies in Theravada Buddhism.* Cultural Report Series No. 13, 175–96. New Haven: Yale University, Southeast Asia Studies Program.

———. 1985. "Khmer." In *Refugees in the United States: A Reference Handbook.* Ed. David W. Haines, 127–47. Westport: Greenwood Press, 1985.

Ebihara, May, Carol A. Mortland, and Judy Ledgerwood, eds. 1994. *Cambodian Culture since 1975: Homeland and Exile.* Ithaca: Cornell University Press.

Egli, Eric A. 1989. "Self-Report of Psychological Distress and Daily Functioning in the Minnesota Cambodian Community." Ph.D. diss., University of Minnesota.

Eisenbruch, Maurice. 1991. "From Post-Traumatic Stress Disorder to Cultural Bereavement: Diagnosis of Southeast Asian Refugees." *Social Science and Medicine* 33(6): 673–80.

Eisenbruch, Maurice, and Lauren Handelman. 1989. "Development of an Explanatory Model of Illness Schedule for Cambodian Refugee Patients." *Journal of Refugee Studies* 2(2): 243–56.

Elias, Christopher J., Bruce H. Alexander, and Tan Sokly. 1990. "Infectious Disease Control in a Long-Term Refugee Camp: The Role of Epidemiologic Surveillance and Investigation." *American Journal of Public Health* 80(7): 824–28.

Espiritu, Yen Le. 2003. *Home Bound: Filipino American Lives across Cultures, Communities, and Countries.* Berkeley: University of California Press.

Etcheson, Craig. 1984. *The Rise and Demise of Democratic Kampuchea.* Boulder: Westview Press.

Fernandez Kelly, M., Patricia Schauffler, and Richard Schauffler. 1996. "Divided Fates:

Immigrant Children and the New Assimilation." In *The New Second Generation.* Ed. Alejandro Portes, 30–53. New York: Russell Sage Foundation.

Fields, Rona M. 1989. "Terror's Children." *Migration World* 17(1): 7–15.

———. 1992. "Life and Death on a Small Island: Vietnamese and Cambodian Refugees in Indonesia." *Migration World* 20(5): 16–20.

Fiffer, Sharon S. 1991. *Imagining America: Paul Thai's Journey from the Killing Fields of Cambodia to Freedom in the United States.* New York: Paragon.

Fifield, Adam. 1998. "Beyond the Killing Fields." *A Magazine,* April-May, 36–41, 82.

French, Lindsay C. 1994. "Enduring Holocaust, Surviving History: Displaced Cambodians on the Thai-Cambodian Border, 1989–1991." Ph.D. diss., Harvard University.

Frieson, Kate Grace. 1988. "The Political Nature of Democratic Kampuchea." *Pacific Affairs* 61(3): 405–27.

———. 1992. "The Impact of Revolution on Cambodian Peasants, 1970–1975." Ph.D. diss., Monash University.

"From Cambodian Captive to Prep School Scholar." 1987. *New York Times,* June 8.

Frye, Barbara A. 1989. "The Process of Health Care Decision Making among Khmer Refugees." Ph.D. diss., Loma Linda University.

———. 1991. "Cultural Themes in Health-Care Decision Making among Cambodian Refugee Women." *Journal of Community Health Nursing* 8(1): 33–44.

———. 1995. "Use of Cultural Themes in Promoting Health among Southeast Asian Refugees." *American Journal of Health Promotion* 9(4): 269–80.

Frye, Barbara A., and Carolyn D'Avanzo. 1994. "Themes in Managing Culturally Defined Illness in the Cambodian Refugee Family." *Journal of Community Health Nursing* 2(2): 89–98.

Galbraith, Jane. 1983. "Refugees Polishing Up Seedy Area." *Los Angeles Times,* March 22.

Gallagher, D., Susan Forbes, and Patricia Weiss Fagen. 1985. "Of Special Humanitarian Concern: U.S. Refugee Admissions since Passage of the Refugee Act." Washington: Refugee Policy Group.

Gann, Peter, Luan Nghiem, and Stanley Warner. 1989. "Pregnancy Characteristics and Outcomes of Cambodian Refugees." *American Journal of Public Health* 79(9): 1251–57.

Germer, Lucie C. 1986. "The Food Their Families Eat: Cuisine as Communication among Cambodian Refugees." Ph.D. diss., University of Utah.

Gibson, Margaret A. 1988. *Accommodation without Assimilation: Sikh Immigrants in an American High School.* Ithaca: Cornell University Press.

Giuriati, Giovanni. 1988. "Khmer Traditional Music in Washington, D.C." Ph.D. diss., University of Maryland, Baltimore County.

Glass, Roger I., Phillip Nieburg, Willard Cates Jr., Cornelia Davis, Remi Russbach, Susan Peel, Hans Northdurft, and Richard Turnbull. 1980. "Rapid Assessment of Health Status and Preventive-Medicine Needs of Newly Arrived Kampuchean Refugees, Sakeo, Thailand." *Lancet,* April 19, 868–72.

Gleason, Philip. 1980. "American Identity and Americanization." In *Harvard Encyclopedia of American Ethnic Groups.* Ed. Stephan Thernstrom, Ann Orlov, and Oscar Handlin, 31–58. Cambridge: Harvard University Press.

Glynn, Ted, and Vin Glynn. 1986. "Shared Reading by Cambodian Mothers and Children Learning English as a Second Language: Reciprocal Gains." *Exceptional Child* 33(3): 159–72.

Goleman, Daniel. 1995. "Severe Trauma May Damage the Brain as Well as the Psyche." *New York Times,* Aug. 1.

Golub, Stephen. 1986. "Looking for Phantoms: Flaws in the Khmer Rouge Screening Process." Washington: U.S. Committee for Refugees.

Gordon, Linda W. 1989. "The Missing Children: Mortality and Fertility in a Southeast Asian Refugee Population." *International Migration Review* 23(2): 219–38.

Gordon, Milton M. 1964. *Assimilation in American Life: The Role of Race, Religion, and National Origins.* New York: Oxford University Press.

Goza, Franklin W. 1987. "Adjustment and Adaptation among Southeast Asian Refugees in the United States." Ph.D. diss., University of Wisconsin, Madison.

Graff, Nancy P. 1993. *Where the River Runs: A Portrait of a Refugee Family.* Boston: Little, Brown.

Grant, Jonathan S., Laurence A. G. Moss, and Jonathan Unger, eds. 1971. *Cambodia: The Widening War in Indochina.* New York: Washington Square Press.

Granville Corporation. 1982. *A Preliminary Assessment of the Khmer Cluster Resettlement Project: Final Report.* Washington: U.S. Department of Health and Human Services, Social Security Administration, Office of Refugee Resettlement.

Groslier, Bernard Philippe. 1966. *Indochina.* Trans. James Hogarth. Cleveland: World.

Groslier, Bernard Philippe, and Jacques Arthaud. 1966. *Angkor: Art and Civilization.* New York: Praeger.

Gross, Jane. 1989. "Where Five Died, a Monk Gives Solace." *New York Times,* May 11.

———. 1990. "In Refugee Community, Killings and a Healing." *New York Times,* Jan. 15.

Gupta, Akhil. 1992. "The Song of the Nonaligned World: Transnational Identities and the Reinscription of Space in Late Capitalism." *Cultural Anthropology* 7(1): 63–79.

Gyallay-Pap, P. 1990. "Khmer Monk Education in the Thai Border Camps." Bangkok: Khmer Buddhist Educational Assistance Project.

Ha, Pamela Hue. 1994. "Child Abuse and Neglect: A Profile of Cambodian and Chinese in the Department of Children's Services." M.S.W. thesis, California State University, Long Beach.

Habana-Hafner, Sally R. 1993. "Samakom Khmer: The Cross-Cultural Adaptation of a Newcomer Ethnic Organization." Ph.D. diss., University of Massachusetts, Amherst.

Hackett, Beatrice N. 1988. "Family, Ethnicity, and Power: Chinese Cambodian Refugees in the Washington Metropolitan Area." Ph.D. diss., American University.

Haines, David W. 1989. "Southeast Asian Refugee Resettlement in the United States and Canada." *Amerasia Journal* 15(2): 141–56.

———, ed. 1989. *Refugees as Immigrants: Cambodians, Laotians, and Vietnamese in America.* Totowa: Rowman and Littlefield.

Haldane, David. 1987. "Cambodians Struggle to Leave Nightmare Behind." *Los Angeles Times,* June 6.

———. 1988a. "Indochinese Businesses Revitalize Once-Anemic Area in Long Beach." *Los Angeles Times*, Dec. 19.

———. 1988b. "A Taste of Cambodia: A Real Horatio Alger Story: Refugee Built Empire on Doughnuts." *Los Angeles Times*, Dec. 19.

———. 1991. "Latino and Asian Gangs Engage in Deadly Warfare." *Los Angeles Times*, April 15.

Hall, D. G. E. 1968. *A History of South-East Asia*, 94–139, 436–43, 656–65, 758–66, 845–50. New York: St. Martin's Press

Hall, Kari R. 1992. *Beyond the Killing Fields*. Hong Kong: Asia 2000.

Handelman, Lauren. 1991. *Cambodian Elderly Explanatory Models for Illness and Help Seeking Behavior*. N.p.: Gerontological Society of America.

Hardman, Joel C. 1994. "Language and Literacy Development in a Cambodian Community in Philadelphia." Ph.D. diss., University of Pennsylvania.

Heder, Stephen R. 1979. "Kampuchea's Armed Struggle: The Origins of an Independent Revolution." *Bulletin of Concerned Asian Scholars* 11(2): 2–24.

Hein, Jeremy. 1995. *From Vietnam, Laos, and Cambodia: A Refugee Experience in the United States*. New York: Twayne.

Helton, Arthur C. 1989. "Asylum and Refugee Protection in Thailand." *International Journal of Refugee Law* 1(1): 20–47.

Hemmila, Herbert W. 1984. "The Adjustment and Assimilation of Cambodian Refugees in Texas." Ed.D. diss., East Texas State University.

Heng Samrin. 1979. "The Overthrow of the Reactionary Regime Kampuchea: Towards Rebirth and Renewal." In *Kampuchea: From Tragedy to Rebirth*. Comp. E. V. Kobelev, 114–26. Moscow: Progress Publisher.

Herbst, Patricia K.R. 1992. "From Helpless Victim to Empowered Survivor: Oral History as a Treatment for Survivors of Torture." *Women and Therapy* 13(1–2): 141–52.

Hiegel, Jean Pierre. 1994. "Use of Indigenous Concepts and Healers in the Care of Refugees: Some Experiences from the Thai Border Camps." In *Amidst Peril and Pain: The Mental Health and Well-Being of the World's Refugees*. Ed. Anthony J. Marsella et al., 293–309. Washington: American Psychological Association.

Higham, Charles. 2001. *The Civilization of Angkor*. Berkeley: University of California Press.

Hillinger, Charles. 1984. "Cambodian Refugees Make First Film Outside Indochina." *Daily Californian*, April 24.

Him, Chanrithy. 2000. *When Broken Glass Floats: Growing Up under the Khmer Rouge*. New York: W. W. Norton.

Hinton, Alexander L. 1996. "Agents of Death: Examining the Cambodian Genocide in Terms of Psychosocial Dissonance." *American Anthropologist* 98(4): 818–31.

———. 1997. "Cambodia's Shadow: An Examination of the Cultural Origins of Genocide." Ph.D. diss., Emory University.

———. 1998a. "A Head for an Eye: Revenge in the Cambodian Genocide." *American Ethnologist* 25(3): 352–77.

———. 1998b. "Why Did You Kill? The Cambodian Genocide and the Dark Side of Face and Honor." *Journal of Asian Studies* 57(1): 93–122.

Holgate, Susan L. 1994. "Early Marriages of Khmer High School Students: Influences and Consequences of Culture, Education and Intergenerational Conflict." M.A. thesis, California State University, Stanislaus.

Holley, David, and John Kendall. 1987. "Folk Opera: Cambodians' 'Memory and Yearning' Satisfied by Long Beach Performance." *Los Angeles Times,* April 12.

Holley, Lynn C. 1998. "Ethnic Agencies in Communities of Color: A Study of Missions, Services, Structures, and Capacity-Building Needs." Ph.D. diss., University of Washington.

Holloway, Alisa. 1989. "Resettlement and Refugee Health Experiences in First Asylum Camps in Thailand." *Migration World* 17(5): 25–29.

"Homeward Bound." 1991. *The Economist,* Sept. 21, 50–51.

Hopkins, Marycarol. 1991. "Learning Culture: A Cambodian (Khmer) Community in an American City." Ph.D. diss., University of Cincinnati.

———. 1996. *Braving a New World: Cambodian (Khmer) Refugees in an American City.* Westport: Bergin and Garvey.

Howard, Katsuyo K., comp. 1990. *Passages: An Anthology of the Southeast Asian Refugee Experience,* 20–24, 123–31, 205–6, 227–28. Fresno: California State University, Fresno, Southeast Asian Student Services.

Howe, Marvin. 1985. "City's Cambodians Struggle to Adjust." *New York Times,* July 25.

Hubbard, Jon J. 1997. "Adaptive Functioning and Post-Trauma Symptoms in Adolescent Survivors of Massive Childhood Trauma." Ph.D. diss., University of Minnesota.

Hubbard, Jon J., George M. Realmuto, Andrea K. Northwood, and Ann S. Masten. 1995. "Comorbidity of Psychiatric Diagnoses with Posttraumatic Stress Disorder in Survivors of Childhood Trauma." *Journal of the American Academy of Child and Adolescent Psychiatry* 43(9): 1167–73.

Hughes, Caroline. 2002. "International Intervention and the People's Will: The Demoralization of Democracy in Cambodia." *Critical Asian Studies* 34(4): 539–62.

Hunt, Paul. 1991. "Battle for Cambodia's Troubled Spirits." *New Scientist,* Dec. 7, 20–21.

Hurh, Won Moo, and Kwang Chung Kim. 1984. *Korean Immigrants in America: A Structural Analysis of Ethnic Confinement and Adhesive Adaptation.* Rutherford: Farleigh Dickinson University Press.

Hur, Mann Hyung. 1990. "Economic Self-Sufficiency: A Study of Southeast Asian Refugees in Colorado." Ph.D. diss., University of Colorado, Denver.

Ima, Kenji, and Ruben G. Rumbaut. 1989. "Southeast Asian Refugees in American Schools: A Comparison of Fluent-English-Proficient and Limited-English-Proficient Students." *Topics in Language Disorders* 9(3): 54–75.

Ima, Kenji, Alfredo F. Velasco, Kota Ou, and Beverly C. Yip. 1983. "Adjustment Strategies of the Khmer Refugees in San Diego, California: Six Ethnographic Case Histories." San Diego: Union of Pan Asian Communities.

Indochina Studies Program, comp. 1985. *The Kampuchean Problem in Thai Perspective: Positions and Viewpoints Held by Foreign Ministry Officials and Thai Americans.* Asian Studies Monograph No. 32. Bangkok: Chulalongkorn University, Institute of Asian Studies.

Ingram, Carl, and Robert A. Jones. 1989. "Gunman Had Attended School He Assaulted, but Motive Remains Unclear in Attack." *Los Angeles Times,* Jan. 19.

International Committee of the Red Cross. 1981. *Kampuchea: Back from the Brink.* Geneva: International Committee of the Red Cross.

International Rescue Committee. 1990. "Displaced Lives: Stories of Life and Culture from the Khmer in Site II, Thailand." Bangkok, Thailand: International Rescue Committee, Oral History Project.

Inzunza, R. 1990. "The United States Refugee Act of 1980: Ten Years After—Still the Way to Go." *International Journal of Refugee Law* 2(3): 413–27.

Isaacs, Arnold R. 1983. *Without Honor: Defeat in Vietnam and Cambodia.* Baltimore: Johns Hopkins University Press.

Jackson, Karl D. 1989a. "The Ideology of Total Revolution." In *Cambodia 1975–1979: Rendevous with Death.* Ed. Karl D. Jackson, 37–78. Princeton: Princeton University Press.

———. 1989b. "Intellectual Origins of the Khmer Rouge." In *Cambodia 1975–78: Rendevous with Death.* Ed. Karl D. Jackson, 241–50. Princeton: Princeton University Press.

———. 1989c. "Introduction: The Khmer Rouge in Context." In *Cambodia 1975–78: Rendevous with Death.* Ed. Karl D. Jackson, 3–11. Princeton: Princeton University Press.

Jackson, Tony. 1987. *Just Waiting to Die? Cambodian Refugees in Thailand: Report of a Tour to the Thai-Cambodian Border and Subsequent Research.* Oxford, Eng.: Oxfam House.

Jarvis, Helen. 2002. "Trials and Tribulations: The Latest Twists in the Long Quest for Justice for the Cambodian Genocide." *Critical Asian Studies* 34(4): 607–10.

Johnson, Kevin. 1991a. "Cambodian Dance Troupe Back on Its Feet." *Los Angeles Times,* Oct. 11.

———. 1991b. "Cambodian Dancers' U.S. Tour Collapses." *Los Angeles Times,* Oct. 5.

———. 1991c. "Debt Hamstrings Dance Troup from Cambodian Refugee Camp." *Los Angeles Times,* Oct. 3.

Johnson, Sally. 1987. "Young Cambodians in Vermont Try to Cope." *New York Times,* July 6.

———. 1988. "Long Road's End for Reunited Asians." *New York Times,* May 1.

Jones, Clayton. 1987. "Cambodians Revive Classical Dance after Near Destruction of Heritage." *Christian Science Monitor,* June 17.

Jorgensen, Karen K. 1989. "The Role of the U.S. Congress and Courts in the Application of the Refugee Act of 1980." In *Refugee Law and Policy: International and U.S. Responses.* Ed. Ved P. Nanda, 129–50. Westport: Greenwood Press.

Jowitt, Deborah. 1996. "Celestial Dancers on American Soil." *Dance Magazine* 70(1): 72–77.

Kalab, Milada. 1994. "Cambodian Buddhist Monasteries in Paris: Continuing Tradition and Changing Patterns." In *Cambodian Culture since 1975: Homeland and Exile.* Ed. May M. Ebihara, Carol A. Mortland, and Judy Ledgerwood, 57–71. Ithaca: Cornell University Press.

Kalb, Jonathan. 2001. "Making Dance of the Killing Fields." *New York Times,* June 24.

Kang, Connie, and Jeff Leeds. 1996a. "Ngor's Death a Blow to Movement for Cambodian Genocide Tribunal." *Los Angeles Times,* March 10.

———. 1996b. "Quest for Justice: Push for Tribunal on Cambodian Genocide Lost Key Leader with Ngor Death." *Los Angeles Times,* March 7.

Kang, Kimberly Eun Sook. 1999. "Acculturation Styles and Struggles of Cambodian Gang Members." M.A. thesis, California State University, Long Beach.

Karp, David. 1994. "Where Cambodians Travelled to Study and Stayed to Cook." *New York Times,* March 20.

Kaufman, Sarah. 2001. "Cambodian Dancers Jump Ship in D.C." *Washington Post,* Oct. 5.

Kelley, Barbara R. 1991. "Cambodian Childbearing Practices and Beliefs." Ed.D. diss., Boston University.

Kelly, Gail P. 1986. "Coping with America: Refugees from Vietnam, Cambodia, and Laos in the 1970s and 1980s." *Annals of the American Academy of Political and Social Science* 487: 138–49.

Kelly, Sheldon. 1991. "The Rebirth of Sichan Siv." *Reader's Digest* 138(826): 138–42.

Kemp, Charles. 1985. "Cambodian Refugee Health Care Beliefs and Practices." *Journal of Community Health Nursing* 2(1): 41–52.

Kennedy, Edward M. 1981. "The Refugee Act of 1980." *International Migration Review* 15(1): 141–56.

Khing Hoc Dy. 1994. "Khmer Literature since 1975." In *Cambodian Culture since 1975: Homeland and Exile.* Ed. May M. Ebihara, Carol A. Mortland, and Judy Ledgerwood, 27–38. Ithaca: Cornell University Press.

Khmer Buddhist Research Center, comp. 1986. *Buddhism and the Future of Cambodia.* Rithisen, Cambodia: Khmer Buddhist Research Center, Rithisen Temple.

Khoi, Sokley. 1998. "The Causal Attributions of Depression among Cambodian Refugees and Caucasian-Americans." Ph.D. diss., California School of Professional Psychology, Alameda/Berkeley.

Kiang, Peter N. 1994. "When Know-Nothings Speak English Only: Analyzing Irish and Cambodian Struggles for Community Development and Educational Equity." In *The State of Asian America.* Ed. Karen Aguilar-San Juan, 125–45. Boston: South End Press.

———. 1996. "Persistence Stories and Survival Strategies of Cambodian Americans in College." *Journal of Narrative and Life History* 6(1): 39–64.

Kiernan, Ben. 1985. *How Pol Pot Came to Power: A History of Communism in Kampuchea, 1930–1975.* London: Verso.

———. 1988. "Khmer (Kampucheans)." In *The Australian People: An Encyclopedia of the Nation, Its People, and Their Origins.* Ed. James Jupp, 658–59. North Ryde, NSW: Angus and Robertson.

———. 1989. "The American Bombardment of Kampuchea, 1969–1973." *Vietnam Generation* 1(1): 4–41.

———. 1996. *The Pol Pot Regime: Race, Power, and Genocide in Cambodia under the Khmer Rouge, 1975–79.* New Haven: Yale University Press.

———. 2000. "Bringing the Khmer Rouge to Justice." *Human Rights Review* 1(3): 92–108.

————. 2001. "Myth, Nationalism and Genocide." *Journal of Genocide Research* 3(2): 187–206.

————. 2002. "Introduction: Conflict in Cambodia, 1945–2002." *Critical Asian Studies* 34(4): 483–95.

Kiernan, Ben, and Chanthou Boua, eds. 1982. *Peasants and Politics in Kampuchea, 1942–1981.* London: Zed Press.

Kim, Young Yun. 1989. "Personal, Social, and Economic Adaptation: 1975–1979 Arrivals in Illinois." In *Refugees as Immigrants: Cambodians, Laotians, and Vietnamese in America.* Ed. David W. Haines, 86–104. Totowa: Rowan and Littlefield.

Kinzie, J. David. 1985. "Cultural Aspects of Psychiatric Treatment with Indochinese Refugees." *American Journal of Social Psychiatry* 5(1): 47–53.

————. 1986a. "The Establishment of Outpatient Mental Health Services for Southeast Asian Refugees." In *Refugee Mental Health in Resettlement Countries.* Ed. Carolyn L. Williams and Joseph Westermeyer, 217–31. Washington: Hemisphere Publishing.

————. 1986b. "Severe Post-Traumatic Stress Syndrome among Cambodian Refugees: Symptoms, Clinical Course, and Treatment Approaches." In *Disaster Stress Studies: New Methods and Findings.* Washington: American Psychiatric Association Press.

————. 1988. "Therapeutic Approaches to Traumatized Cambodian Refugees." *Journal of Traumatic Stress* 2(1): 75–91.

————. 1990. "The 'Concentration Camp Syndrome' among Cambodian Refugees." In *The Cambodian Agony.* Ed. David A. Ablin and Marlowe Hood, 332–53. Armonk: M. E. Sharpe.

Kinzie, J. David, R. H. Fredrickson, Rath Ben, Jenelle Fleck, and William Karls. 1984. "Posttraumatic Stress Disorder among Survivors of Cambodian Concentration Camps." *American Journal of Psychiatry* 141(5): 645–50.

Kinzie, J. David, William H. Sack, Richard H. Angell, and Spero Manson. 1986. "The Psychiatric Effects of Massive Trauma on Cambodian Children. I: The Children." *Journal of the American Academy of Child Psychiatry* 25(3): 370–76.

Kinzie, J. David, Paul Leung, Anh Bui, Rath Ben, Kham One Keopaseuth, Crystal Riley, Jenelle Fleck, and Marie Ades. 1988. "Group Therapy with Southeast Asian Refugees." *Community Mental Health Journal* 24(2): 157–66.

Kinzie, J. David, and J. K. Boehnlein. 1989. "Post-traumatic Psychosis among Cambodian Refugees." *Journal of Traumatic Stress* 2(2): 185–98.

Kinzie, J. David, and Paul Leung. 1989. "Clonidine in Cambodian Patients with Posttraumatic Stress Disorder." *Journal of Nervous and Mental Disease* 177(9): 546–50.

Kinzie, J. David, William H. Sack, Richard Angell, Gregory N. Clarke, and Rath Ben. 1989. "A Three-Year Follow-Up of Cambodian Young People Traumatized as Children." *Journal of American Academy of Child and Adolescent Psychiatry* 28(4): 501–4.

Kinzie, J. David, James K. Boehnlein, Paul K. Leong, Laurie J. Moore, Crystal Riley, and Debra Smith. 1990. "The Prevalence of Posttraumatic Stress Disorder and Its Clinical Significance among Southeast Asian Refugees." *American Journal of Psychiatry* 147(7): 913–17.

Kinzie, J. David, James K. Boehnlein, Crystal Riley, and Landy Sparr. 2002. "The Effects of September 11 on Traumatized Refugees: Reactivation of Posttraumatic Stress Disorder." *Journal of Nervous and Mental Disease* 190(7): 437–41.

Kiv, Khuon. 1997. "The Darkness of My Experience." In *Children of Cambodia's Killing Fields: Memoirs of Survivovrs.* Comp. Dith Pran, ed. Kim DePaul, 101–4. New Haven: Yale University Press.

Klintworth, Gary. 1989. *Vietnam's Intervention in Cambodia in International Law.* Canberra: Australian Government Publishing Service.

Kohn, Hans. 1957. *American Nationalism.* New York: Macmillan.

Kong, Bosseba. 1984. "The Resettlement of a Cambodian Family." M.S.W. thesis, University of California, Los Angeles.

Koschmann, Nancy L. H. 1987. "The Resettlement Process of Southeast Asian Refugee Adolescents: Making It American." Ph.D. diss., Cornell University.

Krasa, Miloslav, with photographs by Jan Cifra. 1963. *The Temples of Angkor: Monuments to a Vanished Empire.* London: Allan Wingate.

Kulig, Judith. 1988a. "Childbearing Cambodian Refugee Women." *Canadian Nurse* 84(6): 46–47.

———. 1988b. "Conception and Birth Control Use: Cambodian Refugee Women's Beliefs and Practices." *Journal of Community Health Nursing* 5(4): 235–46.

———. 1990. "A Review of the Health Status of Southeast Asian Refugee Women." *Health Care for Women International* 11(1): 49–63.

———. 1991. "Role, Status Changes and Family Planning Use among Cambodian Refugee Women." D.N.S. diss., University of California, San Francisco.

———. 1994a. "Old Traditions in a New World: Changing Gender Relations among Cambodian Refugees." In *Reconstructing Lives, Recapturing Meaning: Refugee Identity, Gender, and Culture Change.* Ed. Linda A. Camino and Ruth M. Krulfeld, 129–46. Basel, Switzerland: Gordon and Breach.

———. 1994b. "Sexuality Beliefs among Cambodians: Implications for Health Care Professionals." *Health Care for Women International* 15(1): 69–76.

———. 1994c. "'Those with Unheard Voices': The Plight of a Cambodian Refugee Woman." *Journal of Community Health Nursing* 11(2): 99–107.

Kuoch, Theanvy, Richard A. Miller, and Mary F. Scully. 1992. "Healing the Wounds of the *Mahantdori*." *Women and Therapy* 13(3): 191–207.

Kusel, Ronald J. 1989. "Church Growth Plans in a Multicultural Setting: First Lutheran Church of Long Beach." D.Min. diss., Fuller Theological Seminary.

Kuwahara, Yuri Lea. 1998. "Interactions of Identity: Inner-City Immigrant and Refugee Youths, Language Use, and Schooling." Ph.D. diss., Stanford University.

LaDuke, Mary A. 1998. "Help-seeking Behavior and Empowerment among Cambodian Refugees." M.S.W. thesis, California State University, Long Beach.

Lamer, Brook. 1986. "Many Refugees Flee War in Asia Only to Face New Threat in U.S." *Christian Science Monitor,* April 29.

Law, Chi Kwong. 1988. "Economic Assimilation of Refugees: Human Capital, Job Information and Ethnic Enclave." D.S.W. diss., University of California, Los Angeles.

"Law Paves Way for Tribunal." 2001. *Los Angeles Times,* Aug. 11.

Lawyers Committee for Human Rights. 1985. *Human Rights in Kampuchea: Preliminary Summary of Findings and Conclusions.* New York: Lawyers Committee for Human Rights.

———. 1987. *Seeking Shelter: Cambodians in Thailand.* New York: Lawyers Committee for Human Rights.

———. 1989. *Refuge Denied: Problems in the Protection of Vietnamese and Cambodians in Thailand and the Admission of Indochinese Refugees into the United States.* New York: Lawyers Committee for Human Rights.

———. 1990. *Kampuchea: After the Worst.* New York: Lawyers Committee for Human Rights.

———. 1992. *Cambodia: The Justice System and Violations of Human Rights.* New York: Lawyers Committee for Human Rights.

Ledgerwood, Judy L. 1990a. "Changing Khmer Conceptions of Gender: Women, Stories, and the Social Order." Ph.D. diss., Cornell University.

———. 1990b. "Portrait of a Conflict: Exploring Changing Khmer-American Social and Political Relations." *Journal of Refugee Studies* 3(2): 135–54.

———. 1994. "Gender Symbolism and Culture Change: Viewing the Virtuous Woman in the Khmer Story 'Mea Yoeng.'" In *Cambodian Culture since 1975: Homeland and Exile.* Ed. May M. Ebihara, Carol A. Mortland, and Judy Ledgerwood, 119–28. Ithaca: Cornell University Press.

Lee, Gen Leigh. 1996. "Chinese-Cambodian Donut Makers in Orange County: Case Studies of Family Labor and Socioeconomic Adaptations." In *The State of Asian Pacific America: Reframing the Immigration Debate.* Ed. Bill Ong Hing and Ronald Lee, 205–19. Los Angeles: Asian Pacific American Public Policy Institute and UCLA Asian American Studies Center.

Lee, Matthew. 1996. "With Friends Like These." *Far Eastern Economic Review,* Nov. 14, 22.

Lefreniere, Bree. 2000. *Music through the Dark: A Tale of Survival in Cambodia.* Honolulu: University of Hawaii Press.

Lenart, Edith. 1977. "After War, Another Battle." *Far Eastern Economic Review,* April 29, 21–24.

Lenart, Janet C. 1989. "An Exploratory Study of Cambodian Refugee Women's Childbearing Beliefs, Knowledge and Informational Sources." M.P.H. thesis, University of Washington.

Lenart, Janet C., Patricia A. St. Clair, and Michelle A. Bell. 1991. "Childrearing Knowledge, Beliefs, and Practices of Cambodian Refugees." *Journal of Pediatric Health Care* 5(6): 299–305.

"Letter from Sok An to Hans Corell." 2001. *Critical Asian Studies* 34(4): 612.

Levy, Barry S. 1981. "Working in a Camp for Cambodian Refugees." *New England Journal of Medicine* 304(23): 1440–44.

———. 1986. "Working at Khao I Dang: A Physician's Experience." In *Years of Horror, Days of Hope: Responding to the Cambodian Refugee Crisis.* Ed. Barry S. Levy and Daniel C. Susott, 107–15. Millwood, N.Y.: Associated Faculty Press.

Levy, Barry S., and Daniel C. Susott, eds. 1986. *Years of Horror, Days of Hope: Responding to the Cambodian Refugee Crisis.* Millwood, N.Y.: Associated Faculty Press.

Lew, Gena A., and Brandon Sugiyama. 1995. "The Cambodian Business Community in Long Beach." *LEAP Connections* 8(2): 4–5.

Lew, Lillian S. 1991. "Elderly Cambodians in Long Beach: Creating Cultural Access
to Health Care." *Journal of Cross-Cultural Gerontology* 6(2): 199–203.

Lind, Louise. 1989. *The Southeast Asians in Rhode Island.* Providence: The Rhode Island Heritage Commission and the Rhode Island Publications Society.

Lipsky, Sherry, and Ky Nimol. 1993. "Khmer Women Healers in Transition: Cultural
and Bureaucratic Barriers in Training and Employment." *Journal of Refugee Studies* 6(4): 372–88.

Lobban, William. "The Revival of Masked Theater, *Lkhaon Khaol,* in Cambodia." In
Cambodian Culture since 1975: Homeland and Exile. Ed. May M. Ebihara, Carol
A. Mortland, and Judy Ledgerwood, 48–56. Ithaca: Cornell University Press.

Loescher, Gil, and John A. Scanlan. 1986. *Calculated Kindness: Refugees and America's Half-Open Door, 1945–Present,* 147–69. New York: Free Press.

Long Beach Police Department. 1996. Untitled information pamphlet on gangs. Feb.

Longmire, B. Jean. 1992. "Communicating Social Identity in a Job Interview in a
Cambodian-American Community." *Journal of Asian Pacific Communication*
3(1): 49–58.

Lowenthal, Jeff. 1995. "One Small Step for Women: Helping Torture Victims Heal."
Human Rights: Journal of the Section on Individual Rights and Responsibilities
22(4): 20–21.

Lowman, Sheppard. 1992. "The Cambodian Repatriation: Fall, 1992." Washington:
United States Catholic Conference Migration and Refugee Services. Oct.

Luciolli, Esmeralda. 1986. "Khao I Dang: The Early Days." In *Years of Horror, Days of
Hope: Responding to the Cambodian Refugee Crisis.* Ed. Barry S. Levy and Daniel
C. Susott, 67–72. Millwood, N.Y.: Associated Faculty Press.

Lydon, Julia. 1988. "Finding a Way: Cross-Cultural Adaptation at Home and School
in Nashville, Tennessee." Ph.D. diss., Bryn Mawr College.

Lynch, Maureen J. 1997. "The Experience of Southeast Asian Refugee Families: An
Exploration of Family Identity (Cambodian, Vietnamese)." Ph.D. diss., Oregon
State University.

Mabbett, Ian, and David Chandler. 1991. *The Khmer.* London: Blackwell.

Malnic, Eric. 1996. "Three Charged in Death of Actor Ngor." *Los Angeles Times,* April
27.

Maloney, Colleen A. 1989. "Barriers to Health Care Acquisition in the Cambodian
Refugee." M.S. thesis, University of Massachusetts, Lowell.

Mam, Teeda Butt. 1997. "Worms from Our Skin." In *Children of Cambodia's Killing
Fields: Memoirs of Survivors.* Comp. Dith Pran, ed. Kim DePaul, 11–18. New Haven: Yale University Press.

Mannikka, Eleanor. 1996. *Angkor Wat: Time, Space, Kingship.* Honolulu: University
of Hawaii Press.

Marcucci, John L. 1986. "Khmer Refugees in Dallas: Medical Decisions in the Context of Pluralism." Ph.D. diss., Southern Methodist University.

Martell, Charles, and Kitty W. Shek. 1992. *A Guide to the Oral History Collection of
Cambodians in California.* Sacramento: California State University, Sacramento, the Library, Cambodians in California Project.

Martin, Marie Alexandrine. 1994. *Cambodia: A Shattered Society.* Berkeley: University of California Press.

Martin, Richard. 1988. "Inhabitants Live on Edge in Border Refugee Camps." *Insight* (*Washington Times* magazine), Aug. 1, 15–18.

Martois, James E. 1988. "A Case Study of the Unique Educational Needs of Cambodian Americans." Ph.D. diss., University of Southern California.

Mason, Linda, and Roger Brown. 1983. *Rice, Rivalry, and Politics.* Notre Dame, Ind.: University of Notre Dame Press.

Masson, Mireille A. 1993. "Khmer Spoken Here: Ethnography of a Title VII Classroom." M.A. thesis, California State University, Long Beach.

May Someth. 1986. Ed. and with an introduction by James Fenton. *Cambodian Witness: The Autobiography of Someth May.* New York: Random House.

McFadden, Robert D. 1983. "Seven Families of Cambodian Refugees Flee Brooklyn in Search for Safety." *New York Times,* March 18.

McKenzie-Pollock, Lorna. 1996. "Cambodian Families." In *Ethnicity and Family Therapy.* Ed. Monica McGoldrick, Joe Giordano, and John K. Pearce, 307–15. New York: Guilford Press.

McNamara, Dennis. 1990. "The Origins and Effects of 'Humane Deterrence' Policies in South-east Asia." In *Refugees and International Relations.* Ed. Gil Loescher and Laila Monahan, 123–33. New York: Clarendon Press.

Melnick, Leah. 1990a. "Cambodians in the Bronx and Amherst." *Vietnam Generation* 2(3): 88–105.

———. 1990b. "Cambodians in Western Massachusetts and Bronx, New York." *Migration World* 18(2): 4–9.

"The Message from the Camps." 1988. *The Economist* 308(7557): 28.

Michelmore, Peter. 1997. "Legacy of the Killing Fields." *Reader's Digest* 150(901): 60–66.

Miller, Alan C., and Stu Glauberman. 1992. "Going Back Home to Help." *Los Angeles Times,* Aug. 24.

Miller, Kathleen M. 1986. "An Exploratory Study of the Illness Beliefs and Practices of a Group of Cambodian Refugees." M.S. thesis, School of Nursing, University of Rochester.

Mitchell, Florence S. 1987. "From Refugee to Rebuilder: Cambodian Women in America." Ph.D. diss., Syracuse University.

Mitrsomwang, Supervadee. 1992. "Family Values and Behaviors in the Academic Performance of Indochinese Refugee Students." Ph.D. diss., Vanderbilt University.

Moburg, Mark, and Stephen J. Thomas. 1993. "Class Segmentation and Divided Labor: Asian Workers in the Gulf of Mexico Seafood Industry." *Ethnology* 32(1): 87–99.

Mollica, Richard F. 1990. "Communities of Confinement: An International Plan for Relieving the Mental Health Crisis in the Thai-Khmer Border Camps." *Southeast Asian Journal of Social Science* 18(1): 132–52.

———. 1997. "Effects of War Trauma on Cambodian Refugee Adolescents' Functional Health and Mental Health Status." *Journal of the American Academy of Child and Adolescent Psychiatry* 36(9): 1098–106.

Mollica, Richard F., Karen Donelan, Svant Tor, James Lavelle, Christopher Elias, Martin Frankel, and Robert J. Blendon. 1993. "The Effect of Trauma and Confinement on Functional Health and Mental Health Status of Cambodians Living in Thailand-Cambodia Border Camps." *Journal of the American Medical Association* 270(5): 581–86.

Mollica, Richard F., and R. R. Jalbert. 1989. "Community of Confinement: The Mental Health Crisis in Site Two (Displaced Persons Camps on the Thai-Kampuchean Border)." Baltimore: World Federation for Mental Health, Committee on Refugees and Migrants, Feb.

Mollica, Richard F., Charles Poole, Linda Son, Caroline C. Murray, and Svang Tor. 1995. "Southeast Asian Refugees: Migration History and Mental Health Issues." In *Amidst Peril and Pain: The Mental Health and Well-Being of the World's Refugees.* Ed. Anthony J. Marsella et al., 83–100. Washington: American Psychological Association.

Mollica, Richard F., Grace Wyshak, and James Lavelle. 1987. "The Psychological Impact of War Trauma and Torture on Southeast Asian Refugees." *American Journal of Psychiatry* 144(12): 1567–72.

Mollica, Richard F., Grace Wyshak, James Lavelle, Toan Truong, Svang Tor, and Ter Yang. 1990. "Assessing Symptom Change in Southeast Asian Refugee Survivors of Mass Violence and Torture." *American Journal of Psychiatry* 147(1): 83–88.

Mong, Adrienne. 1994. "A Home in the Bronx: Cambodians Are Joining the American Mainstream with Varying Degrees of Success." *Far Eastern Economic Review* 157(17): 38–39.

Morelli, Paula Toki Tanemura. 1996. "Trauma and Healing: The Construction of Meaning among Survivors of the Cambodian Holocaust." Ph.D. diss., University of Washington.

Morrison, Patt. 1996. "When Parallel Universes Bump." *Los Angeles Times,* March 13.

Morris, Stephen J. 1999. *Why Vietnam Invaded Cambodia: Political Culture and the Causes of War.* Stanford: Stanford University Press.

Mortland, Carol A. 1987. "Transforming Refugees in Refugee Camps." *Urban Anthropology* 16(3–4): 375–404.

———. 1994a. "Cambodian Refugees and Identity in the United States." In *Reconstructing Lives, Recapturing Meaning: Refugee Identity, Gender, and Culture Change.* Ed. Linda A. Camino and Ruth M. Krulfeld, 5–27. Basel, Switzerland: Gordon and Breach.

———. 1994b. "Khmer Buddhism in the United States: Ultimate Questions." In *Khmer Culture Since 1975: Homeland and Exile.* Ed. May M. Ebihara, Carol A. Mortland, and Judy Ledgerwood, 72–90. Ithaca: Cornell University Press.

———. 1997. "Khmer." In *Case Studies in Diversity: Refugees in America in the 1990s.* Ed. David W. Haines. 167–93. Westport: Praeger.

———. 2001. "Tacoma, Washington: Cambodian Adaptation and Community Response." In *Manifest Destinies: Americanizing Immigrants and Internationalizing Americans.* Ed. David W. Haines and Carol A. Mortland, 71–88. Westport: Praeger.

Mortland, Carol A., and Judy Ledgerwood. 1987a. "Refugee Resource Acquisition: The Invisible Communication System." In *Cross-Cultural Adaptation: Current Approaches.* Ed. Y. Y. Kim and W. B. Gudykunst, 286–306. Newbury Park, Calif.: Sage.

————. 1987b. "Secondary Migration among Southeast Asian Refugees in the United States." *Urban Anthropology* 16(3–4): 291–326.

Motherland: CANDO Quarterly Newsletter. 1994. 1(1). Phnom Penh: Cambodian-American National Development Organization.

————. 1995. 1(2). Phnom Penh: Cambodian-American National Development Organization.

Mouth, Sophea. 1997. "Memoirs of a Survivor." *Progressive* 61(9): 12.

Muecke, Marjorie A. 1995. "Trust, Abuse of Trust, and Mistrust among Cambodian Refugee Women: A Cultural Interpretation." In *Mistrusting Refugees.* Ed. E. Valentine Daniel and John Chr. Knudsen, 36–55. Berkeley: University of California Press.

Muecke, Marjorie A., and Lisa Sassi. 1992. "Anxiety among Cambodian Refugee Adolescents in Transit and in Resettlement." *Western Journal of Nursing Research* 14(3): 267–91.

Muldoon, Jeannine D. 1990. "New Immigrants and Their Health: Southeast Asian Refugees in Western Massachusetts." Ph.D. diss., University of Massachusetts.

Munoz, Lorenza. 1996a. "Community Mourns Loss of Its Best Known." *Los Angeles Times,* Feb. 27.

————. 1996b. "Countrymen Honor Slain Actor, Activist." *Los Angeles Times,* March 8.

Muntarbhorn, Vitit. 1992. *The Status of Refugees in Asia.* Chap. 12: "Thailand," 125–42. Oxford: Clarendon Press.

Mydans, Seth. 1991a. "As Cultures Meet, Gang War Paralyzes a City in California." *New York Times,* May 6.

————. 1991b. "Refugees' Fears Survive Even Peace in Cambodia." *New York Times,* Nov. 19.

————. 1995. "From Cambodia to Doughnut Shops." *New York Times,* May 26.

National Association for the Education and Advancement of Cambodian, Laotian and Vietnamese Americans. 1995. *A Profile of the Cambodian, Hmong, Laotian, and Vietnamese People in the United States.* N.p.

Newman, Vicky, William Norcross, and Roger McDonald. 1991. "Nutrient Intake of Low-Income Southeast Asian Pregnant Women." *Journal of the American Dietetic Association* 91(7): 793–800.

Ngor, Haing S., with Roger Warner. 1987. *Haing Ngor: A Cambodian Odyssey.* New York: Macmillan.

"Ngor's Death a Blow to Movement for Cambodian Genocide Tribunal." 1996. *Los Angeles Times,* March 10.

Nguyen-Hong-Nhiem, Lucy, and Joel M. Halpern, eds. 1989. *The Far East Comes Near: Autobiographical Accounts of Southeast Asian Students in America.* Amherst, Mass.: University of Massachusetts Press, 95–164.

Nicholson, Barbara L., and Diane M. Kay. 1999. "Group Treatment of Traumatized Cambodian Women: A Culture-Specific Approach." *Social Work* 44(5): 470–84.

Niedzwiecki, William R. 1998. "The World Turned Upside-Down: Khmer-American Status, Identity, and Cultural Conflicts in Institutional Contexts." Ph.D. diss., Boston University.

Noble, Kenneth B. 1996. "Cambodian Physician Who Won an Oscar for 'Killing Fields' Is Slain." *New York Times,* Feb. 27.

Nordland, Rod. 1983. "Promised Land Is Eluding Many Southeast Asians Here." *Phil-*

adelphia Inquirer, 28 March. In *Newsbank,* Social Relations, microfiche 11, grids B14, C1–3.

Norman, Michael. 1983. "A Long Journey of Fear, a Refuge of Hope for Cambodians." *New York Times,* March 21.

Norodom Sihanouk, and Wilfred Burchett. 1973. *My War with the CIA: The Memoirs of Prince Norodom Sihanouk.* Harmondsworth, England: Penguin.

North, David, and Nim Sok. 1989. *Profiles of Some Good Places for Cambodians to Live in the United States.* Washington: U.S. Department of Health and Human Services, Family Support Administration, Office of Refugee Resettlement.

Northwood, Andrea K. 1996. "Trauma Exposure, Post-Traumatic Symptoms, and Identity in Adolescent Survivors of Massive Childhood Trauma." Ph.D. diss., University of Minnesota.

Nou-Meas, Borina. 1998. "Child Abuse and Neglect in the Cambodian Community." M.S.W. thesis, California State University, Long Beach.

Nyman, Nina W. 1986. "Cross-Cultural Perspectives on Child Development: A Study of the Imaginative Play of Cambodian and Black Preschoolers." D.S.W. diss., University of California, Berkeley.

Office of the United Nations High Commissioner for Refugees. 1989. *Kampuchea: An Emergency Preparedness Profile.* Geneva: Office of United Nations High Commissioner for Refugees.

———. 1993. *Cambodia: Hope for a New Life.* Geneva: Office of United Nations High Commissioner for Refugees.

———. 1995a. *Collection of International Instruments and Other Texts Concerning Refugees and Displaced Persons.* Vol. 1: *Universal Instruments.* "Convention Relating to the Status of Refugees" and "Protocol Relating to the Status of Refugees," 10–43. Geneva: Office of the United Nations High Commissioner for Refugees, Division of International Protection.

———. 1995b. *The State of the World's Refugees, 1995: In Search of Solutions.* New York: Oxford University Press.

———. 2000. *The State of the World's Refugees, 2000: Fifty Years of Humanitarian Action.* New York: Oxford University Press.

Ong, Aihwa. 1995. "Making the Biopolitical Subject: Cambodian Immigrants, Refugee Medicine, and Cultural Citizenship in California." *Social Science and Medicine* 40(9): 1243–57.

———. 2003. *Buddha Is Hiding: Refugees, Citizenship, the New Americans.* Berkeley: University of California Press.

Ong, Aihwa, and Donald M. Nonini, eds. 1997. *Ungrounded Empires: The Cultural Politics of Modern Chinese Nationalism.* New York: Routledge.

Opportunity Systems, Inc. 1979. *Sixth Wave Report: Indochinese Resettlement Operational Feedback (Cambodian Refugee Group).* Prepared for Office of Refugee Affairs, Social Security Administration, U.S. Department of Health, Education, and Welfare. Washington: Government Printing Office.

Osborne, Milton. 1969. *The French Presence in Cochinchina and Cambodia: Rule and Response (1859–1905).* Ithaca: Cornell University Press.

———. 1973. *Politics and Power in Cambodia: The Sihanouk Years.* Camberwell, Australia: Longman Australia.

———. 1994. *Sihanouk: Prince of Light, Prince of Darkness.* Honolulu: University of Hawaii Press.

Ouk, Vibol, and Charles Martin Simon. 1998. *Goodnight Cambodia: Forbidden History.* Santa Cruz, Calif.: Charles Martin Simon.

Packer, George. 1991. "Cambodia: Faces Saved and Lost." *Dissent* 38(1): 29–31.

Paddock, Richard C. 2003. "Cambodia's Black Sheep Return to the Fold." *Los Angeles Times,* March 28.

Palinkas, Lawrence A., and Sheila M. Pickwell. 1995. "Acculturation as a Risk Factor for Chronic Disease among Cambodian Refugees in the United States." *Social Science and Medicine* 40(12): 1643–53.

Pape, Eric. 2001. "The Remote-Control Revolution." *Los Angeles Times Magazine,* June 24.

Park, Robert E. 1923. "A Race Relations Survey." *Journal of Applied Sociology* 8: 195–205. Repr. in Robert E. Park. 1950. *Race and Culture: Essays in the Sociology of Contemporary Man.* New York: Free Press, 158–65.

———. 1926. "Our Racial Frontier on the Pacific." *Survey Graphic,* May, 192–96. Repr. in Robert E. Park, 1950. *Race and Culture: Essays in the Sociology of Contemporary Man,* 138–51. New York: Free Press.

Parker, Martha K. 1996. "Loss in the Lives of Southeast Asian Elders (Cambodian, Hmong, Laotian, Vietnamese)." Ph.D. diss., University of Minnesota.

"Pawns in a Deadly Game." 1988. *Time,* Dec. 19, 55.

Pfeffer, Max J. 1994. "Low-Wage Employment and Ghetto Poverty: A Comparison of African-American and Cambodian Day-Haul Farm Workers in Philadelphia." *Social Problems* 41(1): 9–29.

———. 1997. "Work versus Welfare in the Ethnic Transformation of a Philadelphia Labor Market." *Social Science Quarterly* 78(2): 452–71.

Pfeifer, Mark E. 2002. "Census Shows Growth and Changing Distribution of the Cambodian Population in the United States." "Hmong Studies Internet Research Center" Web-site copyright by Mark E. Pfeifer at <http://www.hmongstudies.org/> accessed on Sept. 15, 2002.

Pho, Hai B. 1991. "The Politics of Refugee Resettlement in Massachusetts." *Migration World* 19(4): 2–10.

Pich, Sohko. 1993. "Autobiography." Unpublished term paper, Asian American Studies 2, University of California, Santa Barbara.

Pickering, Rexann G. 1987. "An Ethnographic Study of the Health Beliefs of Cambodians Living in Memphis, Tennessee." M.N. thesis, School of Nursing, Methodist Hospitals of Memphis.

Pickwell, Sheila M. 1982. "Primary Health Care for Indochinese Refugee Children." *Pediatric Nursing* 8(2): 104–7.

———. 1990. "Journey to the Promised Land: The Health Consequences of Refugee Status for Cambodians in San Diego." Ph.D. diss., University of California, San Diego.

PierSath, Chath. 2000. "Coping Methods: Personal and Community Resources Used among Cambodians in Cambodia and Cambodian-Americans in Lowell, Massachusetts." M.A. thesis, University of Massachusetts, Lowell.

Poethig, Kathryn A. 1997. "Ambivalent Moralities: Cambodian-Americans and Dual

Citizenship in Phnom Penh." Ph.D. diss., Graduate Theological Union, Berkeley, Calif.

———. 2002. "Movable Peace: Engaging the Transnational in Cambodia's Dhammayietra." *Journal for the Scientific Study of Religion* 41(1): 19–28.

"Political Violence Comes to America, Following Those Escaping It." 1996. *Los Angeles Times*, March 9.

Pollack, Sheryl R. 1987. "Food Habits and Factors Influencing the Health Status of Low Income Pregnant Cambodian Women in Long Beach, California." M.S. thesis, California State University, Long Beach.

Ponchaud, Francois. 1978. Trans. Nancy Amphoux. *Cambodia: Year Zero.* New York: Holt, Rinehart and Winston.

———. 1989. "Social Change in the Vortex of Revolution." In *Cambodia, 1975–78: Rendevous with Death.* Ed. Karl D. Jackson, 151–78. Princeton: Princeton University Press.

Poremba, Barbara A. 1991. "Nutrition Education for Cambodian Refugees: Evaluating a Health Intervention Media Project." Ed.D. diss., University of Massachusetts.

Portes, Alejandro, and Min Zhou. 1993. "The New Second Generation: Segmented Assimilation and Its Variants." *Annals of the American Academy of Political and Social Science* 530: 74–96.

Portes, Alejandro, and Ruben G. Rumbaut. 2001a. *Legacies: The Story of the Immigrant Second Generation.* Berkeley: University of California Press.

———. 2001b. "Conclusion—The Forging of a New America: Lessons for Theory and Policy." In *Ethnicities: Children of Immigrants in America*, ed. Ruben G. Rumbaut and Alejandro Portes, 301–17. Berkeley: University of California Press.

Proceedings of the First Meeting of the Cambodian, Hmong, and Laotian Apostolate in the Catholic Church in the United States. 1985. Washington: National Conference of Catholic Bishops.

Press, Eval. 1997. "Unforgiven." *Lingua Franca*, April-May, 67–75.

Quinn, Kenneth M. 1989a. "Explaining the Terror." In *Cambodia 1975–1978: Rendevous with Death.* Ed. Karl D. Jackson, 215–40. Princeton: Princeton University Press.

———. 1989b. "The Pattern and Scope of Violence." In *Cambodia 1975–1978: Rendevous with Death.* Ed. Karl D. Jackson, 179–208. Princeton: Princeton University Press.

Rajatanavin, Araya. 1985. "Language Needs Identification of Cambodian Refugees in a U. S. Urban Area." Ph.D. diss., Florida State University.

Rajeswary, I. 1985. "Cambodian Refugees Hit U.S. Immigration Policy: 15,000 Applicants Rejected." *Washington Post*, Aug. 1.

Ranard, Donald A., and Margo Pfleger, eds. 1995. *From the Classroom to the Community: A Fifteen-Year Experiment in Refugee Education.* McHenry, Ill.: Delta Systems and Center for Applied Linguistics.

Rasbridge, Lance A. 1991. "Infant/Child Feeding among Resettled Cambodians in Dallas: Intracultural Variation in Reference to Iron Nutrition." Ph.D. diss., Southern Methodist University.

————. 2001. "Dallas, Texas, Enclave and Suburb: Patterns and Reactions in Refugee-Host Interactions." In *Manifest Destinies: Americanizing Immigrants and Internationalizing Americans.* Ed. David W. Haines and Carol A. Mortland, 25–37. Westport: Praeger.

Ratliff, Sharon K. 1997. *Caring for Cambodian Americans: A Multidisciplinary Resource for the Helping Professions.* New York: Garland.

Realmuto, George M., Ann Masten, Linda Flies Carole, Jon Hubbard, Andrea Groteluschen, and Bunkhean Chhun. 1992. "Adolescent Survivors of Massive Childhood Trauma in Cambodia: Life Events and Current Symptoms." *Journal of Traumatic Stress* 5(4): 589–99.

Refugee Policy Group. N.d. "Cambodia: A Time for Return, Reconciliation, and Reconstruction." Washington: Refugee Policy Group.

Refugee Reports (Indochinese Refugee Reports during its first year and a half). May 1979–Dec. 1995, vols. 1–16.

Reynell, Josephine. 1989. *Political Pawns: Refugees on the Thai-Kampuchean Border.* Oxford: Refugee Studies Programme.

Rezowalli, Gary J. 1990. "Acculturation and Distress among Cambodian Refugees." Ph.D. diss., Pacific Graduate School of Psychology.

Rim, Cheoum. 1991. "Greensboro, North Carolina." In John Tenhula. *Voices from Southeast Asia: The Refugee Experience in the United States,* 89–91. New York: Holmes and Meier.

Roark, Anne C. 1989. "Stockton—Tending to the Psyche." *Los Angeles Times,* Jan. 20.

Roberts, David. 1992. "Cambodia: Problems of a UN-Brokered Peace." *World Today* 48(7): 129–32.

————. 2002. "Democratization, Elite Transition, and Violence in Cambodia, 1991–1999." *Critical Asian Studies* 34(4): 520–38.

Robertson, Lynda A. 1983. "English as a Second Language for Cambodian Refugees at Houston Community College: A Programme Evaluation." Ed.D. diss., University of Houston.

Robinson, W. Courtland. 1986. "Refugee Protection in Thailand and the Closing of Khao I Dang." In *World Refugee Survey: 1986 in Review.* Washington: U.S. Committee for Refugees.

————. 1996. "Double Vision: A History of Cambodian Refugees in Thailand." Bangkok, Thailand: Chulalongkorn University, Institute of Asian Studies, Asian Research Center for Migration.

————. 1998. *Terms of Refuge: The Indochinese Exodus and the International Response.* London: Zed Books.

Robinson, Court, and Arthur Wallerstein. 1988. *Unfulfilled Hopes: The Humanitarian Parole-Immigrant Visa Program for Border Cambodians.* Washington: U.S. Committee for Refugees.

Rondineau, Rogatien. 1992. "My Ten Years in the Cambodian Catholic Apostolate in the United States: A Missionary's Reflection." *Migration World* 20(4): 26–28.

Rosas, Josette M. 1999. "The Association of Current Life Events and Post-Traumatic Stress Disorder among Cambodian Refugees." M.S.W. thesis, California State University, Long Beach.

Rosser-Hogan, Rhonda I. 1991. "Dissociation and Posttraumatic Stress Disorder in Khmer Refugees Resettled in the United States." Ph.D. diss., University of North Carolina, Greensboro.

Rousseau, Cecile, and Aline Drapeau. 1998. "Parent-Child Agreement on Refugee Children's Psychiatric Symptoms." *Journal of the American Academy of Child and Adolescent Psychiatry* 37(4): 629–36.

Rousseau, Cecile, Aline Drapeau, and Robert Platt. 1999. "Family Trauma and Its Association with Emotional and Behavioral Problems and Social Adjustment in Adolescent Cambodian Refugees." *Child Abuse and Neglect* 23(12): 1263–73.

Rozee, Patricia D., and Gretchen Van Boemel. 1989. "The Psychological Effects of War Trauma and Abuse on Older Cambodian Refugee Women." *Women and Therapy* 8(4): 23–50.

Rumbaut, Ruben G. 1996. "The Crucible Within: Ethnic Identity, Self-Esteem, and Segmented Assimilation Among Children of Immigrants." In *The New Second Generation,* ed. Alejandro Portes, 119–70. New York: Russell Sage Foundation.

Rumbaut, Ruben G., and Alejandro Portes, 2001. "Introduction—Ethnogenesis: Coming of Age in Immigrant America." In *Ethnicities: Children of Immigrants in America,* ed. Ruben G. Rumbaut and Alejandro Portes, 1–20. Berkeley: University of California Press.

Ryan, Angela S. 1985. "The Correlates of Psychological Adjustment of Southeast Asian Refugees in New York City." D.S.W. diss., Fordham University.

Ryan, Christine E. 1987. "Indochinese Refugees in the U. S.: Background Characteristics, Initial Adjustment Patterns, and the Role of Policy." Ph.D. diss., Brown University.

Sack, William H. 1996. "Multiple Forms of Stress in Cambodian Adolescent Refugees." *Child Development* 67(1): 107–16.

———. 1997. "Does PTSD Transcend Cultural Barriers? A Study from the Khmer Adolescent Refugee Project." *Journal of the American Academy of Child and Adolescent Psychiatry* 36(1): 49–54.

Sack, William H., Chanrithy Him, and Dan Dickason. 1999. "Twelve-Year Follow-Up Study of Khmer Youths Who Suffered Massive War Trauma as Children." *Journal of the American Academy of Child and Adolescent Psychiatry* 38(10): 1173–79.

Sack, William H., Gregory N. Clarke, Chanrithy Him, Dan Dickason, Brian Goff, Kathleen Lanham, and J. David Kinzie. 1993. "A Six-Year Follow-Up Study of Cambodian Refugee Adolescents Traumatized as Children." *Journal of the American Academy of Child and Adolescent Psychiatry* 32(2): 431–37.

Sack, William H., Gregory N. Clarke, and John Seeley. 1995. "Post-traumatic Stress Disorder across Two Generations of Cambodian Refugees." *Journal of the American Academy of Child and Adolescent Psychiatry* 34(9): 1160–66.

Sack, William H., Gregory N. Clarke, Ronald Kinney, Georgia Belestos, Chanrithy Him, and John Seeley. 1995. "The Khmer Adolescent Project II: Functional Capacities in Two Generations of Cambodian Refugees." *Journal of Nervous and Mental Disease* 183(3): 177–81.

Sack, William H., Richard H. Angell, J. David Kinzie, and Ben Rath. 1986. "The Psychiatric Effects of Massive Trauma on Cambodian Children: II. The Family, the

Home, and the School." *Journal of the American Academy of Child Psychiatry* 25(3): 377–83.

Sack, William H., S. McSharry, Gregory N. Clarke, John Seeley, P. Lewinsohn. 1994. "The Khmer Adolescent Project I: Epidemiologic Findings in Two Generations of Cambodian Refugees." *Journal of Nervous and Mental Disease* 182(7): 387–95.

Sahagun, Louis, and Mark A. Stein. 1989. "Cambodian Relives Pain of Killing Fields." *Los Angeles Times*, Jan. 19.

Sak, Sutsakhan. 1978. *The Khmer Republic at War and the Final Collapse.* McLean, Va.: U.S. Army Center of Military History Indochina Monographs.

Sam, Sam-Ang. 1994. "Khmer Traditional Music Today." In *Cambodian Culture Since 1975: Homeland and Exile.* Ed. May M. Ebihara, Carol A. Mortland, and Judy Ledgerwood, 39–47. Ithaca: Cornell University Press.

SamSotha, Francis, and Mariam Khambaty. 1992. "Border Needs Assessment Report." Oakland, Calif.: Cambodian New Generation, Inc.

Sandersley, Paola Polacco. 1986. "One Individual's Contribution." In *Years of Horror, Days of Hope: Responding to the Cambodian Refugee Crisis.* Ed. Barry S. Levy and Daniel C. Susott, 47–52. Millwood, N.Y.: Associated Faculty Press.

Santoli, Al. 1988. *New Americans: An Oral History,* 208–33. New York: Ballantine Books.

Sargent, Carolyn, and John L. Marcucci. 1984. "Aspects of Khmer Medicine among Refugees in Urban America." *Medical Anthropology Quarterly* 16(1): 7–9.

———. 1988. "Khmer Prenatal Health Practices and the American Clinical Experience." In *Childbirth in America.* Ed. Karen Michaelson, 79–89. Westport: Bergin and Garvey.

Sargent, Carolyn, John L. Marcucci, and Ellen Elliston. 1983. "Tiger Bones, Fire, and Wine: Maternity Care in a Kampuchean Refugee Community." *Medical Anthropology* 7(4): 67–79.

Savin, Dan, William H. Sack, Gregory N. Clarke, Nee Meas, and Im Richart. 1996. "The Khmer Adolescent Project, Part 3. A Study of Trauma from Thailand's Site II Refugee Camp" *Journal of the American Academy of Child and Adolescent Psychiatry* 35(3): 384–89.

Schafer-Taylor, Mary. 1987. "Factors Influencing Educational Outcomes for Indochinese Students in the Public Elementary Schools of Philadelphia." Ed.D. diss., Temple University.

Scott, James C. 1976. *The Moral Economy of the Peasant.* New Haven: Yale University Press.

Scott, Joanna C. 1989. *Indochina's Refugees: Oral Histories from Laos, Cambodia and Vietnam,* 109–57. Jefferson, N.C.: McFarland.

Seng, Seang M. 1986. "One Person's Story." In *Years of Horror, Days of Hope: Responding to the Cambodian Refugee Crisis.* Ed. Barry S. Levy and Daniel C. Susott, 3–12. Millwood, N.Y.: Associated Faculty Press.

Shaw, Scott. 1987. "Cambodian Refugees: A Study of Their Relocation to Long Beach, California." Ph.D. diss., Pacific Western University.

———. 1989. *Cambodian Refugees in Long Beach, California: The Definitive Study.* Hermosa Beach, Calif., Buddha Rose Pub.

Shawcross, William. 1984. *The Quality of Mercy: Cambodia, Holocaust and Modern Conscience.* New York: Simon and Schuster.

———. 1987. *Sideshow: Kissinger, Nixon and the Destruction of Cambodia.* Rev. ed. New York: Simon and Schuster.

Sheehy, Gail. 1984. "A Home for Cambodia's Children." *New York Times Magazine,* Sept. 23, 44–47, 50–54, 58, 60, 66–68.

———. 1986. *Spirit of Survival.* Rev. ed. New York: Bantam.

Shek, Kitty W., and Charles Martell. 1991. *Cambodians in California: An Information Needs Assessment.* Sacramento: California State University, Sacramento, the Library, Cambodians in California Project.

———. 1996. *Cambodians in California: Nine Oral Histories in One Volume.* Sacramento: California State University, Sacramento, the Library, Cambodians in California Project.

Siegal, Marcia B. 1990. "Cambodian Dance Springs Back to Life." *Christian Science Monitor,* Oct. 16.

Sieng, Sokhany, and Janice L. Thompson. 1992. "Traces of Khmer Women's Imaginary: Finding Our Way in the West." *Women and Therapy* 13(1–2): 129–40.

Simms, Laura, and Arn Chorn-Pond. 2002. "Between Tigers and Crocodiles: An Interview with Arn Chorn-Pond." *Parabola: Myth, Tradition, and the Search for Meaning* 24(4): 24–31.

Sin, Bo Chum. 1992. "Socio-cultural, Psychological and Linguistic Effects on Cambodian Students' Progress through Formal Schooling in the United States." Ph.D. diss., University of Oregon.

Smilkstein, Gabriel. 1981. "Refugees in Thailand and Short-Term Medical Aid." *Journal of the American Medical Association* 245(10): 1052–54.

Smillie, Ian. 1985. "Kampuchean Refugees: Sorrow in the Land of Smiles." BRC/QEH Working Paper Series, vol. 1, no. 3. Oxford, England: Refugee Studies Programme, Queen Elizabeth House.

Smith, Frank. 1989. *Interpretive Accounts of the Khmer Rouge Years: Personal Experience in Cambodian Peasant World View.* Wisconsin Papers on Southeast Asia, Occasional Paper No. 18. Madison, Wis.: University of Wisconsin, Madison, Center for Southeast Asian Studies.

———. 1994. "Cultural Consumption: Cambodian Peasant Refugees and Television in the 'First World.'" In *Cambodian Culture Since 1975: Homeland and Exile.* Ed. May M. Ebihara, Carol A. Mortland, and Judy Ledgerwood, 141–60. Ithaca: Cornell University Press.

Smith-Hefner, Nancy J. 1990. "Language and Identity in the Education of Boston-Area Khmer." *Anthropology and Education Quarterly* 21(3): 250–68.

———. 1993, "Education, Gender, and Generational Conflict among Khmer Refugees." *Anthropology and Education Quarterly* 24(2): 135–58.

———. 1994. "Ethnicity and the Force of Faith: Christian Conversion among Khmer Refugees." *Anthropological Quarterly* 67(1): 24–37.

———. 1995. "The Culture of Entrepreneurship among Khmer Refugees." In *New Migrants in the Marketplace: Boston's Ethnic Entrepreneurs.* Ed. Marilyn Halter, 141–60. Amherst: University of Massachusetts Press.

———. 1999. *Khmer American: Identity and Moral Education in a Diasporic Community.* Berkeley: University of California Press.

Sok, Chivy. 1993. "Reflections on Being Cambodian American." Unpublished term paper, Asian American Studies 199, University of California, Santa Barbara.

Sok, Siphana. 1986. "Khao I Dang: A Refugee's Perspective." In *Years of Horror, Days of Hope: Responding to the Cambodian Refugee Crisis.* Ed. Barry S. Levy and Daniel C. Susott, 83–84. Millwood, N.Y.: Associated Faculty Press.

Soleng Tom, Connie Young Yu, Philip Tse, and Kenneth Meinhardt. 1983. "Santa Clara County Asian Health Survey." San Jose, California: Santa Clara County Health Department.

Som, Siritha. 1991. "The Donut Queen." In John Tenhula. *Voices from Southeast Asia: The Refugee Experience in the United States,* 179–82. New York: Holmes and Meier.

Son, Linda. 1994. "Understanding the Psychological Impact of War Trauma and the Refugee Camp Experience on Cambodian Refugee Children Residing in Site II." Ed.D. diss., Harvard University.

Stewart, Jocelyn Y. 1997. "Reaching Out to Cambodians." *Los Angeles Times,* Nov. 17.

Stone, Sandy. 1992. "Cambodian Artist's Pain Shows in His Sculpture." *Arlington Journal,* Feb. 3.

Strand, Paul J., and Woodrow Jones, Jr. 1985. *Indochinese Refugees in America: Problems of Adaptation and Assimilation.* Durham, N.C.: Duke University Press.

———. 1989. "The Indochinese Refugee Experience: The Case of San Diego." In *Refugees as Immigrants: Cambodians, Laotians, and Vietnamese in America.* Ed. David W. Haines, 105–20. Totowa: Rowman and Littlefield.

Streed, Sarah. 2002. *Leaving the House of Ghosts: Cambodian Refugees in the American Midwest.* Jefferson, N.C.: McFarland.

Strober, Susan B. 1990. "The Impact of Social Support and Psychological Distress on the Acculturation Adjustment of Cambodian Refugees." Ph.D. diss., Catholic University of America.

———. 1994. "Social Work Interventions to Alleviate Cambodian Refugee Psychological Distress." *International Social Work* 37(1): 23–35.

Stuart-Fox, Martin. 1985. *The Murderous Revolution: Life and Death in Pol Pot's Kampuchea.* Chippendale, Australia: Alternative Publishing.

Sughandabhirom, Bhirom. 1986. "Experiences in a First Asylum Country: Thailand." In *Refugee Mental Health in Resettlement Countries.* Ed. Carolyn L. Williams and Joseph Westermeyer, 81–96. Washington: Hemisphere.

Sun, Lena H. 1995. "For Area Cambodians, a Conflict between Young and Old." *Washington Post,* Feb. 19.

Susott, Daniel C. 1986. "Impressions of a Medical Coordinator at Khao I Dang." In *Years of Horror, Days of Hope: Responding to the Cambodian Refugee Crisis.* Ed. Barry S. Levy and Daniel C. Susott, 73–82. Millwood, N.Y.: Associated Faculty Press.

Sutter, Valerie O. 1990. *The Indochinese Refugee Dilemma.* Baton Rouge, La.: Louisiana State University Press.

Swenson, Dick, 1980. "Oregonian Sanitarians Help Cambodian Refugees in Thailand." *Journal of Environmental Health* 42(6): 335–37.

Swenson, Richard, and Terrance Rahe. 1986. "Sanitation." In *Years of Horror, Days of Hope: Responding to the Cambodian Refugee Crisis.* Ed. Barry S. Levy and Daniel C. Susott, 221–28. Millwood, N.Y.: Associated Faculty Press.

Sylvester, Ellen S. 1997. "Inside, Outside, and In-between: Identities, Literacies, and Educational Policies in the Lives of Cambodian Women and Girls in Philadelphia." Ph.D. diss., University of Pennsylvania.

Szymusiak, Molyda. 1986. *The Stones Cry Out: A Cambodian Childhood, 1975–1980.* Trans. Linda Coverdale. New York: Hill and Wang.

Taing, Vek Huong, as told to Sharon Fischer. 1980. *Ordeal in Cambodia: One Family's Miraculous Survival—Escape from the Khmer Rouge.* San Bernardino, Calif.: Here's Life Publishers.

Takacs, Stacy. 1999. "Alien-Nation, Immigration, National Identity, and Transnationalism." *Cultural Studies* 13(4): 591–620.

Tan, Terpsichore N. K. 1999. "Cambodian Youth in Long Beach, California: Parenting and Other Sociocultural Influences on Educational Achievement." Ph.D. diss., University of Hawaii.

Tann, Kim Huor. 1988. "Older Cambodian Refugees' Stories." St. Paul, Minn.: Southeast Asian Ministry.

Tasker, Rodney. 1991. "The Road Back." *Far Eastern Economic Review,* Sept. 26, 26.

———. 1993. "Empty Dreams: Thais about to Close Last Cambodia Refugee Camp." *Far Eastern Economic Review,* April 1, 22.

———. 1997. "Holding Pattern." *Far Eastern Economic Review,* May 8, 20.

"A Temple, and Then a Community." 1991. *Washington Post,* Aug. 21.

Tenhula, John. 1991. *Voices from Southeast Asia: The Refugee Experience in the United States,* 27–31, 46–47, 60–61, 69–73, 77–78, 89–91, 103–4, 114–15, 116–19, 127–28, 130–33, 141, 148, 155, 166–68, 171–75, 179–82, 184–85. New York: Holmes and Meier.

Tharachatr, Bunlert. 1987. "Brief Narrative on the Situation of Refugees on the Thai-Kampuchean Border." *Migration World* 15(5): 19–24.

Thayer, Nate. 1996a. "After Pol Pot, Who?" *Far Eastern Economic Review,* Aug. 29, 24.

———. 1996b. "Unravelling Revolution." *Far Eastern Economic Review,* Aug. 29, 22–23.

———. 1997a. "Ambiguous Alliance." *Far Eastern Economic Review,* July 3, 24–25.

———. 1997b. "Brother Number Zero." *Far Eastern Economic Review,* Aug. 7, 14–18.

———. 1997c. "Day of Reckoning." *Far Eastern Economic Review,* Oct. 30, 14–20.

———. 1997d. "The Deal That Died." *Far Eastern Economic Review,* Aug. 21, 14–17.

———. 1997e. "Forbidden City." *Far Eastern Economic Review,* Oct. 30, 22–23.

———. 1997f. "Pol Pot Unmasked." *Far Eastern Economic Review,* Aug. 7, 19–20.

———. 1998a. "Dying Breath." *Far Eastern Economic Review,* April 30, 18–21.

———. 1998b. "End of Story?" *Far Eastern Economic Review,* Dec. 17, 23–24.

———. 1998c. "Nowhere to Hide." *Far Eastern Economic Review,* April 23, 12–14.

———. 1999a. "Chance of a Lifetime." *Far Eastern Economic Review,* Jan. 28, 24.

———. 1999b. "Death in Detail." *Far Eastern Economic Review,* May 13, 20–21.

———. 1999c. "Party of One." *Far Eastern Economic Review,* Jan. 21, 26.

———. 1999d. "Peace or Justice?" *Far Eastern Economic Review,* Jan. 21, 24–25.

Thayer, Nate, and Nayan Chanda. 1997. "Law of the Gun." *Far Eastern Economic Review,* July 17, 14–15.

Thompson, Ashley. 1993. "Oh Cambodia! Poems from the Border." *New Literary History* 24(3): 519–45.

Thompson, Janice L. 1991. "Exploring Gender and Culture with Khmer Refugee Women: Reflections on Participatory Feminist Research." *Advances in Nursing Science* 13(3): 30–48.

Tollefson, James F. 1989. *Alien Winds: The Reeducation of America's Indochinese Refugees.* New York: Praeger.

Tran Dinh Tho. 1978. *The Cambodian Incursion.* McLean, Va.: U.S. Army Center of Military History.

Tran, Peter. 1990. "The Pastoral Care and Challenges of the People from Cambodia, Laos and Vietnam in the United States." *Migration World* 18(2): 17–22.

Turner, Craig. 1997. "U.N. Examines How to Bring Pol Pot to Trial." *Los Angeles Times,* June 24.

Uba, Laura, and Rita Chi-Ying Chung. 1991. "The Relationship between Trauma and Financial and Physical Well-Being." *Journal of General Psychology* 118(3): 215–25.

Uehara, Edwina S. 2001. "Understanding the Dynamics of Illness and Help-Seeking: Event-Structure Analysis and a Cambodian-American Narrative of 'Spirit Invasion.'" *Social Science and Medicine* 52(4): 519–36.

Ui, Shiori. 1991. "'Unlikely Heroes': The Evolution of Female Leadership in a Cambodian Ethnic Enclave." In *Ethnography Unbound: Power and Resistance in the Modern Metropolis.* Ed. Michael Burawoy et al., 161–77. Berkeley: University of California Press.

Um, Khatharya. 1990. "Brotherhood of the Pure: Nationalism and Communism in Cambodia." Ph.D. diss., University of California, Berkeley.

———. In press. *Born of the Ashes: World Revolution and Exile—the Cambodian Experience.* Berkeley: University of California Press.

Umbach, Andrea C. 1986. "Cambodian Assimilation: Values, Attitudes, and Expectations." B.A. senior honors thesis, University of California, Berkeley.

Ung, Luong. 2000. *First They Killed My Father: A Daughter of Cambodia Remembers.* New York: HarperCollins.

U.S. Bureau of the Census. 1992. *The Cambodian Community of Long Beach: An Ethnographic Analysis of Factors Leading to Census Undercount.* Ethnographic Evaluation of 1990 Decennial Census Report Series, report no. 9. Washington: U.S. Bureau of the Census, Center for Survey Methods Research.

———. 1993. *Asian[s] and Pacific Islanders in the United States.* Washington: U.S. Bureau of the Census.

U.S. Catholic Conference. 1984. *Refugees from Cambodia: A Look at History, Culture, and the Refugee Crisis.* Washington: United States Catholic Conference, Migration and Refugee Services.

———. 1986. *Welcome into the Community of Faith: A Report on the Cambodian, Hmong, and Laotian Apostolate, 1986.* Washington: U.S. Catholic Conference, Pastoral Care of Migrants and Refugees.

U.S. Committee for Refugees. 1982. *Cambodian Refugees in Thailand: The Limits of Asylum.* New York: American Council for Nationalities Service, U.S. Committee for Refugees.

———. 1985. *Cambodians in Thailand: People on the Edge.* Washington: American Council for Nationalities Service, U.S. Committee for Refugees.

———. 1994. *Something Like Home Again: The Repatriation of Cambodian Refugees.*

Washington: American Council for Nationalities Service, U.S. Committee for Refugees.

U.S. Congress. House of Representatives. Committee on Foreign Affairs, Subcommittee on Asian and Pacific Affairs. 1980a. *1979—Tragedy in Indochina: War, Refugees, and Famine.* Hearings. 96th Cong., 1st sess., 1979. Washington: Government Printing Office.

———. 1980b. *1980—The Tragedy in Indochina Continues: War, Refugees, and Famine.* Hearings. 96th Cong., 2d sess., 1980. Washington: Government Printing Office.

———. 1985. *Cambodian Refugees in Southeast Asia.* Hearing. 99th Cong., 1st sess., 1985. Washington: Government Printing Office.

———. 1989a. *Hope for Cambodia: Preventing the Return of the Khmer Rouge and Aiding the Refugees.* Hearing and Markup. 100th Cong., 2d sess., 1988. Washington: Government Printing Office.

———. 1989b. *Indochinese Refugees at Risk: The Boat People, Cambodians under Khmer Rouge Control, and Re-education-Camp Detainees.* Hearing. 101st Cong., 1st sess., 1989. Washington: Government Printing Office.

U.S. Congress. House of Representatives. Committee on the Judiciary, Subcommittee on Immigration, Citizenship and International Law. Legislative and Oversight Hearings Regarding Indochina Refugees (Evacuation, Reception and Resettlement of Indochina Refugees). 1976. *Refugees from Indochina.* Serial No. 43. 94th Cong., 1st and 2d sess., 1976 and 1977. Washington: Government Printing Office.

U.S. Congress. House of Representatives and Senate. Joint Economic Committee. 1980. *Indochinese Refugees: The Impact on First Asylum Countries and Implications for American Policy.* Report prepared by Astri Suhrke. 96th Cong., 2d sess. Washington: Government Printing Office.

U.S. Congress. Senate. Committee on Foreign Relations. 1984. *United States Processing of Khmer Refugees.* Staff report prepared by Carl W. Ford. Senate Print 98–240. 98th Cong., 2d sess., 1984. Washington: Government Printing Office.

U.S. Congress. Senate. Committee on the Judiciary. 1979. *Refugee and Humanitarian Problems in Vietnam.* Hearing. 95th Cong., 2d sess., 1978. Washington: Government Printing Office.

———. 1980. *Refugee Crisis in Cambodia.* Hearing. 96th Cong., 1st sess., 1979. Serial no. 96–39. Washington: U.S. Government Printing Office.

U.S. Congress. Senate Committee on the Judiciary. Subcommittee on Immigration and Refugee Policy. 1982. *Refugee Problems in Southeast Asia: 1981.* Staff report prepared by Richard W. Day and Jerry M. Tinker. 97th Cong., 2d sess., 1982. Washington: Government Printing Office.

U.S. Department of Health and Human Services. Administration for Children and Families. Office of Refugee Resettlement. 1992. *An Evaluation of the Planned Secondary Resettlement Program.* Washington: U.S. Department of Health and Human Services.

U.S. General Accounting Office. 1999. *Welfare Reform: Public Assistance Benefits Provided to Recently Naturalized Citizens.* Washington: U.S. General Accounting Office.

Van Boemel, Gretchen B., and Patricia D. Rozee. 1992. "Treatment for Psychosomatic Blindness among Cambodian Refugee Women." *Women and Therapy* 13(3): 239–66.

Van Der Kroef, Justus. 1987. "The Endless Aftermath of Conquest: Indochina's Refugees and Their World." *Crossroads: An International Socio-Political Journal* 23(3): 15–27.

Veach, Virginia. 1986. "Holistic Health Care." In *Years of Horror, Days of Hope: Responding to the Cambodian Refugee Crisis.* Ed. Barry S. Levy and Daniel C. Susott, 162–68. Millwood, N.Y.: Associated Faculty Press.

Verhovek, Sam Howe. 1987. "For City Cambodians, It's Wedding Time." *New York Times,* June 22.

Vickery, Michael. 1984. *Cambodia, 1975–1982.* Boston: South End Press.

———. 1986. *Kampuchea: Politics, Economics and Society.* London: Pinter.

———. 1990. "Refugee Politics: The Khmer Camp System in Thailand." In *The Cambodian Agony.* Ed. David A. Ablin and Marlowe Hood, 293–331. Armonk: M. E. Sharpe.

Vollman, William T. 1996. "Degrees of Separation: Race, Fear and Life's Sickening Little Meannesses in Little Phnom Penh." *LA Weekly,* Aug. 2, 24–35.

Vong, Nilrith. 2001. "Understanding Cambodian Teenage Marriage and Developing a Community Support System." Ed.D. diss., Fielding Institute.

von Schilling, Jean M. 1988. "A Study to Assess the Level of English Language Proficiency of the Middle and High School Cambodian Population in the Richard, Virginia, Public Schools, with an Analysis of Related Student Characteristics." Ph.D. diss., Virginia Commonwealth University.

Wald, Matthew L. 1986. "Love Story: From Thailand Camp to Massachusetts Wedding." *New York Times,* June 28.

Wallace, Charles P. 1990. "Homecoming Is Hard After Life in America." *Los Angeles Times,* May 5.

———. 1993a. "Cambodia Assembly Holds Seat for Long Beach Winner." *Los Angeles Times,* June 16.

———. 1993b. "Cambodian Election Tests Californians' Political Skills." *Los Angeles Times,* May 26.

Walters, Tali K. 1994. "Acculturative Stress, Social Support, and Trauma in a Community Sample of Cambodian Refugees." Ph.D. diss., Boston College.

Watanabe, Teresa. 2003. "Cambodians Fear Possible Deportation." *Los Angeles Times,* Feb. 21.

Weeks, John R., and Ruben G. Rumbaut. 1991. "Infant Mortality among Ethnic Immigrant Groups." *Social Science and Medicine* 33(3): 327–34.

Wei, Charmaine. 1992. "Health Status, Disease Distributions and Medical Service Utilization among Refugees from Vietnam, Laos, Cambodia and the Former Soviet Union." M.A. thesis, University of Oregon.

Welaratna, Usha. 1993. *Beyond the Killing Fields: Voices of Nine Cambodian Survivors in America.* Stanford: Stanford University Press.

———. 1998. "The Presence of the Past in Conflicts and Coalitions among Cambodians, African Americans, and Hispanics in Central Long Beach, California." Ph.D. diss., University of California, Berkeley.

West, Cheryl D. 2000. "Pathways of Thriving and Resilience: Growth Responses to Adversity and Trauma in Two Cambodian Communities: A Comparative Study between Lowell, Massachusetts and Phnom Penh, Cambodia." M.A. thesis, University of Massachusetts, Lowell.

White-Baughan, Jennifer L. 1990. "The Effects of a Problem-Solving Intervention with

Educational Videos on Symptoms of Posttraumatic Stress in a Sample of Cambodian Refugees." Ph.D. diss., California School of Professional Psychology, San Diego.

White, Mel. 1992. "Rescue by Radio." *Reader's Digest* 140(839): 65–70.

Wilkinson, Alec. 1994. "A Changed Vision of God." *The New Yorker,* Jan. 4, 52–68.

Wilkins, Rob. 1988. "Cultivating the Killing Fields." *Christianity Today* 32(3): 10–11.

Williams, Carolyn L. 1985. "The Southeast Asian Refugees and Community Mental Health." *Journal of Community Psychology* 13(3): 258–69.

Williams, Carolyn L., and J. W. Berry. 1991. "Primary Prevention of Acculturation Stress among Refugees: Application of Psychological Theory and Practice." *American Psychologist* 46(6): 632–41.

Williams, Louise. 1989. "Cambodia's Violent Border Camps: The Only Escape Is a Minefield." *World Press Review* 36(11): 20.

Williamson, Jan. 1981. "Centers for Unaccompanied Children: Khao I-Dang Holding Center." *Disasters* 5(2): 100–104.

Willwerth, James. 1991. "From Killing Fields to Mean Streets: The Street-Gang Virus Is Now Infecting Cambodian Refugees." *Time,* Nov. 18, 103, 105–6.

Winder, Alvin E., Barbara A. Poremba, and Regine C. Beakes. 1991. "Nutritional Education for Cambodian Refugees." *Journal of Nutrition Education* 23(2): 82.

Wiscombe, Janet. 1998. "The Mighty Pen of the New Phnom Penh." *Los Angeles Times,* April 26.

Wolfe, Lisa. 1985. "Ten-Year Search Brings Cambodian Boys to U.S." *New York Times,* March 4.

Wood, Susan P. 1983. "Cambodian Families in a Refugee Processing Center: Parental Attitudes and Childrearing Practices." Providence, R.I.: The author.

World Health Organization. 1986. "Health Conditions in the Kampuchean-Thailand Border Encampments." *Report to the Kampuchean-Thailand Border of the WHO/ UN Health Mission, 20 January to 5 February, 1986.* Geneva, Switzerland: World Health Organization.

World Refugee Survey. 1973–2001.

Wride, Nancy. 2001. "Cambodian Community Makes Banner Statement." *Los Angeles Times,* July 15.

Wright, Wayne E. 1998. "The Education of Cambodian American Students in the Long Beach Unified School District: A Language and Educational Policy Analysis." M.A. thesis, California State University, Long Beach.

Yang, Sem. 1982. *Cambodian Mutual Assistance Associations Project.* Long Beach, Calif.: Cambodian Association of America.

Yathay, Pin with John Man. 1987. *Stay Alive, My Son.* New York: Free Press.

Yau, Tow Yee. 1995. "The Level of Acculturation, Self-Esteem, and Self-Efficacy of Southeast Asian Refugee Adolescents." Ph.D. diss., University of Colorado, Denver.

Yeung, Rosa A. 1988. "Help-Seeking Behavior of Cambodian Refugees Experiencing Posttraumatic Stress Disorder." M.S.W. thesis, California State University, Long Beach.

Yi, Daniel, and Greg Krikorian. 1998. "Three Men Convicted of Killing Ngor." *Los Angeles Times,* April 17.

Yimsut, Ronnie. 1997. "Return to Cambodia: A Kind of Homeward Bound for Khmer Refugees." *AsianWeek*, Feb. 7, 7.

Young, Florence H. 1988. "Problems Encountered by Limited-English-Speaking Adults in Seeking and Gaining Employment and Advancing in the Workplace." M.A. thesis, California State University, Long Beach.

Young, Robert A., Gregory Robinson, Dara Mendyuk, Cathleen Barnes, and Ken Nelson. 1996. *The Cambodian Family: Minnie Street Neighborhood Community Survey*. Fullerton: California State University, Fullerton, Social Science Research Center.

Zaharlick, Amy, and Jean Brainard. 1987. "Demographic Characteristics, Ethnicity, and the Resettlement of Southeast Asian Refugees in the United States." *Urban Anthropology* 16(3–4): 327–73.

Zhou, Min, and Carl L. Bankston III. 1996. "Social Capital and the Adaptation of the Second Generation: The Case of Vietnamese Youth in New Orleans." In *The New Second Generation*. Ed. Alejandro Portes, 171–96. New York: Russell Sage Foundation.

Zucker, Norman L., and Naomi Flink Zucker. 1992. "From Immigration to Refugee Redefinition: A History of Refugee and Asylum Policy in the United States." In *Refugees and the Asylum Dilemma in the West*. Ed. Gil Loescher, 54–70. University Park: Pennsylvania State University Press.

INDEX

The names of authors cited within parentheses are not indexed. The names of local organizations are listed under the cities or states where they are located, but national organizations have their own headings.

SUCHENG CHAN is professor emerita of Asian American studies and global studies at the University of California, Santa Barbara. She is the recipient of two Distinguished Teaching Awards and the author or editor of fourteen books, among them *Not Just Victims: Conversations with Cambodian Community Leaders in the United States* and *Remapping Asian American History.*

The Asian American Experience

The University of Illinois Press
is a founding member of the
Association of American University Presses.

———————————————————————

Composed in 10.5/13 Adobe Minion
at the University of Illinois Press
Designed by Paula Newcomb
Manufactured by Sheridan Books, Inc.

University of Illinois Press
1325 South Oak Street
Champaign, IL 61820-6903
www.press.uillinois.edu